Southern Encounters

Southerners of Note
in Ralph McGill's South

Southern Encounters

Southerners of Note
in Ralph McGill's South

by

Ralph McGill,
1898-1969

Edited with an introduction by
Calvin M. Logue

Mercer University
Press
Macon, Ga. 31207

ISBN 0-86554-050-0

Library of Congress Cataloging in Publication Data

McGill, Ralph, 1898-1969.
  Southern encounters.

  1. Georgia—Biography. 2. Southern States—Biography.
I. Logue, Cal M. (Calvin McLeod), 1935-   . II. Title.
CT230.M34 1983   920'.075 [B]   83-953
ISBN 0-86554-050-0

Contents

Dedicated to
Grace Lundy Tackett

Acknowledgments

The editor expresses appreciation to the following persons for assistance and support: Ms. Virginia Knight Tubbs, Ms. Elise Allen, Ms. Robin Gormley, Ms. Faye Apple, Dr. Eugene Grace, Mr. Edd Rowell, Dr. Watson E. Mills, Dr. Dwight Freshley, the University of Georgia Library faculty and staff, Ms. Ralph McGill, and Ms. Mary Jo Logue.

Illustrations on pages ii, x, 56, 152, and 318 are from the Ralph McGill Papers, Special Collections, Robert W. Woodruff Library, Emory University. Permission from *Atlanta Constitution*.

Introduction

Ralph McGill: "Man of Fire and Poetry"

Calvin M. Logue

Ralph McGill saw himself as "something of a teacher," providing information and inspiration to a society confronting important decisions. He formed strong opinions and expressed them, sometimes in the style of the seeker and other times as severe critic.[1] When the column, essay, or speech involved topics such as the bombing of a synagogue or abuse of the poor, McGill could be blunt. For example, when violence broke out on the University of Mississippi campus in 1962, McGill wrote: "Not all the perfumes of Araby will wash clean the political hands of Mississippi's Governor Ross Barnett." In 1968 McGill condemned Governor George Wallace as "Alabama's political evil."[2] On many occasions,

---

[1]*Atlanta Constitution*, 15 June 1948; National Education Association speech, in Calvin McLeod Logue, *Ralph McGill: Editor and Publisher*, two vols. (Durham: Moore Publishing Co., 1969), 1:246.

[2]*Atlanta Constitution*, 2 October 1962, and 30 May 1968.

however, McGill explored with audiences what were the most feasible and fair alternatives.

He often left something for the reader and listener to decide. McGill developed strong convictions; yet, he remained aware also of the complexities of social issues and the inevitability of change. "There are times," he stated, "when I envy all those editorialists, columnists and news and radio commentators who have been touched with omniscience and who are so very sure about all the answers."[3] "Whatever traveling I have done, and whatever and all I have seen," he reflected, "have taught me just two things—humility and the awful truth of the uncertainty of things."[4] "There are always those, on both sides of any issue, who unfailingly have the answers," he maintained, "but somehow experience teaches us to distrust those with the glib, ready answers."[5] Rather than offer ready-made solutions to every problem, McGill "often" found himself "reflecting," "wondering and concerned" about historical causes and worthy options. He was troubled with the temperament of "seeing both sides of things."[6]

McGill was an inner-directed involver. Although "an optimist by nature," he found life to be "real" and "earnest." He experienced "periodic attacks of melancholia" and "remorse of conscience."[7] Eugene Patterson, McGill's colleague at the *Atlanta Constitution*, referred to the "combination of Calvinist ancestry and Welsh moodiness" that "sometimes settled upon him and gave him a bleak hour."[8] "All mankind," McGill stated, know "hope, despair, joy, sorrow, anger, grief."[9] "The great lack of modern man," he continued, is that of "spiritual self-confidence."[10] "If we look back through history," he explained, "we see mankind groping for two things outside the sphere of physical needs. He is seeking to relate himself to God and he is striving for some order in his life."[11]

McGill harnessed "the forces at work within" for creative public service. He was a "restless rebel"[12] who did not like to see people exploited.[13] The

---

[3]*Atlanta Constitution*, 6 October 1948, and 31 July 1949; *Arkansas Gazette* speech, in Logue, *Ralph McGill*, 2:109.

[4]*Atlanta Constitution*, 28 March 1946.

[5]*Atlanta Constitution*, 16 September 1957.

[6]*Atlanta Constitution*, 4 November 1947; editor's taped interview with McGill, 29 December 1965.

[7]*Atlanta Constitution*, 18 February 1947, and 13 February 1948; later McGill declared, "I am not an optimist"; Birmingham Rotary Club speech, in Logue, *Ralph McGill*, 1:221.

[8]*Washington Post*, 5 February 1969; Patterson was quoting McGill's own words; *Atlanta Constitution*, 12 February 1948, and 17 July 1951.

[9]Oberlin College commencement address, in Logue, *Ralph McGill*, 2:298.

[10]*Atlanta Constitution*, 27 February 1949.

[11]Fayette County Bar Association speech, in Logue, *Ralph McGill*, 2:226.

[12]*Atlanta Constitution*, 18 February 1947.

[13]Editor's taped interview with McGill.

"troubles of others troubled" him. "You wake and remember them all," he wrote, "wondering how their destinies worked out; how many escaped, how many were trapped. And they leave you weary and depressed and sleepless while you wonder."[14] Although he recognized that progress in solving social problems often came slowly and only after sacrifice and debate, he was impatient with persons who failed to try. He disliked the fact that "more and more across America there are people saying, 'Nobody gives a damn any more'."[15] After a lifetime of personal involvement with issues of race, economics, poverty, law, education, politics, and the press, the day he died McGill exhorted high school students with this statement: "You hear people today say, well, in this society the individual hasn't got a chance, he's submerged, he's up against the great technical forces that are running the world, he's a poor lost individual; don't tell me that today's individual is anywhere near as submerged or lost as was a peasant in Europe in the middle centuries. Or don't tell me that he's as worse [off] as he was back in the days I've seen—tenant sharecropper farmer in the cotton-tobacco regions."[16] "A people that loses its self-respect is easily demoralized and made afraid," he told a college audience. "They become willing to barter away their ideals and integrity. Such persons can't help us. We need your faith and idealism for the long, testing pull that is ahead."[17]

To McGill the remedy for self-discouragement and troublesome social problems was personal involvement in the community. In addition to being personally uplifting, he considered "emotional concern for human life . . . perhaps the most significant mark of a civilization and civilized individuals."[18] Although a private person in his preferences and choices, McGill claimed a universal kinship: "I feel that I am, in fact, related to all men," he concluded, "and that the great law of the Creator is in all things, and that only prejudice or bigotry keeps it from being so. This was one reason why I like the Hindu salutation, 'Nemastah.' A very free translation would be, 'I bow only to God, but God is in all things so I bow to God who is in you'."[19] Meaningful social participation depends upon personal integrity. "Whatever is done must eventually meet the test of being right or wrong," McGill taught. "We must first be honest with ourselves."[20] "We cannot grow merely in economic and agricultural wealth. We must grow in conscience. . . . We must

---

[14]*Atlanta Constitution*, 23 July 1949; *Hartford Courant* anniversary speech, in Logue, *Ralph McGill*, 2:332.

[15]*Atlanta Constitution*, 8 September 1946.

[16]Booker T. Washington speech, in Logue, *Ralph McGill*, 2:506.

[17]University of North Carolina commencement address, in Logue, *Ralph McGill*, 2:249.

[18]*Atlanta Constitution*, 22 April 1952.

[19]*Atlanta Constitution*, 10 December 1952.

[20]*Atlanta Constitution*, 3 January 1947.

grow in moral strength."[21] Citizens have "to believe in" themselves, "in the principles of" their "country, and understand the meaning and responsibilities of freedom . . . and we must try and express this in our daily lives."[22]

McGill contended that free individuals have a moral responsibility to oppose wrong: "If in our respective communities and states we are not willing to do unpleasant jobs, to stand out against what is wrong, even though it leads to misunderstanding and criticism, we won't have very happy communities or states."[23] This journalist thought that "if a free society is to reach an established goal, across the board, it must do so to a great extent through individual decisions. This freedom implies a moral responsibility. This responsibility is that of free business, a free press, free churches, free labor, free civic groups, a free bar, and free men."[24] Citizens have to be "able to face our world with rationalizing minds and a philosophic and spiritual courage lest we destroy ourselves with frustration and fear."[25] The common goal is "social, moral, and spiritual improvement." One should strive "to find or to create a better world." A person has "to speak the truth and work constructively to eliminate those things which cripple us and our common country."[26]

McGill decided that because people and social conditions are slow to change, to persist in the pursuit of a better life one must find resolve primarily from within. He called for a "commitment to the centrality of the individual, to love and compassion as we look at and participate in the human condition."[27] Preservation of the worth of the individual would become increasingly difficult. "Our anxiety and lack of comprehension" of "technological developments" and "social revolution will increase," he predicted, "there is no answer. We can only come back to self."[28] "There is a tremendous world contest on," McGill cautioned, "to determine what the image of man shall be in the last years of the twentieth century, and those centuries which are to come. Will it be that of the wholly outer-directed man of the totalitarian state, of science and computer-card motivations? Or will it be in the inner-directed man concerned with himself as a human being, assured of the worth of being human?"[29] "Think twice," he told a college audience, "before you

[21]Harriet Elliott Social Science Forum speech, in Logue, *Ralph McGill*, 2:197.

[22]Cranbrook School commencement address and Elijah Parish Lovejoy convocation address, in Logue, *Ralph McGill*, 2:176, 186.

[23]*Atlanta Constitution*, 5 August 1946.

[24]Ralph McGill, *The South and the Southerner* (Boston: Little, Brown and Company, 1964), p. 231.

[25]Jewish Education Alliance Veterans Day speech, in Logue, *Ralph McGill*, 2:76.

[26]*Atlanta Constitution*, 1 January 1946; Jewish Education Alliance Veterans Day speech and Harriet Elliott Social Science Forum speech, in Logue, *Ralph McGill*, 2:75, 194.

[27]Oberlin College commencement address, in Logue, *Ralph McGill*, 2:295.

[28]De Paul University commencement address, in Logue, *Ralph McGill*, 2:364.

[29]United Negro College Fund speech, in Logue, *Ralph McGill*, 2:236. In discussing the "verities of the values," McGill warned that "technology may itself become a faith. We see that the Communists

give up your individualism for conformity," for freedom of mind is "the only real safety valve our system possesses."[30] "I ask you, whatever job or profession you enter, to believe in yourself, to give commitment, to participate, to listen for an inner drum to which you can march."[31]

Because McGill learned that social problems could be complex and baffling, he searched for "values which sustain one in the loneliness and frustration" of public involvement.[32] The guiding concern should be the "quality of life."[33] "Much of the history of man," McGill decided, "has been written in his search for those values which will enable one to live usefully. The other side of this coin is that such lives create values."[34] To illustrate his emphasis upon lasting values, McGill cited poet Robert Frost as one "whose contribution was not to our size but to our spirit; not to our political beliefs but to our insight; not to our self-esteem, but to our self-comprehension."[35]

When reading McGill's writings and speeches, one finds specific values that form a "public philosophy," a view that guided McGill in his social involvement. For principles to be valuable he argued that they had to be "professed." These guides for public works are founded upon a "standard of the spirit."[36] Meaningful actions depend upon "great convictions" and the fusing of "moral

---

have done this. They assert they can build a secular paradise on earth in which laboratories and factories are the temples of its faith. Western civilization, by intent and design, advances its technology but does not lose sight of man and his relationship with his Creator. Man, after all, is more complex and mysterious than any of the magic machines"; University of North Carolina commencement address, in Logue, *Ralph McGill*, 2:248.

[30]University of Arkansas commencement address, in Logue, *Ralph McGill*, 1:138.

[31]De Paul University commencement address, in Logue, *Ralph McGill*, 2:368.

[32]Oberlin College commencement address, in Logue, *Ralph McGill*, 2:299.

[33]*Atlanta Constitution*, 27 June 1962.

[34]Rosenwal Centennial speech, in Logue, *Ralph McGill*, 2:282.

[35]Huntsville (Alabama) talk, in Logue, *Ralph McGill*, 2:316. McGill nominated other persons for recognition, among them four presidents: "Each is measured, and established in stature, by the measurement of the forces against which they contended. The four are Washington, Lincoln, Wilson, and Franklin Roosevelt. Washington is measured against the great struggle for independence. . . . Lincoln is measured against the great struggle to retain the Union. . . . Woodrow Wilson is measured by the forces of the great World War I and the successful conduct of the war. Franklin D. Roosevelt is measured by two great tests, the greatest depression the world ever knew, and the second great World War II." See McGill's essay on Wilson in this volume. When asked "what ten persons" he would "select to be saved in a specially prepared cavern" should "destruction from a hydrogen and atomic bombing" take place, McGill answered: "Certainly, Dr. James B. Conant, president of Harvard, would be one. . . . Next . . . I would put down Dr. Hugh H. Bennett, chief of the Soil Conservation Service. . . . Then . . . I would name Charles F. (Boss) Kettering, the genius of invention and engineering, in Detroit. . . . Then we would certainly need doctors. . . . I would then name two young men and two young women, all four of whom would have to be recent . . . graduates of vocational high schools and who have won health and intelligence awards from their 4-H, Future Farmer, and Home-Maker organizations. . . . With them I would send the great books of the world"; *Atlanta Constitution*, 1 February 1948, and 3 March 1950.

[36]Ten Club speech, in Logue, *Ralph McGill*, 2:61.

considerations with social inventiveness." These standards form a "compass course for . . . life."[37] Eugene Patterson found that "the simple virtues moved him most deeply—an autumn sky, a quiet wood, an honest, primitive painting."[38] When reading McGill's works, one finds specific values he esteemed. There were the stock virtues of "honor," "integrity," "intellectual honesty," "common decency," "human dignity," and "common justice." McGill isolated other values requisite to constructive public service. He appreciated the basic freedoms: "Civil liberties," "opportunity," and "promise." He praised virtues that function as guides for involvers: "enthusiasm," "plain unselfishness," "realism," "insight," "self-comprehension," "self-sacrifice," "chivalry," "ambition," "wisdom," "kindness," "gentleness," "stubbornness," "unity," "good will," and "plain speaking."[39]

Drawing upon these professed principles, McGill developed six premises that guided his career of social service. From these six beliefs, McGill refracted public arguments for specific issues and occasions. Here are the six premises: Individuals and governments should pursue policies that are feasible; laws should be obeyed; free individuals have a moral responsibility to oppose wrong; education is requisite to individual and community progress; all persons should be granted the rights and privileges of full citizenship; Southern states should ensure the rights and privileges of their own citizens.[40]

Although McGill often took a "practical approach to actual political problems,"[41] he perceived the world more as poet than politician. Eugene Patterson saw McGill as a man who grew "from small town sports writing to international fame as a great *man of fire and poetry*."[42] Seven years later Patterson eulogized: "His source of power was his character. . . . He spoke for the Negro, the one-crop tenant, the linthead of the Chattahoochee Valley, and the children in the threadbare schools. . . . McGill wrote out of abiding affection for the land and his

---

[37]Cooper Union Lincoln Day address, in Logue, *Ralph McGill*, 2:156. In Jesus, McGill found "something new," one of "calm courage," "untroubled," yet a " 'witness to the truth'." McGill continued: "Today, Christ and His ethic are again opposed by the forces of material power, and once more it is about His standard there gather those whose civilization best reflects His teaching. . . . Man's deep and abiding need is for a living, personal revelation of God, for faith in Divine purpose and for faith enough to serve it in imitation of Him who died and arose again from the tomb on a hill in faraway Judaea and gave to us the first Easter and its Promise"; "Visiting the Scene of the Crucifixion," *Atlanta Constitution and Journal Magazine* (25 March 1951).

[38]*Washington Post*, 5 February 1969.

[39]*Atlanta Constitution*, 1 January, 23 April, 24 October, and 26 December 1946; 18 February, 14 September, and 25 December 1947; 27 February 1949; 14 July 1951; 6 June 1952; Logue, *Ralph McGill*, 2:33, 61, 75, 79, 100, 103, 137, 151-52, 156, 169, 175-76, 190, 197, 232-36, 249, 252, 282, 295, 298-99, 309, 316, 364-68, 479, 481, 509; McGill, *The South and the Southerner*, pp. 44-45.

[40]Cal M. Logue, "Ralph McGill: Convictions of a Southern Editor," *Journalism Quarterly* 45 (Winter 1968): 647-52.

[41]*Atlanta Constitution*, 13 February 1947.

[42]*Atlanta Constitution*, 22 March 1962; emphasis added.

people, even the contrariest. . . . The school teachers and indigenous artists of the South found him as much an ally as the Negroes. . . . Sentimental but irreverent, earnest but antic, McGill's company was most often convivial. . . . He was a warm man, possessed of an infinitely generous heart and a hugely adventurous spirit."[43]

McGill trusted the independent spirit of the poet. He identified with the poet's song: "The deeper answers I believe are to be found not in biography, autobiography, news stories, or personal narrative. They may be found, paradoxically perhaps, in fiction."[44] McGill was a persistent student of Southern history, and quoted dates, statistics, events, and situations meaningfully in his writings and speeches. He was most comfortable and most convincing, however, when phrasing scenes poetically which he had experienced firsthand.

"There is a universal yearning toward things not well comprehended or clearly seen," McGill stated. "We sickle over those yearnings with phrases."[45] In the pieces reprinted below, for example, "Behold, Spring Sweeps Over the World Again," "Autumn," and "November in the Hills," McGill attempted to capture some of people's concerns creatively. He wrote of moments "not understood but felt," "mystery and promise," and "ancient, atavistic forces at work within"—that "something that speaks" from mountain and sea of self. And from "Endden," also printed below, one finds this theme: " 'God is'—and man has something from him which struggles against the ruthlessness of the Darwinian contest which goes on continually." "When power leads man toward arrogance," McGill mused, "poetry reminds him of his limitations. When power narrows the areas of man's concern, poetry reminds him of the richness and diversity of his existence. When power corrupts, poetry cleanses."[46]

A few examples will show McGill's poetic awareness and vivid presentation of routine and ceremonial scenes. What would many persons be thinking when waiting in line at the post office? This is what McGill observed; "We waited patiently in the line before one of the parcel post windows. . . . At last the old woman, in a poor dress, and with an old shawl about her face, handed in her form . . . and I saw that it was a money order made out in a man's name for $5.00. And, I saw, that when she took the green form and turned from the window there were tears in her eyes and on her cheek."[47]

When McGill reported his visit to Bethlehem, he combined historical and geographic facts with sacred sentiment, a recurring pattern distinctive in his writing: "It was, one plainly may see, an old caravanerai into which the travelers of

[43]*Washington Post*, 5 February 1969.

[44]Ralph McGill, "The Clearest Truth Is in Fiction: Jesse Hill Ford's Novel of the South," *Atlantic Monthly*, 216 (August 1965): 92.

[45]Oberlin College commencement address, Logue, *Ralph McGill*, 2:298.

[46]Huntsville talk, Logue, *Ralph McGill*, 2:316-17.

[47]*Atlanta Constitution*, 18 December 1952.

those days drove their animals and put down their bedding in the next stall. No one knows in which stall it was the Christ was born—although they have picked one—but it is *the* place. You feel it and know it and even the guides seem less offensive there. You wanted to kneel down there and pray and you felt tears in your eyes and a very great humility."[48]

Bruce Galphin explained how McGill employed factual details to reach an emotional climax. While Galphin is writing about McGill's *Atlanta Constitution* columns, one finds similar patterns in his articles and speeches: "He did indeed 'walk around' a subject . . . drawing on his vast experience to sketch the contextual background before he arrived at the main subject. Often it took only a few brush strokes to finish the picture, because the central figure already stood in bold silhouette. . . . He humanized the thorniest issues, from war to racial justice. He peopled his columns with flesh-and-blood humans, with sights seen and scenes remembered, with farm shacks and palaces, with starving children and potentates."[49] Here is how McGill recreated a meaningful moment he experienced in London, England: "I had left the Navy office . . . and was engaged in a walk. At Hyde Park corner, near the Duke of Wellington's old home, Apsley House, close by the equestrian statue of Napoleon's nemesis, there is a great and heroic monument in marble with bronze figures of artillerymen about it. Carved in it is the message that it was erected to the more than 49,000 members of the Royal Artillery regiments who lost their lives in the great war from 1914-1918. . . . On this there lay a pitiful bouquet of homegrown garden flowers. They were wrapped in a paper sack, with their once gay and pretty blossoms and part of the stems exposed. . . . They looked so small, in their incongruous cheap wrapping there on the great marble pile of beauty and solemnity, and yet they had about them a dignity and a pathos which wrung the heart."[50]

For over forty years this Pulitzer Prize winner wrote and spoke about politics, religion, economics, military, poetry, Southern history, bees, art, Greece, the press, education, blacks, tenant farming, Andrew Jackson, poker, sports, cooking, India, the 4-H Club, Hitler, television, corn, foreign affairs, human rights, Carson McCullers, music, and changing seasons in Georgia. McGill was assistant sports editor of the *Atlanta Constitution* in 1929; associate editor of that publication, 1938; editor, 1942; and publisher, 1960 until his death in 1969. Neither the sports page nor administrative office could constrain him. For example, in his massive sports column, "Break of the Day," on 31 January 1935, he wished for wealth to provide "all the milk" needed by "all the babies and children in the world," to arrange it so "nobody's sister would ever be in need," to allow "every

---

[48]*Atlanta Constitution*, 10 March 1946.

[49]*Atlanta Constitution*, 5 February 1969.

[50]*Atlanta Constitution*, 21 August 1952.

young boy" to see the "log hut" where Abraham Lincoln was born, and to enable 120,000,000 Americans "to look into the face of Franklin D. Roosevelt and see him smile and hear him speak." As publisher, on 3 February 1969 the week he died, he was still explaining in his *Atlanta Constitution* column why racially segregated schools in the South were "viciously unjust."

Not only are McGill's writings interestingly and insightfully written; they are also *important historically* because most of them are *firsthand accounts* of significant people and events. He wrote what he saw and heard! McGill believed that writers should "live closely with the people" and "get out more" among them.[51] "An astonishing and frightening number of things can be learned only by experience," he advised.[52] "Publishers ought, it seems to me, at least insist on their editors traveling frequently about their home states and neighboring ones just to see and know what's going on and what people are talking about," he wrote. "It also is my guess that a great many editors don't read enough books, don't get to know the sheriff, the chief of police, the court rooms, and the prosecutor. But maybe I'm wrong and just getting crotchety."[53] "I like to get by myself and prowl the town," he wrote.[54] His colleague Celestine Sibley found McGill to be "restlessly, insatiably curious, never satisfied that he had all the story and never satisfied with what he wrote."[55]

When speaking at Emory University in Atlanta on the topic, "Russia Today," McGill prefaced his remarks: "Conclusions will be based on, of course, what I saw and heard, but more particularly on the comments and conclusions of our ambassador there and his very excellent staff and also that of the British and French embassies and their staffs."[56] When writing and speaking about life in the city, he was able to relate personal observations: "It has been my opportunity . . . to go to some big city slums, obtain a friendly reporter, usually a Negro reporter, although not always, and to spend say four or five days and parts of nights in the slums of Detroit, Philadelphia, Chicago, Boston, and New York."[57]

McGill explained how he learned about the South, the theme of many of his works: "I suppose that I have spent a great many man-hours in reading and studying and interviewing people through the past twenty-five or thirty years, trying to determine what it is that has made this region what it is."[58] Periodically he

---

[51]Southwestern Journalism Forum speech, Logue, *Ralph McGill*, 2:39.

[52]*Atlanta Constitution*, 1 November 1946; University of Arkansas commencement address, in Logue, *Ralph McGill*, 1:133.

[53]Pulitzer Memorial address, in Logue, *Ralph McGill*, 2:146.

[54]*Atlanta Constitution*, 21 November 1946.

[55]*Atlanta Constitution*, 5 February 1969.

[56]Russia Today speech, in Logue, *Ralph McGill*, 2:203.

[57]South in Transition speech, in Logue, *Ralph McGill*, 2:352.

[58]Seminar on Manpower speech, in Logue, *Ralph McGill*, 2:371.

would begin a column in the *Atlanta Constitution* in this manner: "In the past three weeks I have ridden by car or flown by plane over most of Georgia and the South."[59]

Indeed McGill's writings and speeches are significant historical notes on people, issues, and events. Many of McGill's articles reprinted below are firsthand reports. Before writing about W. E. B. DuBois, for example, McGill traveled to Ghana and talked to that elderly man. What about the article on Tom Watson, a person who had been dead for many years? McGill talked to persons who knew Watson personally. Here are some of the places McGill visited to obtain information. The experiences will be more interesting and insightful if presented in McGill's own words:

- "The first time I saw Edna St. Vincent Millay was [in the 1920s while writing for the *Nashville Banner*] at the airport in Nashville, Tennessee. . . . She was there to give a reading of her poems. . . . One I asked her to write down and sign for me. . . . I recall it inexactly, but it went something like this:"

> See that man standing there,
> The one close there by the stair?
> No, not him, the one in blue serge pants.
> Well, he was born in Paris, France.

- [McGill traveled] "to Scandinavia" in 1937, "where I diligently visited, lived with, and wrote about the farm marketing problems and methods of small farmers."
- "I recall standing in the cold of an April night in 1938 in a big railway station in Vienna to see and hear Hitler talk. They managed the trick lighting for him."
- "My first Atlantic flight was in early 1943 when the sea lanes had hostile submarines and war flamed on the continent of Europe and in the skies above it."
- In 1945 McGill was one of several representing the American Society of Newspaper Editors "in a sort of Johnny Appleseed mission of trying to . . . interest journalists . . . in a freer flow of news," taking him to London, Paris, Rome, Australia, Ceylon, and "then on to San Francisco where . . . the delegates were gathering to write a charter for the United Nations."
- "In January 1945, I arrived at Orly Field, Paris, from London and went to the Scribe Hotel for quarters. . . . So, we went on down and

---

[59]*Atlanta Constitution*, 11 August, and 8 October 1946.

had a seat in a booth. Pretty soon [Ernest] Hemingway came in, his hands full of packages from the PX shop which was in a small room not far from the bar. . . . After a while Hemingway asked why we didn't go to his quarters at the Ritz Hotel."

● "When I finish with this [1951] I will send it to the Western Union Office, check out of the hotel, take a cab to the airport, climb aboard an airplane, and take off for Delhi, India. . . . Ever since I saw a little of it in 1945, I have said if I had my choice, I'd rather have a look at India than any one country."

● "Manchester, England, 12 May 1954: This was my eleventh trans-Atlantic crossing."

● "A few years ago I interviewed King Farouk of Egypt in his Palace at Cairo."

● [After visiting Germany in 1938] "there was the second visit—1946 and 1947. . . . Now [1957] one comes back to Berlin rebuilding. Her shops are full. Her theaters, opera, ballet, her book publishers, her city, all flourish."

● "Moscow recollections [1959]: Sitting in the Baptist Church in Moscow."

● "In the summer of 1959 I was one of the newspaper men accompanying Vice-President Nixon to Russia."

● "Paris, France," June 1960, "Charlie, I did just what you asked me to do. I found Charmaine. . . . She's older, Charlie."

● "Thoughts after climbing Fuji," Japan, 1962.

● "West Africa," Nigeria and Kaduna, 1963.

● To study candidates and the issues, McGill, a strong supporter of the Democratic party, accompanied the following persons in their campaigns: Franklin D. Roosevelt, Robert A. Taft, Adlai E. Stevenson, Dwight D. Eisenhower, John F. Kennedy, Lyndon B. Johnson, and Richard M. Nixon. Also, as the articles below show, he traveled widely throughout the South to observe Southerners in all walks of life.

● In 1967, he wrote: "An American, who in the span of a few months has been, even for a few weeks, in Vietnam, Hong Kong, Japan, England, Ghana in West Africa, and a number of East Africa's developing nations, finds himself thinking—in the rare hours of rest—on his country. He thinks of the vast changes which everywhere take place so rapidly that he feels, at times, he actually sees changes in motion all around him."[60]

[60]*Atlanta Constitution*, 9 June, and 29 September 1948; 23 October 1950; 5 September, and 21 November 1951; 15 August 1952; 25 January, and 13 May 1954; 2 September 1957; 12 August 1959; 25

ℓ

One final example will illustrate McGill's presence in unexpected places. When editing the essays below, the editor was checking a passage quoted by McGill in his article on Tom Watson from a 1936 speech of Richard B. Russell. To determine the accuracy of McGill's borrowed passage, the editor searched for a text of the speech in the *Atlanta Constitution*. Who covered that speech for the newspaper? Yes, sports editor Ralph McGill, writing as a "staff correspondent," heard, noted, and reported the Russell speech in the *Atlanta Constitution*. So this editor found himself comparing a passage written by McGill in the *New Republic* in 1948 with a press report written by him in 1936! The results of that comparison are presented in a footnote in the article on Tom Watson.

Eugene Patterson told how McGill "would go to the North Carolina mountains and sit on the porch of the late Carl Sandburg and drink goats' milk and sing." Then this restless Georgian would travel to the "North Georgia mountains for a visit with the fragile poet Byron Herbert Reece, or down to Milledgeville for a visit among the peacocks with the late Flannery O'Connor. Carson McCullers, Erskine Caldwell, Margaret Mitchell, and Lillian Smith," Patterson continued, "were McGill's friends. He looked upon them as resources of the South as well as admirable achievers."[61] By reading the articles below, we can travel with McGill from mountain to sea. First we share McGill's exploration of the mysteries of life's changing seasons. Then, against that backdrop, McGill introduces us to poets, clergymen, educators, journalists, sportsmen, businessmen, and politicians who lived in the South. The book ends with an interview with "Reb" Gershon, longtime friend of Ralph McGill.

June 1960; 13 and 14 September 1961; 8 August 1962; 13 and 15 March 1963; McGill, *The South and the Southerner*, pp. 178, 186.

[61]*Washington Post*, 5 February 1969.

Essay 1

Behold, Spring Sweeps Over the World Again!¹*

Once again a troubled earth has turned on its slow wheel and it is spring.

Shelley sang of it:

Behold! Spring sweeps over the world again,
Shedding soft dews from her ethereal wings:
Flowers on the mountains, fruits over the plain,
And music on the waves and woods, she flings,
And love on all that lives, and calm on lifeless things.²

And so spring does sweep over the world again. The fields clothe themselves with grass, the trees with leaves. Flowers bloom. Birds busy themselves nesting. There is a surge of renewal that comes with that mysterious time

---

*Some of editor Calvin Logue's notes to the McGill essays are necessarily rather lengthy. In order not to interrupt the essays with the imposition of these sometimes long notes, the editor's notes occur as *endnotes* at the end of each respective essay. This, it is hoped, will prove to be of best advantage to the reader.—Editor, MUP

called the Vernal Equinox, causing man to feel ancient, atavistic forces at work within him. Primitive peoples, when confronted with it, saw all their best gods at work. Pagans celebrated with festivals of praise and dancing. It was almost as if they were trying to answer something within them.

All about them death was being conquered. Fields which had lain sodden and sere all the long, cold months of winter were showing green. The bare, barren branches of trees were budding. Plants were thrusting themselves out of the dark, dumb earth.

Seeing all this, pagan peoples felt a surging response and celebrated with festivals.

For almost 2,000 years now we have known that this rich and responsive symbolism has a deeper meaning. It is still a surging emotion within us. It still is a great and wondrous thing to watch the swift sweep of spring. We do not yet know all about the mystery of chlorophyl. It is the key which unlocks the doors of spring in all our plants. But we do have the key to the Creator's symbolism. It is in our own Easter Day—the Resurrection. Man, too, has within him a spiritual chlorophyl which will enable him, too, to live again in after life.[3] Out of his death will rise a new life as mysterious as that of new leaf, of flower, of grass, of grain, of fruits and gardens richly colorful with varied vegetables which emerge each spring from seed which have been buried in earth.

So spring is a promise.

It was that which the pagans sensed but could not know.

It is fitting that such a promise should be both mysterious and magnificently beautiful. There was a time when flowers were wild things—Lilies of the fields and forests. But when agriculture was invented and man fixed his abode on earth, he began to bring flowers to him, answering some urge to keep the symbolic promise about him. And so, increasingly, with gardens, plants, trees, and with pots and boxes, he has brought flowers closer to his life.

So we see lawns, borders, and gardens glorious with daffodils, the butter-gold of jonquils, the soft yellows of forsythia, the oriental richness of colors in tulips, the Mediterranean beauty of anemones, the cascading purple of wisteria, the flaming crimsons of azaleas, the ivory of gardenias, the old-South language of camelias—all these and more, cry eloquently of the eternal promise, saying,

"Behold, spring sweeps over the world again!"

Notes—1

[1]Reprinted from *Atlanta Journal and Constitution Magazine* (13 April 1958), by permission of the author, Mrs. McGill, and Atlanta Newspapers, Inc.

[2]McGill appreciated poetry. He "memorized a dozen or so poems, mostly Kipling's" for the Daniel Webster Literary Society at McCallie School. At Vanderbilt he read and memorized Tennyson, Milton, Keats, and Shelley. See Ralph McGill, *The South and the Southerner* (Boston: Little, Brown and Co., 1964), p. 55; *Atlanta Constitution*, 20 December 1960; Huntsville talk, in Calvin McLeod Logue, *Ralph McGill: Editor and Publisher*, two vols. (Durham: Moore Publishing Co., 1969), 2:316-17.

[3]Having watched average citizens and world leaders close-up for many years, McGill developed definite conclusions about the nature of Man. Although "Man, generally, is pretty fine" and capable of heroic acts, he judged, "man by nature is somewhat primitive." Thus one should "not expect too much" from people. "By and large" they "are not informed and it usually is rather easy to lead them off on false trails by appealing to old prejudices. . . ." The result of this is that citizens seldom "act swiftly on issues" so "man progresses by inches" and "never by leaps." *Atlanta Constitution*, 10 December 1946; 23 March and 25 December 1947; 1 March and 26 September 1948; 14 February and 3 September 1950; 2 October 1957; 12 February 1960; Air Defense Command speech, Logue, *Ralph McGill*, 2:68, 70, and Dayton speech, 2:87, 92.

Essay 2

Top of the World[1]

This is dawn at the top of Georgia's
    world. And an old song
       comes to mind:

> *Day, oh Day—*
> *Yonder comes Day.*
> *Day done brake into my soul—*
> *Yonder comes Day.[2]*

And a poet's lines come, too:

> *Night's candles are burnt out, and jocund day*
> *Stands tiptoe on the misty mountain tops.[3]*

This is the earth's ritual and mystery of the coming
      of light. And in north Georgia it is Brasstown Bald
which gets an early glimpse of it. Brasstown Bald is itself
    a mystery. It is the highest peak of Mount Enotah, rising
4,784 feet above sea level. It is forested now—save for the
      area about the peak. Even in ancient days, when only
the Cherokees lived there, there was a "bald" at the

top. And, somehow, a twisted, stunted white oak
tree has managed to grow there, lifting its
dwarfed arms upward as if it were a sun worshiper greeting
its god. The Cherokees thought the feet of the gods
had touched the mountain's top and that thereafter
nothing would grow there. They had a village down
in the valley and, to English ears, the Indian pronuncia-
tion sounded like "Brasstown." In their language it
meant "Town of the Green Valley." But the first settlers
who came through the dark passes of the tumbled
folds of the Appalachians called it "Brasstown," and the "bald"
on the mountain above it came to be called by the
same name. So, this is where we stand—you and I—on top
of the world in Georgia—watching day break
into our souls. There is a thin frost on the hills. Below us
are the forests, the valleys, the homes tucked into the
slopes, the plumes from their chimneys rising straight for
a while until the winds which blow always at dawn
catch them and diffuse them into disappearance. Below us is a
segment of road. Below us are the trickles, the tiny little
streams which join others to become rivers.
Below us are dark areas where no sun has yet penetrated.
Below us is no sign of life. In the houses and the cabins
they have just waked to put wood on the fire. If one were
down in the valleys there would be an occasional smell of coffee
riding the cold, sharp winds. But above us there is only
the vastness, the emptiness, of the unknown outer
spaces. Somewhere out there the Russian Sputniks whirled
around and around the earth. Millions of miles out there
are the stars and satellites of earth. And somewhere,
too, are planets and constellations. And over
it all broods the sense of eternity—of creation:
In His hand are all the corners of the earth,
And the strength of the hills is His, also.
The sea is His, and He made it: And His hands
prepared the dry land.[4]
This is the top of the world—in Georgia.

Notes—2

[1]Reprinted from *Atlanta Journal and Constitution Magazine* (23 February 1958), by permission of the author, Mrs. McGill, and Atlanta Newspapers, Inc.

[2]McGill wrote that he heard a man singing this while plowing with a mule: "I have seen him with his mule going out to the field where the plow was left last night. I have heard him singing as he went in the early morning," "A Southern Editor Talks With Philadelphia Negroes," *Philadelphia Sunday Bulletin* (17 September 1961).

[3]McGill quoted these lines from William Shakespeare, *Romeo and Juliet*, Act III.

[4]McGill quoted this passage from "Morning Prayer," *Book of Common Prayer and Administration of the Sacraments and Other Rites and Ceremonies of the Church* (New York: Seabury Press, 1928), p. 9.

Essay 3

Autumn[1]

Life is a road and all the roads of our lives run to meet the seasons; spring's symbol of renewal, summer's surge of growth, winter's wand of death—

But none comes so suddenly as autumn with her ritual of harvest, her mystery of maturity, her mists of early morning, her hazy dusks, and the wonder of her paint-splashed hills where the hand of God has been, and is.

The slopes look warm and soft as an old hooked rug. They are as gay as a coat of many colors. They glow like a tent of many-tinted silk. They might be grandma's old quilting bag turned out on each tree, or a massed army with myriad banners.

Autumn is fulfillment. It is the season of fullgrown manhood and womanhood. The spring of birth and the summer of growth are behind. Autumn is the harvest of both.

Autumn is the symbol of a life which has brought forth abundantly, which has justified the gift of life and the process of growth.

Autumn is mystery and promise. The sun-splashed, color-gay coolness of the hills beckons to us.

And so we take the curving, man-made roads that climb into them. We stand at some high peak and look across a valley to the hills beyond, seeing the mists in the morning and the smoky haze that comes with dusk. And the great mystery of life seems close about us and ancestral voices out of the long past whisper in the ears of our mind, causing a stir within our deepest being.

Children do not give much more than a glance at the beauty. They are spring. Young men and women "oh" and "ah" and bring out the camera to make color shots. They are summer.

Autumn is the season of maturity and harvest.
And all the roads of our life run to it, and
our hearts lean toward it
in a spiritual ritual of mystery
not understood, but felt.

Notes—3

[1]Reprinted from *Atlanta Journal and Constitution Magazine* (13 October 1957), by permission of the author, Mrs. McGill, and Atlanta Newspapers, Inc.

Essay 4

November in the Hills[1]

For the poets of England and other northern climes November is a dour and surly month of cold blasts and cheerlessness.

But not in the South.

With us November is the month when in the hills the long slopes of the ranges seem to reach out and pull a farm house and its barns, or a small town itself, warmly against the great breast of the dark mountain where the last color of autumn leaves still holds.

In the valleys and along the climbing reaches of the slopes in the early days of the month, where the still-warm sun holds through the day, the hardiest autumn wild flowers still bloom. The diligent bees seek them out in the warmest hours and, pollen-laden, hum back to their hive on farm or in some distant, hidden tree.

Cattle still find fescue grass to crop in the pastures. In the farm gardens, bright greens of collards and turnips are fresh and sweetened by the coolness of night and the mists of fall. Along the edges of the fields where hay was, and among the dry, brittle stalks of corn, the golden globes of pumpkins glow warmly with a color which frustrates artists. Autumn's fire still burns in the woods, but day by day the leaves fall and the dark, deep green of fir and pine show clear.[2]

The mountain mists do not taste of fever as they do along the coasts or the slow, yellow inland rivers. The early riser, in that hour when the freshened log fire on the hearth sends up the chimney the mysterious, nostalgia-producing aroma of its smoke, can almost feel the stillness as the dark, brooding convolutions of the hills "stand shadowless like silence listening to silence." There is something that speaks from the mountains as there is from the sea.[3]

But the sun comes and the mists of morning melt. In the garden the broad leaves of greens glitter with iridescent drops. In the fields the stubble of hay and wheat gleam and glow with myriad sun-lit droplets and on the ranges the many colored leaves have clean, moist faces, waiting to be dried by the sun.

November is the month of harvest and the time of fulfillment. November is the time when faith visibly is confirmed. The men who plowed and dropped the seeds in the spring, see in November's fields the physical products of those inert seeds with their symbol of resurrection and life. Good seed to bring forth good fruit. The meaning of harvest touches all who see November beyond the paved streets and crowded buildings.

But it is best in the hills!

Notes—4

[1]Reprinted from *Atlanta Journal and Constitution Magazine* (1 November 1959), by permission of the author, Mrs. McGill, and Atlanta Newspapers, Inc.

[2]As a classmate of McGill's at Vanderbilt University, Allen Tate predicted that McGill "would become a powerful journalist rather than a 'creative writer'." Actually he became a creative journalist. At McCallie School he wrote two short stories for the *McCallie Pennant*. Although he was never an actual member of the Fugitives, McGill told an audience: "My great happy school years were the twenties at Vanderbilt University when we had The Fugitive group and we were all trying to write poetry and novels. . . ." Although his "energies, after bitter frustration with verse, turned to the weekly student newspaper, the *Hustler*," McGill never lost his love for words. When asked by journalism students how they could learn to write, he replied that it is good to be "a teller of tales who can put into them the language of persons and the feel of the soil and the people. It also is a fine thing for a writer . . . to have an eye for trees and hills and birds and animals and a memory for smells and sound." See Letter from Allen Tate to Calvin M. Logue, 12 July 1966; *McCallie Pennant*, 1914, p. 29; Reynolds Lecture, Logue, *Ralph McGill*, 2:466; McGill, *The South and the Southerner*, p. 76; *Atlanta Constitution*, 7 May 1948.

[3]"Brooding" came easily to McGill. Underlying his writings was the "slogan, 'Life is real, life is earnest'." "I tell you. I'm a serious-minded sort of person, I'm

afraid," he wrote. A recurring theme in his discourse was "something that speaks from the mountains and the sea": "Riding through the Blue Ridge Mountains . . . a voice within one wants to cry out, 'Oh, God, I am terribly alone and lost and somehow afraid.' There is a mystery which always at this moment seems about to explain itself to me. . . . But always it goes, though it touches your cheek and mind like the black wing of a ghostly bird, and it is night and the feeling of mystery and stillness and the fear that comes like the fear in a dream are gone, and it is nothing but night and the road long and winding. . . . But that moment, when it was neither dark nor light—what was it trying to say?" *Atlanta Constitution*, 4 and 22 August 1946; 13 February and 4 November 1947; 31 May and 13 September 1949; 19 July and 30 August 1951; 10 August 1955; Calvin M. Logue's taped interview with McGill, 29 December 1965, Atlanta, Georgia, in Logue, *Ralph McGill*, 2:26.

Essay 5

Endden Revisited[1]

We arrived for our second visit to Endden in mid-afternoon of Saturday, 29 May 1954. My heart went out to the place last year. And again, this time, I felt immediately at home and soothed by the peace of it. So did we all.[2]

The beach draws me and seduces me into blistered arms, shoulders and nose. But, I cannot stay away. So many things happen.

That first afternoon, walking south, close to the dunes, I noted a sandpiper running to my right, apparently seeking to draw me away. (Do they nest in the dunes?) I began to run with the bird. For a span we ran along together, a few yards apart. I stopped. He (or she) stopped. I ran. The bird ran. I stopped. It stopped. So we went, running, stopping, running, until we had gone quite a way. At last I stopped and burst out laughing at the bird. It regarded me gravely as if saying, "What an idiot is man!" When I turned to go back it followed behind until I was safely past the spot from which it had drawn me.

A philosopher could say the beach is a segment of life. There goes on, between sandpipers and the tiny marine life; between gulls and pelicans and small fish; between crabs and other minute life, the eternal struggle for survival. In the sea, when schools of porpoise and sharks go by, we can see the same struggle as the fleeing fish leap from the water, or when we see a splash and know the fish has been caught. Small children on the beach fight over sand shovels and inner tubes. An adult, looking at the beauty of the beach and sea, and watching these struggles of bird, fish, crab, the sand fleas, tiny boring shell fish—cannot fail but to think on himself. "God is"—and man has something from Him which struggles against the ruthlessness of the Darwinian contest which goes on continually. Endden is a good place to think and meditate on these things. No matter how much alone man is, there is always a witness.

One day on the fishing pier a man caught a shark weighing eighty-seven pounds. It was cut up for shark bait. Others were hooked, but all were large enough to break away. Days later a woman fishing on the pier caught a sand shark weighing about five pounds. She was about to throw it back when a fisherman asked for it, saying, "To catch a shark the best bait is another shark." (Meditate on that, you philosophers.) He baited with it and caught a shark weighing more than 100 pounds. Two days later I saw, off the beach, a school of what at first I took to be porpoises—but on second look were not. They were sharks, about fifteen of them, a tan, or yellow color, moving slowly. Fish ran ahead of them. I saw some fish leap desperately from the water and though they were some distance out I am sure they weighed a good twenty pounds. Now and then there would be swirling splashes—a fish caught. The sharks moved back and forth for half an hour, obviously in a school of large fish. Then they went away. They are not the type which attacks people, and they do not come in close to shore.

The beach at Endden is magnificent in its safety. The sand bar sluices of last year are gone. The bar is much wider and the beach improved. The surges of last winter were good for the sands.

By our measurement it is nine-tenths of a mile from Endden steps to the pier. I walked it every morning and then went in swimming, astonished that a walk of almost two miles was not really tiring. One morning, toward the pier, there was a down pillow on the beach—marked USN. Some poor sailor or coast guardsman had it deducted from his pay. On the day of our arrival the beach was heavily strewn with reed-like deposits. A day later sea weed came in. A day after that I read where ships were late in New York because of gales in the Atlantic. Our reeds and weeds came from that, torn from their beds many miles away. After that nothing came in save the usual pieces of wood, bottles, milk cartons and—of all things—the pillow.

I thought of things on the beach one night when reading "Visit and Search, the Dialogues of Whitehead," in the May *Atlantic*.[3] Whitehead recalled that in the 1880s when he went to Cambridge, everything was supposed to be known about physics that could be known save for a few spots such as electromagnetic phenomena. But for the rest physics was supposed to be a closed subject. By the middle of the 1890s there were a few tremors and a slight shiver as of not being quite so sure, but none sensed what was coming—by 1900 the Newtonian physics were demolished and done for. "Speaking personally," he said, "I'll be damned if I'll be fooled again. . . . The danger is dogmatic thought. It plays the devil with religion and science is not immune from it. . . . It doesn't strike me as at all impossible that the smallest pebble might contain within it a universe as complex as the one we know, and that the universe of universes which we have recently begun to apprehend may be as minute in the scale of what lies beyond as that in the pebble to the one we know: or that the vastness might be as much greater in the opposite direction—the direction of what we consider the infinitely small."[4]

Shells make one think of that even more than pebbles.

Certainly nature cannot be all chance. Chance would not spend so much time in the almost infinite variety and beauty of shells, making each different. The sand dollar, for example, with its exquisite five petals flowering in the center, could have been as utilitarian without the carefully shaped petals. The Angel's Wing, the razor clam—these and others may be accepted as merely the product of the laws of evolution. Yet, they are all on the same beach and quite obviously nature is more than evolution.

I am quite willing to believe that the universe we know is quite small and that what lies beyond is greater and better, more beautiful and wonderful. After all, it is only sixty-four years since the Newtonian laws were demolished. And we are on the verge of much new knowledge.

The beach with its shells is a good place to think.

Lying in bed, waiting for sleep at Endden (and the wait is never long), one is more conscious of the surf. Eternally it rolls and makes its soothing, retreating, recurring sound in which the sibilants are so flung together they become a hissing, muted roar.

Thought, I believe, is like that. Especially so is it true in these times when new dangers, crises, and decisions come in on us like a surf. They, too, change our shorelines, remove or create sandbars, make for high tides and low. But they will never stop coming.

One afternoon, sitting in "Rachael's Roost," the children ran down on the low-tide beach to play. It was at that wonderful moment when the sun has just gone but the light remains—a translucent, Mediterranean sort of light. There were Ann and Mary Clelan, Ralph, Jr., and two more children on the beach. They had on various colored dress—and they ran playing in a tight pattern. I remember thinking I had never seen so much grace and such natural choreography. It was a really beautiful ballet. And somehow, with the sea behind it, and the figures running, turning, whirling, it seemed to have meaning, though I could not put it down in tangible words.

Endden, we think, is wonderful. Nothing about it cloys.

Notes—5

[1]Reprinted from manuscript in the McGill papers provided by Mrs. Ralph McGill.

[2]Frank H. Neely, honorary chairman of the board, Rich's Inc., Atlanta, Georgia, wrote to Logue on 4 February 1970: "He visited us at Endden, which is at Fernandina Beach, Florida, and wrote one of the most beautiful stories, Mrs. Neely feels, that was ever written. It is pasted in a book at Endden. Endden is the name of the house that I built for my grandchildren. The "E" is for Eve, "N" is for Nathan, the "D" is for Daniel; then we reversed it and produced the name Endden, which has been the name of the place ever since. . . . It is on the road that the Navy built during the War. . . . The road is on one side and the ocean is on the other, so it makes a very beautiful place for the children to go and fish and swim."

[3]See Lucien Price, "Visit and Search: Dialogues of Whitehead," *Atlantic* 193 (May 1954): 53. Lucien wrote *Dialogues of Alfred North Whitehead* (Boston: Little, Brown and Company, 1954.)

[4]The first sentence McGill quoted from Lucien's quotation of Whitehead actually reads: "Still speaking personally, it had a profound effect on me; I have been fooled once, and I'll be damned if I'll be fooled again!" The word, "of," in "universe *of* universes" should be "or," thus reading, "universe or universes"; Lucien, "Visit and Search: Dialogues of Whitehead," p. 53. For more on Frank H. Neely, see McGill's article in this volume.

Essay 6

Carl Sandburg Says: Don't Let Others Spend Your Time[1]

"A man must find time for himself. Time is what we spend our lives with. If we are not careful we find others spending it for us. . . ."

Carl Sandburg was talking, forcefully, strongly, entertainingly. We sat on his front porch. Before us the slope of the mountain above the village of Flat Rock, North Carolina, fell sharply away and across the tops of the tall, majestic hemlock firs, there stretched a long vista of the folded blue peaks of the ancient Appalachians, turquoise and dark, with Mt. Mitchell's peak blue above them all at the farthest reach of the horizon.

"It is necessary now and then," he said, expanding his point, "for a man to go away by himself and experience loneliness; to sit on a rock in the forest and to ask of himself, 'Who am I, and where have I been, and where am I going?' Once I met a man who took pride in the fact he had listened to 600 radio programs by a well-known comedian. He didn't seem to realize he was allowing the comedian to spend his time for him. Radio and television have many fine things to give, as do other diversions. But if one is not careful, one allows them to spend one's time—the stuff of life."[2]

The marching hills seemed to nod affirmatively.

Born in Galesburg, Illinois, of Swedish parentage in January of 1878, Carl Sandburg has become perhaps the greatest American singer, or Singer of America, put it either way.[3] Some have sought to compare him with Walt Whitman, and that is not sound. Whitman saw much of America. He could write well. But he couldn't smell America, or feel it, or read the eyes and faces of the people. His verses sing, but there is not in them the American images which come crowding out of Sandburg's poetry. Who, for example, can make us see, smell, and know a city as he did Chicago, in the poem with that title which begins:[4]

Hog Butcher for the World,
Tool Maker, Stacker of Wheat,
Player with Railroads and the Nation's
        Freight Handler;
Stormy, Husky, Brawling,
City of the Big Shoulders.

There are sensitive, gentle images, too, in this man's mind and his fingers have put them down. "The Harbour" will do, or maybe a brief one, "Fog."[5]

The fog comes
        on little cat feet.
It sits looking
        over harbour and city
        on silent haunches
        and then moves on.

There is great imagery, too, in "Grass," which begins:[6]

Pile the bodies high at Austerlitz
        and Waterloo.
Shovel them under and let me
        work.
        I am the grass; I cover all.

But he, of all the poets, has taken the stuff of America, the building of her, the sweat, the fields and factories of her, and made poems of them. There was a famous evangelist once who didn't like one of his poems titled "To a Contemporary Bunkshooter"—but everyone knew who it was—[7]

You come along . . . tearing your
        shirt, yelling about Jesus.
Where do you get that stuff?
What do you know about Jesus?

Poetry is not all. This man Sandburg with his Swedish ancestry, was so in tune with the country of his birth, that he was drawn to become the greatest scholar and researcher into the life of perhaps the greatest American—Abraham Lincoln. Sandburg had come along the hard way. He did common labor. He worked for an education. He was one of the Wisconsin progressives of whom Bob LaFollette, the elder, was leader. Always ahead of him was the American dream which he saw had to be interpreted in the lives of people, and never shining up in distant skies out of their reach. All this was fused in Lincoln and Sandburg picked all the locks in six magnificent volumes, "The Prairie Years" and "The War Years."[8]

He did a great novel, too—*Remembrance Rock*.[9] All in all, poems, articles, songs and sixteen fine books have come from his heart, mind, and his dream.

We sat there on his front porch and talked. It is a nice porch. Christopher Gustavus Memminger built it in 1838.[10]

The house had been empty two years when Carl Sandburg bought it and restored it.[11]

It was cold weather that started Sandburg and his family on the journey which ended there on the slope of an Appalachian Mountain. Yet, paradoxically, it was cool weather that dictated the selection.

They had been living on the shores of Lake Michigan. It was grievously cold there in winter. And the sandy soil was not good for a garden. (Something of his frugal, careful Swedish ancestors is within Sandburg and urges him to insist on a semi-subsistence sort of living.) So, they packed up about a freight car load of books and said they would send for them and the furniture one of these days, arranged for the goats to be fed and milked, and set out to look for a place. It was a hot summer of five years ago and the heat was dreadful. So, when they began to climb the grade out of the flatlands up to Asheville, and the air began to be cooler, Carl Sandburg and his family began to revive. And when at last they were on top of the slopes he said, "This is the place," just as Brigham Young said when he led his flock to the valley of the Great Salt Lake.

A real estate man took them around and at last showed them the old Memminger place, deserted, and given over to chipmunks, squirrels, and memories of departed glories.

The books and the goats came along later.

Everyone asks about the goats. Carl Sandburg, when he goes traveling, sometimes startles a fellow passenger on a train by taking from his bag sandwiches of homemade cheese (Mrs. Sandburg is an artist at making it) and a water bottle filled with goats' milk which he quaffs between bites.[12]

There are 164 goats on the Sandburg farm, and they not only are one of the finest herds in America, with orders coming, and being filled, from South American countries and many American states, but their milk is much in demand

and is marketed through the famed Biltmore dairies near Asheville. Arthur and Helga Golby manage the dairy. Helga is Helga Sandburg, youngest daughter, and something like a Norse goddess herself, handy with the English language in prose or poetry, with oils and canvas, and with goats. She also does typing for her father and is a very busy young lady indeed. Her husband is a veteran of the Pacific campaigns, a fine young writer and actor who came to North Carolina for the North Carolina Playhouse season. After he met Helga, he never left.

The goats happened to become a part of the Sandburg household because of a small shed on the Lake Michigan place. One day Sandburg said they ought to have a cow. The shed was too small for a cow. But it was just right for a goat. So, said Sandburg, get a goat. They did.

None of the family had ever tasted goats' milk. But from the start they liked it. All, that is, but Mrs. Sandburg. She didn't know if she'd like it or not. She was quite ill with a gall bladder infection, and physicians were gravely concerned as to whether she would survive. (She is sister to Edward Steichen, internationally famous photographer and plant breeder of note, and is a wonderful person in her own right.) Because of her illness she could not drink milk because of the fat content, and butter was, of course, strictly taboo. But, one day, weary of hearing the family praise goat milk, she secretly drank a large glass and went to bed again, expecting a severe attack. Nothing happened. She tried again a few days later, this time with a piece of bread well buttered with goats' milk butter. Again, there was no reaction.

"I found out," she said, "that because nature homogenizes goats' milk, and because it has so small and soft a curd, it is digestible in about twenty minutes as compared with two hours or more for cows' milk, which is not naturally homogenized and has a large, tough curd. I began to drink the milk, eat the butter, and make cheese to eat. I gained in health every day. Now look at me."

She is a picture of health, jolly, radiant and intelligent. She makes a fine yogurt from the milk, too, and as an expert consumer of this delicacy, I can testify it is as good as the cheese and milk.

Mrs. Sandburg, Helga, and Arthur would like for one correction to be made. Bill Sharpe, the indefatigable publicist for North Carolina, wrote of a Sandburg goat which gave three or four gallons of milk. Hopeful, wistful farmers have driven three and four hundred miles to see the "three-gallon goat." There is no such animal. Three *quarts* is a fine production.

Also, visitors arrive ready to hold their noses. They always are surprised. There is no odor to milk goats. Only the males smell bad, a fact which seems to amuse ladies who arrive with husbands or male escorts. Also, as Mrs. Sandburg says, the milk goat is a dainty, neat, and clean animal and makes the cow look like the dirty, careless animal she really is.

The Sandburg household consists, in addition to those already mentioned, of a daughter, Margaret, who is a splendid pianist and who assists her famous father in research; a third daughter, Janet, who is second in command to her mother in running the domestic side of things, and two grandchildren, Helga's Paula and John.

Sandburg, at 73, is straight as one of his hemlock pines, and his mind and memory are as alert and as agile as his legs—which take him on long walks of five miles and more every day the weather is good. Some days he disappears at noon and returns at dark, having spent the time in the woods walking, thinking, or sitting on a rock or stump writing down notes.[13]

He usually works all night. The family never knows when he goes to bed. Every morning at nine a breakfast tray is outside his door. It varies only slightly. There is a thermos jug of coffee. There are two large slices of homemade dark bread, well buttered. There are two ripe tomatoes in summer and a large glass of tomato juice in winter. Sometimes he comes down the stairs with his tray as they are eating lunch. Or he has it upstairs and appears about two o'clock.[14]

Since he is the greatest scholar and writer on Lincoln (his books on Lincoln, *The Prairie Years* and *The War Years,* sold better in the South than did Freeman's life of Robert E. Lee), visitors ask him what Lincoln would do today. He answers them, grinning, "He'd eat, sleep, and think a lot. And he'd get the subject thoroughly in his head, and try to compromise it out."

Sandburg likes North Carolina and the South. Alexander Stephens, of Georgia, who was vice-president of the Confederacy, is one of his favorite historical characters.

Both Asheville and Chapel Hill are becoming writing-colony centers. In addition to Sandburg at nearby Flat Rock, Asheville has Mr. and Mrs. Demaree Bess, and Tom Polsky. Bess is one of the editors of the *Saturday Evening Post,* and a really distinguished writer on foreign affairs, who spent thirty-five years in Europe. Polsky is a writer of mystery novels, his best known being *The Cudgel.* And, of course, the ghost of Tom Wolfe will always be there.

Notes—6

[1]Reprinted from *Atlanta Journal and Constitution Magazine* (6 January 1952), by permission of the author, Mrs. McGill, and Atlanta Newspapers, Inc.; that *Magazine* reprinted the article with some alterations 28 October 1962. McGill wrote a similar article on Sandburg, "The Most Unforgettable Character I've Met," for the *Reader's Digest* (May 1954), pp. 109-13. Because McGill provides additional information in that article, the editor will quote extensively from that essay. This material is reprinted with permission. Copyright 1954 by the Reader's Digest Association, Inc.

²In the *Reader's Digest*, pp. 109-10, McGill wrote: "I waited on the porch, rocking in one of the big, old-fashioned chairs and thinking on the man with the boyish heart who, at 76, still pours forth writing and song possessing the simple beauty and strength of the marching, blue mountain ranges of the Appalachians on which I looked. Soon there was a booming voice and Carl Sandburg came out. We sat and talked. As always on a visit to Connemara, the first subject is the view. It looks across miles of tumbled, folded ranges all the way to towering Mt. Mitchell, clothed in the eternal haze of blue which the Indians said was the shadow of the Great Spirit. . . . 'A man must get away now and then to experience loneliness,' he said. 'Only those who learn how to live with loneliness can come to know themselves and life. I go out there and walk and look at the trees and sky. I listen to the sounds of loneliness. I sit on a rock or a stump and say to myself, 'Who are you, Sandburg? Where have you been, and where are you going?' 'Time,' he continued, 'is the coin of our lives. We must take care how we spend it. . . . A man must discover his own life, and how to spend time, the stuff of which existence is made'."

³Sandburg was born 6 January 1878, and died 22 July 1967. For further reading see Carl Sandburg, *Always the Young Strangers* (New York: Harcourt Brace Jovanovich, Inc., 1952); Harry Lewis Golden, *Carl Sandburg* (Cleveland: World Publishers, 1961); Richard Crowder, *Carl Sandburg* (New York: Twayne Publishing Inc., 1964); William A. Sutton, *Carl Sandburg Remembered* (Metuchen, New Jersey: Scarecrow Press, Inc., 1979).

⁴Carl Sandburg, *Complete Poems* (New York: Harcourt Brace Jovanovich, Inc., 1950), p. 3. Reprinted by permission of Harcourt Brace Jovanovich, Inc. © 1944 by Carl Sandburg. In the poem, "Chicago," McGill capitalized "h" in "husky," and "b" in "brawling." In "An Evening with Carl Sandburg," a typed paper from the McGill papers about Bette Davis coming to Atlanta to read Sandburg's poetry, McGill wrote of Sandburg's family: "They settled in Galesburg, Illinois. They were poor. The father was a laborer in the railroad shops. The boy grew up there. He shined shoes in the barber shop. He worked in a dairy. He was a fireman. He went to school some. But somehow, in one of the great mysteries of creation, the young child of Swedish immigrants was soaking up America. The prairies spoke to him, as did the cities. But mostly, it was people who communicated with him in the silence of understanding. He was a hobo for a while, and a dishwasher in greasy-spoon restaurants. He was a worker on farms and in shops. He went off to the Spanish-American War. And all the while there was building within him poems and stories, images and emotions, the prairies, the blossoms, the storms, the corn, wheat, the cities, noble and scabrous, the rivers and—always—the people. Whoever gave us such a picture of Chicago."

⁵Sandburg, *Complete Poems*, p. 33.

[6]Sandburg, *Complete Poems*, p. 137. McGill substituted a period for a dash, after "work."

[7]Sandburg, *Complete Poems*, pp. 29-31. There should be ellipses after "tearing your."

[8]Carl Sandburg, *Abraham Lincoln: The Prairie Years*, two vols. (New York: Harcourt Brace Jovanovich, Inc., 1926); Sandburg, *Abraham Lincoln: The War Years*, four vols. (New York: Harcourt Brace Jovanovich, Inc., 1939). McGill wrote: "Many writers become celebrities, but few indeed become personalities, associated with the essence of American life. . . . Sandburg has lived in more American situations than any writer since Mark Twain. He knew the prairies as a wanderer, a worker in fields and shops. He was part of what Golden calls 'the terrible adjustments of immigrants and farmers to an industrial society'. . . . This enabled him to write *The Prairie Years* of Lincoln's life—and to add the four volumes of *The War Years*. (Millions of words about a man whose mother couldn't sign her name by a man whose father couldn't sign his.) There is a beauty and a sensitiveness in these books never attained in any other biography." Typed review from McGill papers of Harry Lewis Golden, *Carl Sandburg* (Cleveland: World Publishers, 1961).

[9]Carl Sandburg, *Remembrance Rock* (New York: Harcourt Brace Jovanovich, Inc., 1948). McGill wrote: "His novel, *Remembrance Rock*, had the bad luck to be published at a time when a number of historical novels had surfeited the market. It remains a remarkably fine book about America—three books in one." Review of Golden, *Carl Sandburg*.

[10]"Sandburg and his family took Connemara to their hearts. First there was much carpentering and plastering to do. 'There came a time,' said Sandburg, 'when I began to look in the crannies and under old stones to see if the secretary of the treasury had left any money around—even Confederate—to help pay the contractor.' But at last it was done. 'Then came the great move,' Sandburg recalls, 'mostly books and goats'." See McGill, *Reader's Digest*, pp. 110-11; Paula Steichen, *My Connemara* (New York: Harcourt Brace Jovanovich, Inc., 1969), pp. 5-30.

[11]"His working quarters consist of a neat, Spartan-like bedroom and a small workroom with a window which looks out on the 'writin' out dere.' He begins work in the late afternoon, and often keeps at it into the dawn. He wears an old-fashioned green eyeshade, such as newspaper editors once wore, and most of the time there is the stub of a 'seegar' in his mouth." *Reader's Digest*, p. 111. In "An Evening With Carl Sandburg," McGill stated: "What a man he is—a poet, a novelist, a teller of children's tales, a writer and singer of ballads, an essayist and, of course, the biographer who caused Lincoln to come back and be one of us. When one has finished the six books of Lincoln, or even the one volume edition on the man, one feels that he has known Abe Lincoln a long, long time. He knows what

went on in that lonely man's heart and mind, what he thought and felt and dreamed, and what his sorrows were, and his joys."

¹²"From that one milk goat the herd grew to 160 pure breds, known and respected by all the nation's goatkeepers. This has now been reduced by sale to a nearby dairy, leaving only enough to supply the Sandburgs' needs. There is a pitcher of cold goats' milk on the table at lunch and dinner, along with butter and cheese. Mrs. Sandburg is a genius in the kitchen, and her cheese, yogurt, and breads are prized by appreciative visitors." *Reader's Digest*, p. 111.

¹³"The fact that Sandburg practices the old virtues of temperate living and plain, wholesome eating has helped keep him young in body, spirit, and mind. Once, before a walk, I waited while he changed to a warmer shirt. I noticed how firm and smooth the flesh was on his arms and shoulders. His legs are sound, too, and much younger men are soon walked down—as I discovered." *Reader's Digest*, p. 111. McGill wrote: "What a life Sandburg has had—and what a man he is. He soon will be 85. Yet, his schedule of writing, traveling, speaking, performing for television, is much heavier than that of [a man] of 55 years." Review of Golden, *Carl Sandburg*.

¹⁴In the *Reader's Digest*, pp. 111-13, McGill added: "Sandburg still relaxes with his old guitar, used in hundreds of lectures in which he has sung folk ballads or some of his poems. He likes to sit on the front porch and make up songs as the mood comes to him, about the hills, the visitors, or a big news story of the day. His voice has almost the quality and timbre of a musical instrument.

"He has the natural simplicity of a truly great person. It might be said that he inherited simplicity and faith. Among Sandburg's earliest recollections is that of his father, who toiled ten hours a day in the railroad shops at Galesburg, Illinois. The elder Sandburg couldn't write, but could read a little. The son remembers him bent over the Bible—a Swedish Bible from the old country—and he remembers, too, his mother's prayers and her whole way of life, which was, in a real sense, a living testament of faith.

"A letter his mother wrote in 1926, a few days before her death, helps to explain Sandburg's gentleness and humility and deep feeling for humanity. In her groping words can be seen the foundations for some of her son's later poems.

" 'Life is short if early days are lost. . . . With thought and love in the home so much can be overcome. . . . I find so much comfort in the thought of wise men; the Bible is full of it. . . . The larger wisdom behind the veil is yet strong and able to uplift the crushed. . . . Crushed I am many times, but not to death. The apron of silence is with me. Silence is a gift. Be silent.'

"During a visit with Sandburg last summer, our talk turned to his six Lincoln books. And then he was off:

" 'You take Lincoln when he floated a canoe down the Sangamon River in the summer of 1831—going to New Salem. It was a town of just about a dozen families at the time, yet for the young man from the prairie it was a cosmopolitan metropolis. Think what it meant to him, the raw-boned young fellow out of the backwoods!

" 'At New Salem there was a gristmill run by the Rutledges and Camerons. (Sandburg spoke as if they were actual aquaintances of his.) A man could hear all sorts of talk there as the farmers, from all parts of the new country and the old, came to grind their corn and wheat. And there was a school taught by Mentor Graham, a college graduate. Graham developed a special friendship for young Lincoln and soon had him devouring books. A debating society was organized, and Lincoln made his first real speech before it.

" 'There was talk and enterprise there to sharpen the mind. It was in New Salem that the young Lincoln began to find himself, to take on polish and to react to the best in his environment. When he moved on to Springfield he was ready for life.'

"There was more of Lincoln. Sandburg seemingly has never forgotten a single scrap of information discovered in twenty years of research on Lincoln. He lives closely with his writing. He felt so near to Lincoln that when he wrote the last chapters of *The War Years* he had to stop work from time to time to control his tears.

"Later the conversation turned to the recent success of *Always the Young Strangers*, the story of Sandburg's first twenty-one years. It is not merely a warm and inspiring picture of the son of a Swedish immigrant growing up in a small Illinois town but a moving portrayal of the making and shaping of what we call the American Dream. It was published on Sandburg's seventy-fifth birthday, the thirtieth book by a man whose father had never learned to write.

"It is a lot easier to be with Carl Sandburg, listening or just sitting looking at the 'writin' of the blue ridges, than to write about him. He is a rugged man whose face and figure might fittingly be chiseled out of rock in some carving of great Americans. He is, himself, so much the story of what America is supposed to mean in opportunity and life that one's inclination is to think of the great man, the man who had fulfilled the dream.

"One forgets that this famous, gentle man was once a poor, lonely and bewildered boy; was once a barbershop bootblack; was once a hobo, a dishwasher, a day laborer. Now and then, as you sit and talk with the man, and feel his philosophy sink in, he seems almost like one of the old prophets who came out of the desert's loneliness with a vision.

"The parents' hard-working, humble life shaped the philosophy of the son. The father never thought to be other than a plain, honest working man, living decently and paying his way. The faith in work and the knowledge of what those 'to fortune and fame unknown' have added to the sum of progress and human existence are strengths Carl Sandburg had from his father and mother. He has little patience with cheapness of mind or work. Nor with intolerance. He suspects the glib men who know all the answers. . . .

"People mean a lot to Sandburg: he thinks of them as human beings, not as problems or statistics. He is patient with all persons with dreams—especially young writers. (He had never forgotten the friends who encouraged him, and who listened to him read and sing.) He still goes, when he can, to the homes of young writers or newspapermen and talks with them, his viewpoints as fresh and vigorous as theirs.

"Meanwhile, he has work in the blueprint stage which will keep him busy for years to come. He faces the future with a faith from the pages of his father's old Swedish Bible and from his mother's life.

" 'The Chinese,' he says, 'have a saying that after seventy a man is like a candle in the wind . . . but sometimes the winds are soft . . . and if, when a man comes to die, he has a boy's heart, is that a bad thing?' "

In a letter to McGill, Carl Sandburg wrote that, "Sometime I may try to figure out who are the ten richest men in the country and you would be one of them." Quoted by "Reb" Gershon, life long friend of McGill's, in interview with Logue.

Essay 7

Little Woman, Big Book: The Mysterious Margaret Mitchell[1]

"Peggy's book is coming out on June thirtieth," said the book buyer at Davison's, "and the publisher is allowing us to release it a bit earlier; so we are having a luncheon for some of her friends. . . ." (It was 1936.)

At lunch that day Peggy was excited; she had been for months. She was keyed to laughter and a sort of role Don Marquis's cockroach Archy would describe as *toujours gai*. She was weary from weeks of reading galley proofs with her husband. If Macmillan was going to publish the novel, then, by damn, there would be no errors in it.

There were friends around the table, and some of them were a bit resentful because she hadn't told them she was writing a novel. "Why didn't you tell us, Peggy? We'll never forgive you."

"Me? Tell secrets?" she replied, and laughter went about the table. Anything and everything was gay and bright that day because Peggy was there and her book was ready. There were copies of it on the table, side by side with the flowers—big fat books with dark yellow dust jackets, with an Old South scene on them, and the large letters *Gone With the Wind* at the top.

"Any news from the publishers about the advance?" asked the man to the right of Peggy, while the eager gabble of conversation went on. ". . . . Honestly, you'd think she would have told someone. . . ."

"They're pleased," she said. "Pleased. I don't know exactly what that means. I've read about first novels. If you sell 2,500 copies it's average. I have hopes this one may go at least 5,000 copies." She paused and her face lighted up. "If all the Southern lending libraries buy a couple of copies," she said, grinning, "it may go 10,000. Wouldn't that be grand?"

It was an innocent luncheon, an innocent author and guests. In two months, *Gone With the Wind* was a runaway best seller. The Book-of-the-Month Club took it for July. Macmillan added 50,000 copies to a planned first edition of 10,000. In a little more than three months, it sold over 500,000 copies.[2]

Those of us who gathered for lunch that day to celebrate Peggy's novel did not know it, but that was the last time we'd ever see the complex little woman of many paradoxes whom we knew so well. *Gone With the Wind* was to fall in on her. The weight of success became heavier. She made a gallant fight to remain Peggy Mitchell. She and her husband kept the same apartment, the same cat, and servant. They held fast to the old friends and rather wistfully sought to retain the simple routines. But it was not to be. A new image grew of Peggy Mitchell. Her health and that of her husband became a problem. Success did not spoil her, but it changed her life.[3]

Gone With the Wind was issued against the background of a savage depression. It was a time in which the nation was surfeited with the corrosive sorrows, frustrations, and the griefs produced by economic defeat. But it also was a time of resolution in the face of disaster and need.

The world was as badly off. There were civil wars and rebellions. There was the sound of collapsing thrones; the creaking of others could be heard. Mussolini and Hitler were making the trains run on time and preaching a super race and a master philosophy. There was something in *Gone With the Wind* for all who read it—and European editions, both pirated and legitimate, soon were appearing. Tough and secular Scarlett O'Hara, ruthlessly resourceful; compassionate, gentle Melanie; and Rhett Butler, the gallant black-market operator of 1861-1865 and the Reconstruction, who had turned to "the cause" in its death struggle—all these, and others, were akin to persons everywhere in the sick and hurt world of the 1930s. Letters were to come from Poland and Spain saying, "We have lived the things which you have written."

The book kept selling. In mid-1961, Macmillan announced that more than 10,000,000 copies had been sold, not counting paperback or pirated editions. *Gone With the Wind* had been printed in twenty-five languages. These included Chinese, Japanese, Czech, the Scandinavian languages, Arabic, Slovak, Polish and, of course, the less exotic languages of the world. Thirty foreign countries have accounted for sales of almost 5,000,000. (English-language editions have sold more than 5,000,000.) A number of countries pirated editions. Peggy Mitchell, daughter of a lawyer, fought these with some success, winning royalties in Holland, Chile, Yugoslavia, and Japan. In time she developed a grudging admiration for their brazen knavery. "The bastards always send me copies of their illegal editions," she said. "Usually, there is a letter telling me how much they liked the book."

Years ago, a critic who didn't care for the Mitchell writing style and who thought the plot commonplace, confessed to having been overwhelmed and silenced by the huge success and perpetual momentum of the book. *Gone With the Wind*, said the critic, "is not a book, but a phenomenon."

It is both book and phenomenon. It is no exaggeration to say that if all the stories and articles on Margaret Mitchell and the book (factual, fantastic, and false) were published, they would make half a dozen or more volumes as thick as the novel itself. That the deluge of interest and curiosity in her and it has never halted is eloquent evidence of the book's healthy longevity. It is a geriatric literary curiosity, a veritable Methuselah insofar as life is concerned.

The young woman who wrote it has been dead since 11:59 AM, 16 August 1949. She died in Atlanta's Grady Hospital, to which she had been taken five evenings before after having been struck down on Peachtree Street, just a few blocks from her home, by a speeding automobile driven by Hugh D. Gravitt, aged twenty-nine, an off duty taxi driver in a hurry. Margaret Mitchell Marsh and her husband were crossing the street to attend a neighborhood movie. Gravitt later was tried and convicted on a charge of involuntary manslaughter and sentenced to twelve to eighteen months imprisonment.

Margaret Mitchell was born on 8 November 1900. Her father was Eugene Mitchell, a highly competent and esteemed attorney. Two years after the birth of his daughter, who was christened Margaret Munnerlyn Mitchell, he purchased a twelve-room, two-story Victorian house near the corner of Jackson Street and Highland Avenue. It was here she spent her childhood; it was in this house she began to "write" impressions of her childhood. It was here, also, that she was interested enough to sit quietly in a corner and listen to the conversations of old lawyers and guests, men and women, who had lived through, or been soldiers in, the Civil War. She developed, or had, a retentive memory, and she unquestionably had an instinctive ear for colorful speech.

Her brother, Stephens Mitchell, has said of those young days on Jackson Street that his sister was a very much alive and energetic girl. She put down thoughts in writing. She rode a bicycle, climbed trees, rollerskated, played baseball, participated in the mudball battles, and ran foot races with the boys. She and brother Stephens built a tree house. She remembered how they lifted up kittens in a basket. She and he took turns riding a pony named Nellie. Later, with father's permission, they swapped the pony for a horse.[4]

The horse introduces an element which some psychologists find of interest. Are some persons "accident prone"? Whether they are or not, injuries were influential in Margaret Mitchell's life. One led her to make the decision to settle down and write a novel. Another accident brought her to Grady Hospital and five days of coma and delirium before death came for her. When she was eleven years old, her horse fell, pinning Margaret beneath. Her left leg was severely injured; her face was cut; a tooth was chipped. But she liked horseback riding and stubbornly continued—on other horses.

In 1911, when Margaret was eleven, her father built a house on Peachtree Street. (It was this house, the center of what was a happy growing-up with no Freudian feeling of being unloved, that the complex woman of many paradoxes would direct, in some of her last instructions, be torn down.) There she was to grow through her teens to womanhood. She wrote plays which were acted out, with a community cast, in the living room.

In 1918, she was graduated from Washington Seminary, a school for young ladies of the gentility, and that fall went to Smith College. Friends often have wondered what Peggy Mitchell might have become, or done, had she stayed on four years at Northampton. But the death of their mother caused her father to suggest that she return home and become the head of the house. Her father wished her to become a proper Southern lady, and she herself was drawn toward this image.[5]

It was in these years that the paradox of Margaret, or Peggy, Mitchell began to show. Perhaps it had been apparent all along in the life of this happy, enormously energetic, ebullient, tomboy-lady-girl. In 1920, the contradictions were plain to observing friends. But paradox merely added to her charm. She was very much the unreconstructed Southerner, and was to die unreconstructed. She had almost a reverence for the Old South traditions and legends, though sometimes, to be sure, she mocked at them. But she also was a rebel.

Peggy Mitchell was considerably influenced by Frances Newman. This Old South lady was the first Deep South literary feminist and rebel. She was twelve years older than Peggy and also a success. "The Hardboiled Virgin" was a shocker to proper ladies and gentlemen. Even so, Frances Newman, for all her rebellion, was "Old South," and believed that young Southern ladies from the right side of the tracks could do no wrong in the company of young Southern gentlemen from the right side of the tracks. Looking back at those years, it is possible to say, and believe, that Peggy Mitchell and Frances Newman saw no contradiction in that attitude.

Scarlett O'Hara emphatically was not an autobiographical character. But Peggy Mitchell was a part of Scarlett. She was harum-scarum and rebellious, but intensely feminist. She liked parties; she enjoyed hearing and telling bawdy stories; she was the natural life of any gathering of friends. There was nothing studied about her joy or verve. She was right out of the Southern Scott Fitzgerald era. She was a John Held girl. If, as Atlanta folklore has it, she went to a dance with small jinglebells on her garters, everyone would laugh and say, "Isn't that just like

Peggy?" It was the time of flasks and corn liquor, of a joyous freedom from the old Calvinist restraint, *Toujours gai, toujours gai,* as Archy would say.

There was the second accident in 1920; another horse fell with Peggy. She suffered injuries which were to trouble her the rest of her life.

In 1922 a big love came. There had been an earlier sentiment, but no one really knew the truth of it. A young man was killed in France with a picture of Peggy in his wallet and heart. However, they both were young, and if there was an engagement it was tenuous. But in 1922 she and a merry young man, Berrien K. Upshaw, were married. A friend of Upshaw's, John Marsh, was at the wedding. Marsh was a quiet man, and had never told his friend Upshaw, or the blue-eyed Peggy, that he, too, had been smitten.

The newlyweds needed more income. Peggy had a friend who was quitting a job on the Sunday magazine section of the *Atlanta Journal;* she talked herself into the job; the salary was $25.00 per week. She weighed then about ninety pounds, wore a beret, and looked like a little girl playing at being grown-up.

Peggy loved the work. Her energy exploded. She climbed out on window-washers' platforms, had herself let down in a sling from the top of a seventeen-story building, rode elephants at the zoo. She interviewed Rudolph Valentino; she had a photographer snap the Great Lover lifting her in through a window.

Old-timers recall that Peggy would come from the magazine offices to the city room to use the big dictionary which was on a stand by the city desk. (She was a stickler about spelling and the use of words.) There are two stories. One is that she was so tiny she stood on tiptoe to look up a word; this caused the short skirts of that time to lift and two or three inches of white skin would show above her stocking, to the great distraction of the city room copyreaders and rewrite men. The other is that Peggy would say, "I think I'll go in and give the middle-aged men a thrill."

In 1924 she and Upshaw were divorced. It had been a sad mistake. He was a bright fellow, but he was second fiddle to Peggy's job. It apparently did things to his ego.

On 4 July 1925, a date deliberately selected as symbolic of independence, she and John R. Marsh, a young Kentuckian and a newspaperman, who had been present at the first wedding, were married. They were not really independent. John had a lot of medical debts, the inheritance of an earlier illness. But Peggy Mitchell, for all her *toujours gai* qualities, had a never-failing ability to discipline herself.[6]

"John and I are poor so we will live poor as hell until we get out of debt," she said.

They moved into a small, shabby apartment which Peggy soon made bright. They called it "The Dump."

Friends thought this marriage to solemn, slow-talking, serious John Marsh would not last. It did. Perhaps modern psychologists would say he provided the father image. Whatever it was, they got along. There were parties. "The Dump" was a favorite gathering place. But they got out of debt.

The injured leg and ankle were a bother. In 1926 John had a better job and more money, in the advertising department of the Georgia Power Company. Peggy, heeding a doctor, quit work. For a time she was on crutches. She began to write; there was nothing systematic about it; nor was it her first writing. This was a mysterious and complex little woman who never, at any time or to anyone, fully revealed herself, not even to John Marsh. She was never the marble statue of the symbolic Confederate woman. She always was flesh and blood. But she could keep her counsel and be as reticent as ice.

Once she was to say, in irritation at all the queries about whether she would write a sequel to *Gone With the Wind*, "I have written a lot of novels."

That she did write one other is known. It was based on the establishment of an officer's training station, Camp Gordon, on the outskirts of Atlanta, at the outset of the First World War. There came to Camp Gordon men from all over the nation. They entered into the social life of Atlanta. They brought cultures, ideas, and attitudes. They fell in love and married Atlanta girls. Peggy destroyed this novel.

Gone With the Wind was not germinated until Peggy Mitchell sat down to write it. She had, of course, thought for years of the historical background of that period, but never in connection with writing a book. Nor had she really "thought" of the background. She had been raised on it, or absorbed it. In 1926, having quit her job because of the old injury, she determined to write a novel. She sensibly used what she knew.

She did not know—and therefore did not follow any technique. The last chapter was written first. From then on she wrote whatever chapter was uppermost in her mind. As each was written, it was placed in a separate, labeled envelope, along with any rewrites she had made. Some chapters were rewritten many times. This did not, however, involve any change of plot, characterization, or scene. The alterations were aimed at a better telling of the story. By 1929 the novel was practically completed. There are interveiws in which Peggy Mitchell says she spent ten years on the book; this includes the background years. The slow writing of it took a little more than three years. For the next three years the novel remained almost untouched. It had not been "polished."

Only a few friends knew she had been working on a novel. One of these was Lois Cole, who had been in the Atlanta office of the Macmillan Company. In 1932 Miss Cole was transferred to the New York office. In the spring of 1935, Harold S. Latham, trade editor and vice president of Macmillan, set out on a trip to the larger cities of the South and West in search of manuscripts. Miss Cole wrote her friend Peggy, urging that she show Latham the manuscript. She wrote also to a mutual friend, Medora Perkerson, assistant editor of the *Journal's* Sunday magazine, and asked her to see that Latham saw Peggy. Peggy met the distinguished publisher. She drove him about to see the dogwood and the residential area. But, she said, she had no manuscript worth showing to him.

Late in the same afternoon John Marsh called home. He was the only person who had read the manuscript. Peggy related Latham's request. John persuaded her to let him have it so that a professional opinion might be had.

Peggy Mitchell put down the receiver and bundled all the many dusty envelopes, with their several versions of chapters, into a great package. The first chapter was not ready; she sat down at her typewriter and did a synopsis of what she had in mind. She then drove to Latham's hotel and called from the lobby. He came down to see a tiny woman sitting by a pile of envelopes which reached to her shoulder. He went to a nearby luggage shop and bought a large suitcase; the manuscript filled it. He was leaving for the West Coast. He read it—with growing excitement—on the way.

The rest is history. A contract was signed. A few weeks later, so the story goes, Peggy Mitchell opened a letter. Her eyes widened.

"Let me lie down," she said to her husband. "Here is a check for $500."

He took it and looked.

"Move over," he said. "It's for $5,000."

The presses could not print pages fast enough. A unique publishing phenomenon had moved onstage.

On the night of 11 August 1949 Margaret Mitchell failed in a desperate attempt to dodge the speeding car.

A human being is a many-sided prism, reflecting many lights, but also changing inside itself. It is difficult, perhaps impossible, to know another human being—be it wife or husband, mother, father, son, daughter, friend, or lover. No one will ever be able to pin down, or gather, all the complexities of life that were in Peggy Mitchell. Many persons have sought to understand or "know" her. This was the more difficult because there were two images of her—one before publication and the other after the immense and overwhelming success of the book.

The surprise of that success, the many silly and baseless rumors that someone else must have written the book, all helped to reveal one of Peggy Mitchell's deep and dominant traits. Not one of the merest handful of persons who knew she had written a book had seen it or had the faintest idea of what it was about. Candor compels one to say that the most loyal friend would not have believed that even by rubbing an Aladdin's lamp could she have written the book. She hid herself completely, inwardly, and in many things, from her best friends.

What was she like? It is perhaps easier to look into the soul and mind of a creative artist than of those who are not. An author, in a very real sense, is what he or she writes. So we turn to *Gone With the Wind*. There is much bitterness in it, and violence, too. Those characters in it who love are never understood. Not only that, they are with the exception of Rhett, weak in the eyes of Scarlett, the central character. Those who have tried to pick the locks of the armor of reticence and reserve with which Peggy Mitchell covered herself think often of two telling scenes in the novel. One is when Scarlett is foraging in the fields, hungry, weary, almost defeated. But she shakes a defiant fist against a hostile sky and cries out that she will never be hungry again. Was it hunger mere food would satisfy? The other scene is the death of Melanie. Ashley says, when his wife dies: "She is the only dream I ever had that lived and breathed and did not die in the face of reality." Once, in 1936, Peggy Mitchell suddenly and inexplicably broke into tears when a friend quoted that sentence. Nor did she explain why she wept. Was she never hungry again? Did she ever realize the dream? Was there ever fulfillment? There are no answers.

Her will was a simple thing. She, daughter of a lawyer, sat down one day and wrote her last will and testament. It began very simply and directly: "I want John, Steve Mitchell, and the Trust Company of Georgia to be the executor of my will. I want Bessie Jordan (her long-time Negro servant) and her daughter, Deon Berry, to have the house and lot at 446 Ripley Street, N.E.—which they now occupy. . . ."

This was her first concern. This was in the old tradition—Peggy Mitchell almost certainly would have been greatly disturbed by the 1954 U.S. Supreme Court decision, and those following, voiding segregation in education because of color. People, of course, change. Had she lived, she might, too, have developed new attitudes. But she was always the unreconstructed Southerner, with a fierce pride in, and loyalty to, the old code that a Southern white person scrupulously "looked after" servants and decent colored persons in distress.

The will carefully disposed of all real and personal properties. Her husband inherited the copyrights. They were, in turn, left to her brother, Stephens, in John's will.

Sometime before her death she had exacted two promises. One was that the old home place on Peachtree Street, in which she had grown up, would be torn down. The other was that the manuscript of *Gone With the Wind* and all her papers would be burned. Why? There are surmises, but no answers.

John Marsh, ailing and grieving, said that he had burned them all, save for a few pages of the manuscript, with his wife's handwritten changes and notes. He made a statement about it in a codicil to his will:

"My wife, Margaret Mitchell Marsh, wanted her private papers destroyed. She did not wish them to fall into the hands of strangers. . . .

"Peggy left me discretion as to the disposal of her papers. I have decided that some of the *Gone With the Wind* papers should be saved, as a means of authenticating her authorship of her novel. If some schemer were to rise up with the claim that her novel was written by another person, it would be tragic if we had no documentary evidence and therefore were unable to beat down the false claim. So I am saving these original *Gone With the Wind* papers for use in proving, if the need arises, that Peggy and no one else was the author of her novel. . . ."

The fact that there is so little religion in the book is curious and speculative. The Civil War had aroused a fervent, nationalist revival of religion. Yet, the novel does not touch on it. Peggy Mitchell was separated from her church. This was a blow which deeply affected her, though she never made talk about it.

She had no children. How badly this hurt no one knows. She was a warm, friendly, loyal person, fiercely devoted to her friends—who could do no wrong. What loneliness, regrets, or unfulfillment she knew, she never discussed. She strove mightily publicly to be what she always had been. Neither she nor her husband piled up possessions, nor made any grand tours. Neither was well, but neither complained. John was husband, father, business manager, friend, and watchdog.

We know a great deal about him and her—But the first person, singular, Margaret Munnerlyn Mitchell—?

Notes—7

[1]Reprinted from *Show*, October 1962, by permission of the author, Mrs. McGill, and Huntington Hartford.

[2]See Finis Farr, *Margaret Mitchell of Atlanta: The Author of* Gone With the Wind (New York: William Morrow & Co., 1965), pp. 97-122.

[3]Ibid., pp. 149-67.

[4]Ibid., pp. 13-40.

[5]Ibid., pp. 41-51.

[6]Ibid., pp. 56-57, 69-73.

Essay 8

In Memoriam: Byron Herbert Reece[1]

The years no longer concern Byron Herbert Reece, so there is no need for me to search out the date. It was long years ago and winter that I went to Young Harris College with the late Walter Rich. He had given a building to the school and there were to be some dedicatory services.[2]

During the course of the day I met the professor of English and as we talked, I remembered something.[3]

"I read a poem I liked the other day," I said. "It was in the *Mercury* magazine and it was by a man named Reece in Blairsville. Do you know him?"

"Why, he is one of our students," he said. "Would you like to meet him?"

I said I very much would like to meet him. So we walked through the cold mountain rain to a small dormitory building and knocked on a green door. Someone called to come in. The teacher turned the knob, and we entered a disorderly room with a small coal-burning stove in the center. There were three single, cot-like beds by the walls and as many chairs. I was introduced.

Byron, perhaps more then than later, had the looks of the young Lincoln. He was gaunt and so thin as to seem taller than he was. He was almost painfully shy, but was enormously pleased that the poem in the *Mercury* had been seen. The teacher asked if he had any more and Byron found an old clipbook and showed a half dozen more. His teacher suggested he read them aloud. I saw Byron hesitate. He was ready to do so. But he cut his eyes at the two roommates and looked distressed. The old mountain reticence was on him. He felt it would be pretentious to be reading his poems aloud. It was obvious he had never done so in their hearing. Being mountain bred and born, I understood and said we'd wait on that until another time. He gave me a grateful look, and after a few minutes we left. It was about time for the visitors from Atlanta to start their journey back home.

That was my first meeting with Byron Reece. It began a friendship which was to continue until that night not so long ago when, for reasons entirely reasonable and valid to himself, he put a shot through his thin chest and the long-tortured, sick lungs behind it, and made a quiet, still exit from life.[4]

There were several other meetings in Blairsville, in Atlanta, and at the old mountain home of the Reeces. The heart of it had been a log cabin in which his mother had been born and in which she had been married and had reared her own children. It had been built there at the time of the Cherokee removal, or perhaps before. My memory is not clear as to the date. He told me about it in a casual conversation, saying his grandfather had to be careful about wandering bands of Indians who had hid out and escaped the long trail of tears to the territory of Oklahoma. Other rooms had been added, but it was a small house for all its warmth and comfort.

Byron's only work place in winter was a small table in the short hallway, which served as a tiny living room. He kept his portable typewriter on it. A naked light bulb hung above it, suspended by a cord. Here, after all the family had gone to bed, he worked on poems and novels during the winter nights. In summer he often worked out of doors by day, but even then he would go back to the little table and the portable when the coolness of late night had come to the mountains and the waters of Nottley.

Once, when a speaking engagement kept me in Blairsville, Byron came to the hotel and we talked and read poetry aloud far into the night. We read his poems and others, too. I remember he liked especially Edgar Arlington Robinson's "Mr. Flood's Party."[5]

There was another fine evening, a winter one, when Harold Martin and I picked up Byron at his house by the side of the road and went on in to Blairsville. Harold, also of the *Atlanta Constitution* and even then a nationally known writer of magazine articles for the *Saturday Evening Post*, was very fond of Byron and he of him. His son, Harold, Jr., then in high school, was along, having been pressed into service as a driver.

They had dinner in a room at the hotel and read poems to each other—Sandburg, Keats, Yeats, Stephen Benet, and, of course, Reece. I, alas, was speaking to some group in the dining room. So were some others. It was 10:00

P.M. before we were in the car and on the road to Byron's. There we stayed until near 2:00 A.M. talking and reading aloud. Most of these poems were Byron's. He had a great sheaf of them. A selection of them became the manuscript of his second volume of poems. His family had all gone to bed, but, quiet as we were, we must have kept them awake. I remember how pleased he was—and this he told me later—that young Martin had listened with "such patience." Actually, Harold, Jr., was enchanted. He, too, was trying to write poetry, and it was a great evening for him to be with a very fine poet and two men who liked to read it.

All of us have within us an inexplicable loneliness. Byron had the mountain silence. He was not an outgoing man. In talks in Atlanta and the mountains he would reveal a little of his inner self, but only glimpses. The fact that he had tuberculosis made him feel himself cut off from falling in love with a girl. He knew, or believed, he could not, with honor, fall in love, marry, and have a family. So, he withdrew. But what sorrow and grief this was to him, only he knew. He never shared it. What fires of resentment at his fate burned in his brain none of us ever knew. But that he was a Prometheus bound to the harsh rock of tuberculosis, with the vultures of a cruel fate pecking at his liver, was undoubtedly true.

Now and then he would go to a doctor and the sanitarium. But it was no good. Once there he wanted out. The last time he went to the hospital he wrote me of how intolerable it was for him. There were those who died. They hurt him. But, worst of all, he seemed to think that for all of them as sick as he there was no real hope of a full life. And so, one day, he left.

He had a growing fear of the future. He was afraid of becoming a burden—of being unable to care for himself. Fires other than tuberculosis were burning within him and consuming him. He told me once that when, a couple of years before his death, he went to California to teach for a summer, he was weighted with a great sense of insecurity. In his last year of life, he had so far deteriorated psychologically that he felt this unease when he left his home or his room at Young Harris. Just a few months before his death he had developed a slight tremor and growing nervousness. About three weeks before he made that quiet exit, he went abruptly to the college clinic and said he wanted an examination. He was put to bed and given a sedative in preparation for the examination the following morning. But he arose about 6:00 A.M., dressed, and slipped out, without a word to anyone.

This was his final concession to medicine and doctors. Lying awake in the early morning hours, he apparently had again reached his old conclusion—that nothing really could be done for him.

He was lonely. He felt he could not offer or receive love from a woman. He did not feel he should visit the homes of his friends, especially if they had children. Even in the times when his tuberculosis was in check, he was unduly sensitive about it, feeling that friends might be afraid to have him come and stay in their house and sleep in their guest room. He never spoke of this, but it was a part of the consuming fires. And, of course, he was lonely, and inevitably he felt himself isolated and deprived.

But he never winced or cried aloud. He had a fierce pride and a great courage. The fox was gnawing away at his vitals, but he kept his cloak about him and never let it be known. He lived with loneliness and hopelessness for as long as he could. And only when the tremor came, the increasing nervousness, and the old disease hung on, did he put a favorite record in his record-player, listen for awhile to the swelling beauty of the strings and brass, and then put the prepared revolver to his chest and pull the trigger.

He was either too honest, or could not trust himself to be strong, to write any farewell notes. He knew all who knew him would understand. If he had tried to write a few notes, he might have become maudlin or allowed others to see his old agonies of spirit. He had never done that. So, he would not.

This last decision of a fine and sensitive mind, this final move by the slender poet's fingers, was not arrived at impulsively. He had work to do. He wanted to finish it. In his last letter to me he was writing of a long poem once the novel was done. He sent, too, some poems.

What happened was that the frail mechanism swiftly was running down. It was almost at an end. In a hospital he might have dragged on for months, or even a year or so. But he could not have worked. He would have been, in his mind, a burden. Loneliness came about him like a fog. Life is a candle in the wind, another poet has said. For him the cold winds had begun to blow across that River Jordan, about which he had written so often in his poems. He snuffed it out himself, without that last, helpless waiting.

He will live in the hearts of those who knew him. Appreciation of him as a poet will increase his stature across the years ahead. What he might have been, how far he might have gone as a poet, none may say. He left us enough of poetry and of friendship to give him a place as one of the best and most sensitive poets of our time. This he would accept as epitaph enough.

Notes—8

[1]Published by permission of the author, Mrs. McGill, and *Georgia Review* 12 (Winter 1958): 372-75.

[2]Raymond A. Cook, *Mountain Singer: The Life and the Legacy of Byron Herbert Reece* (Atlanta: Cherokee Publishing Co., 1980), pp. 19-20.

[3]Professor W. L. Dance; see Cook, *Mountain Singer*, p. 17.

[4]Reece was born 14 September 1917 in the North Georgia mountains, and died 3 June 1958.

[5]McGill studied this and other poetry at McCallie School and Vanderbilt University; see Logue, *Ralph McGill*, 1:25-44.

Essay 9

Carson McCullers: 1917-1967[1]

A call came from the Associated Press. It was a message that Carson Smith McCullers had died. I was glad she was at last free from the weeks of coma, the years of sickness, and the pain and frustration of arthritis and paralysis. For more than half the life of this tall, frail woman with gray-blue eyes, her fragile person was a battleground for unrelenting attacks by various illnesses and, later, small strokes. She had borne all these afflictions, as she had earlier, grievous burdens, without complaint or without any sense of martyrdom. Yet, with her going, all who had known and loved her for the wonderful person she was felt themselves lessened.[2]

Carson saw beauty in the most unusual things. Once, in a letter on a journey South, she wrote: "There is a strange sense of poetry in the ugliness, the drabness of things, and there is always the poetry of house and childhood, no matter how ugly it seems to others."

That she was a lonely, withdrawn child and woman is true. But her spirit always was warm and friendly. She was somehow fated to be an exceptional person, "not like the other children."

There was an appealing quality of youth and almost fey innocence in Carson McCullers when I first met her in 1940. She was then twenty-three. *The*

Heart Is a Lonely Hunter, which was receiving enthusiastic critical attention, was selling well. Learning that she had come home to Columbus, Georgia, for a visit, I telephoned, and asked to go there to talk with her. She said that by a happy coincidence she and her mother would be in Atlanta for some hours between trains en route to New York, and we could talk then. A date was set.

Carson looked like a very thin but self-possessed little girl as she stepped from the train. She was wearing a blue, pleated light woolen dress with a sailor blouse to match. Her stockings, a heavier woolen, stopped short of the knee.

I had arranged a private room at the Atlanta Athletic Club. We had cocktails. "I am almost embarrassed to talk," she said. "I like to take a few sips of Port wine when I am working long hours. I suppose it is the sugar in the wine. It gives me energy. But," she said, "in Columbus I could find only a very cheap quality of Port, and it has stained my teeth a light blue." She smiled broadly and her teeth were, indeed, stained a light blue. With much laughter we made a note never to drink that particular brand of Port.

She was understandably excited about the book's success. A new novel, *Reflections in a Golden Eye*, was almost finished, she told me. It is now being made into a movie. The material for the novel, formed and amplified by the creative imagination of the author, came out of listening to tales told at Fort Benning, where Carson had taken music lessons from Mrs. Albert Tucker. She considered Mary Tucker the finest music teacher she had ever known. Carson remembered Fort Benning as a happy place of laughter and fun during the weekends that she spent with Colonel and Mrs. Tucker. At lunch she talked about some of those memories and of how she had turned from music to writing. Carson had gone to New York when she was seventeen to study at Columbia and the Juilliard School of Music. Subways fascinated her. During a ride in one on her second day in the city, she kept staring out the window at the stations, trying to soak up the feel of speed and the people crowded into the train. Somewhere along the way her pocketbook, which she had put down beside her, was stolen. It held her tuition and expense money.

She tried many jobs, working as waitress, salesgirl, and dishwasher. Her health went bad. Although the diagnosis was tuberculosis, other (and better) diagnosticians later believed it to have been rheumatic fever.

In 1936 she joined a writing class at Washington Square College, taught by Sylvia Chatfield Bates.[3] At the end of the class year Miss Bates published, in mimeograph form, those stories she considered the best. Among them were some of Carson's, which helped her to get editorial attention. One of the stories so published, "Wunderkind," is about a young girl, a talented pianist, who somehow loses the feel for music and the ability to interpret it. She is no longer a *Wunderkind*. It is a poignant story and perhaps reveals one reason why Carson turned to writing.[4]

Mrs. George Swift, who knew Carson all her life, has told me that from early childhood she had a passion for music.[5] "She voluntarily, even eagerly, worked many long hours at the piano each day, while neighboring children were out playing. She was an "A" student in school, leading most of her classes. At an early age she began to write little stories, which she took to a neighbor, who was a newspaperman, for advice.

"Throughout her entire childhood," said Mrs. Swift, "Carson was an exceptional individual—somewhat different from the average run of children. This, unfortunately, resulted in her being rather lonely and very often unhappy, introspective, and alone. She seemingly compensated for this by living within her imagination. . . ."

Carson herself later was to confirm Mrs. Swift's deduction about her ability to live within her imagination. "I never in my life have known a deaf mute," Carson wrote in reply to a magazine query. "It would be difficult to explain just how *The Heart Is a Lonely Hunter* (which includes a deaf mute as one of the central characters) came to be written. . . . It seems to me that writing, or any art, is not dependent on an act of will but is created spontaneously from some objective source. . . . The writer can only shape, control, and form. . . . All the characters in my books would perhaps be called entirely fictional. . . ."

The characters were imaginary—all, that is, save the lonely girl and woman whose relatively short life had been one in which love, so terribly needed, was elusive. In never-failing supply, however, were sensitiveness, courage, and nobility of spirit.

Carson's social sense was natural, not acquired; she was not merely the first Southern writer but probably the first American novelist to convey so truly the inner vision and the "knowing" and reflective mind of the Negro in the South.

Once, while talking about the poverty of the South and the changes for the better, she, who could see the poetry and terrible sadness in the drab and ugly, reminisced about the mill-town section of Columbus, which in her young girlhood was typical of its time, with rows of company-owned shacks on unpaved streets, outdoor privies, and no drains.

"I remember," she said, "being with my grandmother once, when I was a child, on a Christmas visit to the mill section. I saw a baby sitting on a chamber pot by an open door in a cold, two-room house with only a puny blaze in the fireplace. The degradation and desolation of that single scene have never left me, although decades have passed. . . ."

The heart of one forlorn child reached out toward another. In Carson's character there was nothing mean or small. She was kind and gentle. This made all the more noticeable the toughness of her will and courage. During her last years her hands were so crippled with paralysis and arthritis that a page of copy per day was all she could manage. Yet, she wrote a novel, *Clock Without Hands*' and a play, *The Square Root of Wonderful*, assisted in the stage adaptation of *The*

Ballad of the Sad Café, and produced several short stories and articles. She left also some unpublished manuscript.

Carson married Reeves McCullers in New York City in 1937. It was not a success. She again became ill and returned home to Georgia. There was a divorce.

In Columbus she met Marjorie Peabody Waite, who invited her to Yaddo, at Saratoga Springs, to study and write. *The Member of the Wedding* was written there. A Guggenheim Fellowship enabled her to go to Europe in 1942; however, poor health forced her to leave.

She remarried Reeves, and another separation followed. McCullers was not a bad man. But he was very bad for himself and for Carson. By all reports, he had romantically envisioned himself as an author, and had insisted on going to France, believing that he could "write." The consensus was that he cracked up because of his inability to do so. He died in Paris in 1953. The second marriage involved heavy debts, not of Carson's making or knowledge. Legally she could have evaded responsibility. Instead she paid them all, even though to do so took much of the large sum earned by the Broadway success of *The Member of the Wedding.* She never expressed rancor or criticism but saw that McCullers had a decent burial.

On 17 May 1954 the Supreme Court of the United States handed down the unanimous decision declaring segregation in public schools unconstitutional. We corresponded about it. Carson was excited and happy. She wanted mightily to write about it. *Clock Without Hands* was her contribution. Typed in much pain, with a gnarled, swollen hand, the novel has some of the "Wunderkind" genius.

I think Carson was one of the two or three best Southern writers. She belongs with Faulkner. Health did not allow her to come near the Mississippian's magnificent output, but in quality she ranks with him, and in sensitivity to and interpretation of the juxtaposition of loneliness and love she excels.

Carson would not care for comparisons. She was what she was. If bad luck restricted her work, that was just bad luck. She was a very great artist and human being. Let it go at that.

Notes—9

[1]Published by permission of the author, Mrs. McGill, and *Saturday Review* (21 October 1967). © Saturday Review, Inc.

[2]Lula Carson Smith McCullers was born 19 February 1917 in Columbus, Georgia, and died 29 September 1967.

[3]Bates was at New York University; Virginia Spencer Carr, *The Lonely Hunter: A Biography of Carson McCullers* (Garden City, N.Y.: Anchor Press, 1976), p. 44.

[4]See ibid., pp. 28-29.

[5]Swift was the "closest friend" of Carson McCullers's mother; ibid., p. 421.

Essay 10

The Caring People[1]

When the news came on the morning of Sunday, June 3, that 121 Americans, most of them from the Atlanta area, had been killed and burned in the flaming take-off crash of an Air France jet at Orly Airport, Paris, grief and tears seemingly were everywhere. There were weeping men and women who left churches to go and comfort orphaned children or a new-made widow or widower. There were orphans, widows, and widowers who left their pews, seeking the comfort of priest or pastor, or who were taken home to grieve in familiar surroundings. If sorrow is sharper there, it also is more bearable. Voices sobbed over telephones. There were tearful meetings on streets and in homes.

It was days later that one heard of weeping in the most unexpected place. The therapy-art class for the criminally insane at Georgia's huge, sprawling mental hospital at Milledgeville, Georgia, wept for William David Cogland, twenty-six. Twice a month, for more than a year, David Cogland had made the two-hundred mile round trip, without compensation, to give patient instruction in art to those whom society had classified as being so mentally ill as to be dangerous.

Cogland was one of the many dead whom a grieving officer of the Atlanta Art Association (which had sponsored the tour for its members) had in mind when he said, "These were the caring people."[2]

Cogland, son of a small tenant farmer, now blind, had come with his parents to Atlanta. Somehow, out of the mystery of genes, he had a genuine talent for painting. He earned a living as a commercial artist, but in the last several years his paintings had gained attention. They hang in local galleries and in private homes. Out of his own struggles he had been drawn to travel, by bus, to the mental hospital and try to bring, with the self-expression of brush and oils, some light to the dark and deranged minds of the criminally insane.

Sidney A. Wien, his wife, and daughter, Joan, whom friends knew and loved as Toni, died in the cherry orchard where the Air France jet burned. He was retired from business. His brother is Larry Wien, a New York financier and real estate dealer whose syndicate recently purchased the Empire State Building. Sidney Wien was a quiet man who did volunteer work at the Atlanta Art Institute. His chief pleasure was in discovering young painters and in buying their work. His knowledge of art was extensive. One reason he went along on the charter tour was to begin a search for paintings to be given Brandeis University. A friend once asked Sidney Wien why, long ago, he had become so deeply interested in art. "For me," he said, "it was just like the good book says, 'What is good and beautiful— dwell on these things.' "

These two are symbols of "the caring people"—and of their range.

There were thirteen artists who died in the sudden and calamitous crash. At least three were highly professional persons with rising reputations. Best known of these was Douglas Davis, thirty-two, a portrait and mural artist. It was his death which stirred much of the inevitable talk of the blind sisters of fate, snipping threads of life; and, of course, of Thornton Wilder's *The Bridge of San Luis Rey*.

Doug Davis lived in Paris. He had his first show there in 1955. His professional competence was such that he rather quickly earned a sound reputation as a portrait painter. Viven Leigh, Rex Harrison, and Rise Stevens are among those who sat for him. His father had been one of the pioneer aviators who, in the old Flying Jenny planes, made aviation history in Atlanta. Doug Davis, Sr., lived through a dozen crashes. He did wing walking and stunt flying. He died in an automobile crash. His artist son did not care for flying. He had many friends on the Art Association flight and, learning that a seat was vacant, decided to come home and pay his mother a visit in Hapeville, a suburb of Atlanta.

Helen Seydel was another whom critics of stature regarded as possessing a very considerable talent. She serves, perhaps, as an illustration of one of the very human aspects of the tragedy of lost lives and talents. Well educated, with art study in Zurich a part of it, she had suffered the trauma of a sudden and, to her, inexplicable, end of a marriage she had found good. She had taken a job and done little painting. The journey to Europe was, to her, she told a friend before departure, an opportunity to find herself and start life over. "A sort of spiritual resurrection," she said. "I want to go only to Florence." The friend wrote letters which opened doors. A letter came back. "I am ready to begin again."

There were a number of such intimate, personal stories. One lovely woman had relatively recently returned to normal life after years of mental disturbance. She had looked forward to the journey as a new inspirational start in life—of books, music and art. She had written back from Greece: "I have found here peace and beauty and understanding. Now, for the first time I want to come back and read Homer and all the new and old books about the Greeks. I could feel all this stirring anew in my mind and I felt well and sure. . . ."

There were a dozen or more along who had been painters in their younger days and who had found that marriage, children, and household duties effectively had interfered. Some of these had written back of a determination to begin again. One of these was Mrs. Julia Jones. She and her lawyer husband, Baxter, both died. They were wonderful, gentle, scholarly persons. Baxter Jones had been one of those who years ago offered as a candidate for Congress in Georgia's Fifth District to give the people an alternative against incumbent James C. Davis, whose racist prejudice had become intolerable to many. Baxter Jones was defeated, but from that time on there were more and more persons who stood to be counted. His attractive wife had been one of those who had looked forward to the tour as a prelude to "getting started again."

The Psalmist has said that we spend our years as a tale that is told. All tragedies in which many lives are lost testify to the truth of this ancient observation. There were, of course, many personal stories. Some went on the tour because it was a cheap way to go to Europe. There were those who couldn't be dragged into a museum, art gallery, or to an exhibition. A few of these sent back night-club pictures of themselves with champagne on the table and semi-nude entertainers in the background. One or two signed to go to get away, even briefly, from routines of life which had come to be burdensome. Some insight into the hidden troubles of at least one on the trip was had by those who went to call on a person orphaned by the crash. "Do not come to offer me sympathy; it is not wanted," was what they heard before the door closed.

Many were the motivations behind decisions to make the tour. But the overwhelming majority of those who went were "the caring people."

It is not true, of course, that the civic and cultural life of Atlanta was ended or paralyzed by the mass loss of more than 100 of those who were affiliated with her civic and cultural activities. It was not merely the Art Institute which lost members. Among those who died were individuals who have helped Atlanta build, and support, a well regarded symphony orchestra, a civic ballet which for years has attracted a growing following, and the little theater groups as well. Some were persons of wealth and influence. Most were not. There were those who held important positions with large corporations or were successful in their professions. Others would be classified as being in the lower middle class income brackets. A few had a hard time making ends meet.

Mayor Ivan Allen, Jr., who promptly flew to Paris to do what could be done for the processes of identification and the return of the terribly burned bodies, and to give personal attention to any other details, said before departure:

"This was my generation . . . my friends. . . . One was my first teen-age crush. . . ." Mayor Allen is fifty-one years old. Most of them were of the Mayor's generation. A few were older—and younger. They were all bound by a common tie.

Perhaps because of the recognition of this sincere commitment, there was an almost immediate "we must-not-let-them-down" response to their passing. Atlanta had just had put before it bond issue plans which include the establishment of a cultural center for the performing arts in her Piedmont Park. Within hours after the first news came, the *Atlanta Constitution*'s news desk began to receive telegrams and phone calls. One wire will illustrate the mood of that hour: "I have never been to the Art Institute, but I am now going and I want to urge that we all join in support of what must be done in memory of these people."[3]

William B. Hartsfield, who for more than twenty years was nationally known as Atlanta's positive and progressive mayor, and who, at seventy, declined to run for another term and supported Ivan Allen, summed up public reaction and the Atlanta mystique which has made it unique among Southern cities, in response to a request for comment for this article:[4]

"We may take solemn pride in the fact that the people may have, in death, accomplished much which they wanted to do in life. It is written that the blood of the martyrs is the seed of the church, and likewise, the Atlantans may have done in death what they had hoped to do in life—promote the cultural life of Atlanta.

"Not only the Art Museum lost supporters, but many of them were likewise supporters of the Atlanta Symphony, the ballet, and other cultural facilities of our city. Atlanta can ill afford to lose people of this kind, interested as they were in the arts and in a more beautiful city, but Atlanta can take solemn pride in the fact that there are many others who will step forward to fill the void and to carry on both as a challenge and a memorial to those whose interest in the better things of life for our city had led them to take this fatal trip. After all, let me repeat, Atlanta being what it is, they have done in death what they had hoped to do in life."

This is what a city has come to feel—out of its great grief and sorrow.

Notes—10

[1]Reprinted from *Life* magazine (15 June 1962), by permission of the author and Mrs. McGill.

[2]The sculpture, "The Shade," by famous French sculptor Auguste Rodin, was given to the Atlanta Memorial Arts Center by the Republic of France to honor Atlantans killed in Orly, France, 3 June 1962.

[3]The dedication of these people "to the arts—and to the meaning that only the arts can give to life—served as the stimulus for the" conception and construction of the Memorial Arts Center in Atlanta. The center combines "spaces for the performing and visual arts." See Martin Sharter, *The Atlanta Arts Alliance: 10 Years and Beyond*, The Atlanta Arts Alliance, Inc., 1979, p. 8. Bruce Galphin wrote, "When Atlantans decided to memorialize their dead from the Paris air crash in a living arts center, contributions ranged from the 'anonymously' given $6.5 million of Robert W. Woodruff—half the construction cost—to literally nickels and dimes from school children." See "Paying the Piper: Funding the Arts," in *The Atlanta Arts Alliance: 10 Years and Beyond*, p. 30. For more on Robert W. Woodruff, see McGill's article in this book.

[4]For more on Hartsfield, see McGill's article in this book.

Essay 11

Martin Luther King, Jr.: 1929-1968[1]

On first being introduced to Dr. Martin Luther King, Jr., I said to him that he was the best known unknown man in the South. He was just then in the home stretch in winning the fight against the harshly discriminatory practices of segregation on the Montgomery Bus Co.

Dr. King had gone to Montgomery from Boston where he had been a graduate student working on his Ph.D. dissertation. He had, indeed, been commuting from his studies at Boston University once a month to preach at the Dexter Avenue Church. This was regarded by Negroes as a "silk-stocking" church in the cradle of the Old Confederacy (Dr. King was to change that). But, after receiving his doctorate in June, 1955, he had gone there as the regular pastor.[2]

There had been a growing fear among Montgomery Negroes. The United States Supreme Court decision of May, 1954, had stirred the segregationists. The ghost of old Jeff Davis was walking. And in the beer halls and taverns there was talk that if the crazy Supreme Court, Communist influenced, kept on, it would make the Nigger forget his place and there would, sure as hell, be trouble. The South, by God, was saying "never."

On 1 December 1955, a forty-three-year-old seamstress at a Montgomery department store was going home on a bus. Her feet hurt. Christmas shopping was beginning and she was tired. The bus driver, following company rules, ordered her to move and allow a white woman to have the seat when a number of white passengers got on at one of the stops.

Mrs. Rosa Parks, somewhat to her own astonishment, found herself saying she would not move. She had moved on many previous occasions. But things were changing. There had been an increasing number of arrests of Negro bus riders. So, she refused, was arrested, fingerprinted like a criminal, and jailed.[3]

Dr. King was not called in on the first or second meeting of local Negroes planning action. But, he had become known to a small circle. He was developing a reputation as a charismatic man, although, to be sure, that now so familiar word was not then employed. At any rate, Dr. King was asked in. Within a few days he was the leader.

On that day when I met him he had the bus company on the run. The nation had been reading about him. The South's preposterous preoccupation with where people would sit on a bus or where children would sit at school was beginning to appear as stupid and as ridiculous as it really was. Dr. King, admitting that Gandhi was his model, was a minor national figure.

A mere thirteen years have passed since the victory in Montgomery and the end of the shabby system of segregated seating in public transportation. If one considers all that has been accomplished in that period of little more than a decade, it is remarkable. Yet, in the hours that have followed Dr. King's assassination, one realized how much is yet to be done and how deeply engrained in the American mores, especially in those of the South, are the many racist attitudes and prejudices.

The stubborn quality of those prejudices and attitudes is starkly outlined by events in the life of Dr. King after Montgomery. There were the police dogs and fire hoses in Birmingham, used as defenders of the immoral and unconstitutional practices of discrimination. At Selma there were killings in the town and on the highway. But always the nonviolent movement endured these and continued to win.

One wonders where the nation would have been in its struggle to attain equal citizenship for all its people had it not been for Martin Luther King.

I asked him at another time where he got all the strength he had in his backbone and all the undisputed courage that was his.

"If I have it," he said, "it is in my genes. You know my dad, I got a lot of it from him." I nodded.

I did indeed know his father, a big man, with a lot of strength and muscle, both physical and mental. There was, along with the blood of African kings, some Irish in Martin Luther King. His paternal grandfather was James Albert King; the post-Civil War years had not been kind to him.[4]

James Albert King was a sharecropper and, in fact if not in law, a peon, owing the plantation store more than any crop brought in. Martin Luther King's father was born on that plantation. He walked away from that plantation as a young boy, going to Atlanta, There he worked to get an education. He entered the then small Negro college, Morehouse. He became a preacher. He married a fine young woman whose father was a minister. He begat a family. They grew up in Atlanta.

The young boy, Martin Luther Jr., never forgot the lessons his father taught. "Once," he related to me, "my father told off a policeman for calling him 'boy.' I was frightened. The officer had ordered my father to pull his small car, a Ford, as I recall, to the curb. 'What's your name, boy,' he said.

" 'Here's my boy,' said my father, indicating me. 'Speak up Martin, and tell him your name.'

" 'I mean you,' said the officer.

" 'Well, I'm a man, not a boy. If you want my name speak to me as a man.' "

Martin Luther King, Jr., remembered how the officer reddened but, finally, wrote down the name and walked away. Nor was there ever a summons to court.

In the South's gothic structures of segregation, there were many varieties of humiliation. One was in shopping. This was worse in the small towns. Shoe stores were perhaps worst of all. There was a great dislike on the part of the owners to fit shoes on black feet and, later, try them on Caucasian feet. Possessors of the latter would sometimes come into the country stores and say: "Don't put any shoes on me you've been letting Niggers try on."

Young Martin Luther King once told me he often despaired of having any shoes at all. "My father," he said, "would take me into a shoe store. He would sit in the front row. The clerk would order him to move to the back. He would not. The clerk would insist. My father would then get up, take me by the hand, and walk out. Only now and then would a clerk, after being sure no other customer was near, allow us to buy a pair of shoes on the front row.

"My father used to say to me, 'Martin, son, I have never accepted segregation and I never will. I don't want you ever to make any concessions to it.' "

It was much easier to talk with Dr. King, Sr., than with his famous son. The latter had no small talk and his sense of humor was small. He could joke and laugh; but he was serious by nature. Thoreau was often in his talk. He had become interested in the great dissenter of earlier days of the Republic, and had he not discovered Gandhi, might have used him as a model.

I once asked him why he had chosen Gandhi. The reason was a realistic one. Gandhi, he said, was a man known to Negroes of today. The movies of the Gandhi years, especially the newsreels and Gandhi's fight for Indian independence, had reached the Negro masses.

"Sometimes," he said, "they would laugh when I talked about Gandhi and ask me why he, such a skinny little man, wore all those bunched-up diapers instead of pants to hide his pipestem legs. I soon learned that they knew who he was."

In 1951, while visiting Hindu friends at their home in the small village of Ayanah, some twenty miles from Etawah in the United Provinces, I came across, for the first time, a message of Gandhi to American Negroes.

Some nine years later, in a talk with Dr. King, I learned that this message had been influential with Dr. King and that he had used it in meetings to inspire rural Negroes.

Gandhi had written, in 1929, the year Dr. King was born:

> Let not the twelve million Negroes be ashamed of the fact that they are the grandchildren of slaves. There is no dishonor in being slaves. There is dishonor in being slave owners. But let us not think of honor or dishonor in connection with the past. Let us realize that the future is with those who would be truthful, pure, and loving. For, as old wise men have said, truth ever is, untruth never was. Love alone binds, and truth and love accrue only to the truly humble.

There were those who insisted that Martin Luther King made cynical use of Gandhi. I could never agree. He modified Gandhi's principles somewhat to fit an American problem, but he never ceased to believe in the possibility of Gandhiism.[5]

Critics also charged that while Dr. King preached non-violence, his protests usually ended up in violence. This was, on the face of it, a false bit of reasoning. Dr. King's marchers never did an act of violence. They often were attacked, but they themselves were never aggressive.

The attack came always from the entrenched forces of segregation defending what they called, and what really was, "the Southern way of life" and "Southern customs."

After Dr. King came to Atlanta from Montgomery, in 1956, seeking a broader base for the organization he had conceived, the Southern Christian Leadership Conference, I had talks with him and letters from him.

He found another Atlanta from the one he had known as a boy. He had not been an entirely happy youngster. He was intense and "high strung."

At fifteen he had read and learned enough to be admitted to Atlanta's Morehouse College.

President of the college was Benjamin Mays, himself often a victim of indignities inflicted by segregationists, including one severe beating and a few ejections from trains. Mays remembers the young man as a serious, sensitive student and became a second father to Dr. King.[6]

"He was a great one," Dr. Mays says. Dr. Mays asks us, with unavoidable logic, to think what the nation would have had to endure had Dr. King come preaching violence and hate instead of nonviolence and humanity?

When Dr. King won the Nobel Prize for Peace in 1964, there was some dissension, even among some of the Negro leadership. Little of it got to the surface.

The thinking of the Nobel committee was, I believe, correct. It is true that Dr. King had not brought peace to his own country. And there were racial conflicts in Africa. Yet, it should by now be plain that what the Nobel committee had in mind was that Dr. King's nonviolent policy had produced substantial results. More than that, it had provided a policy which, if adopted elsewhere, would bring peaceful solutions. Passage of the civil rights legislation and the energetic support of implementing laws by the president of the United States were also a factor that was aiding the prospects of a peaceful solution of an old problem. Dr. King was a phenomenon.

In Atlanta there was opposition from some of the power structure to giving a recognition and testimonial dinner to the Nobel Prize winner. Protestant ministers who were approached to join in sponsoring the dinner retreated in haste with many excuses. But there were prominent business and professional men who stood firm and said the dinner must be held.

The Roman Catholic archbishop, the late Paul Hallinan, became a sponsor. So did Atlanta's well-known rabbi, Jacob Rothschild. Dr. Mays, of Morehouse, and this reporter completed the sponsoring committee. To our delight the response was great. One of the companies which had tried to prevent the dinner came around on the last day and meekly asked for forty tickets. There was some unchristian pleasure in informing them there were but eight left. The dinner was sold out with some four hundred persons waiting in the lobby hoping for no-shows.

Dr. King's attractive wife, Coretta, and the two oldest of their four children were present.[7] The huge ballroom was packed with a happy, integrated crowd, almost half being white. Dr. King made a magnificently simple address. It was a successful evening, and Atlanta's good name was saved.

Later on Dr. King told me the dinner had meant a great deal to him. "I would have been badly disappointed," he said, "had my hometown let me down because I have disrupted some of the old ways and the old customs."

That Dr. King was deeply concerned about the growing movements for separateness and for violence is no secret. Before he returned to Memphis, he said that if Memphis authorities did not do what was right in what was much more than a strike of Negro garbage workers, he, Dr. King, feared the policy of nonviolence might never again be useful. Negro militants worried him. He could not agree to apartheid in reverse. Nor could he agree that retaliatory violence made sense.

So he went back to Memphis. And Memphis stalled. And at last the killer, slave to his own hatreds and guilt, destroyed the one prestigious voice that called for nonviolent action.

The loss is enormous. Extremists see an opportunity to gain ground and power, especially if there are not other voices and personalities to come forward to fill the power vacuum before the violent bear it away. Then, indeed, will the disaster at Memphis assume more ominous overtones.

It is a piece of irony that subsequent riots matched those that followed Gandhi's assassination in India.

Notes—11

[1]Published by permission of the author, Mrs. McGill, and the *Boston Globe* (14 April 1968).

[2]King was graduated from Morehouse College in Atlanta, 1948 (and ordained into the Baptist faith), from Crozer Theological Seminary, Chester, Pennsylvania, 1959, and Boston University, with the Ph.D., 1955. See David L. Lewis, *King: A Critical Biography* (New York: Praeger Publishers, 1970), pp. 17-45.

[3]See Martin Luther King, *Stride Toward Freedom: The Montgomery Story* (New York: Harper Publishing Co., 1958).

[4]See Martin Luther King, *Daddy King: An Autobiography* (New York: Morrow Co., 1980).

[5]See Charles Chatfield, ed., *The Americanization of Gandhi: Images of Mahatma* (New York: Garland Publishing, Inc., 1976), pp. 723-58, 773-84; Amiya Chakravarty, "Satyagraha and the Race Problem in America," in Sibnakayan Ray, *Gandhi: India and the World: An International Symposium* (Philadelphia: Temple University Press, 1970), pp. 300-18; Mohandas Karamchand Gandhi, *Non-Violent Resistance (Satyagraha)* (New York: Schocken Books, 1951); Ralph McGill, "Report on India," *Atlanta Constitution*, 21 November 1951 through 8 January 1952; McGill, "New Truth in a New Nation," *Saturday Review* 37 (25 December 1954): 14-15.

[6]See Benjamin Elijah Mays, *Born to Rebel: An Autobiography* (New York: Scribner, 1971).

[7]See Coretta Scott King, *My Life With Martin Luther King, Jr.* (New York: Holt, Rinehart, and Winston, 1969).

Essay 12

Arthur James Moore: The Bishop's in a Hurry[1]

In 1935, in the Central Belgian Congo village called after its chief, Wembo Niama, a Methodist missionary bishop named Arthur James Moore was approached by the tall, massive tribal ruler, closely followed by a retinue of twenty-three wives, reduced to that low figure from some one hundred sixty-odd by the Christian influence, and certain members of the royal family. As an influential ally and convert of the church, the chief occupied a special status. And he had a request to make.

For some time he had been watching the ease with which missionaries rode their bicycles, and the chief wished for one with all the yearning of a small boy.

A month later at a town some four hundred miles away, the bishop found a red bicycle of French make and purchased it for his friend. It was duly presented, though not without some trepidation. Before the admiring eyes of the village, the delighted chief swung his great bulk upon the saddle and pushed off down the slight slope before his house. He careened forward a few yards and then fell in a wild tangle of legs and wheels, to the accompaniment of gasps from the court and shrill cries of alarm from his wives. He disentangled himself and, with great dignity and never a glance at the treacherous vehicle, the bishop or the wives, retired to his house.

Soon thereafter, a worried bishop, who was calculating the trouble a hostile chief could create, received a letter from the chief, written by a graduate of the mission school who served as scribe to the tribal ruler. It was short and to the point:

Dear Friend-Chief: You have given me a bicycle which will not stand up. Please send me one that will.

The bishop brooded unhappily over this, and it was some months before a stroke of luck enabled him to make good. It was the sight of a large and sturdy invalid's chair on a ship at a coastal port which inspired him to inquire as to its origin and to order a duplicate from a New York department store. Weeks later it arrived, was uncrated, demonstrated and presented to the chief, who beamed not at all, but looked on, dubious of mien, as did the anxious wives and the royal court.

But when the chair was pushed before him, he lowered his bulk into it and, having noted the demonstration with care, called imperiously to his wives to push. With great glee and delighted cluckings and giggling, they worked in relays to wheel the chief about the village and back before the bishop.

The chief stepped out, beaming. "This," he said to the bishop, "is a true bicycle that knows how to stand up."

Since April, 1909, when Arthur James Moore, as a young flagman for the Atlantic Coast Line Railroad, was converted at a service in Waycross, Georgia, his admirers say that the man who now is president of the Council of Bishops of the Methodist Church and its more than fifty different fields in Asia, Africa, Latin America, and Europe has been giving to all peoples who hear him vehicles of faith that will stand up.

At sixty-two, sturdy and stocky, with a young face and boundless enthusiasm and stamina, he is something of a living legend in the Methodist Church, which is, since the union in 1939 of the Methodist Episcopal Church South and the Methodist Protestant Church, the largest Protestant group in America.

In the service of this church, the president of bishops has been circuit rider, evangelist with nationwide assignments, pastor of outstanding churches, a member of the Council of Bishops since 1930, president of the Board of Missions since 1932, with oversight of church affairs in fifty-two countries, and president of the council since early 1951.

From 1934 to 1940, he went more or less breathlessly up and down the world, doing the work previously done by three missionary bishops. For six years his schedule placed him with the churches in China, Japan, and Korea from September to April; in Poland, Czechoslovakia, and Belgium through May, June, and July; and the rest of each year in the Congo. He began flying when to do so was an event. Thomas and Jan Masaryk, Eduard Benes, Josef Pilsudski, Leopold III, Generalissimo Chiang Kai-shek, Gen. Douglas MacArthur, Gens. Jiro Minami and Iwane Matsui, of the Japanese war party, Ambassador Hiroshi Saito, and others of the Japanese military and civil life were either friends or well-known acquaintances made during those years.

In the postwar years his official duties have sent him on trouble-shooting jobs to most of the countries of Europe and the islands of the Pacific, including a journey to the state of Sarawak, in Borneo. There he ate dinner with a new convert who had swinging from the rafters a net of dried human heads.

"Mostly Japanese," he said modestly to the inquiring bishop.

When he went to the First Methodist Church at Waycross for the spring revival service in 1909, Moore was twenty years old, a railroad flagman since eighteen, married at eighteen and one-half, the father of a son, and on the threshold of his young life's most coveted goal—promotion to a full-time freight conductor's job. He was not an irreligious man, but he had given to the church only routine attendance.

In fact, at fourteen he had been "read out" of the Baptist church in his hometown of Glenmore, near Waycross, where his father, an Atlantic Coast Line section foreman, then lived. In those days all small, rural towns frowned on the sinful pleasure of dancing. One night young Arthur Moore, in company with other curious boys of the town, was drawn to the home of a non-churchgoing citizen where a dance was in progress. Boylike, they peered through a porch window at the goings on. For this sampling of worldly joys, he was summoned by the board of the Baptist church to explain his erring ways. Resenting what seemed to him an unfair accusation, the boy, who had never then nor since danced a step, refused to go. His name was removed from the list of members of the church.

So, on this night of the eventful service of 1909, preached by Dr. Charles Dunaway, now in retirement in California, the young railroader had no sense of impending change. Yet something in the sermon moved him to go down to the altar and seek membership in the church on confession of faith. For years, now, a bronze plaque at the church has commemorated that conversion.

The young convert had no thought then of becoming a minister. But his job no longer interested him. He became a lay worker, seeing to it, for example, that the church was cleaned and that cooking fires at the summer camp meetings were supplied with wood.

Bishop Moore was born at Argyle, Georgia, one of the small towns on his father's railroad section, on 26 December 1888. It is in the flat wire-grass and piney-woods area not far from the great Okefenokee Swamp. His father, John Spencer Moore, was first-generation Irish, son of an immigrant who came over from North Ireland and took up land in Clinch County, South Georgia, a few years before the outbreak of the Civil War. When volunteers were called, he joined the 26th Georgia Infantry and died in a charge at Gaines' Mill, one of the grim struggles of the Seven Days' Battles.

The grandfather had come alone to Georgia. He had been married but a few years when he went to war.[2]

"My grandmother knew little of her husband's life in Ireland except that it had been hard and he had left the poverty of it to seek opportunity in America," says Bishop Moore. "She was left a widow in what was almost frontier country and had a cruel, hard time of it with her young son, my father. When the railroad came, he took a job with the construction crews and then stayed on as a section foreman."

Arthur Moore's first memories center about Brookfield, another town of the section. It was at this town that he met, at the age of eleven, the granddaughter of a Waycross Methodist minister, visiting in an uncle's home. This was Martha McDonald, his first and only sweetheart. They were married on 26 April 1906. They have three sons and a daughter. The eldest son, Harry, is a minister who has triumphed over blindness which came to him about five years ago. Wardlaw, the second son, is a businessman in Corpus Christi, Texas, and the third son, Arthur, is with the Columbia University Press. The daughter, Alice Evelyn, is Mrs. Lowell V. Means, of San Antonio.

"I was always deeply interested in church membership," Mrs. Moore recalls, "and I wanted to be completely proud of my husband. I tried quietly but persistently to bring him to membership, and I will never forget my joy and pride the night he rose and went down to the altar."

In August of that year, while Arthur was still with the railroad, the presiding elder sent for him. Down at St. Marys, Georgia, an old pre-Revolutionary seaport town at the mouth of the river of the same name, an elderly minister named John W. Simmons was critically ill.

"I want you to go down there and preach in Doctor Simmons' place," the presiding elder told him. "You've got it in you. Pray with Doctor Simmons and preach."

So, at twenty years of age, possessed of only a common-school education, an unlicensed layman, he obtained leave from his job and preached for six weeks at St. Marys.

Bishop Moore has had many experiences and satisfactions, but he recalls those at St. Marys as among the superior ones. When he presented himself before the conference in late October to request a license, there was also before the bishops a request from the St. Marys congregation to send back the young preacher. He received the license, but the assignment was a circuit of seven isolated rural churches in agricultural McIntosh County.

The Moores remember those days well. Their parsonage consisted of two rented upstairs rooms, one of them a kitchen. Mrs. Moore, who is a small person, recalls that she had to carry water, wood, and supplies up the steps—the circuit rider was gone most of the time. But it was a happy year. The people were kind. The doctor was a Baptist, but he sent no bills. The neighbors provided frequent gifts of milk, butter, chickens, and vegetables.

The seven towns echo yet to the preaching of the young circuit rider. He was a sort of ministerial Paul Bunyan. Elisha Thorpe, of Townsend, had lent him an old, half-blind white horse which would not step over logs—a handicap on a circuit where much of the riding was through woods with years of accumulated logs felled by age and storm. But Moore went everywhere. There are men there yet who recall the young preacher walking up and down beside plowmen in the fields, talking to them about the gospels. He and his old horse would arrive at a lonely clearing at dusk. The minister would chop wood, help to milk, and that night about the fire or, if in summer, out in the yard in straight kitchen chairs, he would talk of God's mercy, to the family about him.

He visited every house in his wide circuit, seeking out lonely cabins in distant clearings. The first time he preached at Jackson's Chapel, twenty-three persons joined the church. He never got another member there. Every unsaved soul in the community joined that first night. It was that way at all towns. Great crowds came long distances on Sundays to hear him preach. He was, as his listeners said, "on fire with the Word."

Until his conversion he had never made a talk in his life. Now the cabin clearings and the schoolhouses were filled with his eloquent, moving exhortations.

"It was a miracle to me to hear him," says Mrs. Moore. "All I can believe is that God gave it to him that night before the altar at Waycross."

Toward the end of the year, the Thorpes, who admired him mightily, came to him and said, "Brother Moore, you ought to go to Oxford College" (Old Oxford, at Oxford, Georgia, now Emory University, near Atlanta).

Brother Moore, who by then was the father of two children, thought it was a good idea, but on $440 a year there didn't seem to be much chance. The Thorpes offered to donate twenty-five dollars a month to the cause, and so the Moores unhesitatingly picked up and moved to Oxford and Emory College, a small Methodist school about thirty-five miles east of Atlanta, which includes among its alumni Vice-President Alben W. Barkley.[3]

There was neither time nor background for a routine beginning. The college wisely assisted Moore to select certain necessary courses. A four-room house was found, as were students who would rent two of the rooms and thereby add to the meager income. Lights regularly burned late as the young man attacked his texts with the inadequate tools of the poor grade schooling offered in rural communities in his day. He did find time to play on the baseball team and to take up tennis, which he enjoyed more because it could be played at odd hours. He liked best the hour before dinner in the evening. He would take the two babies with him to the tennis court, put them on a blanket in one corner, and by this method of baby sitting have his game and also give Mrs. Moore time to prepare their evening meal.

The college rules required church attendance each Sunday. Student Moore met this by preaching in nearby towns, where he soon was in great demand. Flocks of fellow classmen accompanied him, and the congregations of the small rural churches often complained that if they did not arrive early, Moore's mobile congregation took all the seats.

At the end of two work-packed years, he knew more about preaching and people than any other student, but less Greek. He also faced a decision. When he had quit railroading to preach at $440 per year, he had left some debts behind. He had gone to each person he owed—and they were but few—and told them his story. He wanted to preach. If he did, he could not be sure when they would get their money, but he promised that they would in time receive it. Now three years had passed, two at school with no income at all beyond bare subsistence. There was a demand for his services in the church's field of evangelism, so, reluctantly, he gave up the idea of more schooling.

Today, he is an unusually well-educated man. He has never ceased to study, read, and learn. He is the author of several scholarly religious books and is a careful researcher and student in all addresses, sermons, and writings. He has accepted only a few of the many honorary degrees offered him.

On leaving college, he was appointed a district revivalist, and as such took a tent and went to preaching. He followed his old custom of going to backwoods towns and communities, where preaching had been scarce. He organized almost one hundred churches and won thousands of converts.

Dr. William N. Ainsworth, pastor of the large Mulberry Street Methodist Church in Macon, Georgia, sent for him on the basis of the enthusiasm he had aroused about the state, and had him pitch his tent on the outskirts of Macon at a place called Cherokee Heights. Thousands came, and a church was organized. Today it is one of the largest congregations in the state, numbering well over 2,000, and the church plant is a large and efficient one. The word began to get around that, when Arthur Moore converted someone, it "took." Minister Ainsworth began to tell laymen and ministers that he had never before met a man with the power of preaching which the district evangelist had.

The next step was that of general evangelist—a post that enabled him to preach in more than two-thirds of the forty-eight states. It was not at all uncommon for special trains to be run to his meetings, and it was almost the rule that when he had completed a revival the people of that town would follow him on to the next.

In the fall of 1920, Doctor Ainsworth, then bishop, wired him at San Angelo, Texas, where a typical Moore revival was at its height, saying, "Arthur, the time has come for you to take a church. I am today appointing you to Travis Park Church in San Antonio." This was, and is, one of the largest and most successful churches in the Methodist domain.

Moore was there for six years. In a church which seated 2,400 there was rarely a service, day or night, when there were not many persons standing. In those six years an average of twelve persons joined the membership each Sunday.

In 1926, Dr. George R. Stuart, one of the great preachers of Southern Methodism, died suddenly of a heart attack. Bishop Warren A. Candler, who had taught Moore at Emory College, moved him from San Antonio to fill Stuart's pulpit at Birmingham, Alabama. In four years there he duplicated his San Antonio success. In the ten years at the two pastorates he received more than 6,000 persons into church membership. The man who had been so convincing in the cabin clearings and the weather-beaten one-room schoolhouses of McIntosh County was just as effective in the large city churches.[4]

In 1930 at the General Conference in Dallas, Texas, the pastor of Birmingham's First Methodist Church was proposed for election to bishop. It is not unusual for 200 or 300 ballots to be taken in such deliberations. Pastor Moore was elected overwhelmingly on the very first ballot, a rare and glowing compliment.

He was sent to the frontier of Methodism in America—the Western states of Arizona, Montana, California, Washington, and Oregon. His salary was about half what it was when he was pastor, but he was happy on a familiar assignment. It has always seemed to him that lonely people are lonely chiefly for the word of God. The distant ranch houses, the wagons of sheepherders, the small Western towns, sun-baked in summer and raw-cold in winter, as well as the cities, came to know his voice. He used automobiles and he rode horseback. He attended round-ups and rodeos. He founded churches and revived old ones. He lived with the people, and it is no figure of speech to say they loved him. There was, and is, much tangible evidence of it everywhere he has been. A well-known minister spoke of this at a dinner tendered the bishop on the occasion of his election as president of the council.[5]

"While the rest of us were learning Greek and Hebrew, Arthur was learning how to reach the hearts of people," he said.

At the General Conference of 1934 at Jackson, Mississippi, the financial problems of the church were pressing. The world depression was at its worst. The Board of Missions was heavily in debt. Of the council of sixteen bishops, two had died and three had reached the age of retirement. It was determined to ask eleven to do the work which sixteen had been doing before. Prior to 1934 there had been three bishops in the foreign field. One was based at Shanghai, serving China, Japan and Korea. A second ministered to Poland, Belgium, and Czechoslovakia; and the third was in charge of vast mission developments in the Belgian Congo.

"Let's leave them all to Arthur," said one of the bishops. And they did. For six years he moved constantly about a world preparing for its second great war.

China and Japan were already at war. In Korea, the Japanese were ruthlessly squeezing out the Christian church. Everywhere there was growing fear and concern. One of the problems Bishop Moore faced then was the same one that confronts the Christian church in the Russian satellite countries today.

There was pressure in those years in Korea to resist the Japanese antichurch moves, even if it meant being sent out of the country or arrested, and the closing of the churches. In Korea, for example, the Japanese required all the children, those of Christian schools included, to bow before the Shinto shrines and gods. They had shrewdly ordered this on two grounds—religious and patriotic. Failure to bow could be classified as unpatriotic and subversive.[6]

Bishop Moore, with the hardheaded, practical sense that has characterized his career, said, "We'll stay. Let the children bow. Would they not be required to bow if we left? As long as we are here, we can continue to teach the truth."

Gen. Jiro Minami was governor general of Korea in those days. Bishop Moore's able diplomacy and always-good-natured resistance interested him. They became well acquainted and were, in a sense, friendly enemies.

In 1950, at dinner with his good friend, Gen. Douglas MacArthur, in Tokyo, Bishop Moore asked what had been the disposition of General Minami, who had been one of the war criminals and who had received a life sentence.

"Did you know him?" asked the astonished General MacArthur.

"Well," said the bishop.

The next day a quiet interview was arranged. Bishop Moore waited in a room at the end of a prison corridor. Soon he saw a shuffling figure, clad in a prisoner-of-war uniform, come down the hall, not at all resembling the glittering governor of a few years before.

"We talked about forty-five minutes," said Bishop Moore. "I recalled to him something that had happened in Korea. He had imposed a restriction on us because of an offense by another religious group. I protested, and he said, 'Bishop, you must suffer for the sins of others.' I told him that, in my opinion, he was doing just that, and that I had prayed for him and forgiven him. He did an unusual thing for a Japanese," the bishop continued. "He put his arms about me and held me tightly and wept."

To this day, Bishop Moore regards as a sort of minor miracle the fact that he was not jailed in Japan. In those years he was going back and forth between China and the emperor's domain. One of his books, extremely critical of the Japanese, had been published. But even after severe fighting between China and Japan had begun and the Japanese had taken Shanghai, he was able somehow to do much of his job. A shadow crosses his face as he recalls the International Settlement, jammed with refugees in those days when the Imperial Army clique had launched its determined invasion of China. Thousands died of hunger and disease. At least 250 bodies were picked up off the streets each morning, in addition to the hundreds who died elsewhere.

Japanese officials refused him permission to visit churches outside Shanghai. He particularly needed to go to Soochow (Wuhsien), about fifty-five miles west of Shanghai.

One day while trying to break down official resistance, the bishop recalled a letter which had been most helpful on numerous occasions in Japan. Two years earlier he had visited his friend, Ambassador Saito, in Washington and requested a letter which would facilitate travel in Japan. He had obtained a generously worded letter in which the ambassador vouched for him and urged all those to whom the document might be presented to give to the bishop full cooperation in travel. The ambassador had put his personal "chop" on the letter, as well as the official imperial seal. It was an impressive-looking document.

The bishop plucked it from his files. He then put on his cutaway coat and striped pants, and approached the sentry at the Soochow Creek bridge—presenting the letter with a flourish. The troubled sentry read it, sucked air through his teeth, and called the officer in charge. This soldier, too, read it with care and was also greatly troubled. As he stood in doubt and irresolution, the bishop took the letter, said "Thank you," and walked by.

At General Matsui's headquarters they were also astonished to see him and disturbed by the letter. There was a great scurrying, but at last the letter and the bishop were sent in to the general. The general appeared dubious, and the bishop said he would be most unhappy to report to America that the Japanese refused to allow inspection of church property. Since they were not quite ready for Pearl Harbor, the general at last consented for the bishop "and his entourage" to make the journey under escort. The bishop, of course, had no entourage, but he supplied one, taking along other missionaries as "clerks" and "chauffeur." They were escorted by a Colonel Oka, who slept lightly in the room with the bishop at each stop.

From Colonel Oka the bishop learned, with some discouragement, of how the winebibbers of earth have been able to spread an obscure Biblical verse about the world to annoy good Methodists, who emphatically do not look with favor upon wine or strong drink. One cold night, as they sat around a fire near Soochow, the colonel obtained some sake and offered a drink to the bishop.

"No, thank you," said the bishop.

"Doesn't your Bible say to take a little wine for the stomach's sake?" asked the grinning Shinto sinner.

When the party returned to Shanghai, the bishop felt that prestige, custom, and appreciation called for a dinner. Colonel Oka was among those invited. Naturally, no wines were served. The colonel arrived in jovial mood, smelling loudly of sake. About midway of the meal, he had lost his edge, and the bishop was startled to hear him call, "Oh, beesh-opp. There is something wrong with my stomach."

Some years later, General Matsui, chief guest at that dinner, was hanged as a war criminal in Tokyo.

Bishop Moore is a firm admirer and old friend of General Chiang Kai-shek. He believes him to be a sincere Christian. In one of his rare ventures into political controversy, he was outspoken in his support of the Chiang government and has endorsed continued aid to and alliance with the generalissimo. He has visited Chiang on Formosa and believes the army there is loyal and that it and Chiang merit confidence.

Chiang was baptized a Christian and a Methodist by a Chinese bishop, Kiang Chang-chuan, who apologized a few months ago for having performed this symbolic ritual. In the course of a speech in behalf of the new organization of the church in China under communist direction, Bishop Kiang also denounced Chiang as a tool of imperialists and an enemy of the Chinese people.

Bishop Kiang and Bishop Moore were warm friends and associates, and although greatly distressed by the reported speech, the president of the Council of Bishops refused to pass judgment on its maker.

"I will retain confidence in Bishop Kiang and all others in his position in other countries under communist rule until we know the facts," he says. "We do not know what pressures they are under. I recall my own less arduous days in Korea."

Recently the bishop received a letter smuggled out of China. It was from a young Chinese minister whom the bishop had confirmed and started on his way.

"Do not send any letters, cables, or literature to any of us in China," the letter said. "When the General Conference meets, do not seat any Chinese in America as representing the church in China."

That letter has meaning far beyond the instructions, he believes. "Until we can get behind those curtains and know the truth," he says, "we must not cease to believe in the men whom we knew and loved."

The bishop does not believe either the Chinese or Russian communists will be able to conquer forever the Christian, democratic spirit in the countries they now control. He was in Czechoslovakia when the Germans took the Sudetenland. He went to call on his friend, Eduard Benes. The Czech president, in deep sorrow and foreseeing the agony ahead, told him he had that morning gone to the grave of Thomas Masaryk and prayed there.

"Tell the world that Masaryk and I did our best to build here a democratic nation with a free religious life," he said as they parted.

"The world is poorer because the Czech flame is temporarily extinguished," Moore said, "but it is not gone forever. It burns in the hearts of millions in that unhappy country. The Christian, democratic spirit is immortal."

One of his greatest thrills came at a conference held in Frankfurt, Germany, in 1946, the first after the war's end. Representatives were there from all over Europe. Many German pastors had been imprisoned, and fifty-two had lost their lives during the war. The conference opened with a hymn which begins, "And are we yet alive, and see each other face to face?"

"It was a magnificent, emotional moment. Most of those singing had tears in their eyes, but triumph in their voices and hearts. A great revival has continued in Germany ever since, and much of it is in the Russian zone.

"I believe the Christians of the communist-held countries will one day be able to meet with their old comrades and brothers and sing the same hymn," says Bishop Moore. "If any man has had a chance to see these monstrous forces which have been turned loose in the world and which threaten us today, I am that man. I hold tenaciously and triumphantly that out of this insanity and horror will come a better world. I believe this because I believe in the character and sovereignty of God. He has not abdicated. He will not allow the folly of man to rule forever. One day God will break in on that folly. This is not the end of things."

Notes—12

[1]Published by permission of the author, Mrs. McGill, and *The Saturday Evening Post* (10 November 1951). Moore died in June 1974.

[2]See Arthur J. Moore, *Bishop to All Peoples* (Nashville: Abingdon Press, 1973), pp. 15-34; "Address by Robert B. Troutman, Sr.," in *Georgia-Wide Dinner Honoring Bishop Arthur James Moore on the Occasion of His Retirement* (Atlanta: The Ruralist Press, Inc., 1960), pp. 1-4.

[3]Moore, *Bishop to All Peoples*, pp. 33-46.

[4]Ibid., pp. 49-53; Bishop Moore, "I Remember," in *Georgia-Wide Dinner*, pp. 5-12.

[5]Moore, *Bishop to All Peoples*, pp. 54-62.

[6]Ibid., pp. 63-89.

W. E. B. DuBois[1]

A luncheon given in early 1963 by Conor Cruise O'Brien, vice-chancellor of the University of Ghana, beautiful on the gentle hills of Legon near Accra, made possible a subsequent talk with William Edward Burghardt DuBois. Until one met him, he was myth grown out of some seventy-five years of the often turbulent and tragic history of the South's and the nation's trauma of race. I did not expect the first question, after greetings, to be concerned with the author of the *Uncle Remus* stories. But it was.

"Did you know Joel Harris?"

"No," I replied, "he died some years before I went to work on the *Atlanta Constitution*. After going there, I got to know three of his sons and a daughter. He wrote some of the *Uncle Remus* stories at the old double-rolltop desk I have in my office."

"I had a letter of introduction to him after I went to Atlanta," he said. "One day I decided to present it. Walking to his office, I passed by a grocery store that had on display out front the drying fingers of a recently lynched Negro."

He fell silent. No one else said anything. Outside the windows of his spacious house, provided by the government, in the old residential section of Ghana, there was a sound of children at play. A breath of air blew in past the flowering shrubs near the windows. We waited—his wife, his stepson, David,

Mark Lewis, of the U. S. Information Agency office in Accra, a wide-eyed, solemn-faced young Ghanaian girl who was nurse to the aged and ailing man, and I.

The frail body of the ninety-five-year-old man lay stretched on a sofa. He wore trousers, a soft white shirt, and socks and slippers. His mustache and goatee were carefully trimmed. He had been asleep when we arrived. We had waited perhaps half an hour for him to awaken and then be dressed. Neither illness nor a prostate operation in a London hospital some months before, where Ghana's president, Kwame Nkrumah, had insisted he go, had reduced the fire of his mind, though he said his memory was not as quick as before.

There was a lot of history in the slender, sick, and slowly dying man. At ninety-four he had become a citizen of Ghana, where he had resided since 1960. Three years before, he had requested membership in the Communist Party, because he had ceased to believe, he stated, that any other system would produce the sort of world he wanted. But in keeping with his controversial past, he denounced the U. S. Communist program to set up an all-Negro state somewhere in the South. The idea was repellent to him.[2]

Always the fiercely independent, sensitive intellectual, he had been for more than fifty years a passionate fighter for full civil rights and equality of citizenship for the Negro. This placed him in opposition to Booker T. Washington well before the turn of the century.[3] He had helped found the NAACP but had broken with it in 1948 because of its "timidity" and his own growing obsession with Communist causes and ideology.[4]

As I waited for him to speak and studied his face, revealing that his mind was going backward in time and memory, he seemed to me somehow alien to the old colonial house that some long-departed English civil servant had occupied in the Gold Coast days. On its walls were richly and beautifully wrought red hangings of Chinese silk and a few paintings. There were busts of Marx, Lenin, and Mao Tse-tung. Save for the sculptured head of Marx, there was no evidence of Russian art, though DuBois had made a number of journeys to Moscow.[5] One sensed that perhaps the Chinese intellectuals, with their polished manners, had more attraction for the man who for most of his life had himself been somewhat formal in manner and had often worn a pince-nez, carried a cane, and kept carefully trimmed both goatee and mustache. The Chinese had honored him in Peking on his ninety-first birthday with a dinner at which Premier Chou En-lai had been present.[6] Ghana's President Nkrumah, as a student in the United States, had become an apostle of DuBois's Pan-Africa policy. Ghana honored him as a citizen-scholar. Yet the feeling persisted that although the DuBois concept of the Negro's proper status in America was coming into being, the old fighter seemed lonely and unrequited by life.

At last he spoke, his ivory-colored face changing from reflection to anger.

"I saw those fingers. . . . I didn't go to see Joel Harris and present my letter. I never went!"

"I wish you had gone," I said. "Joel Chandler Harris was a good man, as were his closest associates."

"No," he replied, "it was no use. He and they had no question in their minds about the status of the Negro as a separated, lesser citizen. They perhaps were kind men, as you say. They unhesitatingly lived up to a paternalistic role, a sort of *noblesse oblige*. But that was all. The status slowly had become immutable insofar as the South's leaders of that time were concerned. Booker T. Washington had helped them rationalize it. I do not think that he meant to do so. But he did. In fact, he put a public stamp of acceptance on it there in your city when he spoke at the Atlanta Exposition."[7]

"I've read that address many times," I said. "I also have talked with men who saw and heard him deliver it. They've told me of the tremendous drama of that day. They said that when he came to his key paragraph, he began it by holding up both arms, the fingers of each hand spread wide, and said, 'In all things that are purely social we can be as separate as the fingers, yet as the hand'—and here Washington quickly clinched each hand—'in all things essential to mutual progress.' "

DuBois nodded.

"I know," he said, "and in that same speech he implicitly abandoned all political and social rights."

There was a long pause.

"I never thought Washington was a bad man," he said. "I believed him to be sincere, though wrong. He and I came from different backgrounds. I was born free. Washington was born a slave. He felt the lash of an overseer across his back. I was born in Massachusetts, he on a slave plantation in the South. My great-grandfather fought with the Colonial Army in New England in the American Revolution." (This earned the grandfather his freedom.) "I had a happy childhood and acceptance in the community. Washington's childhood was hard. I had many more advantages: Fisk University, Harvard, graduate years in Europe. Washington had little formal schooling. I admired much about him. Washington," he said, a smile softening the severe, gaunt lines of his face, "died in 1915. A lot of people think I died at the same time."[8]

"Could you pinpoint the beginning of the controversy and break between him and you?"

"The controversy," he said, "developed more between our followers than between us. It is my opinion that Washington died a sad and disillusioned man who felt he had been betrayed by white America. I don't know that, but I believe it. In the early years I did not dissent entirely from Washington's program. I was sure that out of his own background he saw the Negro's problem from its lowest economic level. He never really repudiated the higher ends of justice which were then denied.

"As Washington began to attain stature as leader of his new, small, and struggling school at Tuskegee," DuBois continued, "he gave total emphasis to economic progress through industrial and vocational education. He believed that if the Negro could be taught skills and find jobs, and if others could become small landowners, a yeoman class would develop that would, in time, be recognized as worthy of what already were their civil rights, and that they would then be fully accepted as citizens. So he appealed to moderation, and he publicly postponed attainment of political rights and accepted the system of segregation.[9]

"I know Washington believed in what Frederick Douglass had crusaded for from emancipation until his death in 1895. But he made a compromise.

"We talked about it. I went with him to see some of the Eastern philanthropists who were helping him with his school. Washington would promise them happy and contented labor for their new enterprises. He reminded them there would be no strikers. I remember once I went with him to call on Andrew Carnegie—with whom he had a warm and financially rewarding relationship. On the way there Washington said to me:

" 'Have you read Mr. Carnegie's book?'

" 'No,' I replied, 'I haven't.'

" 'You ought to,' he said; 'Mr. Carnegie likes it.' "

DuBois chuckled softly. "When we got to Mr. Carnegie's office," he said, "he left me to wait downstairs. I never knew whether Mr. Carnegie had expressed an opinion about me or whether Washington didn't trust me to be meek. It probably was the latter. I never read the book."

Washington came to national prominence by way of the Atlanta Exposition speech in 1895. It is possible that his decision toward acceptance of the political status quo was influenced by the frustrations and failures of Frederick Douglass. Douglass had been a crusading abolitionist, and he carried his fervor into the years from 1865 until his death, demanding full and equal citizenship. Washington had watched the party of Lincoln cast off the Negro in the historic compromise with Southern leaders that enabled Rutherford B. Hayes to be elected in 1876. The price of this steal of a national election was a removal of occupying federal troops and an end to the radical reconstruction that had been imposed after Lincoln's assassination. This deal had left the future of the newly freed, largely uneducated Negro to "states rights" decisions. By 1895 the several Southern states had about completed total disfranchisement of the Negro by way of constitutional amendments and legislative statutes.

Washington's decision may have lacked a certain idealism, but it was born out of present reality. He may have died feeling a certain betrayal; he nonetheless had made a substantial contribution to preparing many thousands of Negroes for participation in the drive for long-denied rights that began after his death. It came to fruition in the late 1940s and culminated in the 1954 school decision and others that quickly grew out of it. There was a greatness about Washington.[10]

"As I came to see it," said DuBois, "Washington bartered away much that was not his to barter. Certainly I did not believe that the skills of an artisan bricklayer, plasterer, or shoemaker, and the good farmer would cause the white South, grimly busy with disfranchisement and separation, to change the direction of things. I realized the need for what Washington was doing. Yet it seemed to me he was giving up essential ground that would be hard to win back. I don't think Washington saw this until the last years of his life. He kept hoping. But before he died he must have known that he and his hopes had been rejected and that he had, without so intending, helped make stronger— and more fiercely defended— a separation and rejection that made a mockery of all he had hoped and dreamed. I felt grief for him when I learned of his death because I believe he died in sorrow and a sense of betrayal."

There was time for one more question. Booker T. Washington's influence was supreme in racial leadership for twenty years. He was frequently attacked by Negro intellectuals. But he had so successfully appealed to what was a national mood that developed in the years after the Hayes-Tilden election of 1876 that he easily put down all opposition. He had the support and friendship of powerful figures in the industrial and political life of the nation. He was a guest in their homes and in their private cars. And always he came away with money to help educate greatly disadvantaged young Negroes. Many historians believe that Washington's postponement of a decision on Negro rights was largely influential in the U. S. Supreme Court's separate-but-equal decision of 1896, a year after Washington's separated fingers were upraised in the Atlanta Exposition address. Certain it was that Washington's appeasement view, however temporary he anticipated it to be, came to be accepted, North and South, as the view of the Negro himself. Washington was confronted with that conclusion on those occasions when his speeches called attention to the fact that the Negro must, one day, be admitted to the ballot and to full citizenship. Southern editors and leaders invariably took him sharply to task, demanding to know what he meant and why he had changed his mind after the Atlanta speech.

There was no doubt in DuBois's mind. He was sure, he said, that without Washington's position there would have been no Plessy-Ferguson decision in 1896.

There was a sense of unreality in talking about all that was past with DuBois, who after 1915 had been one of the stormy, and sometimes storm-tossed, leaders in the struggle for civil rights. He was always a bit arrogant, or so those who worked most closely with him felt. Except for one summer early in his teaching career spent in the South's poorer plantation region, he had never been directly interested in the masses. W. E. B. DuBois was an intellectual and a scholar. He dreamed, his associates and biographers say, of creating a "talented tenth" that would supply the leadership necessary to winning rights and full equality for the Negro. He was most comfortable with small groups of intellectuals and good conversationalists. In the 1930s he proclaimed in *The Crisis*, the NAACP magazine which he edited, that he wrote his personal column for sophisticated persons, not for "fools and illiterates."

He was best at polemics. Delay and contradiction drove him to frustration and frequent outbursts of invective and criticism that revealed the storm within him. He once admitted that he, opposing racial prejudice, was "one of the greatest sinners" in the intensity of his prejudice against white persons. He was honest enough to say that he expected prejudice and therefore may have even caused it by anticipating it. In *Darkwater*, published in 1920, he concluded a section of verse which condemned "The White World's Vermin and Filth" with the lines:

> I hate them, Oh!
> I hate them well,
> I hate them, Christ!
> As I hate hell!
> If I were God
> I'd sound their knell
> This day.

Oswald Garrison Villard, who admired DuBois very much and who had worked with him in the NAACP, wrote in 1920 of the personal bitterness "that so often mars his work." In the same year, in a letter to a friend, he said, "I think I pity Dr. DuBois more than any man in America."

The Crisis was founded in 1910 with encouragement from Villard and others who disagreed with Booker T. Washington's policies. The magazine legally was the property of the NAACP, but in making DuBois editor and promising him independence of action, they asked him only to agree not to make *The Crisis* a personal organ and to avoid personal rancor. This pledge was not well kept. But DuBois made *The Crisis* a dynamic and forceful voice for the major objectives of the association. In 1910 the magazine condemned the proposal to establish segregated public schools in Chicago; Philadelphia; Columbus, Ohio; and Atlantic City. In 1913 DuBois joined with Villard and others in a written protest to President Wilson against segregated practices in government employment. In 1917 DuBois launched an attack on the white primary system, which was the chief barrier to Negro participation in the ballot. Some of the white social reformers of his time who gave him consistent support, although occasionally they became dismayed by his polemic excesses, were Jane Addams, John Dewey, William Dean Howells, John H. Holmes, Lincoln Steffens, Stephen S. Wise, William H. Ward, and Lillian D. Wald.

By 1916 the NAACP board and many of DuBois's most ardent supporters were becoming increasingly embarrassed by his extremes of editorial expression. His race prejudice was more and more apparent. Typical of these editorial comments in *The Crisis* was one stating that "the most ordinary Negro is a distinct gentleman, but it takes extraordinary training and opportunity to make the average white man anything but a hog."

Slowly DuBois's bitterness narrowed his one piercing view. He broke with Walter White, executive secretary of the NAACP. Editors of Negro newspapers who dared criticize him were dismissed as "croaking toads." DuBois left *The Crisis* editorial chair in 1934 to go to Atlanta to teach, and the magazine ceased publication soon after. For a long time it had been mostly a personal organization for DuBois, and he was beyond question, as Walter White said, "one of the chief molders of modern thought regarding the Negro," but he had to rule. The Negro in America, despite harsh discriminations and segregation, was making great advances and producing new leaders for the changing times. DuBois could accept neither them nor the changing scene.

Ten years after his retirement from *The Crisis*, he was back with the NAACP, but his influence and position had lessened. Four years later he was dismissed with a pension. Paul Robeson, chairman of the left-wing Council on African Affairs, welcomed the old man as he left the NAACP. Dr. DuBois worked for various Communist front organizations, but it is likely he believed he was using them to further his own ends. The Russians interested him, but they were not Negro.

By 1952 he simply abandoned the struggle for Negro rights to give full time to world movements for world peace, for socialism, and later, to team with Kwame Nkrumah and others in promoting a Pan-Africa movement. It has never been possible to separate the man from the myth in considering W. E. B. DuBois.

Mark Lewis and I said good-bye. There was a feeling of having emerged from a place far back in time as we came out of the cool, high-ceilinged house—where the talk had been of Atlanta, of the South, and of a man's more than seventy-five years of participation in the revolutionary background of changes in American educational, political, and social life—into the sun and beauty of Accra's best residential area of old walls, gardens, verandas, and flowers. Six months later in faraway Ghana W. E. B. DuBois died. It was 28 August 1963, the eve of the march on Washington, the largest demonstration for civil rights ever held.[11] One could not help experiencing a feeling of destiny linking both events. The man who for many years had spoken with the loudest and most articulate voice was now silent while his objectives were being realized.

Notes—13

[1]Copyright 1965, by *The Atlantic Monthly* Company, Boston, Massachusetts (November 1965): 78-81. Reprinted with permission. DuBois was no "Southerner," although he taught at Atlanta University for a time. He is closely tied to concerns of the South.

[2]See Henry Lee Moon, *Emerging Thought of W. E. B. DuBois: Essays and Editorials from* The Crisis (New York: Simon and Schuster, 1972), pp. 267-68; *Autobiography of W. E. B. DuBois: A Soliloquy on Viewing My Life from the Last Decade of Its First Century* (International Publishers, 1968), pp. 396-408.

[3]Moon, *Emerging Thought of W. E. B. DuBois*, pp. 26-30, 307-308; *Autobiography of W. E. B. DuBois*, pp. 209-65.

[4]Moon, *Emerging Thought of W. E. B. DuBois*, pp. 215, 400-401; *Autobiography of W. E. B. DuBois*, pp. 291-92.

[5]Shirley Graham DuBois, *His Day is Marching On: A Memoir of W. E. B. DuBois* (Philadelphia: J. B. Lippincott Co., 1971), pp. 259-71, 295, 351; *Autobiography of W. E. B. DuBois*, pp. 269, 290.

[6]*Autobiography of W. E. B. DuBois*, p. 409.

[7]See Booker T. Washington, "Atlanta Exposition Address," in Wayland Maxfield Parrish and Marie Hochmuth, eds., *American Speeches* (New York: Longman's, Green and Co., 1954), pp. 461-65.

[8]W. E. Burghardt DuBois, *Dusk of Dawn: An Essay Toward An Autobiography of a Race Concept* (New York: Schocken Books, 1968), pp. 8-49; *Autobiography of W. E. B. DuBois*, pp. 61-131.

[9]DuBois, *Dusk of Dawn*, pp. 216-43.

[10]In praising Washington's willingness to compromise as a means of helping blacks (as compared to DuBois's strategy of assertiveness) McGill reflected his own approach to social progress. McGill wrote: "I cannot be a good crusader because I have been cursed, all my life, with the ability to see both sides of things. This is fatal to a crusader." He also believed that "extremists in either direction almost inevitably provide dangerous and damaging leadership"; *Atlanta Constitution*, 13 February and 4 November 1947; 31 May and 13 September 1949; 19 July and 30 August 1951; 10 August 1955; Logue, ed., *Ralph McGill* 2 vols. (Durham: Moore Publishing Co., 1969), 2:21-22, 160, 189, and 1:138.

[11]Reports differ on the day of DuBois's death including 27, 28, and 29 August 1963. He died in Ghana, probably on 27 August 1963. See Moon, *Emerging Thought of W. E. B. DuBois*, p. 412.

Essay 14

Four Teachers
Remembered Best[1]

The editors have asked me to reminisce about teachers who stimulated me in the days I was on and off the reservation on the city's borders—

I cannot recall the name of the teacher who most often stimulated me when I was a student at Vanderbilt University. He was an assistant in the chemistry department and as such had a key to the storeroom where alcohol was kept for experiments. The year was 1919 and I was back after being out more than a year and was one of the Lost Generation.

By using a simple physics demonstration, it was possible to draw alcohol from the barrel. By placing a few dried apricots in a large balloon flask and mixing in water and alcohol in even amounts, a splendidly rewarding chemistry experiment could be carried forward with the aid of a Bunsen burner, a special rubber stopper, and a foot or so of glass tubing. The result was an amber fluid, of pleasant taste, with a proof ranging from 100 to 150. On many of the weekends he kept my mind pleasantly stimulated and on occasion in midweek we would stimulate our minds with research, working late in the dingy laboratory of Furman Hall while the sluggards of the faculty and the student body were stultifying their minds and bodies with sleep and ease.

This assistant faculty man, noble fellow that he was, was the patron saint of the Lost Generation group at Vanderbilt that year and the next. When he left at the end of the school year, we drew out some ten gallons which I secreted in the attic of the old Sigma Chi house on Garland Avenue. It was thus possible for our small group of serious students to sacrifice our vacation and carry on chemistry experiments all that summer. Lacking laboratory equipment, they were necessarily crude. As I recall, they consisted of pouring about three inches of fluid from a bottle of Virginia Dare non-alcoholic wine, filling it with the ingredient from the chemistry barrel, and shaking well. The result was also quite stimulating. Alas and alack, I cannot recall his name, and I mention him merely as prelude to those I do remember.

The students in my time were harried and harassed a lot by some pretty dismal Y.M.C.A. meetings. I attended one and the saccharine quality of it caused me to avoid all others thereafter. A student is interested in religion, and it was good to have a Reinke clear matters up and put things in perspective. It is a pity Reinke could not have been called upon to handle the Y.M.C.A. meetings in my time. I don't know how they are now, but I trust they have changed.

He, as much as any other man, is responsible for the quality of Vanderbilt's medical school. When his biology pre-med students reached medical school, they were prepared. He coincided with the expansion of that school. The foundation of its standing was Reinke's graduates.

Once I recall going to Reinke with a tough personal problem. Actually it seemed a difficult one only because of my immaturity, but he was enough of a teacher to treat it as seriously as it seemed to me to be, and to advise me properly. Long after I had given up any hope of becoming a doctor, a fact which saddens me yet, I used to go by and look in on Reinke. From Dr. Mims I got an accelerated interest in poetry and in memorizing it. From Doctors Jackson and Mayfield I received an impetus to learn about Germany and France, their literature and art. And from Reinke I learned to know and recognize the keen blade of truth and its place in life.

The man on the Vanderbilt faculty who gave me what mental discipline I possessed when I left there, and who became my good friend and who stimulated me (without benefit of chemistry experiments), was the late Edwin E. Reinke, head of the biology department. He was a very great teacher, in the full meaning of the word. I wanted to be a doctor in those days, and would have been could I have found the money. Reinke was my hero. I was stimulated to think far beyond the biology classes. I found myself dropping in at his flat and meeting his pleasant, shy wife. He led me beside few still waters, but into the deep ones of philosophic depth. He taught me the value of doubt—and to ask, "How do you know that's true?" I recall how thrilled I was when he defied the witch hunters at the time of the ridiculous evolution bill. I learned a lot of religion from Reinke, and no pious cant at all. He was your true intellectual and his life and teaching were essays in intellectual honesty.

Dr. Eddie Mims and George Pullen Jackson sparked my imagination and started me off into rewarding fields of reading and thought, but it was Reinke who gave me discipline. The nerves of his rabbits were there and they had names. The kidneys of his earthworms were there and functioned in a precise manner which could only be explained with accuracy. The muscles had names, and they were attached at specific points which had definite names.

It was possible to direct Dr. Mims away from a factual reply, by a discussion of some poem or flight of prose. He inspired me to a love of poetry I have never lost. I attended Dr. George Pullen Jackson's German classes and was acclaimed by him as the student with the finest "Ya! Ya!" and "Neine! Neine!" vocabulary he ever had. He could be diverted from a direct answer by a discussion of the place of woodwind instruments in a symphony orchestra, or by a query as to the nuances of Chopin's nocturnes. I learned almost no German, but was so driven to music that I almost married a neurotic young thing who could play a piano like an angel, but who later was sent to a mental institution. I was propelled to the German poets and philosophers and I learned a great deal about Germany so that when I went there years later and remained for some months I felt at home with the physical aspect of it, however much the political dismayed me.

Reinke inspired, but insisted also on discipline. For him there had to be right or wrong answers. I studied for his classes, and until I lost all hope of becoming a doctor, I made good grades under him. Even when I slacked off, I studied enough to pass because I did not wish to face his scorn. Also, I felt that I couldn't go around and call on him at home if I had made an ass of myself in his classroom.

Another who helped me by stimulating my imagination was Dr. George Mayfield. He is a grand man, with a gift for talking with students outside the classroom. I was not long in his German class, being transferred for some reason not now in my memory. But, Dr. Mayfield, too, created interests for me.

These are the four I remember best.

Reinke is gone, now, and perhaps because I cannot tell him so in person, I seem to think of his doing the most to stimulate my mind to inquire, to doubt, to examine, and to know the value of facts.

Reinke had been dead for months before I learned it. I was overseas most of 1945 and learned of his passing by the merest chance. It saddened me for days and I felt guilty in that I had not in some years seen him and had never adequately told him of what he had meant to me and of how much I thought of him—although I think he knew the latter. I remembered the stink of his shabby old lab and the smell of the corpses of formaldehyde-soaked rabbits as we unwrapped them for recitation and study. Later on he got his big building and a first-rate lab and his department became the largest in the University. I am glad he had that before he left us.

Dan McGugin meant a lot to me in the way of inspiration. I will always nurse a tight ball of resentment because of the decision to kick Dan upstairs and go seeking the highly dubious values of big-time football. I think the decision shamed Vanderbilt and created a weakness which persists to this day. But, I assume only a few of us feel this way. I happen to feel it strongly.

I don't know how good my evaluation of teaching is. In the meager records in the registrar's office the results wouldn't add up to much. But, my idea of a teacher is one who sparks the interests and imagination—causes a man to try and keep on learning all his life. That's what Reinke, Mims, Mayfield, and Jackson did for me. They were never just classroom teachers.

Notes—14

[1]Published by permission of the author, Mrs. McGill, and *Vanderbilt Alumnus* (March 1952). McGill wrote that "hero worship for an older cousin who had graduated from Vanderbilt Medical School has persuaded me to register in the pre-medical department"; Ralph McGill, *The South and the Southerner* (Boston: Little, Brown and Co., 1964), pp. 70-71. On 19 December 1961, McGill wrote in the *Atlanta Constitution* that after one year at Vanderbilt he joined the Marine Corps, returning to the College of Arts and Sciences in 1919. He recalled that he took his "discharge and caught the train" from Quantico, Virginia, "with high hopes."

Essay 15

Donald Randolph Wilson: Oglethorpe's New President[1]

Most of the time a man never truly knows why he gives up something which is going well for him, with the future opening up toward a big horizon labeled "Success," to go into something new, untried, and providing less material return.

As, for example, Donald Randolph Wilson abandoned a thriving law practice in Clarksburg, West Virginia, with the further promise of a political career his for the asking, to come to Atlanta as president of Oglethorpe University. He assumed his duties on 1 October 1956.

He is thirty-nine and possessed of a unique combination of education and experience. In 1951-52 he was national commander of the American Legion. In 1951 he had been selected as one of the nation's ten outstanding young men. Earnest efforts were made to launch him in politics in West Virginia, following his successful year as national commander of the Legion. But he stayed with the law.

Yet, all the while, and most persistently since 1952, there was some inner urge which would not let him be. It was not one of those still, silent voices about which one hears now and then. This was almost a compulsion.

Why? He isn't sure. He thinks it was in his background as a child, but it never really began to worry him until he was at Princeton. He believes, too, that Woodrow Wilson had something to do with it. At the university, Woodrow Wilson's tall, gaunt ghost still seemed to stalk the halls with the students and to sit in on the classroom lectures. Years before, the great Democratic leader had been a vigorous, magnetic executive who caused controversial ideas and issues to be a part of the life and legend of the great school. He spoke to Don Wilson through his books in the library and in histories of the tremendous, tumultuous years when a great war was fought and won, and a magnificent ideal and mechanism for peace, the League of Nations, almost was gained, only to be lost through the greed and blindness of little men.

Woodrow Wilson was a part of Donald Wilson's thinking. Maybe a big one.[2]

There was another influence. He entered the second great world war as a private. He was placed in the medical corps. As the war advanced he moved with it to the battles and in rank as well. He served in, and about, the campaigns in North Africa, Italy, Sicily, and France. In the last years he was a captain in charge of one of the hospital ships which moved in and took off the wounded as the invasion battles were being fought. His work caused him to be decorated by the French Legion of Honor. He received, too, the Republic of France's medal to her liberators and the National Guard of Honor's Distinguished Service Medal. He also was a recipient of the Flag Foundation's Americanism award.[3]

But one does not see, work, and live with men broken and shattered by war without thinking, remembering, and weighing.

The war, the wounded and suffering men, were a part of his decision.

Whatever the urge was, it would not let him be.

"I came to see," he said, talking about his acceptance of the presidency of Oglethorpe University, "that if I meant to get into the work of serving my country, it had to be done through two fields, education or politics. I do not mean to be immodest when I say I believe I had opportunity in politics. And I was interested. I consider politics to be a magnificent field of public service. Looking back on it, it seemed to me that when I was a student at Princeton I felt an urge to become a teacher. But when I took my A.B. degree there in 1939 I had become interested in law. In 1942 I graduated from the University of Virginia School of Law.[4] It was my good fortune to become associated later with the law firm of Steptoe and Johnson of Clarksburg, West Virginia, and Washington. I was happy, but I kept thinking about doing something which would seem to me like service to my country.

"The issues which will confront the next generation, on which will hang the fate of mankind, are in fact being decided right now by how well our colleges educate the young manhood and womanhood of America. Since I had decided against politics, I began to believe my place was with some college with that sort of understanding and with that kind of forward look.

"It was about this time that Oglethorpe approached me. I came down and I was impressed with what seemed to me opportunity, and also with those connected with it. But I didn't want to give an answer just then. I went back home and thought it all over, every person I'd met, and all I had seen. And then I made my decision. But," he concluded, smiling, "I guess I had made it all along."

Dr. Wilson is of average height and size. He has blond hair with a touch of red. He has a face which is pensively serious in repose. He looks even younger than his years, which are not yet many. But he also has the scholar's look. It also is apparent that he has a deep interest in life and people. Certainly, there is nothing of the cloistered life, or the ivory tower, about him. He was a Phi Beta Kappa at Princeton. He has studied, written, traveled, and seen much of life and war. And he thinks he knows what sort of education the future will need. And he has thrown in his experience and training with the future of Oglethorpe, Atlanta, Georgia, and the South.

"I have no unusual plans," he said. "Nor do I entertain any ideas that something 'new' is needed in education. The sum of human knowledge is there to be taught. It is teaching and the concepts and values of instruction which are important. One does not need to do 'new things' if one is a teacher. Teaching is communication. We shall try to do that at Oglethorpe. It seemed to me that there was on the campus when first I came here a sense of dedication on the part of the faculty. We will need that, as all universities need it."[5]

Dr. Wilson was born at Detroit, Michigan, 17 May 1917, the son of Abram Bain and Edna Lucille [Lehr] Wilson. His father was engaged in one facet of the steel and iron industry. The son does not recall any unusual childhood. It was a normal sort of one, with a good home and a mother and a father who gave him a background of freedom and unobtrusive guidance and an education. Later, the family transferred to West Virginia.

He is married to the former Miss Mary Virginia Hornor, of Clarksburg. They attended high school together in Clarksburg. He was one class ahead of her. They have two sons, Donald Randolph and Thomas Hornor.[6] He and his family are members of the Baptist church. Dr. Wilson is a former member of the National Lay Council of Churches of Christ, U. S. A. In the more secular field he is, of course, a member of the American Bar Association and those of West Virginia and of Harris County, where his home was. He also is a member of the Reserve Officers Association, American Ordnance Association, and the Military Order of the World Wars.

Dr. Wilson is the fourth president of Oglethorpe. The Oglethorpe which attracted the new president because of its dedication reflects most the character, integrity, and courage of one man. It would not be amiss to say (indeed it would be remiss not to say), that Dr. Philip Weltner, former chancellor of the

University of Georgia, is the man who saved it and who slowly, and with great unremitting labor and affection, has molded it into what he believed to be needed in the field of small, liberal arts colleges.[7] He, too, wanted men and women taught how to live and serve their country and mankind by reflecting the values attained at Oglethorpe in their everyday life as well as in the service of their country.

As Dr. Wilson talked, informally, to provide the basis for this story, Dr. Weltner sat quietly, seemingly lost in thoughts of his own. But he was listening. And there was on his face a look of contentment. It seemed to be saying that he had found what Oglethorpe needed.

Dr. Wilson's election was announced to the student body at the time of the spring commencement exercises by Pope Brock, chairman of the board of trustees, and by Dr. George S. Seward, who as acting president has done a fine job for the university while the trustees sought for the man "fitted for Oglethorpe."

There is a strong feeling at Oglethorpe that now, beginning with this administration, the university will become more and more a part of the educational life of the city, state, and region, and that its growth, both in plant, endowment, students, and results, slowly but surely will have an effect in the life and issues of our times.

Looking at Dr. Donald R. Wilson, and talking with him, one shares that confidence.[8]

Notes—15

[1]Reprinted from *Atlanta Journal and Constitution Magazine* (21 October 1956), by permission of the author, Mrs. McGill, and Atlanta Newspapers, Inc.

[2]See McGill's article on Woodrow Wilson in this book.

[3]He entered World War II as a private in 1942 and was discharged as a captain in 1945.

[4]Wilson was graduated from Salem College in 1952 with the LL.D.

[5]In 1956, Wilson saw "his new job as comprising the following: (1) achieving a smooth administrative operation so that the business end of the school will run efficiently; (2) interpreting the school to the community and 'in a sense to the nation and state'; (3) acting as an assistant to the faculty in providing things they are too busy to handle themselves, and (4) aiding the students in any way to help them 'develop their faculties to the fullest'." *The Flying Petrel,* November 1956, published by National Oglethorpe Alumni Association.

[6]In 1956 Randy was twelve years old, and Tommy, nine.

[7]Wilson was the college's fourth president; its founder, Dr. Thornwell Jacobs, died in 1956. Dr. Philip Weltner was president from 1944 until 1953; he began the strong liberal arts program for the college. Dr. J. Whitney Bunting resigned as president in 1955 to accept a position with General Electric Corporation.

[8]Donald Wilson served as president of Oglethorpe College, 1956-1957. Wilson joined the law firm of Charleston, West Virginia, attorney Stanley Preiser in the 1960s. In January 1976, Wilson was named by West Virginia Governor Arch A. Moore, Jr., to the state Supreme Court.

Essay 16

Jack Tarver:
A Newspaper Man's
Newspaper Man[1]

I remember that a good many years ago Jim Gillis, who, of course, has been chairman of the Georgia Highway Department forever, invited me to come down to South Georgia, near Lyons, to speak at the Yeoman family reunion. I recall that I wanted to go for several reasons. High on my priority of reasons was that I wanted to see a young weekly newspaperman named Jack Tarver.

He was not trying to hide his light under a bushel. His weekly writings had humor, bite, and style. The symbolic Tarver candle even then was casting a light that had managed to project its rays a long way from Vidalia, and later Lyons, from where he really got going on the *Toombs County Democrat*.[2]

When Jack Tarver came to the reunion, he was driving an imposing, gleaming Packard car with a long, rakish hood. The hood was decorated with a shiny black leather belt, which was a creation of a good ad man. We were not then completely out of the horse age and the heavy belt made one think of saddle girth belts on all the mighty horses in the engine. The Packard was the Cadillac of its time. I was then the owner of a second-hand Ford, and I recall that when I saw the

Tarver Packard I began to wonder if it might not be advisable to consider moving from the daily to the weekly field.

One of the things I had planned for the trip was to talk with Jack Tarver about the possibility of coming up to work on the *Atlanta Constitution*. I did get around to discussing this possibility. His reaction was that while he would like some day to come to Atlanta, he did not believe he was ready. He thought, he said, that it would be better to work on a daily in a smaller city before moving to the state's capital city.

There was a certain familiar logic in the argument. It is my opinion, however, that one of journalism's hoary myths is that working on "a smaller paper" is a necessary step to a larger one. I did not try to override his idea, seeing how firmly he held it. (I did not know at the time how stubborn he was, and is, so it was just as well I did not belabor the matter.) Also, events have justified him.

He now is, and for a good many years has been, president of Atlanta Newspapers, Inc., which includes both the *Atlanta Constitution* and *Journal*. He is in his third term as chairman of the Sixth Federal Reserve Bank. For some years he has also been a director of American Motors. In his own profession he has held a number of top positions in national newspaper organizations.[3] He is, without argument, one of the two or three best young newspaper executives in the country. (I think he is the best of the younger ones, but then I admit to a certain prejudice.) Certainly Mercer University, from which he graduated in 1938, can claim considerable credit for polishing up his native intelligence and for assisting him into a newspaper career.

Before making the move from the weekly to the daily field, Tarver took an important non-journalism step. In 1940 he married Margaret Taylor, the prettiest girl in Macon. Fortified with a wife, he moved on from Lyons to the *Macon News* about two months after the mutual pledging of vows.

At Lyons he had learned to set type, sell and set ads, make up the paper, and write most of it. It was this eager-beaver characteristic, plus his writing talent, that had brought attention to him. In Macon he could not man the linotypes or sell ads, but he did pitch in everything else that had to be done.

It was a column written from Lyons just before coming to Macon that distributed his name and ability thoroughly over the state. In point of fact, the column received some national reprints and comments. Movie critics had tried very hard on reviewing Margaret Mitchell's great epic as seen on the new wide screens of the time. Tarver was somewhat irreverent. The opening paragraph read:

There was a land of cotton and cavaliers, called *The Old* South. A land of *lords* and their *ladies*, of master and of slave. Look not for them hereabouts, for they are no longer to be found. They are *all* down to the picture show seeing *Gone with the Wind*.

The column, like the book, may be a bit dated by the passing years and by change, but both the book and the column are still good. I think Mercer's alumni may be pleased to have a few top paragraphs from the Tarver review printed in the column titled "In the Wash"—the same title, incidentally, he used in the student paper at Mercer:

> Gerald O'Hara was Scarlett's pa. By nature, he was most animal-like. Proud as a peacock, he roared like a lion and rode like a dog and pony show.
>
> Anyhow, Scarlett was in love with Ashley Wilkes, who was in love with his cousin Melanie, who was in love with Ashley, and so they were married. (Ashley and Melanie in case you are getting confused.)
>
> This irritated Scarlett no end and so, in quick succession she married for spite and cash, respectively, a couple of fellows whose names we didn't get. But then, neither did Scarlett for long.
>
> The other major characters were Rhett Butler, Belle Watling, and a colored lady exactly like the one on the flapjack box.
>
> If Rhett had joined the Lost Cause in the second reel instead of after intermission, the Confederacy would have won the war.
>
> And Belle. You'd have loved Belle. Everybody did. (This was somewhat daring writing for rural Georgia. *Everyone* knew that Belle was madam of the Atlanta brothel.)
>
> During the siege on Atlanta, only three places were running—Belle's place, Prissy's nose, and the laundry that kept Rhett's white suits white.
>
> Melanie's baby arrived about the same time Sherman did. Both were equally welcome to Scarlett.
>
> It was, as far as our painstaking research revealed, the first baby ever born in Technicolor.
>
> Anyway, the South lost the war again in the picture. (What could you expect with a lot of Yankee producers?) And Scarlett married Rhett to get even with him.
>
> Their married life was just like setting in hell's fire and listening to the heavenly choir. Scarlett was as changeable as a baby's underwear.
>
> However, Rhett had enough of her foolishness and when he told her he was leaving and she asked what would happen to her, he says: "Frankly, my dear, I don't give a damn."
>
> Neither, by this time, did the audience. They were glad to see the end, their own having become number than somewhat from seats harder than a landlady's stare.

The years in Macon were good ones. Tarver established a reputation that brought him a number of offers. By late 1943 he was ready to come to Atlanta.

In addition to the qualities of intelligence, ability, personality, and stubbornness already noted, the list of assets requires still another asset—canniness.

The *Atlanta Journal* also had made him an offer and he properly went to see them. But the gentleman who was conducting the interview made an error. He dismissed the column Tarver had so well established and told him what kind of column he would expect from him in the future. Stubbornness wrestled with a salary increase and the former won. Tarver came to the *Constitution* where he had been told he could write what he pleased as associate editor.[4]

The writer recalls his great satisfaction in that decision. There followed some happy, trying, testing years. Now and then, in these days when editorial staffs have grown in numbers, Tarver and I like to recall when each turned out several columns per week, wrote all the editorials, and did the make-up. When one of us was absent, all the editorials were written and the make-up done by the one remaining.

In late 1944 the American Society of Newspaper Editors named the writer as one of a committee of three to visit all possible foreign capitals for discussions about a post-war international association that would further a freer flow of news. The journey stretched out about six months.

Tarver got even in 1949. His work won for him an Ogden Reid Foundation fellowship, which enabled him to fulfill an ambition to travel in South America and report and comment from there. He almost died at the outset of a never really accurately diagnosed illness that involved a heavy fever, suggestions of oncoming paralysis, and a coma. He came out of it his old smiling self and for six months did a superb job of feature writing and wise analytical comment.

The Tarver column, always bright and widely and loyally read, had been nationally syndicated. Tarver wrestled with decision, however, and, as usual, made the right one. He determined to move into management. The *Atlanta Constitution* was at that time in desperate need of such management, and Tarver made a good beginning. In early 1950 the late Clark Howell, owner of the *Constitution*, decided to accept an opportunity, brought to him by a close friend in the investment world, to merge into a holding company, Atlanta Newspapers, Inc., with the late Governor James M. Cox of Ohio.

Governor Cox and his son, James M. Cox, Jr., had well before recognized Tarver's unusual competence and ability. He quickly was moved in as assistant to the late George Biggers, local executive head of the new company. Later on when illness incapacitated Biggers, Tarver became acting President of Atlanta Newspapers, Inc., and following Mr. Biggers' death, was elected president. In his years as president the papers have made greater progress than at any previous period in their history.

Maybe because he has a touch of it himself, Tarver tolerates eccentrics, if they can write and do their job well. In this he was fully supported by the late Governor Cox and, in the years since his death, by Jim Cox and his associates.

They all believe newspapers have a duty to serve their time and generation by participating in all things affecting the public interest. They and Tarver have worked as a team to give leadership and confidence to the editorial staffs.

Alas, the space assigned me is used up. I forgot to say Jack Tarver was born.[5] Savannah was his natal city. His father, O. M. Tarver, from whom the son inherited considerable personality, was in the hotel business and so the young Tarver lived in Savannah; Murfreesboro, Tennessee; Dublin; and Macon. He has two fine children, Jack, Jr., and Margaret Tarver Jason. Jack has already made him a grandfather. Tarver senior is, as one might expect, a doting grandfather who tries so hard not to show it that he makes it obvious he enjoys being a grandfather and will be all the happier with any and all grandchildren yet to come.

Mercer can be very proud of this now prematurely graying grad. All of us are at 10 Forsyth Street, Atlanta, Georgia.

Notes—16

[1]Reprinted from *The Mercerian* (September 1967), by permission of the author, Mrs. McGill, and Mercer University.

[2]Tarver worked on the *Vidalia Advance*, 1938-1939. He began the *Toombs County Democrat*, Lyons, Georgia, 1939-1940, and was associate editor and editor of the *Macon Evening News*, 1940-1943.

[3]He served as president of Southern Newspaper Publishers Association, 1976. See *Editor and Publisher* 109 (13 November 1976): 16-19.

[4]Tarver became associate editor, *Atlanta Constitution*, 1943-1950; assistant to president of Atlanta Newspapers, Inc., 1950-1953; general manager, Atlanta Newspapers, Inc., 1953-1958; vice-president, Atlanta Newspapers, Inc., 1956-1958; president, Atlanta Newspapers, Inc., 1958; publisher of Atlanta Newspapers, Inc., 1970; president of Cox Enterprises, Inc., 1969-1978; chairman of board, Associated Press, 1977-1982; vice-chairman, Cox Enterprises, Inc., 1978-1982; retired, April 1982.

[5]Jackson Williams Tarver was born 2 March 1917.

Essay 17

Bobby Jones: Great Man and Great Golfer[1]

A group of senior friends of Robert Tyre Jones was gathered in the East Lake Club locker room a few days ago discussing his exploits. They were somewhat disturbed to recall that they were graying, paunchy adults, when he, in his twenties, was winning all the golf titles at home and in the British Empire, and that on March 17 the young man, who retired at twenty-eight with no more golfing worlds to conquer, will celebrate his fifty-first birthday. "What does that make us?" they asked one another.

But, they called a hovering waiter, turned all the mirrors to the wall so as to hide the unpleasant facts, and went on with their talk.

"If Bob were to hear me say it," said one, "he would undoubtedly suggest that I hasten to the nearest chapter of Alcoholics Anonymous. But, just the same," he concluded, "there is a lot about the fellow that reminds me of my conception of what sort of a man General Robert E. Lee must have been."

Robert Tyre Jones, who became one of the best-known supporters of Candidate Dwight D. Eisenhower by doing a typical Jones job—working hard at it—would undoubtedly hoot at the comparison, but in some aspects, at least, it isn't too far off the putting line. He has always had a great sense of duty, and of responsibility, and he learned that he who conquers himself is greater than he that taketh a city.[2] And despite the fact that he lived for a good half of his life in the brightest floodlight of public attention, he never said or did a wrong thing. Also, he managed to learn how to be not merely a good loser, which is easy, but to be a good winner, which is vastly more difficult.

During the years when he was compiling the greatest record golf has ever known, he was perhaps even more popular in Scotland and England than at home, where he was taken somewhat for granted, like the national parks, Old Faithful, or the Natural Bridge.

After one of his jaunts to the British Isles, Robert W. Woodruff, a close friend who accompanied him, came back and was talking about it.[3]

"Bob just went out at St. Andrews for a practice round," he said. "There wasn't any announcement of it. But, before he had gone two holes, the gallery was large and growing every minute. And every blessed Scot in it was beaming of face and talking fondly about him. See if you can get down on paper the qualities which make for that."

"You can't," I said. "It's like the riddle of Greek proportion. It's just there. Or it isn't."

The riddle of that perfection continues. It was said that when General John B. Gordon entered a railway car or a hotel in the years after the War Between the States, men and women would stand up, their faces alight, and cry, "Gordon," as they hurried to shake his hand or embrace him. It is the same with Jones. He retired in 1930 (after setting a golf record, of which more later), but the public kept calling on him, and whenever there was a public service job he felt fitted to do, he took it. He never liked being in public. He never really enjoyed tournament golf, especially the last years of it. He never liked being called "Bobby" although he was known with affection the world over by that name. He detested signing autographs and putting up with all the pests and hangers-on that go with fame and championships, but he did it without resentment or in any way avoiding it. Whatever he felt it was his duty to do—he did it. And without, of course, making any mention of it being his duty. It was the same way with the Army. He didn't have to go. But he went, and served overseas. If he ever had an ego, he never revealed it.

All of which is by the way of prelude to the story of his political activity in behalf of his friend who has become president of the United States and who sees to it that he and Bob Jones have frequent conversations on the telephone, when they can't be had in person.

Some few years ago Bob Jones began to be worried by a pain in his back. Later on, there was a numbness in one foot. The doctors put their X-rays to work and discovered a crushed spinal disc. It was an old injury, and one he never knew he had. Nature had tried to heal it by growing scar tissue around it so that the broken pieces were almost a part of the spinal cord. There wasn't too much the surgeon's knife could do through a long, tedious operation. Also the pain didn't go away. More than a year later there was a second operation to see if there was anything new to be done. There wasn't. Pain remained. He learned to live with that. And he kept on going places, and walking, even if it meant going slowly and using a couple of sticks. He said nothing about it, and complained not even once.

There was no real reason for him to go to the political wars. He has his law practice. His home is a beautiful and comfortable one, and he has it wired so that when he wishes he can hear his favorite records anywhere he happens to be. Each Saturday afternoon he selects a complete symphony and gives himself, the family, and any guests present a concert. And he likes books. But, there seemed to him a reason to be active politically. He felt there ought to be a new administration in Washington. And, feeling that way, he considered, although he did not say so, he had a duty. So, not only did he make contributions and join a committee, he became chairman of one.

Chairmanships meant meetings and travel. He did it. He went all over the state of Georgia to attend rallies. He must have suffered a lot of pain and been terribly weary at times. Indeed, now and then I'd see him when I thought there was a gray spot at the corners of his lips where the quiet smile always is, but the smile was never gone, and he was his usual thorough, courteous self.

Georgia was having a factional fight in her Republican Party, and Jones and a lot of others couldn't understand it. But he was as patient as any old-timer, and he helped work out many a knot.

When the convention time came along, there was a dispute about the delegations from Georgia and Texas, and the Georgia case was to be heard first. Bob Jones got himself out to the airport and into a plane and arrived in Chicago, where he secluded himself in the apartment of a friend, Harry Kipke, who was one of the greatest punters football ever knew, and who is on all the all-time Michigan teams selected by the experts. He sent word to General Elbert Tuttle, chairman of the disputed delegation, the eventual seating of which swung the tide to General Eisenhower, that if he needed a witness named Bob Jones the witness was on hand and ready, willing, and able to testify. As it turned out, the opposition wouldn't allow any new witnesses, but Jones was there. It is his way. Only his family and a close friend or so knew he was going, and in Chicago only General Tuttle and a few others were informed he was on deck if needed.

He came back home and watched it all on television. He and Ike had a talk when that victory was won.

Then he went to work again. He was patient with his Democratic friends, although I am sure he couldn't understand supporting anyone else when General Eisenhower was available. But he never mentioned it to them. He went to work, despite the pain and the physical discomfort of it all—and, I suspect, the mental, because, after all, he doesn't really care for the mechanics of politics. He had no real hope he and his associates could carry Georgia, but he had promised the general they would give him a record vote. And they did.

The night of the election he sat up until it was conceded. Then he and Ike were on the telephone.

"I sure liked the way you sank that long putt," said Jones, and the weary president-elect of the United States laughed as he had not laughed all day.

Then, of course, the winner came to the Augusta National Golf Club, where he has long been a member, and where he played with Bob Jones before the spinal injury halted the latter's play. And the General and Mrs. Eisenhower lived at the Jones cottage while they were there.

In late February, President Eisenhower began to pine for Augusta and golf, and the White House office suddenly announced the President of the United States would fly down for a weekend of golf, again the guest of Bob Jones. The president, his staff, and the regular White House correspondents arrived February 26 and departed March 1.

There are plans for a cottage next door to the Jones dwelling at the Augusta National. And the president very well may make it the Little White House, because he long ago came down with the golf virus, and there is no cure for it.

If he does, as he is almost sure to do, he will be the third president to select Georgia as a winter "home." President William Howard Taft wintered at Augusta "On the Hill," and President Franklin D. Roosevelt, of course, had his "Little White House" at Warm Springs.

The Georgia Republicans from Richmond County (Augusta) entered an Augusta National Club float in the inaugural parade, and it drew from the just-inaugurated president perhaps the only really spontaneous reaction of a long afternoon. When he saw it, he flashed the famed Eisenhower smile and then laughed out loud in delight, while Mrs. Eisenhower applauded. The new president then leaned over and whispered to ex-President Herbert Hoover (perhaps an explanation of the float), and the Californian smiled, too. And to top it off, the president of the United States has painted a portrait of Bob Jones. "The toughest job was Jones' hands," said the president. "Hands are difficult even for experienced painters, and Bob's hands are so fine and sensitive they gave me a lot of trouble."

One ought not, I assume, to write about Jones without going into his golfing record, despite the fact it has been done so often. It is so amazing an accomplishment it always sounds new. A few weeks ago Jones went to New York to be present at the unveiling of a portrait of himself in the Hall of Golf, a companion piece to baseball's Hall of Fame. He said there in an interview he expected the record to be duplicated, or excelled. And he meant it. But, it will take a lot of doing even to match it. In considering this record, it must be kept in mind that he played when golf club shafts were hickory, and no two were alike in torque, or response. A man literally had to learn the smallest characteristic of each club. Today, with the shafts made of machine-tooled steel one obtains accuracy and conformity. Also, the golf courses of today have less rough. They have been manicured, perhaps sensibly so, to make the game more enjoyable for the duffers.

So, here goes with the Jones record:

He played in thirteen amateur championships in the United States. Of these he won five and twice finished second.

As an amateur playing against the best professionals in the world, Jones played in eleven United States open championships. He won four and four times was second.

He played in four British open championships and won three.

The British Amateur was his most difficult. He was in three and won once.

This, of course, was in 1930 when he won all four—the United States Amateur and Open and the British Amateur and Open—with the pressure and the odds increasing terrifically each time he won.

So much for the record. He is still the greatest golfer the world has ever known.

All through these years he has had the saving grace of laughter and of being able to see, and laugh at, the ridiculous aspects of life, golf, or politics. He can be very serious, and he always plays to win if he is in competition. But, he never took himself, or his feats seriously enough to stuff his shirt with them.

All the while he has had that rare combination of strength and gentleness.

St. Patrick doesn't mind a bit sharing March 17 with Bob Jones.

Notes—17

[1]Reprinted from *Atlanta Journal and Constitution Magazine* (15 March 1953), by permission of the author, Mrs. McGill, and Atlanta Newspapers, Inc. Robert Tyre Jones was born in Atlanta on 17 March 1902 and died 18 December 1971.

[2]See Grantland Rice, from the writings of O. B. Keeler, *The Bobby Jones Story* (Atlanta: Tupper & Love, 1953), p. ix. See also Robert T. Jones and O. B. Keeler, *Down the Fairway: The Golf Life and Play of Robert T. Jones, Jr.* (New York: Blue Ribbon Books, 1927); Robert Tyre (Bobby) Jones, Jr., *Golf Is My*

Game (Garden City, NY: Doubleday & Co., 1959); Dick Miller, *Triumphant Journey: The Saga of Bobby Jones and the Grand Slam of Golf* (New York: Holt, Rinehart and Winston, 1980).

[3]See the article in this book by McGill on Woodruff.

Essay 18

Frank Neely: One of Atlanta's Great Builders[1]

A knowledge of forbears often is essential to understanding today's man. This is true of Frank Henry Neely, who has had, perhaps more than any other one person, a hand in the shaping of the burgeoning Atlanta of our time.[2]

A stubborn, persistent man, his tenacity and unrelenting pursuit of an idea or plan have been compared with the traditional bulldog's grip and the singleness of purpose of one of Oliver Cromwell's famed "Roundheads." Once in a discussion of Neely a friend said that he held on in the legendary manner of the turtle. "No," said one in the group, "according to legend the turtle lets go when it thunders. Frank, in the presence of thunder, holds on the harder."[3]

There is, in truth, a lot of the "Old Dutch" in him, as well as Scottish patience. On the maternal side this reaches back to William Longstreet, and his wife, who was Hannah Randolph. They moved from Monmouth County, New Jersey, in 1785, to Augusta, Georgia. The name had been Americanized in the course of a century. William's forbear was Dirck S. Landstraet, who had come to America from the Netherlands in 1657.[4]

Once settled in Augusta, William Longstreet applied himself to constructing a steam engine. Such was his progress that on 1 February 1788, the General Assembly of Georgia passed an act securing to "Isaac Briggs and William Longstreet, for a term of fourteen years, the sole and exclusive privilege of using a newly constructed steam engine invented by both." Longstreet invented other machines, one for rolling cotton. He also built a few steam-operated cotton gins. Because of carelessness and lack of knowledge, these were destroyed by fire. The *Augusta Herald*, of 23 December 1801, mourned this loss editorially, declaring they had worked successfully and produced, with little expense, "800 to 1,000 weight of clean cotton per day."

He also designed portable sawmills, erecting and operating a number of them in South Georgia. One, near St. Marys, was destroyed by the British in 1812. As early as 1790 he sought state funds to aid in building a steamboat. Sixteen years later, without help, he did construct a small steamboat which ran on the Savannah River against the current at the rate of five miles an hour. Both he and Robert Fulton were at work at the same time on the same idea, Fulton then being in France. But it was 1807 before Fulton's Clermont steamed on the Hudson, a year after Longstreet's success on the Savannah. One wonders what the story might have been had Georgia assisted him in 1790.

William Longstreet died in 1814, leaving a widow and six children. One of these was Augustus Baldwin Longstreet. He, too, was to leave a name in Georgia. He was writer, Methodist minister, president of Emory College at Oxford, Georgia, and later of the University of Mississippi and South Carolina. One of his daughters married Lucius Q. C. Lamar. A nephew was James Longstreet, the famed and controversial "Old Dutch" Longstreet, one of General Robert E. Lee's commanders. Frank Neely is descended from one of the sisters. He comes naturally by his "Dutch."

On his father's side, too, were preachers and teachers. His father ran away to sea as a young boy. He came back home master of five languages, his intelligence sharpened by study and experience. During the four years of the War Between the States he served with distinction and success in the Confederate intelligence service. He spent much of his time in Federal-held cities and behind the lines. He also was used in Confederate negotiations with foreign powers. The pity is he did not write his memoirs. His bent always was toward teaching. After the war he led in establishing the public school system in Richmond County and, later, in Floyd County. In both he demanded, as a condition of employment, that he be allowed to build equal school facilities for Negroes and teach in both schools. Neely High School, named for him, has continued at Rome into our time. One of Frank Neely's great sorrows is that he cannot remember his father, he being not quite five years of age when the beloved teacher died. There were nine children. He was the youngest.

Relatives assisted in the care of the children. Somewhat to the despair of those who cared for young Frank, he showed no liking for school, and a great dislike in particular for Latin. There was one exception, a doting sister at Cedartown, who urged him on to school and books. Even so, he was not enthusiastic until one day he and other school friends saw new farm machinery demonstrated at a nearby farm.

It is significant that this machinery drew his interest. He went home to his aunt and told her he was going to study hard, go to Georgia Tech, and become an engineer.

A relative in Atlanta took him in and, after a summer of intensive study, he took the entrance examinations. There were no questions on Latin and young Neely, at sixteen, found himself a freshman at the Georgia School of Technology. He graduated in 1904 with highest honors and the mathematics medal.

This record attracted scouts of the Westinghouse Electric Company just beginning to look South for talent, and he was hired at a starting wage of $40.00 per month. He was a design engineer, but after a few months surprised his superiors by asking transfer to plant operations, the first engineering graduate to make such a request. As a boy, it had been the sight of new and wondrous machinery which had inspired him. Now, as a young man, it was the writings and teachings of Frederick Taylor and Henry L. Gantt on scientific management which drew him. Gantt was consulting engineer to Westinghouse on production problems, and Neely wanted to be close to him. He worked hard. He invented and patented. He became supervisor of production in the building of the first electric locomotives for the New York, New Haven, and Hartford Railroad. And he got to know Gantt. He was encouraged to learn as much as he could of production and management methods and return South where there was not yet much industrialization and even less management skills. Gantt encouraged him also to understand that management skills included participation in the civic life of the community and the establishment of good working conditions and employee relationships. Neely never forgot.

In 1908 he came South to marry Rae Schlesinger, daughter of Harry and Ella C. Schlesinger, whom he had courted for several years. It had been a mutually helpful courtship during their school years. She had helped him with English literature and themes. He had assisted her with arithmetic and algebra.[5]

In 1910 with Gantt's blessing, he came back to Atlanta and set up home and office, specializing in plant layout, production methods, and quality control. He became a student of developing Southern economic conditions, manufacturing, and distributing.[6]

There was not too much income. It was a new venture for the South. Mrs. Neely had a job of management, too. Out of sentiment she kept, from those days, a teapot for which she paid twenty-five cents. It reminds her of the time when, looking at it, she had to debate whether twenty-five cents could be spared, and also of the joy and pleasure she had in assisting her husband to set his feet in the path of both spiritual and material success.[7]

But jobs came to the young consultant. He carried out fuel tests and coal production studies in Kentucky and Tennessee, which successfully increased the quality and quantity of production. Candy manufacturers, textile plants, food producers, cottonseed oil and gin operators came to him with problems. As a result of his demonstrated ability, he was asked in 1915 to join the Fulton Bag and Cotton Mills, which operated six plants in about as many states, as director of production. By 1924, during which years he had been vice president and, finally, director, he had instituted a complete change of methods, plant layout, design, operation, and maintenance. Production and efficiency zoomed to record heights. Norman Elsas, chairman of the Fulton Bag Board, said Neely's application of the "Gantt task and bonus" method of payment was the first in the textile industry. Elsas also testified to the greatly improved employer-employe relationships. Gantt, by this time, regarded Neely as one of his favorite pupils and was often a house guest in Atlanta.

In 1924, when Neely was forty, Walter Rich, head of M. Rich and Son, now Rich's, Inc., had a problem of management. The store was in its new six-story building at Broad and Alabama. The stocks were much larger; the problems of inventory, sales, and production were greater. Some records had been lost in the transfer. Walter Rich knew about Neely's work with Fulton Bag. He sent for him. Neely demurred. After all, a department store is not a factory. Walter Rich was insistent. Neely deliberately named a figure well above his Fulton salary. Rich didn't hesitate.[8]

"When," he said, "can you come to work?"

So it was that into the department store, via coal mines, candy factories, and textile mills, came Frank Neely, with Gantt's charts and his own. It was a crossroads. Now and then Frank Neely must have sought to imagine where he might have gone in engineering and production had not Rich's called. He transformed Rich's. He was the first man in America to introduce engineering principles to retailing. A system of stock and classification control, studies of vertical and horizontal movement of goods, traffic, merchandise flow, the establishment of manufacturing workrooms on a scientific basis, a quota bonus plan, a free clinic, mutual aid, a credit union, improved working conditions, insurance, pensions—all these came after he arrived.

Walter Rich soon came to refer to his protege as "The Master Builder." Neely always was building something. He was forever having experts in about lighting, the colors of walls, the display counters. Additions were planned, and built. In sixteen years there were four large expansions of space. In 1924 the sales volume was roughly five million dollars a year. Last year it was more than sixty million.

The material story is a fabulous one.

The intangible one is greater.

Neely led the way in putting himself and his associate executives into civic affairs. He had come to know this part of Gantt's dual theory was equally as important as the business planning. If the community in which the business is located does not grow and prosper, the business cannot.

He made himself clear in all his meetings.

Nothing of a civic nature must be planned or supported which had the narrow interest of benefiting their own business. In the long run such activity would hurt. All their energies must be directed at making Atlanta and Georgia a better and more prosperous city and state. In such increasing prosperity they would have to hustle for their share of it.

It is a tribute to Frank Neely that even his most ardent competitors agree, sometimes grudgingly, that he has hewed to this line. "I must admit," said one, in a recent discussion of him, "I never knew him to advocate anything which first of all wasn't good for Atlanta."[9]

In 1950, for example, as chairman of the board of the State Commerce Department, he presented to Governor Herman Talmadge the committee report favoring enactment of a "no exemptions" sales tax. Such a tax, anathema to all retailers, increasing bookkeeping and employe costs, was necessary to the progress of Georgia, especially her schools. "Public Servant Neely puts himself ahead of Merchant Neely," said an editorial.

In 1926 Atlanta was a city in three segments. The railroad yards made gulfs through it. In 1926, as president of the Atlanta Improvement Association, he promoted the building of wide viaducts over the yards—nine main lines come into Atlanta. He was responsible for the organization and establishment of the first Fulton County zoning and planning commission. Later he had a hand in the merging of county and city planning and zoning activities.

In 1926 he was chairman of the bond commission which spent $10,000,000 in improving the city's streets, schools, and making growth possible. He is vice-chairman of the bond commission which is pushing through the popular expressway system and its necessary limited-access-highways which have put Atlanta ahead of her sister cities in this field. Indeed, it is fair to say, that while many men had a vital and valuable part in it, Neely was the first to begin prodding city officials and the public with the necessity for such a system to care for a city expecting a population of 1,000,000 by 1970.[10]

In 1937 during the depression, when city and county were locked in a desperate political debate over welfare programs and costs, he agreed to take the chairmanship of the County Welfare Board. He remained until the problem was worked out and operations proceeded smoothly.

The year 1938 saw him become chairman of the board of the Sixth Federal Reserve Bank. There followed an application of engineering techniques to the bank, a reorganization of staff, of flow of work and product handling, and an exchange of information system between member banks which compares with a running inventory such as is used in industrial and merchandising operations. Research and statistics, as a service to banks and business in the district, also came out of his planning. He saw to it, too, that all executives came out of their cloisters and assisted in all proper civic problems, such as planning, community boards, and the like.

His war-time work as regional director of the War Production Board for the South brought him official commendations. After the war he served admirably in converting plants to peace-time activities.[11]

He advocated, and caused to be created, a Georgia State Department of Commerce and was its first chairman.[12]

He has a great ability to get work done by indirection. Indeed, in times of civic crisis his friends are known to fear they may find themselves on a committee, a board, or doing research into some aspect of a problem. At least two mayors have been needled so much that they have at times complained of difficulty sitting down. At times the City Hall, and the county commissioners, have waved arms and shouted with Frank Neely in red-faced exchanges. But always they cool off with the realization that both want the same thing, the only difference being that Neely's schedule is always too fast for them. It is his method for emphasizing the need to get off dead center.[13]

These are but the skeleton outlines of some of the major civic jobs in which he has been one of the prime movers for a better Atlanta.

But perhaps because of his father and other teacher forbears, he himself has more satisfaction from his work with education than any other thing he has accomplished. And, on examination, this contribution stands up as the best, possessing as it does so much long-range value.[14]

He has been instrumental in bringing about bond issues for school buildings, equipment, and salaries. He served as chairman of the present Joint Bond Commission schools committee. The committee report, as submitted to the Boards of Education and executives of Atlanta and Fulton County in 1946 was "so broad in scope and so basic in its fundamental simplicity, that the entire school system of Atlanta was reorganized on the basis of its recommendations."[15]

Earlier, during the depression years, he engineered the financing of Atlanta schools by private enterprise, maintaining a school organization which would have collapsed without such support. Through the Rich Foundation, and on his recommendation, the public school system was presented a radio station and equipped classrooms to receive educational programs broadcast by it. The station has received three national citations.

As chairman of the board of the Alumni Foundation, he assisted in the selection of the late Blake R. Van Leer as president of Georgia Tech and in a campaign which raised the millions necessary to expand the plant and faculty. He serves, too, on the board of the Georgia Tech Research Institute, which engages entirely in research in the interests of industry in the state.

He has worked, too, with Emory University, the University System, and Tallulah Falls School.

A number of thick scrapbooks, kept by Mrs. Neely, reveal that his greatest affection has been for the public schools. The books are filled with letters from grateful children, teachers, and parents. These, and other mementos, including many letters from some of the nation's and world's leaders, are for his three grandchildren, Daniel, Nathan and Eve, sons and daughter of his and Mrs. Neely's only child, Mrs. Benjamin Parker.

The story of his transformation of a worn-out, red-clay farm into one of the most successful demonstratfons in the state, is but another aspect of his career as a builder, though not technically a part of the Atlanta story.

Dick Rich, president of Rich's, once said of Chairman of the Board Neely:

> Frank Neely is an engineer, and a great one. But he could not have succeeded in the department store business had he not had something else—namely, the ability to apply the coldly scientific methods in such a way that they required happy and interested human beings to make them work best. Neely has always been more of a teacher than an engineer anyhow. Teaching ran in his family blood, and he has never stopped holding classes.[16]

It is a fine summation of the career of a real public servant.[17]

Notes—18

[1]Reprinted from *Atlanta Journal and Constitution Magazine* (3 June 1956), by permission of the author, Mrs. McGill, and Atlanta Newspapers, Inc.

[2]Neely was born 19 January 1884, and died 24 May 1979. "The son of a Confederate veteran and the youngest of nine children, Frank Neely was born in Augusta . . . and grew up in Floyd County in northwest Georgia. His father . . . served in the intelligence service for the Confederate Army during the Civil War. After the war, he helped establish public school systems in both Richmond and Floyd counties." David Morrison, *Atlanta Constitution*, 25 May 1979.

[3]"Neely was the son of Benjamin and Henrietta Eve Carmichael Neely. His father, an Episcopal clergyman, taught in Augusta before the Civil War and established Richmond County's first public school system. Later, the elder Neely

was to set up a Rome-Floyd County school system as well. In both Augusta and Rome, the father insisted that the public schools should benefit blacks as well as whites." Raleigh Burns, *Atlanta Journal*, 25 May 1979.

[4]"Neely's mother was, on her maternal side, the great granddaughter of William and Hannah Randolph Longstreet and the grand-niece of Augustus Baldwin Longstreet. The latter was author of *Georgia Scenes*, president of Emory College at Oxford from 1840 until 1848, and later president of the University of Mississippi and of South Carolina College." *Atlanta Journal*, 25 May 1979.

[5]"His wife, Mrs. Rae Schlesinger Neely, whom he married 4 February 1908, survives him. Other survivors include a daughter, Mrs. Rachel Neely Parker, grandchildren, Mrs. Howard (Eve Parker) Hoffman, Daniel Neely Parker and Nathan Neely Parker, and eight greatgrandchildren." *Atlanta Journal*, 25 May 1979.

[6]"He was graduated from Georgia Tech in 1904 with a degree in mechanical engineering and moved to Pittsburgh to go to work for the Westinghouse Electric and Manufacturing Company, then producing the first electric locomotives for the New York, New Haven and Hartford Railway.

"His four years with Westinghouse had a powerful impact. He came to know . . . Frank and Lillian Gilbreth, . . . who were pioneer efficiency experts, although they preferred to call their field scientific management.

"Neely acquired their expertise and came home to Atlanta in 1908 to set up his own consulting firm. He also worked for his father-in-law, Harry L. Schlesinger, who owned a leading candy factory in Atlanta in that era.

"In 1915, Neely was lured to the Fulton Bag and Cotton Mills and placed in charge of production in the company's bag factories in Atlanta, Dallas, New Orleans, St. Louis, New York, and Minneapolis. He also was made a director of the company." *Atlanta Journal*, 25 May 1979.

[7]"After his marriage to Rae Schlesinger, Neely went to work at his father-in-law's candy factory. He rebuilt the factory and applied to it some of the management techniques and engineering skills he had learned at Westinghouse. . . .

"It was that background that Neely brought to Rich's in the mid-1920s. The family-owned department store in Atlanta was on the brink of crisis. A new Rich's store had been built at the corner of Broad and Alabama streets, a part of downtown Atlanta that was considered to be dying. New York-based Macy's was buying out Davis-Paxon and building a big new store in a better location on Peachtree Street. And Sears, Roebuck & Company had successfully broadened its mail-order catalog business and was about to build its ninth retail store in the nation in Atlanta on Ponce de Leon Avenue.

"Walter Rich, nephew of the store's founder, knew the Neelys socially and had been impressed by the novel approaches that the then-forty-year-old Neely had taken in three unrelated businesses.

"Neely's first endeavor was to convert Rich's from what he said was 'still a country store' to a department store that could compete successfully with Macy's. He hired New York designers and lighting experts to redesign showcases and flood the store with light. He instituted a method of inventory and stock control that helped the store eliminate overstocking in unpopular sizes and colors of items, a system that was considerd revolutionary at the time. . . .

"Meanwhile, he had time to work in the public arena. He served on the bond commission for the city of Atlanta that financed construction of viaducts over the crisscross maze of railroad tracks." *Atlanta Constitution*, 25 May 1979.

[8]"Neely's tenure at Rich's . . . spanned an era of expansion of both the department store and the city. He funded that expansion with intelligence and drive and an almost imperial vision that if the city prospered, so would Rich's." *Atlanta Journal*, 25 May 1979.

[9]"He served the company successively as executive vice-president and secretary, as president, and, beginning in 1947, as chairman of the board of directors. . . . One of Neely's early actions at the store, and one of lasting significance, was the elimination of Rich's adjustment bureau, the place where customers went to voice dissatisfaction with articles they had bought and to get replacements or refunds of their money.

"Mr. Neely said henceforth, customers would make their own adjustments. Effectively, his step was the root of a Rich's credo, that the customer is always right. The store became famous for its liberal exchange policy, which was publicized in a series of institutional ads that Neely initiated." *Atlanta Journal*, 25 May 1979.

[10]"In 1931 he organized the Special Relief Commission and got involved in other relief projects during the Great Depression. He served three years as president of the Community Chest and was chairman of the Fulton County Department of Public Welfare.

"Neely worked to have Fulton County establish its first planning and zoning agency and became chairman of the county's planning and zoning commission when it became reality. . . . He was also among those instrumental in having Bell Aircraft Corporation bring wartime aircraft production to Atlanta. He participated in the conversion of many Atlanta industries to war production.

"In 1953 Neely was invited by former President Herbert Hoover to serve as a member of the committee on Business Organization of the Department of Defense, a unit of the second Hoover Commission.

"Neely was a member of President Kennedy's White House Committee on Youth Employment." *Atlanta Journal*, 25 May 1979.

[11]"He served for sixteen years as chairman of the board of directors of the Federal Reserve Bank in Atlanta and was a member of the prestigious commission formed in 1954 by former President Herbert Hoover to implement modern business management practices in the U. S. armed forces." *Atlanta Constitution,* 25 May 1979.

[12]"In 1952 Neely became chairman of the Georgia Better Roads Committee, which sponsored the escrowing of motor fuel taxes for highway construction. In 1956 he helped organize the first Georgia Nuclear Advisory Commission and as that body's chairman was instrumental in obtaining the Georgia Tech nuclear reactor that bears his name.

"Neely was appointed a director and deputy chairman of the Federal Reserve Bank of Atlanta (Sixth District) in 1937 and was chairman of the board for sixteen years beginning in 1938.

"Neely was president of the Rich Foundation, which made grants to religious, charitable, scientific, literary, and educational causes. During his presidency, the foundation made grants to Emory University for its School of Business Administration; to Georgia Tech for the Rich Laboratories of Industrial Engineering and the Rich Electronic Computer Center. . . .

"The foundation also made notable contributions to Georgia Baptist Hospital, for an out-patient clinic; to St. Joseph's Infirmary; to Agnes Scott College, and to Shorter College.

"Neely was a charter member of the Georgia Tech National Alumni Association, received the Tech Alumni Distinguished Service award in 1941, was a trustee emeritus of the Georgia Tech Foundation Inc., and was a former member of the board of trustees of the Georgia Tech Research Institute." *Atlanta Journal,* 25 May 1979.

[13]" 'He was a great fellow,' said former Governor Marvin Griffin, a regular visitor to Neely's office at the department store for over-the-desk luncheons. 'He was a man of integrity and honesty, but a man of vision who wanted to get his job done and see his plans materialize.'

"Griffin appointed Neely chairman of the Georgia Nuclear Advisory Commission. In that post Neely went to work to develop the nuclear research center at Tech.

" 'If he thought he was right,' the governor said, recalling many a verbal skirmish with his friend, 'he was damned hard to get around. He was not the kind of person you could just turn off and on to suit you.' " *Atlanta Constitution,* 25 May 1979.

[14]"In 1941, Neely received Georgia Tech's distinguished alumni award, the same honor the institution bestowed on President (Jimmy) Carter [in 1979].

"George Griffin, former dean of men at Tech, said Thursday that Neely 'was a man the whole institution leaned on when it was in trouble. He was a number one citizen of Atlanta and a godsend to Georgia Tech.' " *Atlanta Constitution*, 25 May 1979.

[15]"The outstanding memorial to his vision may be the Atlanta expressway system. Starting as World War II drew to a close in 1945, Neely and Rich's began prodding local government officials and the Atlanta public to develop an expressway system.

"They saw to it that Harry Lochner, a Chicago planner, was brought to Atlanta to make preliminary plans for such a system. In 1946, voters in Atlanta and Fulton County approved a $20 million bond issue that, matched with state and federal dollars, was to finance constructin of the first part of today's $300 million-plus urban highway system." *Atlanta Journal*, 25 May 1979.

[16]"He stepped down as board chairman in 1961, relinquishing that post to the late Richard H. Rich. That effectively was the end of Neely's dominant role in management of the store, but as chairman of the executive committee of the board he kept a hand in Rich's affairs for at least another decade." *Atlanta Journal*, 25 May 1979.

[17]"Neely died at Neely Farm, his country estate on the banks of the Chattahoochee River near Norcross. With advancing years his health had declined, and he had been seen in recent years by few except members of the immediate family." *Atlanta Journal*. See *Mechanical Engineering* 102 (February 1980): 117.

Essay 19

Edgar J. Forio[1]

Once a newcomer to the Coca-Cola Company had a thorough briefing from Edgar J. Forio.

"That fellow," the newcomer later said to a company old-timer, "draws you an accurate picture of a cow and then just to be sure you recognize it, writes the word 'cow' under it."

"Yes," said the veteran, "that way you don't bring in many bulls."

It is necessary to write this article in perhaps a somewhat personal manner because Ed Forio won't see what is being written about him until it appears. What's more, he doesn't even know what's going into it.

It was about twenty years ago I first met Forio, now a staff vice-president of the Coca-Cola Company. Harrison Jones had been named as state chairman of the Georgia campaign for the National Foundation for Infantile Paralysis. He engaged me to help organize the state committees and to see that the newpapers, weeklies and dailies, received regular news releases. He gave me a desk in a corner of Ed's office to use for an hour or so each day. I became a Forio *aficionado* then and there and have remained one ever since.[2]

Early in December William E. Robinson, president of the company, and H. B. Nicholson, chairman of the board, pinned a thirty-five-year service pin on him at a surprise anniversary luncheon in his honor in New York. He is the first officer in the history of the company to be honored with a thirty-five-year service award.

It would be safe to assume that all through the Coca-Cola industry there was a fine warm glow of pride in that award and in the man receiving it. Through those thirty-five years Ed Forio's life has touched the lives of many of his co-workers. He knows them and their families, perhaps even the names of their children and what sorrows and joys they have experienced. They have all learned to know him for a fellow who gives to his job hard work, intelligence, and loyalty.

Through his thirty-five years he has had to learn a great deal about a great many of the jobs in the Coca-Cola Company—chemistry, the raw material, promotion, bottles, crowns, contracts, and so on. He has done, and is continuing to do, each job in the Forio manner—thoroughly, honestly, and diligently.

All the old copy-book maxims are in his career, and if today it is trite to say that a man gives to his job his earnest best, applies himself so as to be of the most possible value, does in addition his share of civic work, and is a good husband and father, then so be it. But it's true just the same about Ed Forio.

Harrison Jones, for whom Forio worked in the company for a number of years, has a typical "Harrisonism" to describe him. "I believe," he said, "you could turn Forio loose on a pitch-black night in a dangerous mountain area and he would instinctively stop short six inches or so from a precipice."[3]

Forio was born 19 March 1901, missing St. Patrick's Day by a mere two days, a fact which his father, Rene Forio, regretted. He attended the University of Tulane. When, in 1923, he took a law degree from Loyola, attending the night classes, he had been working for the Coca-Cola Company almost three years.

Joining the company 2 December 1920, Forio was in fountain sales at New Orleans until 1925.[4]

In 1926 he was transferred to Chicago as assistant to the regional vice-president. In 1929 he became manager of the Chicago district and in this capacity represented the company at the World's Fair in Chicago. He was in charge of the beautiful crowd-pulling display for Coca-Cola and was responsible for distribution throughout the sprawling fair grounds.[5]

In the post-fair months, Forio was transferred to Atlanta in charge of the dispenser department. He was promoted two years later to be assistant to Harrison Jones, then executive vice-president of the Coca-Cola Company. He was there until 1942 when the government called on the company for some executive assistance. Forio was one of those "lend-leased" to Washington. He was industry consultant to the beverage and tobacco section. The next year saw him elected a vice-president and stationed in Washington. In a very real sense he assisted the entire industry in many aspects of adjustment to the war time restrictions.

A gentleman who heads up one of the companies manufacturing a major item used by the soft drink industry thinks Forio, with his patience and his indefatigable attention to details and duty, deserves as much credit as any single person for keeping the industry going during the war—the producers of bottles, crowns included.

"There was a regulation concerning crowns," he recalls, "known as M104. Within a short while we all referred to it as 'M-1-0-Forio' for it was Ed's knotty problem to see that the industry got enough vital tin and cork to keep it going, but no more than its rightful share."

It was during this Washington stint that the business of national contracts for the company were made his responsibility.

In 1947-1948 he became vice-president in charge of bottle sales and in 1952 was made staff officer in charge of the office of information industry relations, contracts with bottlers, and public relations.

This still is his job. It keeps him almost always on the go. He spends much of his time making speeches here and there over the nation. He is a familiar figure as a speaker and company representative at medical conventions, public health assemblies, national food association meetings, gatherings of state and national dental associations as well as those of the industry he represents. He is in great demand as a speaker.[6]

He has put the problem of public and press relations into as memorable a phrase as one is likely to hear:

"People are down on what they ain't up on."

"This philosophic axiom was picked up in conversation with an old colored employee of the company. Forio offers the theory that the basic philosophy of public relations is 'getting people "up" on the things they don't know about American business.' "[7]

With all of his many activities, Forio finds time to be a good, doting father to two boys, and has moved easily into the business of being a grandfather. He was married to Miss Vivia Marks of New Orleans in 1922. Their two sons are Ed and Robert, both graduates of the University of Georgia and settled in jobs. Bob is married and has two children.

Ed Forio's friends believe that perhaps the greatest measure of him as a man and a citizen is that, despite the full time given to work, he always has given generously of his time and talents to civic work and to the activities of his church.

In Atlanta he is a director of the American Red Cross, has served as co-chairman of the Community Chest campaign, as an officer of the Metropolitan Community Services, as an executive of the Atlanta area council of the Boy Scouts of America, as state polio chairman. He also has done many civic chores as a member and officer of the Atlanta and Georgia State Chambers of Commerce. He and his family are communicants of the Co-Cathedral of Christ The King and he is a member of the committee on Catholic Social Services for Atlanta.

Because of his interest in having billboards liked, Forio has won a place as a director of the national organization known as "Keep America Beautiful." He is a trustee of the Nutrition Foundation, Inc., a director of the Food Law Institute, member of the Advisory Council of the Tax Institute and the National Public Relations Council of U.S.O.

All this adds up to a busy, well-balanced life and business career.

His military record is in keeping with the business and civic depart-ments. He served overseas in World War I with the Fifth Marines. There is no need to amplify that. The Fifth Marines are a part of our history.[8]

In one of his speeches to a group of businessmen he made an observa-tion which all who heard him have remembered:

"Every business is but one generation from oblivion . . . it must tell its story over and over again to each generation which comes along."

He has been one of those telling the story of Coca-Cola for a long, long time. As the pin, which President Robinson put in his lapel, testifies, he has been telling it for thirty-five years.

And there are a lot of good years left for a fellow who was born in 1901.[9]

Notes—19

[1]Reprinted from *Refresher* 3 (January 1956), published monthly for the employees of the Coca-Cola Company by the office of information, the Coca-Cola Company. In the footnotes that follow, the editor includes statements included by McGill in a draft of this article omitted in routine editing for publication.

[2]In an early draft of the piece, McGill added, "It is a little difficult to write about him because he is one of those quiet, deeply conscientious men without any 'front' or cultivated eccentricities to make him colorful copy. Also, for a fellow who makes a lot of speeches, he is by nature a reticent sort of man." Draft provided by Mrs. Ralph McGill.

[3]In the draft McGill had included more from Harrison Jones: "Now and then when I was out of reach and something came up concerning work which was our responsibility, I might occasionally come back to find no headway had been made. But never once had he made any holes that had to be filled up. That's the real test."

[4]The draft had included: "His first job was with a retail candy company. It consisted not of selling, but of keeping merchandising records. One day Neil Harris, Coca-Cola branch manager in New Orleans, happened to mention to the candy manufacturer that he was looking for a young man who might fit into

Coca-Cola sales. Forio was recommended. So it was that on 2 December 1920, the name for the first time appeared in the company's employment records."

[5]In the early draft, McGill included: "The job he did there caused executives to put their heads thoughtfully together and decide to make him assistant regional manager in the big city on Lake Michigan. Three years later he was promoted to the district managership and, in 1933, handled another World's Fair at which Coca-Cola introduced the revolutionary fountain dispenser."

[6]The draft included: "He typically prepares his speeches carefully as to facts, and consequently they have always stood up. This has earned him the respect, confidence, and affection of business and professional men and women across the nation. He also is called upon for talks on trade marks, good will, public press relations, as well as business subjects."

[7]The draft added: "After thirty-five years of unflagging zeal for the job at hand, Forio can still routinely carry out an itinerary which calls upon him to ride a plane most of the night, make a speech the next morning, and ride a plane to another appearance in the evening—and so on throughout the week."

[8]The draft also stated: "Forio is a prodigious reader of books—most of them serious. 'Ed,' said a friend, 'probably reads more books on economics, analyses of business trends, and heavy tomes on legislation and court decisions than any fellow outside the law or teaching professions. Now and then he gets around to biographies and an occasional twenty-five cent paperback detective story while on long airplane hops. But mostly he is trying to learn something when he reads a book.' Being from Louisiana, he naturally likes to fish and hunt."

[9]"Edgar Joseph Forio, seventy, retired senior vice-president of the Coca-Cola Company, died '8 November 1971, at his home in Fernandina Beach, Florida. . . . He was studying chemical engineering at Tulane University and attending night classes at New Orleans College of Oratory and Loyola University when he took his first job with the company in 1920. Forio received his law degree from Loyola (New Orleans) three years later. . . . He was elected senior vice-president in 1956, ten years before his retirement'; *Atlanta Journal*, 8 November 1971. Forio was honorary member of Beta Gamma Sigma and held an honorary Doctor of Laws degree from the University of Tampa, Florida. He served as member, executive board, Atlanta Area Council, Boy Scouts; advisory board, Salvation Army,; president, Atlanta Chamber of Commerce; and with many other professional service organizations."

Essay 20

Robert Woodruff: The Multimillionaire Nobody Knows[1]

Some years ago, a Sunday-supplement feature writer was assigned to do an article on Robert Winship Woodruff, chairman of the executive committee of the Coca-Cola Company. A week later, deeply frustrated and well into his fourth highball, he said to those gathered about him:

> This fellow Woodruff is no story. He has his original wife after more than thirty years and they still get along. He's rich enough for yachts, but he hasn't even got an outboard motor. The guy likes poker, but is no gambler. He has never owned a race horse or backed a Broadway show. He has a ranch out West, but the only persons he takes there are his wife, relatives, and family friends. All I can find out about him is that he's a successful man who's done a lot of good he won't tell you about. The hell with him! Pass me the bottle.

The story of Robert W. Woodruff is basically one of a well-known drink and a little-known man whose policies have made of it probably the most universally vended, branded food or drink product in the world. Every day last year approximately 50,000,000 persons around the globe had a Coke. But the publicity-shy man whose direction created this world-wide acceptance is so little known that he walks the streets of his home city, which he and his father have had a major share in building, with only an occasional recognition.[2]

At sixty-one Woodruff is a tall, well-set-up man with no fat or suggestion of paunch. His face is fixed in well-defined, severe lines, but his smile is warm and disarming. He wears conservative, well-tailored clothes and is careful of his appearance, but no clotheshorse.

He is patient, sometimes exhaustively so. He frequently wears out associates and friends by the thoroughness of his examination into an idea, coupled with his belief in an old axiom picked up along the way—that it is not wise to make a decision when tired. The latter led to an associate's saying wearily one afternoon that it was a good thing Woodruff was copper-riveted and possessed of a distance runner's stamina, as at the end of one of his conferences everyone else was too damned tired to come to a decision.

He plays as hard as he works. Men soft from many years at a desk have been known to grow pale on receiving an invitation to come down for a return visit and hunt quail on the Woodruff plantation in South Georgia. They know they will be up on the heels of dawn. They will climb off a horse for each covey point, shoot, hunt out singles, mount again, and ride after the dogs to the next point, quitting only when it becomes too dark to shoot. They know, too, that after dinner there will be poker or gin rummy until midnight or later, but the waking call will come each morning at about the hour the more merry night clubs close. At the end of a week, they will depart, as one guest said, with "even their hair follicles hurting," Woodruff happily greeting another group.

The only visitor ever to out-Woodruff Woodruff was General Dwight D. Eisenhower, who accepted an invitation to come from a week of golf at the Augusta National Golf Club to the plantation near Newton, Georgia, for a few days of shooting. When Woodruff appeared the first morning with the earliest streaks of dawn, he found General Eisenhower standing before the big fireplace in the living room.

"What's holding things up?" asked the general, who had been told there would be an early start and had got up before his call. This left Woodruff nonplused, and he is not a man who nonpluses easily.

Woodruff's physical endurance is the more remarkable because he takes no regular exercise, indulges in no diets, has not the slightest idea of how to relax, and devotes his vacation periods to strenuous hunting or long horseback rides at his T. E. Ranch—once Buffalo Bill's holdings—thirty miles out from Cody, Wyoming. He is a chronic stayer-upper and an early riser. Restless always, but often lonely and given to deep moods of introspection, he has a saying that the future belongs to the discontented.

The early decades of the nineteenth century found restless men everywhere in the new republic on the move, especially to the new lands of Georgia, Alabama, and Mississippi, from which the Indians were being withdrawn. New England supplied a goodly number of discontented on the hunt for new opportunity. Among these were Woodruff's forebears. George Waldo Woodruff, with the brand of transcendentalism on his name and the regional virtues of thrift and work in his bones, arrived at the new town of Columbus, Georgia, a few years after it had been laid out in 1828. The Chattahoochee River fall line is at that city, and the swift descent of the waters over large rocks provides a ready source of power, which was later to attract textile mills. George Woodruff built a gristmill, which was profitable. He invested in other enterprises and died a millionaire at ninety-one. His son, Ernest, married Emily Winship, whose father, Robert, had brought his family from New England to Georgia a few years before the Woodruffs arrived.[3]

The first of the three sons of Emily and Ernest Woodruff was born on 6 December 1889, and christened Robert Winship. He was a child when the family moved to Atlanta. The town had been rebuilt after General Sherman's fires had destroyed it, and was flourishing mightily. It was attracting those who could see opportunity in its development, and Ernest Woodruff's canny New England blood was singing prophetically in his ears. He saw the raw city's need for a horse-pulled street-railway system which one day could be parlayed into an electric-power-and-transit company; for a plant to manufacture ice; for banks and investments—and he was chief among those who brought them all into being.

Young Robert grew up in the staidly fashionable Inman Park residential section. One of his playmates was Harrison Jones, now chairman of the board of Coca-Cola. Another of his schoolmates was William B. Hartsfield, currently and for fourteen years mayor of Atlanta. His Sunday school teacher, Asa Griggs Candler, was a member of a leading family in the Methodist Church. Candler owned the wholesale-drug firm of Walker and Candler and was pleased with a recently acquired sideline which was catching on amazingly—one of the new-fangled soda-pop drinks called Coca-Cola.

Candler's Sunday school pupil was apt with the prophets and apostles, but the New England trader strain was evident in him even then. Young Woodruff was one of several boys who rode ponies to school. He was given fifty cents a week to buy feed for the pony, a sum ample in those uninflated days. This weekly half dollar was a challenge to his Connecticut chromosomes. The stables from which the Candler wagons and drays moved in carrying freight and deliveries was near Robert's school. Woodruff and the Negro stableman became friends—a friendship which endured until ended by stableman Jim Key's death a few years ago. Woodruff's pony was stabled and fed at his Sunday school teacher's stables all through the school hours. And Woodruff had for the nine months of the school year a net profit of fifty cents a week.

Years later when Woodruff, as the new president of Coca-Cola, reported for his first day on the job, he met Jim Key by the elevator.

"Jim," he said as they shook hands, "I haven't been upstairs yet, and I don't know the rules, but you are on the payroll for the rest of your life, and you don't have to hit another lick from this minute on."

Woodruff moved from grade school to Georgia Military Academy, and when he had graduated there, he spoke up for a job. His father ordered the boy into Emory College—now Emory University, of Atlanta—at Oxford, Georgia. Young Woodruff stayed not quite a year and quit.

"You're going back and get something in your head," said his father. "Damn it, boy, it's only three generations from shirt sleeves to shirt sleeves!"

"I'll take the shirt sleeves now," said Robert. And he did.

"The college bills are yours," said the old man grimly—and let him go. Between the two, father and son, was a deep affection, but they were too much alike to get along smoothly.

Young Woodruff took the first job he found—helper in a foundry. He moved from that to a sales job with the General Fire Extinguisher Company, where his natural talents for selling brought in quick results, and his commissions mounted to totals quite respectable. News of this reached his father, who relented and sent for him. Ernest Woodruff had by then successfully organized the Atlantic Ice and Coal Company, and he offered his stubborn son a job as salesman and buyer at $150 a month. He took it. This was in 1911. The next year, after months of persistent salesmanship, Robert Woodruff was accepted by Miss Nell Hodgson, of Athens, Georgia, and they were promptly married. They still are, devotedly.

Marriage gave young Woodruff added incentive to get ahead. He made a survey which demonstrated to his satisfaction that trucks would be more profitable and efficient in the ice-and-coal business than horses, mules, and drays. After long and skillful trading with Walter White, of White Motors, Woodruff contracted for trucks. This caused Father Ernest, who had not been consulted by his buyer and who also was unconvinced the automobile was here to stay, to become temporarily incoherent. When the power of speech returned, he fired the buyer and urged him never to darken the door again.[4]

White promptly hired the young man, explaining later that Woodruff's ability in the truck deal was such that he didn't want him working for someone else. "I thought I had a sucker when I got hold of the youngster and started selling him trucks. I ended up with a deal in which my profit wouldn't have bought the shirt I almost lost," he said. White assigned Woodruff to South Georgia, but he soon out-grew that territory and White moved him up. He became the nation's top truck salesman.

Georgia's famed Ty Cobb and Woodruff were friends and bird-hunting competitors at that time. The bird-dog fraternity still recalls an episode of those early days when the star truck salesman and the great Detroit outfielder put their favorite dogs down with sizable bets on their covey-finding abilities. At the end of the first day, Woodruff's Lloyd George was ahead of Cobb's Connie Mack by two coveys.

"Hold the covey count, double the bets, and we'll hunt again tomorrow!" stormed the angry Cobb.

When the soft, smoky haze of a deep-South autumn twilight fell through the pines and fields on the following Saturday to close out six consecutive days of hard hunting, Lloyd George was still ahead. The hard-losing Cobb looked blackly at his dog and walked off.

"That damned dog of Woodruff's has got his nose for prospects," he said, in deep disgust, and refused even to speak to his friend for the next six or seven months.

Woodruff was still with the White Motor Company, where he had advanced to first vice-president and general sales manager, when, in 1923, a group of nail-biting men in Atlanta, including a chastened Ernest Woodruff, asked him to head up the Coca-Cola Company, which they had purchased four years before. The going had been a little rough, and the truck salesman was a unanimous choice for the presidency.

It could be said with no great strain on the imagination that Coca-Cola had been waiting around for Woodruff. Both were born in the same town and each was moved to Atlanta in infancy. Until they met, the real possibilities of neither had had full opportunity for development.

Less than three years before Woodruff had his natal spanking in Columbus, Colonel John S. Pemberton had departed that city with an idea born to him there. He had not done well with a small wholesale-drug company, and Atlanta beckoned. He believed that in the larger city he could develop his idea. There was great interest in soda water and the new fruit-flavored soda-pop drinks. The colonel had an idea for a new type. In Atlanta, he hopefully stirred his mixtures with a new boat oar in an open cast-iron kettle in a small building near the present site of the Sixth Federal Reserve Bank. He carried samples to be tested by the clerks and hangers-on at Venable's Drugstore near Atlanta's Five Points, until he had one which caused them to beam upon him and purchase a jug of syrup. This was 1886. Old records reveal that Colonel Pemberton sold less than thirty gallons of his beverage that year.

F. M. Robinson, a bookkeeper who wrote in a flourishing script, named the drink Coca-Cola. The world-familiar form of it is a copy of his original writing of the trade name.

In 1887, Colonel Pemberton, sick and discouraged by the poor progress of his drink, sold a two-thirds interest for $283.29. The purchasers had no idea of its potential value, and the rights kicked around Atlanta until 1889. That year Woodruff was born, and Asa Griggs Candler began to collect the Coca-Cola holdings. By 1892 he was sole owner. His company employed traveling salesmen and an advertising and sales manager named Samuel Candler Dobbs. It was he who put out the first oilcloth signs with the words "Coca-Cola" on them. He also produced the first soda-fountain displays and put the product on billboards. Candler gave the United States bottling rights to two insistent young Chattanoogans, warning them their idea of putting the drink in bottles was not sound. It was a fortunate decision in more ways than one, in that almost from the beginning Coca-Cola was a local business wherever it was found.

By 1898 Coca-Cola sales were almost $500,000. They were up to $3,300,000 in 1907, and by 1917 had climbed to $15,700,000. Sales were still rising in 1919, but profit lagged well behind volume. In 1919 the home-office staff, including all employees down to janitors, totaled only thirty-three persons, although that year the company took in almost $25,000,000.

By this time Asa Candler was a bit tired of it. The drink seemed about at its peak. His sons were interested in other enterprises. In September, 1919, he sold out to a group of Georgia capitalists, of whom Ernest Woodruff was the leader. The Candlers received $10,000,000 in cash and $15,000,000 in preferred stock—since retired.

The managerial gears did not mesh too well, and in April, 1923, the directors sent for the vice-president and sales manager of the White Motor company. The two Columbus products at last had met.

From the beginning, Woodruff's first loyalty was not to the company but to the product. His concept is that if a man produces an honest product and gives his loyalty to it, he will bring into play all the better human values in his promotion of that product. He will thereby make of it, his company, and profits something helpful and part of the community. Woodruff's belief that the free-enterprise system has community obligations amounts almost to an obsession.

Woodruff spends a lot of his time engaged in what he refers to as trying "to see over the hill."

"It's easy to see down into the valley and up the slope," he said one day to a friend, "but it's tough as hell to see over the next hill."

It was in his early years with the company that he managed to get a quick look over the hill and thereby chart a course and reach certain decisions. He determined that the soundest success could be had if the manufacturing, whole-sale processing, and distribution facilities should be owned, controlled, and managed separately from each other, and each should be independent of the retailers. Coca-Cola would, he and his staff decided, develop as a single-product institution and, as manufacturer of that one product, would refrain from taking over a multiplicity of related operations which easily could have been integrated. Save for intimate control of the character of a few ingredients, Coca-Cola would, he directed, buy its requirements from suppliers in the market. Coca-Cola would, for instance, own and control no sugar plantations, mills, or bottle-manufacturing plants. Today, Woodruff is gratified that of all its suppliers, Coca-Cola owns and controls not one, and that, even in foreign countries, it can be said that but for an already-steadily-decreasing few exceptions, everything used in the manufacture of Coca-Cola is produced in the country where it is sold.

Woodruff is proud of the fact that at both the wholesale and retail levels, Coca-Cola is shot through with economic independence. Of the jobbers one hundred per cent, of the bottling plants more than ninety-five per cent, and of the retailers one hundred per cent are under ownership independent of the manufacturing company. A long time ago Woodruff "saw over the hill" that if he could make of Coca-Cola not an empire, but instead a cooperating set of independent local businesses, his company would win support wherever its product was marketed, because of the local roots. Also, it would assist the competitive system, which, he believes, explains and maintains American productive genius.

When foreign expansion began, he imposed the same rules. Coca-Cola would sell the syrup to local processors, who would buy from local suppliers all they could of bottles, crowns, cases, coolers, cartons, and the thousand other things needed.

To these independent businessmen at home and abroad, Woodruff preached personally and through his associates that in each town "the Coca-Cola Man" must be active in community and civic work, so that he might become "not merely the representative of the product but the personification of the institution."

Between 1923 and 1930, sales went from $24,000,000 to $35,000,000 and net profits, where the Woodruff influence was most apparent, rose from $5,000,000 to $13,000,000. By 1940, under Woodruff's Argus-eyed direction, Coca-Cola had become the best-known, most widely distributed and extensively mass-produced item in the world. Beginning in 1886, fifty-one years had been required to sell the first 500,000,000 gallons of syrup. The second 500,000,000 gallons were sold in seven years, and by 1949 the global sales were at a rate of about 500,000,000 gallons every three and a half years. The company's sales in 1949 were about $221,800,000, with profits of about $38,000,000 after taxes. At the same time, Coca-Cola's more than 270 foreign bottlers, private enterprises all, and 300,000-odd nondomestic retailers, also independent businesses, were grossing an approximate $150,000,000.

In France last year, Communists persuaded some of the many small vineyard owners that Coca-Cola was a competitor of wine. The French Assembly, which reacts to farm pressure in much the same manner as a state legislature in Georgia or Iowa, adopted an anti-soft-drink measure, loudly opposed by French manufacturers of trucks, bottles, and other items purchased by Coca-Cola and providing jobs for Frenchmen. From the Kremlin, apparently disturbed by the European success of this American product which assisted so many private suppliers around the world without any connection whatsoever with or aid from the Marshall Plan, came a steady flow of anti-Coca-Cola propaganda.

Hatchet-Essayist Ilya Ehrenburg was called upon to produce angry essays which hinted that from drinking Coca-Cola to robbing banks was but one short step. Nothing is likely to seem more strange to the researchers of the future than the preoccupation of the Soviet Union with a soft drink costing five cents, or the equivalent thereof, almost anywhere in the world at the peak of the controversy.

Woodruff's stubborn refusal to become a public figure largely explains why he is not well known nationally. But the further fact is that he privately is a difficult man to know. Even those closest to him reluctantly admit they do not know the pattern which fits him. Woodruff himself seems to have friends whom he seeks out to match whatever carefully concealed mood may be upon him. He is greatly drawn, for example, to one of his directors, Ralph Hayes, whom some in the company refer to as "Woodruff's conscience." One of the reasons for this, aside from executive skill, is Hayes' ability to talk and write well. Woodruff has been known to carry about with him some of Hayes' letters containing phrases or paragraphs of excellent prose until the pages were worn and smudged. Another of his intimates, Robert Tyre Jones, the great golfer, is esteemed by him for his forthright answers on business subjects, as well as for his companionship.

Only a severely limited few know the Woodruff who will sit by a fire and listen to poetry or some well-written paragraph read aloud. Not many more know the Woodruff revealed on infrequent two-man quail hunts through the piney woods and the fields of the South Georgia plantation.

The late O. Max Gardner, former governor of North Carolina, was one of Woodruff's close friends. A few hours before Gardner was to sail for London to begin his duties as ambassador to the Court of St. James's, he succumbed to a heart attack. Woodruff was at breakfast at his plantation, expecting a good-by telephone call. There was a call, but it informed him of the death of his friend. There was one guest in the house. He and Woodruff hunted that day into darkness. Woodruff, silent, in deep thought much of the time, chose the periods when he and his friend were riding along between covey shots, in which he rarely participated, to talk quietly but movingly about human values and what a man could do with his life to give it genuine meaning.

This is a side of Woodruff's personality which he guards with a deep shyness, based, his friends think, on a fear that he might be misunderstood. This same reticence marks his attitude toward religion. He has assisted many churches and is a major supporter of two. He has many sincere Negro friends and has helped their churches and boys' clubs. Organizations which have known his aid are many, but known only to him and his secretary. It is fair to say he is a religious man. He looks for this quality in businessmen and has, for example, privately referred to Charles E. Wilson, of General Electric, now head of the Office of Defense Mobilization, as a man who manages to be a spiritual statesman in business.

These two Woodruffs—the tough, exacting business executive and what his friends call "the other Woodruff"—undoubtedly complement each other. Yet, if they do, only he knows it. He apparently possesses the ability to turn the two on and off as he desires.

One day there arrived at his Atlanta office a requested color print of a portrait of James M. Cox, publisher, 1920 presidential nominee, and former Democratic governor of Ohio. In a well-turned inscription on the photograph, the donor had commented on Woodruff's innate "sense of what citizens and dollars owe to our lives." The picture arrived during Woodruff's absence, but a close friend who was present when it was opened and the inscription read said of him: "Bob's almost tormented concern with the obligation of the free-enterprise system and its dollar profits to society derives from the fact that all of his life the ancestral shades of a shrewd, ruthless New England trader father and a warm, generous, and gentle mother have been carrying on a debate inside his skull. The tug and pull of it are expressed in his life. As soon as he had made a business profit, he frets until a part of that profit has been put to what he conceives to be useful human service. And the worst of it," wryly concluded the friend, "is that he insists on his friends doing likewise, whether they want to or not."

When Robert Woodruff's mother died, one of her servants said of her, "Miss Emily was the sort of person who could go to heaven without changing her clothes." It is obvious to those who know him best that from his mother Woodruff derived a pressing awareness of human values. This has made of him, among other things a builder of hospitals. It has caused rural, deep-South counties, long darkened by malarial scourges, to be made well and safe.

Down on Woodruff's Ichauway Plantation, thirty-six miles southwest of Albany, Georgia, in great peanut-growing and bird-hunting land, the Negro hands think the Lord gave Woodruff a sign. Shortly after he bought the place in 1930, an old Negro patriarch of one of the tenant families drove over in a one-mule wagon to see the "new boss" who he had heard was there for the day. As he stood talking to Woodruff, a severe malarial seizure of chills struck him, and he all but collapsed at the feet of the new owner. This was Woodruff's first introduction to malaria, and with characteristic thoroughness he had doctors in to give inspection to every person on the plantation. Malaria and some venereal disease were found. In the course of the health examinations, Woodruff learned that Baker County, in which the plantation is located, had a high incidence of malaria, with a death rate which was shocking. The county was poor, because it had been hard hit by the boll weevil in the early '20s. There was no county health department.[5]

An average man, emotionally aroused as was Woodruff, would likely have given the county a health department. Woodruff did, but not until he first had put dollars to work in research to determine what the problem was and what a health department would need. He set up a field station, deeding land to it, and financing it through Emory University's School of Medicine. It was provided with a modern laboratory. This station has kept on growing. The United States Public Health Service long ago was invited in and has profited greatly from the malarial studies. So has Baker County.[6]

Out of this, Woodruff was directed, or led, to the field in which he wanted social-welfare dollars, derived from competitive-enterprise profits, to go to work. He had seen that a well person was happier and more interested in his job and in opportunity. All of Woodruff's plantation staff are promoted from the ranks. He turned to Emory University Hospital and its School of Medicine. He interested friends. The result has been a steady enlargement of that plant and its efficiency, until both the hospital and school are among the outstanding departments in the Southeast. An extra and substantial contribution there of his own was the Robert Winship Memorial Clinic, equipped with the most modern cancer-detection and -treatment equipment and a staff of high quality. In addition, he has initiated or greatly influenced through friends and foundations the development of the Grady Clay Eye Clinic, a Private Diagnostic Clinic, a Department of Physical Medicine, a Department of Internal Medicine, the Crawford W. Long Hospital, affiliated with Emory, the School of Dentistry and a Medical Research Building, now under construction—all at Emory University, where he envisions a medical center for the Southeast on a par with that of the Mayos at Rochester. A fine coordinated program between Emory and Atlanta's municipal Grady Hospital has long been in effect.[7]

These are hard years for medical schools everywhere, and for about ten years Woodruff has, with the cooperation of others, paid off the Emory deficit, which, in the process of expansion and rising costs, has not infrequently run as high as $200,000 and more. He has aided other private and state educational institutions. He has not been unaware of the problems of general education and has been helpful in that field, although hospitals and medical-school problems frankly occupy most of his attention.[8]

In the fall of 1950, Woodruff was elected to the board of trustees of Tuskegee Institute, the magnificent school at Tuskegee, Alabama, founded by Booker T. Washington. Acceptance of this election to the board had a significance beyond mere membership on another board. The fact that Woodruff, tremendously busy with his business and the board memberships he already had, went on the Tuskegee board meant a determination to expand his energies to assist with the whole field of Southern education. His dreams, ambitions, and plans fit naturally into the New South, about which the oratorical and promotional voices have been talking for more than half a century, but which now may be seen on the horizon. He has already been responsible for bringing important industrial board meetings south and has pointed out the region's assets to industrialists looking about for a place to go, though he is never regionally chauvinistic in these approaches. "A region is built, as a nation is, by enterprises which create other jobs and raise standards, including education," he says. "In a free economy like ours, trained initiative is the vital ingredient."[9]

That is why he objects so strongly to socialization and to increasing federal controls and supervision, which create more bureaucratic jobs, but fewer productive ones. He saw much to oppose in the Roosevelt Administrations, and did so forthrightly. Some things he approved, for he never made the error of closing his mind to what was going on and to the damage the free enterprise system could do to itself by not shouldering its responsibilities in a competitive system. He sees that an economy expanding through research and risk capital will produce jobs, and they, in turn, will produce wages to buy the products of the jobs. Therefore, Woodruff wants the fight against socialism to be carried on by a dynamic economy which will maintain employment and produce profits, a fair percentage of which will be plowed into the activities which are helpful to people.

"The people will buy that," he insists, "and leave socialism on the shelf."

Woodruff knows that the future is challenging this sort of system to meet and defeat the chaos in currencies, ideologies, and world economics. New methods and original techniques will be required. These, he is sure, will develop out of the competitive system and the American genius for it, if they are not shackled. If left free enough, he is confident, the American system has the stamina, vitality, and skill to overcome and out-produce, in jobs, goods, and the humanities, any other system in competition. But, he insists, American businessmen have got everlastingly to be trying to see over that always-present hill ahead. Those who dig in the valley will die there.[10]

Notes—20

[1]Reprinted from the *Saturday Evening Post* (5 May 1951), with permission of the author, Mrs. McGill, and *Saturday Evening Post*.

[2]McGill wrote a second article on Robert W. Woodruff for the *Atlanta Journal and Constitution Magazine* (19 August 1956). Passages from that article are quoted by permission of the author and Atlanta Newspapers, Inc. From that article McGill wrote:

"The Woodruff name and deeds are written deep in the economic history of the city [Atlanta] and state across the long span of the past 100 years. His paternal and maternal grandfathers were industrialists before the great War Between the States. His father, Ernest, was one of the great figures in Atlanta and Georgia's raw years of growth when mines, trolley lines, power companies, and banks were being created, sold, traded, merged, absorbed.

"Almost everyone has heard of Robert W. Woodruff. He is, even in retirement, one of the nation's business titans, on the boards of many of the nation's great financial organizations and industrial corporations, and chairman of Coca-Cola's France [Finance] Committee.

"But somewhat paradoxically, since so many have heard of him, not many know him. It has been said that each person who does know him knows a different man, but this is a part of the legend that grows up about any highly competitive, greatly successful man who shuns the spotlight of publicity, cafe society, and the gossip columns."

³"Woodruff's restless driving energy probably isn't a matter of choice with him. It's in his blood—the thoroughness, ingenuity, and drive of New England ancestors.

"When New England, generations ago, was sending so many of her sons to sea in the clipper ships, two of them chose to go south instead, to a pioneer country that was Georgia.

"Joe Winship went from Massachusetts. He started a machine shop in Atlanta which made guns for the Confederacy until Sherman's troops came and burned it. After the war this business became a cotton-gin factory which today is one of the largest producers of cotton gins in the world. Joe Winship was Bob Woodruff's great-grandfather.

"Sherman's raiders also burned out George Woodruff, who had come from Connecticut to build a flour mill on the river at Columbus, Georgia. He came back and was a millionaire when he died at the age of ninety-one. He was Bob's grandfather.

"These New England Yankees married Southern women. His father, Ernest Woodruff, born in Columbus, married Emily Winship of Atlanta. Robert was born 6 December 1889. Soon afterward the family moved to Atlanta, where two younger brothers, George and Henry, were born." *Atlanta Constitution and Journal Magazine* (19 August 1956).

⁴"The bridegroom figured out a family budget and decided he must earn more income. To accomplish this he became an automobile salesman for the White Company. With one of those famous old Whites to drive, Bob and Nell lived in a cottage around the corner from his parents in Inman Park, Atlanta.

"He was general sales manager of the company in Cleveland when, in 1923, a worried Coca-Cola board called him to Atlanta." *Atlanta Constitution and Journal Magazine* (19 August 1956).

⁵"Woodruff's introduction to public health and hospital needs came to him suddenly, and with no preparation whatever. It was about a quarter century ago on an old dirt road in deep south Georgia that a destiny 'shaped his charitable ends.' A short while before, he had bought an old, all-but-abandoned cotton plantation in Baker County. It was called 'Ichauway,' from the creek of that name which ran through it. The word is Creek Indian, meaning 'where deer sleep.' Riding with the manager on a back road one day, planning how to put old fields back into production, they came on an old wagon, pulled by an aged mule and driven by an ancient Negro. They stopped and the old man climbed down to greet

the new owner. As he stood there talking, he began to tremble. His voice faltered, and as the horrified Woodruff watched, the old man fell suddenly to earth, his body twitching.

"It was a violent malarial seizure. The manager shrugged, helplessly. 'Almost everybody down here has it,' he said. 'He'll be all right after a while.'" *Atlanta Journal and Constitution Magazine* (19 August 1956).

[6]"Woodruff did not know it then, being merely a greatly disturbed, sensitive man in a hurry to reach a telephone, but he had found a purpose and a channel through which to direct his interest and the money available for responsible, charitable use.

"He telephoned Atlanta. He placed probably the largest single order for capsules of quinine in the history of the state, and had it rushed to the farm. It was distributed to the 'hands' there and, later throughout the county. . . .

"It was learned that roughly sixty percent of the county's population, white and colored, showed positive malarial reaction. Hookworm and pellagra also were encountered. The work attracted the attention of the Rockefeller Foundation, and of Tom Parran when he was the able Surgeon General of the United States.

"Within a very few years there was not a single active case of malaria in the county, and hookworm and pellagra also were reduced to the elimination point.

"Woodruff began to soak up public health statistics from his friend, Tom Parran, and to startle associates with intimate discussions of various viruses and germs and their constant warfare with man. 'It got so,' a friend recalls, 'that I used to go to see my doctor after leaving Woodruff. After listening to him tell of the battles with malaria I'd feel feverish and all my bones would be aching.'" *Atlanta Journal and Constitution Magazine* (19 August 1956).

[7]"Inspired by her son's enthusiasm, his mother, a sweet and gentle woman, persuaded her husband to establish the Emily and Ernest Woodruff Foundation. A few years later Mrs. Woodruff succumbed to cancer. Most of her fortune, several millions of dollars, went into the foundation, which was created to minister chiefly to the health and educational needs of the South. Woodruff himself personally established, and endowed, at Emory University Hospital, the Robert Winship Clinic. Named for his mother's father, Robert Winship, it was patterned after and staffed by doctors from Memorial Hospital, New York. It was, and is, devoted entirely to research and treatment in the field of cancer." *Atlanta Journal and Constitution Magazine* (19 August 1956).

[8]"Being a good listener and also an asker of questions, he and his friends arranged for other income for the medical school through the establishment of a clinic especially fitted to the teaching and income needs of the school and hospital.

"This was a successful development, and the need arose for a building to house it. Woodruff, and the foundation which bears his mother's and his father's name, presented it to the hospital at a cost of more than $2,000,000.

"When Crawford Long became associated with Emory, its buildings were old and inadequate. Woodruff moved to meet what had been a long-standing emergency. He and the foundation presented a large and magnificent, many-winged building and memorialized his mother by naming it the Emily Winship Woodruff Memorial Building. Originally planned as a maternity hospital, it was large enough, and the need was so desperate, that it became the major, general-use hospital. This gift was something about $2,500,000.

"No one, not even Woodruff himself, knows when the idea of a great medical center came to him. It may have come gradually. But, at any rate, somewhere along the way after the old Negro farmer fell in a severe malarial seizure, he began to dream of such a development. The malarial field station had early given him the important knowledge that research is the bedrock foundation of any, and all, true medical centers.

"So on the schedule which had grown in his mind, he and the foundation constructed and equipped a tremendous research building on Emory Campus. It will house the Robert Winship Cancer Clinic, and its important research, along with general research in all designated fields. It is easily the finest research facility in the Southesast. The cost here was in excess of $2,000,000.

"Woodruff's personality is forceful and his enthusiasm persuasive. Emory University Hospital badly needed expanding. While Woodruff brooded over this he was visited by Mrs. Lettie Pate Evans, an old friend. She had become infected with his medical-building bug and wanted advice. The result was the Conkie Pate Whitehead Surgical Pavilion, a large, magnificently modern wing costing in excess of $2,250,000. In addition, the entire front of the hospital was changed for architectural reasons, and the lawn landscaped.

"These contributions, plus others of a lesser, though substantial nature, mean that Woodruff and the Woodruff Foundation have put about $12,000,000 into medical buildings at Emory Hospital. When to this is added the several millions given by his friends who were inspired by him, the result is indeed a major one." *Atlanta Journal and Constitution Magazine* (19 August 1956).

⁹"Woodruff and the foundation have given most generously to educational institutions, both secondary and college. It was he who advised with Mrs. Evans in constructing the Lettie Pate Evans Hall at Agnes Scott. He personally has been one of the chief supporters of the annual cancer and polio campaigns. His benefactions in all fields of charity have been generous, and like his major ones, unsung. His wife, Mrs. Nell Hodgson Woodruff, shares his enthusiasm for work in the medical field. She has always been interested in nursing. During the war she served as a nurse's aid. Since then she had held office in a number of organizations, and was an official delegate to one of the international meetings on public health.

"Recently, because of his long experience in the field, Woodruff was named to a special committee by the Ford Foundation. It will advise in the allocation of the huge sum of $90 billion to American hospitals and medical schools.

"It was Woodruff who called, and paid for, the luncheon meeting of citizens who formed the Atlanta Safety Council, an organization which has done much in safety and in traffic reform. Contributions came from local business, but Woodruff underwrote the first year and has remained a generous contributor.

"As far as I know, this is the first summing up of the impressive multimillion-dollar contribution by Woodruff as a 'builder' of the metropolitan Atlanta city and area. Because of his insistence on no publicity, the public is almost totally unaware of the magnitude and worth of his participation. A brooding man, given to long moods of introspection, he still has dreams about doing even greater things for his hometown and native state.

"The story of Woodruff and Coca-Cola is one of the truly great business stories and romances of our time.

"It has been told before, and since this is concerned with his contribution to the physical and spiritual growth of his city, does not belong here. It is nonetheless, one of the epic stories of the American system." *Atlanta Journal and Constitution Magazine* (19 August 1956).

[10]"A man whose streak of New England granite clashes always with the gentleness inherited from his mother, he is courtly of manner, and kindly of disposition.

"Reticent, never voluble about his plans, he still works for his company—though in retirement. And he still dreams dreams—and foremost among them is the old one—of a great medical center in Atlanta, with all hospitals cooperating around the big research building which bears his father's name.

"Among those who have helped—and who continue to assist—in building an even greater Atlanta, none has a higher place than Robert Winship Woodruff." *Atlanta Journal and Constitution Magazine* (19 August 1956). Mrs. Julia Howe, director of news services, Emory University prepared this press release, 28 October 1981:

"Since 1937, the Emily and Ernest Woodruff Foundation and its successor, the Emily and Ernest Woodruff Fund, Inc., have donated more than $225 million to Emory University and its affiliates for building construction, renovation, and general support. In addition to his substantial gifts to Emory, Mr. Robert W. Woodruff and his family's foundations have supported many other medical, academic, and cultural organizations throughout the city, state, and region.

"Mr. Woodruff's ties to the university date to his days as a student at Emory College, when the entire college was at Oxford, Georgia. He later served as a member of the Emory University board of trustees, from 1935-1948, and he was also a member of the executive committee of the board.

"He was vice-president and sales manager of the White Motor Company trucking firm, when the Coca-Cola Company offered him its presidency in 1923, which Mr. Woodruff accepted. His father, Ernest Woodruff, was one of a group of businessmen who purchased the soft drink company in 1919.

"For thirty-two years, Robert Woodruff guided Coca-Cola from a national company to a multi-national corporation, offering diversified products in a world market. He officially retired in 1955, but in later years he continued to serve on the finance committee of the company.

"Much of the Woodruff generosity has been for the medical facilities and programs at Emory. His gift of $50,000 in 1937 enabled the creation of the Robert Winship Clinic, named for his grandfather.

"His philanthropy was extended in 1944, when he offered to underwrite the annual deficit of the medical school so it could modernize the teaching format by developing a full-time faculty. Mr. Woodruff eventually assumed the entire deficit, which averaged almost $250,000 per year.

"In 1952, the Emily and Ernest Woodruff Foundation informed the university that it would like to review an overall development plan for the medical center, which would include the schools of medicine, dentistry, and nursing, the hospitals, clinic, and related health activities. If approved, the foundation would consider underwriting the cost of the plan's implementation. The plan was approved, and it has remained the basic guide for the medical center's development ever since.

"In the early 1970s, a five-year, $50 million construction plan in the medical center was financed by the foundation, and included a $7 million administration building, a $7.5 million center for rehabilitation medicine, a $39 million expansion and modernization of the Emory University Hospital, and additions to the Emory University Clinic.

"Other areas of the Woodruff family philanthropy at Emory include: an addition to the Anatomy-Physiology Building; the construction of Goodrich C. White Hall and the new Chemistry Building; and at Oxford College, the building of a new gymnasium and the renovation of Seney Hall.

"Although recipients of Mr. Woodruff's good will frequently have assumed the identity of the donor, the philanthropist has preferred to cloak his gifts in anonymity. But his generosity has benefitted people throughout Atlanta and Georgia.

"Among his gifts have been financing the purchase and development of three city parks, support in the construction and endowment of the Atlanta Memorial Arts Center, and grants awarded to the Atlanta Historical Society, the Martin Luther King Memorial, and the Fernbank Science Center. Mr. Woodruff has also supported the Tuskegee Institute in Alabama and the Atlanta University Complex.

" 'It always gave me pleasure to do something for somebody without being asked to do it,' Mr. Woodruff once said. 'I don't like to be asked. I didn't want to be given credit.' "

"In 1974, the 'anonymous donor' was honored with the Shining Light Award, sponsored by the Atlanta Gas Light Company and WSB Radio. The plaque now stands outside of the Coca-Cola world headquarters in Atlanta, and the inscription reads: 'Business genius. Counselor of presidents. Sportsman, Humanitarian.

Benefactor of education, medicine and the arts. He enlarged the vision and soul of Atlanta.'

" 'Thank God Almighty you came this way,' said Dr. E. Garland Herndon, Jr., vice-president and director of the Woodruff Medical Center, at the time of the award. Dr. Herndon's words speak for many."

Essay 21

Peter Knox and Sons: They Stuck to the South—and Won[1]

Over sawdust-and-honeysuckle-scented Thomson, Georgia, lay the deep tranquillity of an August afternoon. There was the customary withdrawal from the heavy heat, save at the Knox home, where Peter Knox, that day five, was entertaining with a birthday party. Perspiring mamas, still steaming from having wrestled their young darlings into the party suits and the long, ribbed stockings then considered as polite garb for public functions of the young, were herding their chirping little ones along walks toward the Knox residence. Young Peter himself stood, as his mama had coached him, at the top of the veranda steps, welcoming his guests one and all, but also putting a calculating eye upon each with an efficiency that any White House Secret Service agent might have envied.

Suddenly he flung himself very vigorously upon a starched and startled young guest who was halfway up the steps. They rolled down into the walk, to a crescendo of youthful shrieks, with deeper contralto exclamations from their mamas. The harried guest tore himself away and headed speedily for home with his host in pursuit, giving cry like beagle hound after hare.

The awakened citizens leaped from their siestas in rooms darkened against the sun. They hurried to their doors to see the two youths zigzagging up the tree-shaded street, and to witness the fleeing guest reach the haven of his home a step ahead of young Knox. Thus thwarted, the host returned homeward, moral outrage written on his face. His bug-eyed young guests, their accusing mamas, his hand-wringing mother, and puzzled father awaited him on the steps.

"He didn't bring a present!" he shouted in justification from the gate.

Long after his agitated mother had dragged him back to reluctant apology, hours after the ice-cream-and-cake-stuffed young celebrants had departed, Peter Knox, Sr., still was clapping his young son upon the back with mighty thwacks, protesting it was the finest damn sight he ever saw, and that he was indeed proud to have sired such a son.

"I'll never worry about Pete," he said, as he told the tale to every lumberman who came and went. And he never did.

Knox, pater, was a curious mixture of Calvinism and the goings-on at a Gaelic wake. He was a great hand to call every morning the roll of his sons—Wyck, Peter, Lawrence and Robert—and to remind them that it was sinful to let a dollar remain idle. A dollar was meant to be put where it would spawn and produce hundreds of fingerling dollars of its own—a dollar was not to be left somewhere in a bank vault to grow old and dry and brittle, like an old maid hoarding her charms.

The old man deliberately was building himself a business team. He tinkered around with each part of it, polishing and fitting and hammering when he had to.

Today the old man's young team is still playing on the home grounds, where he started it in 1932. None of the four is yet forty years old. Yet, in a town of about 3,500 persons, it has built an organization that grosses about $11,000,000 annually. It is a group of separate corporations.

One of the corporations is one of the nation's few successes in the field of prefabricated housing. With obvious pain, the Prefabricated Home Manufacturers' Institute reports that at one time there were several hundred prefabricators of houses who were "prefabricators in name only." The insititute seems to think they were attracted by the glowing promises of the then Housing Administrator, Wilson Wyatt, and that they gathered from far and near to flutter about the optimistic glow which Mr. Wyatt gave off. But, alas, like the proverbial moths, most of them got singed and fell, as the institute says with ill-concealed relief, "by the wayside." The institute hastens to add that this was by no means a reflection on the industry. Between the lines, the institute seems to consider this a very healthy thing indeed, because the production for the first six months in 1948 was forty percent over 1947.

"There are now perhaps sixty-five real home fabricators in the country today, of which it can safely be said that the Knox Corporation is one of the outstanding leaders, with an excellent product, a fine plant and an efficient organization," reports Mr. Harry H. Steidle, manager of the Prefabricators' Institute.[2]

Another of the Knox corporations is a new industry for the South, that of automotive suppliers, with national outlets through Montgomery Ward and International Harvester. This began, at government request, as a war plant, and turned out half of all the bearings used in all the Liberty ships built, from Maine on down the coast and out to Kaiser's yards, a sizable job for four young men who smelled of sawdust and shavings. It also turned out sixteen-inch shell casings, 100-pound bomb casings and other war items. The government was very happy about them, testimonials prove.

There are three other corporations in the group, covering lumber manufacturing and wholesale lumber brokerage, backed by forestry holdings large enough to guarantee a perpetual cut. They carry out the old man's idea that in the lumber business it is a good idea to control the whole thing, from the trees and the land on which they grew, to the sale of the finished product—including the key to the door, if the product be a house.

While the old man was getting his team of boys in shape, he was careful to follow up the sermons about idle money with illustrations from life. Risk money and venture money were the life-blood of business success, he would say. He would follow up this text with some lurid chapters from his own successes and failures or maybe with a little light demonstration in which he emphasized his instruction with handy peach-tree switches, the switch from the peach tree being keen and limber like a light buggy whip.

This instruction by the senior Knox, as he sought to incline his four twigs, often took a turn which would cause a psychologist versed in the training of the young to leap into the air with wild cries of anguish and protest.

There was the time the fond father returned home from the funeral of a cousin, frugally bringing with him six packs of cigarettes from the more personal effects of the deceased. A day later he discovered Wyck and Pete, his two eldest, initiating themselves into the exquisite pleasure of the forbidden weed behind the barn. He marched them into the living room where an old-fashioned "circulating" heater took the slight winter chill off the mild East Georgia air. Closing all the doors to the room, he carefully opened the remaining packages. He then stripped his erring sons to the waist and switched them vigorously.

That done, he said, very pleasantly indeed, "Boys, I've smoked for thirty years. I don't want to take an unfair advantage of you, so you will now smoke up all these cigarettes, and when you've done we will all quit."

Soon the air was worse than that at any smoke-filled political convention since Sir Walter Raleigh introduced this new-world flora. And the puffing sons were showing a marked lack of enthusiasm for their happy privilege. Whenever one of his progeny slowed down his puffing too much, Father Knox would lay about him with his peach-tree switches, causing his sons to cavort about the room like young colts stung by bees, and to puff with renewed vigor.

It was in one of those nimble leaps that young Wyck Knox flung a just-lighted cigarette into the open door of the heater. His father promptly collared the offending son and administered a stern lecture on the evil of waste, with a generous dose of "peach-tree tea," as he termed it, to wash it down. For years thereafter the two oldest Knox boys would grow glassy-eyed and pale at sight or smell of tobacco in any form. To this day they approach the weed with a delicate touch, as if at any moment they might have to put it down and rush for air. None of them admires peach trees either, although a peach tree in bloom is as lovely as a ballerina in Swan Lake.

Despite the marked success of the boys in odd jobs, such as hawking saw-mill slabs in a pony wagon, delivering papers for the Atlanta and Augusta publications, and in before-and-after-school jobs in the father's enterprises, the old man seemed a mite disappointed in Wyck, the eldest, who was a bit mule-headed anyhow and inclined to reckless waste, as the cigarette episode plainly showed.

It was not until Wyck drew out his savings of $200, told his parent where he could go, and went off to the Florida boom at the age of sixteen that the old man began to cheer up. When Wyck came home a year later in a new suit and with $250 in cash, the old gentleman happily awarded him his diploma, *magna cum laude*, and took him to his heart along with Pete, who had earned his diploma at the famous fifth birthday.[3]

Other citizens of Thomson were climbing off chicken wagons, on which they had hitched rides, or dropping off freight cars in their retreat from the Florida boom. The old man bored his cronies for a year or more with the boast that Wyck was the only damn man in the United States to come home from Florida with no patches on his pants and with extra money in his pockets. Thereafter, he vowed, he would never worry about anyone save their competitors as long as Pete and Wyck remained a team. He took the two younger ones, Lawrence and Robert, and inclined the former toward a course in business administration and the latter to law school, so as to round out his business team. And before Pete and Wyck had got out of college—both in the class of 1932, because of Wyck's one year in the boom—he had picked out the field on which his team was to play, the home grounds of Thomson, in a gloomy year of the depression.

A year before Pete and Wyck were out of college, the old man had started a small building-supply business as a side line to his planing mill, but the young fellow who was running it for him had died and the doors had been locked. Upon their graduation, he and the boys looked in. There was some sheeting and some molding. It was about $1,000 worth of cull lumber.

This became "Knox Brothers, Retail Building," Wyck and Pete proprietors. The third day in business a neighbor came to see them and said he wanted to build his colored cook a three-room house in his back yard. The proprietors figured on it separately, and the old man screeched happily—like his planing-mill blades—when the results were within fifty cents of each other.[4]

By 1935, the boys persuaded the old man to put his business, valued at $15,000, in with theirs, which had an estimated value of $10,000. It became the Knox Brothers Lumber Company. Lawrence meanwhile had graduated and had done a year and half's work outside. But by 1935 he was in the firm as salesman and supervisor. By 1938 the firm at last was complete, with Robert as its attorney and a full associate.

Wyck was a fine man to go out and look at trees and see them standing there as so many feet of cut timber. Pete's nimble mind produced copious ideas. He saw that the more construction he could get, the more lumber had to be bought from the retail salesman, Lawrence. This developed so fast that in 1938 Pete bought an old planing mill and stock of lumber at Greensboro, Georgia, which now ships about 400 to 500 cars of lumber a year. All this produced considerable work for a lawyer.

After the old mill was in shape, Pete's mind picked up an item in the morning paper about the great need for houses at Camp Gordon, near Augusta, where the Army was going to train a lot of men. Pete went down and watched the slow work going on, with carpenters sawing and measuring lumber. He got an idea. He formed a new company to handle the necessary FHA business, and he put the mill to work precutting lumber to plan. When it got to the site of the house, there was nothing to be sawed. That company, the King Development Company, built 400 houses near Augusta in so short a time that the Army people were hollering for others to come look, and were shoving contracts at Pete Knox. From precutting lumber, the next step was to prefabricated houses, although other types of construction still went on as before. The company has now built about 4,500 houses throughout the South. Of these, the last 2,000 have been prefabs.

Pete's new idea was to sell the house as a literal package.[5] He also insisted on sticking to the old man's teaching of controlling the house from the time it was standing as trees on their own timberland until it was a completed house. This meant buying land, subdividing it, putting in streets, utilities, landscaping it, and selling the houses.

The packages move out of the $300,000 prefab plant at Thomson, which turns out houses on assembly lines, on a special trailer truck. The whole house is stacked on it in a neat, efficient plan. It's all there—the windows and doors already hung, the kitchen cabinets ready, the bathroom medicine cabinet in place, glass in the windows, screens in place, and every small item there. When it reaches the site, the house goes right up on the waiting foundation. All that is lacking in the package is the plumbing, the wiring and heating units. The houses are adaptable to any type of heating. These are waiting in a materials dump on the site. There are four types of packages—houses of four, five, six and seven rooms—but each fits on the trailers. The last item added is a big sign on each side—" 'another Complete Knox Home.'"

The raw lumber from trees on the Knox reserves, the Knox mills, and the Knox kilns comes into the Knox prefab plant for framing and finish. It runs through the planers and is sized. Three conveyor belt lines then carry it to eleven saws, where it is cut into framing lengths. From there it moves to five assembly lines. From a mezzanine deck above the lines, precut wallboard material is dropped down to complete the insulated wall panels. The completed panels are picked up by quarter-ton hoists and dropped into the packaging platform, where packages of three or four "bundles," depending on the size of the house, are tied together. In the packages are inside walls, outside walls, roof, ceiling and other items. A ten-ton crane picks up the packages and deposits them on the Knox-built trailer. There are sixty-five of these specially designed trailers. At peak production, the plant can turn out about one house an hour.

With foundations laid, the house can be put up by a crew in about eight hours. Title Six of the FHA law was removed by the last Congress. It allowed builders to put up houses, clear them through FHA for specifications, and then find buyers. Title Two remains. It requires finding the customer for each house or group of houses before they are built. Operating under this restraint, the plant now is turning out a mere four houses a day, but plans are ready for a speed-up. Pete has plans for going not merely to individuals, but to cooperative groups who might want to transform an old field into a community of homes, and for construction of new-type industrial communities.

In the days when prefab houses were going up in about twenty communities and three states, to say nothing of the big Army hospital near Augusta, Pete Knox got to be a sort of living legend, with folks making bets on how soon he'd be a dead one.

He went night and day, and he learned to drive his car with his legs crossed, so he could have one foot on the gas and a handy knee to put a pad on for figuring while he drove. He would foolishly drive sixty and seventy miles an hour, figuring on his pad and giving the road what seemed to his passengers to be no more than a casual glance at odd moments.

He developed units of carpenters and bricklayers, many of them teams composed of Negro boys with whom he had played as a boy around Thomson, and he usually had a crew with him. Sometimes they wake up at night, muttering and sweating, as the bomber combat crews used to do, dreaming they are riding with Mr. Pete, and him with his legs crossed, his eyes on his estimate figures there on his knee, and the speedometer hitting seventy. But they think of him just the way the crews used to think of a pilot who always got them there and got them back. They are proud of their jobs, they swear by Mr. Pete, and they regard him as having some sort of divine protection.

The senior Knox had included a number of nonbusiness courses in his school. The Calvinist in him led him to frown very vigorously on the evils of drink. But the Gaelic in him rarely let him refuse a proffered drink. He almost never took the second, but he sometimes made the first one a slug that would have opened the eyes of a seaman in his first Sands Street bar after the long run from the China Seas.

One of the stories around Thomson concerns the young salesman who walked into the Knox office and offered a drink from a full half pint. Friend Knox poured the whole half pint into a tumbler and drank it off as if it were spring water. Nevertheless, liquor in amounts of more than one drink was an evil, and he was tougher on overindulgence than any parson in town. Sunday found the Knox family in the First Methodist Church for Sunday school and church. There was no more religious-minded family in town, and no more sincere. His sons carry on. They are stewards of the Thomson First Methodist Church.

The old gentleman regarded a really pretty girl as God's finest handiwork. He also brightened to the sound of fiddles at a dance, and he thought home was the place to have fun. The Knox home was, almost nightly, filled with merriment and play. The boys got their dates and brought them home. Father Knox, immaculate as always in a white, stiff-bosomed shirt and black string tie, never failed to kiss each one on arrival. The home was so constructed that by taking up rugs a large front room and hallway could be converted into a sizable ballroom. But a dance never got under way before the old gentleman had kissed all the girls.

"Marry a girl from your own section and replenish the earth," was one of the Knox axioms. The boys obeyed teacher. Pete married Mary Lyles Aiken, of Florence, South Carolina, near his mother's home place. He was twenty-three. Wyck married the next year. His bride was Byrnice Purcell, of Cochran, Georgia, who had been at the university with Wyck and who was teaching school in Thomson. As a member of the school board, Wyck Knox had recommended her for the teaching job. He was twenty-five. Lawrence was twenty-five when he married Margaret Evans, of Warrenton, Georgia, twelve miles up the road from Thomson. Robert was an old man of twenty-seven when he married Ruth Hall, daughter of the then Methodist minister at Thomson. Lawrence has three children, the others two each.[6] The families remain closely knit, with more or less routine recreation, broken only by Pete or Wyck, who will suddenly interrupt their heavy schedule of work to go off for a week at some resort or to a football or major-league baseball game. In Thomson the families are a normal part of the social life found in any town of 3,500.

Knoxes have been in the region of what is now McDuffie County for more than 100 years. The county, of which Thomson is the county seat, was "laid out," as they say, after the Civil War. Before that, it was part of more ancient Wilkes County. The Knox clan came over from Scotland in the 1730s.

The town has had the Knox name on it since the end of the Civil War. Charles Edward Knox, who had gone off to war with a Georgia regiment as drummer boy and courier, aged fourteen, fought the last three years of it as a soldier. He came home after Appomattox on shanks' mare. At Crawfordville, about thirty miles from home, he followed his nose to a farm kitchen where a pretty girl was baking a pan of biscuits and frying a chicken. She fed the weary soldier, and as he limped on homeward he made up his mind to marry the girl.

He did too. When he took her back to Thomson, they both decided that her talent for cooking shouldn't be wasted. The economy of the late Confederacy was flat on its face, and the Yankee dollar was hard to come by. They founded the Knox Hotel and opened a livery stable near by. The Knox Hotel is still in the charge of a member of the Knox family. So is the Terrace Hotel, the town's other hotel. Both are famous for fried chicken and hot biscuits.

The son of Charles Knox was Peter Knox. He saw men about him put imagination and any idle dollars they had to work, and while some went broke, some didn't. He exacted all he could in the way of information from those who didn't.

He learned, too, that keeping an ear to the ground was good business. He was fooling around with two old secondhand sawmills, still a young man in the business, when one day he accepted an invitation to have a drink with a salesman who already had had four or five. The salesman allowed as how he had it on good authority the Atlantic Coast Line Railroad was planning a short cut in their line to speed up freight traffic. Peter said a hurried farewell to his friend. By the next day he had acquired timber options along the reported new right of way, soon to be official. He cashed in heavily. By 1905 he was married and had taken his bride, Gertrude Austin, from South Carolina, to his lumber camp at Hickox, Georgia. It was a frontierlike life, but the tall, wiry man was already effecting the immaculate dress which was to become a sort of trademark.

The birthdays of his boys mark also periods of stress and strain in his life and work. Wyckliffe Austin Knox was born in the turbulent lumber-camp days at Hickox, 1 October 1909. When Peter Seymour was born on 11 August 1911, the event took place in a house in Thomson where the old man had moved after his attorney had negotiated the purchase of a farm, for which the lumberman yearned with all the passion of a sailor or a magazine writer. The fact the farm covered most of the north end of the county and totaled about 20,000 acres, much of which was worn-out cotton land, didn't daunt him. He had an idea that dollars, spent intelligently on a farm, would pay off. This was in the days before soil conservation and modern farming methods. The floods and the droughts came, and on the day before William Lawrence Manning Knox was born at the farm, in October of 1913, a Negro hand, sent for supplies, came back from Thomson with an empty wagon and reported that the gentleman at the store said he had to have some money. The land was sold off and the family moved back to town. The elder Knox thereafter viewed big farming operations as something akin to dice or roulette. Robert Edward Knox was born in March, 1916, with the old gentleman on top of the wave again, in lumber.[7]

He turned more and more of the business over to his boys, until at last they were doing it all. But he was always at his desk at 7:00 every morning. He took more time off for little pleasure trips, and on 6 December 1946, he and Mrs. Knox registered at the Winecoff Hotel, Atlanta. They died in the fire which took more than 100 lives early the next morning. It shook the boys and their families deeply, but the more they remembered him and their mother the more they were comforted. They remembered their father with laughter and with tears. He left a lot of wisdom, stories, and legends. But none was shady. Not even his critics could say he hadn't been straight as a string and a good man for the town.[8]

There was something of the old man in Pete Knox when he stood up before the Rotary Club, of Augusta, Georgia, and told them why the Knox Company was not going to stay on in Augusta when the war contracts were done. They were going to build a plant to cost somewhere in the neighborhood of a half million and they were going to give the South a new industry. But not in Augusta.

He didn't think it was good for the town, he said, for a businessman to have to do business with politicians in order to do business. He thought taxes ought to be what they should be, and that it should not be necessary for a businessman to see a politician about them. Augusta was then in the hands of a machine grown fat and corrupt with too many years of power. It was in the habit of bringing in the sheaves by putting businessmen under obligation to the machine. Pete didn't play ball. He just paid the bill and said his piece. As it turned out, this was one of the factors which helped bring political reform in Augusta. The Knoxes do considerable building there now.

The Knox brothers had gone into Augusta at the request of the Navy when a war-contract company had failed. They were asked to supply management. As Pete said, all the Knoxes had ever had in their heads was sawdust, and this job was in metals. But they took over the old Lombard Iron Works, which for 100 years had been peacefully plodding along with about twenty employees, and went to work. After they signed up, they discovered certain liabilities not revealed in the agreements, and some of the new corporation officers wanted to take the loss and quit. They were up in the high-tax brackets anyhow. But Pete said no. So they stayed. For a time the Knox shirt in this particular project hung in the balance, but after a year they had it going. Their production of bearings, shaftings, other seagoing gear, and of shell cases for 100-pound bombs and sixteen-inch shells was so good that the Navy gave them all the pretty testimonials which good producers got. This, plus the vital production of timber and housing, caused the Navy and War Departments to pin down three of the boys on the jobs. Robert, the lawyer, they let go. He served with the antiaircraft outfit in the Canal Zone for four years, one of the many forgotten men kept there in anticipation of a German or Japanese sneak attack on that vital waterway.

The new plant was built at nearby Waynesboro, Georgia. It is turning out truck and trailer bodies for International Harvester, farm trailers for Montgomery Ward, hubcaps for the Kelsey-Hayes Wheel Company, of Detroit, parts for the General Motors diesel plant, plus smaller contracts for other firms. It does general metal stamping, steel fabrication, and chrome plating. Despite steel shortages and lack of a good quota, it being a new business, it did about $2,500,000 worth of business last year.[9] Early in 1949 plans were made to establish a new lumber mill at Soperton, Georgia. It will be ready by fall.

Poking around the Knox plants, you can turn up an occasional oldtimer who was back there at Hickox with the old man. They were easier to find, in fact, than boys who had gone to school with the Knox brothers. Most of these had gone off to other places, seeking better opportunity—an exodus which the South has experienced annually and painfully for many years. John Fullbright, a foreman in the prefab plant, is one of the men who started with the senior Knox.

"There ain't no mystery about these four boys staying in a country town and making millions," he said. "Havin' old man Pete for a daddy explains it. Little Pete takes after him. He's just like the old man. The old man wouldn't gamble and wouldn't buy stocks. But if he had ten thousand dollars in the bank, it nearly drove him crazy. He had to put them dollars to work. He was always thinkin' up somethin' for dollars to do. And Little Pete is the same way. Always thinkin'. Wyck, now, he never give much of a damn till he got out of college. He gets better all the time. But when he was young he fretted the old man considerable. He and his daddy used to butt heads. But they always settled up. Lawrence was lazy as a boy, but he could just laugh at the old man and get away with it. He still is the easiest-goin' one. Robert is a lot like Pete. A lot of them say Pete is the leader, but it takes the output of all of them. Just like the old man used to say, 'It takes four posts to hold up a house.' "

Notes—21

[1]Published by permission of the author, Mrs. McGill, and *Saturday Evening Post* (30 April 1949).

[2]As of 24 November 1981, Knox Homes had merged with National Homes of Lafayette, Indiana, along with two other prefabricating plants that they owned in other states. The mobile home plant in Thomson was also included in the merger.

[3]Wyckliffe Austin Knox died 8 June 1976. He was graduated from Thomson High School and the University of Georgia. His principal business activities were lumber, housing, construction, and real estate development. His active participation in the lumber and housing business ended when that business was merged with National Homes in 1959. Since that time his principal business activities were

with Knox Rivers Construction Company in Thomson, one of the largest road-building companies in the state, and in the real estate development business in the Central Florida area where he maintained a part-time residence up until the time of his death.

His primary civic activities included service on the McDuffie County School Board for sixteen years, twelve as chairman. He also was an active Boy Scouter, having served as president of the local council. He received both the Silver Beaver and the Silver Antelope awards. He was recognized in 1963 by the Business School of the University of Georgia, of which he was an alumnus, for outstanding business accomplishments. He managed Governor Carl Sanders' successful campaign for governor in 1961, and thereafter served one term in the Georgia State Senate.

A son, Wyckliffe Austin Knox, Jr., is a lawyer in Augusta and head of his own firm, Knox and Zacks. In addition he serves as chairman of the board of Knox-Rivers Construction Company which now has operations in Thomson, Macon, and Augusta. He is married to the former Shell Hardman of Commerce, grand-daughter of the late Governor L. G. Hardman, and they have four children. He also operates a family investment company, Knox Properties, and serves as a director of Georgia Railroad Bank and Trust Company in Augusta. He is active in alumni activities of the University of Georgia, and is a member of the Athletic Board, and formerly was a member of the Board of Visitors at the Law School in Athens. He has been president of both the local Scout Council and the Rotary Club.

Wyckliffe Knox's daughter, Harriet Knox Fleming, lives in Augusta with her husband, S. Stetson Fleming, an accountant, and three children. Wyckliffe Knox's wife, Byrnice, was recently married to Denver Swanson of New Smyrna Beach, Florida, who retired as vice-president of the St. Paul Companies in Minnesota, and divides her time between Thomson and this Florida city.

[4]Knox Brothers Retail and Knox Lumber Company were made a part of Knox Corporation, which included the Prefabricated Housing Plant. In 1959 Knox Homes was merged with National Homes of Lafayette, Indiana. The brothers remained to manage this operation for a short while—then all left National Homes to head their own businesses.

[5]Peter Seymour Knox, Jr., was graduated from Thomson High School and Davidson College. As of 24 November 1981, he has led a very successful life as head of Knox Realty Investment Corporation, a real estate and development company based in Augusta, Georgia. His residence is still in Thomson where he has large farming and forestry interests. He was former chairman of the board of The Bank of Thomson. A son, Boone, is now president of The Bank of Thomson. The oldest son, Peter, III, is president of Merry Companies—a large brick manufacturing company located in Augusta. This company, which has several subsidiaries, was recently sold to a large Australian conglomerate.

His chief interests lie in the restoration of several sections of downtown Augusta—including the business district and a residential section in Old Augusta now called Olde Towne. Here he has restored in a very authentic way several hundred residences, commercial buildings, etc. His Telfair Square project has received recognition and awards from numerous historic and restoration groups.

A daughter, Nanci, is an outstanding horsewoman, having recently won several world championships with her stable of gaited horses, and is manager, Seymour Farms, a horse and cattle farm.

His wife, Mary Lyles Aiken, is a native of South Carolina, and the daughter of the late Jefferson Boone Aiken, outstanding Carolinian.

He has maintained a special interest in his alma mater, Davidson College, Davidson, North Carolina, where he was recently honored for his gift of a dormitory building, Peter Knox Hall. He is a member of the Davidson Board of Visitors.

Other businesses and activities include partner, Aiken Investment Company, and Knox Investment Company; trustee, Reinhardt College; member, board of directors, Augusta Chamber of Commerce.

[6]William Lawrence Manning Knox was born 8 October 1913, and was graduated from Thomson High School and the University of Georgia. As of 24 November 1981, he had remained for several years as production manager of National Homes after the merger. He then opened a land planning office in Thomson, having been one of the early graduates of the Department of Landscape Architecture at the University of Georgia. The company, LK Land Planners, does architectural drawings and planning for shopping centers, parks, and commercial and residential landscaping. He is particularly interested in restoration of some of the historic homes and buildings of McDuffie County.

He served for thirty-two years on the McDuffie County Hospital Board, eighteen of those years as chairman. He retired from the authority in 1977. He is a director of Knox-Rivers Construction Company and a partner in Knox Investment Company. He is a director of W. L. Knox and Company, an investment banking firm in Atlanta which is headed by his son, Larry Knox, Jr.

He and his wife, Margaret Evans, have four children. Gabrielle Knox Vaughan is married to Dr. William Vaughan, general surgeon, practicing in Thomson. They have two daughters.

Peggy Knox Morrison lives in Concord, North Carolina, and is married to John H. Morrison, Jr., of that city. She has two sons and a daughter.

Larry Knox, Jr., is president of W. L. Knox and Company of Atlanta. He is married to the former Paula Copenhaver. They have two daughters.

John Charles Knox is a graduate of Emory University Medical School. He is a pediatrician—chief resident at Grady Hospital and Egleston Children's Hospital—soon to enter private practice in Atlanta.

[7]Robert Edward Knox was born 28 March 1916, and was graduated from Thomson High School and the University of Georgia. He is head of his law firm, Knox and Evans, in Thomson. He has served in the Georgia State Senate and for several terms as mayor of Thomson. He operates a farm in McDuffie County and oversees the activities of Knox Investment Company. He is married to Ruth Hall. They have four children.

Robert E. Knox, Jr., was graduated from the University of Georgia. He is a partner in the law firm of Knox and Evans, and is presently mayor of Thomson, Georgia. He is also vice-president, Georgia Municipal Association. He is married to Dorothy Ellen Meadows, and they have a child, Mary Ann.

Mary K. McNeill was graduated from the University of Georgia, and is married to Donald T. McNeill, president, McNeill, Lauff and McNeill, Inc., box manufacturers. They have two children, Virginia Ruth and Donald T., Jr.

Andrew H. Knox was graduated from the University of Georgia. He is president of Watson and Knox, Inc. an insurance and real estate company, and First of Thomson, Inc. He is married to Anne Tomlinson, and they have a child, Caroline.

Ruth A. Knox was graduated from Wesleyan College and the University of Georgia. She is an attorney with Kutak, Rock and Huie, Atlanta, Georgia.

[8]Peter Seymour Knox, Sr., was born 15 September 1868, in Crawfordville, Georgia. He died 7 December 1946 in a hotel fire. He was the first child of Charles Edward and Leila Williams Knox. Mrs. Peter Seymour Knox, Sr. (Gertrude Austin) was born 18 April 1878, in Greenville, South Carolina. She died 7 December 1946 in a hotel fire. She was the daughter of John Wyckliffe and Emma Latimer Austin.

[9]As of 24 November 1981, a mobile home division of this Waynesboro plant had been started and later moved to Thomson. The Waynesboro plant itself was sold to Perfection Industries which later sold to a large German company.

Essay 22

Alexander H. Stephens: Hamlet of the Confederacy[1]

When one enters the gate and starts up the drive to the house, lifting the eyes to the white house which sits serenely on a knoll, the world seems to fall away. In the drowsing heat of summer, grasshoppers leap in the grass. Birds hop about in search of unwary insects. There is a deep, quiet peace as if here it was always drowsy afternoon.

So deep is this feeling that one unconsciously looks for the slight figure of Liberty Hall, Alexander Stephens, "Hamlet of the Confederacy," and for a moment the mind pictures him as seen in old portraits, waiting there on the wide porch which stretches across the front of the white, two-story frame building with the ell of two rooms in the rear. This house, and the memory and legend of the man, are the heart of the memorial state park near Crawfordville, Georgia, that bears his name. All who pass that way go there to feel the stillness, to see the beauty of old things, and to recall the indomitable spirit of the man who was ill and in pain all his days; who never weighed more than 100 pounds; who came from great poverty to grandeur of place and spirit; who conquered sorrow and affliction and left the name of Alexander Hamilton Stephens as a simile for honor and for civilization.

He drew to him men of like sensitiveness and character. One such was Abraham Lincoln. It is likely that Stephens was one of the very few men in public life in 1860—perhaps the only one—who admired and respected Lincoln and did not regard him as an ignorant buffoon. They had served in Congress together and had jointly opposed the Mexican War.[2] On 2 February 1848 Congressman Lincoln wrote his law-partner and friend, Bill Herndon:

"I take up my pen to tell you that Mr. Stephens of Georgia, a little, slim, pale-faced consumptive man, with a voice like [Stephen T.] Logan's, has just completed the very best speech of an hour's length I ever heard. My old, withered eyes are full of tears yet."[3]

The honesty of purpose which ruled the lives of both these men drew them toward one another. They were friends. So it was that Lincoln, reading of a speech Stephens had made to his own state and to others in the South, urging them to remain in the Union, wrote, on 22 December 1860:

"I fully appreciate the present peril the country is in and the weight of the responsibility on me. Do the people of the South really entertain fears that the Republican administration would directly or indirectly, interfere with the slaves, or with them, about the slaves. If they do, I wish to assure you as once a friend, and still, I hope, not an enemy, that there is no cause for such fear. . . . I suppose, however, this does not meet the case. You think slavery is right and ought to be extended, while we think it is wrong and ought to be restricted. That, I suppose, is the rub. It certainly is the only substantial difference between us."[4]

Stephens, whose ruling passion was the Constitution of the United States, and the Union, strongly opposed secession until his state voted it—by a margin made narrow by his argument and that of Howell Cobb.[5] He followed his state, sorrowing spiritually and practically. He had told them that even with Lincoln elected, the South still would rule the Congress and nullify Lincoln. But, while many listened, not enough did. So, he went into the war, and became the vice-president of the Confederacy. Almost from the start he ran counter to Jefferson Davis. From all points of view, Stephens was the superior man—intellectually, politically, and especially psychologically. Twice he would have, in all probability, worked out an honorable peace for the Confederacy, had not the stubborn Davis interfered. When the last try failed, though he took it all the way to Lincoln and Grant, Stephens retired to Liberty Hall, embittered at Davis's blindness which had so limited him and made impossible a deal with Lincoln. He stayed there until he was arrested, at war's end, and taken to prison in Boston Harbor.[6]

Always, like Hamlet in another field, he was seeking to justify his act of leaving the Union. And when the war was done, he put his longest soliloquy in book form, *The Constitutional Views of the War Between the States.*.[7]

Lincoln, noting him when he first saw him wheeled to the floor of Congress, and a valet removed the many wrappings from the frail figure, said, jestingly, "I never saw so much shuck and so little cob."

One day, a Georgian, who had made Stephens his hero, upon learning that the great man was to be on a train passing through his town, crowded on the car when the train stopped. Stephens was pointed out.

"Good Lord," said the astonished spectator, and then turned his back and departed.[8]

What he saw was "a small, boyish figure, a little more than five feet high, weighing about ninety pounds, with a shrunken, consumptive chest, a sallow, mummified face, in which the bony structure stood forth like a death's head, capped by a vampirish wisp of brown hair, the unearthly aspect of the whole lighted by a pair of fierce, piercing eyes, deep sunken in their sockets."

So frail was he that even after he was a successful and famous lawyer, men used to take him for a boy. Once a man patted his head and asked, "Do you expect to go to college, sonny?"

At the age of twenty-two, Stephens wrote his own description: "My weight is ninety-four pounds, my height sixty-seven inches, my waist twenty inches in circumference, and my whole appearance that of a youth of seventeen or eighteen. When I left college two years ago my weight was seventy pounds."[9]

Stephens' friend and biographer, Richard Johnston, wrote: "His chestnut hair was brushed away from a thin, white brow and bloodless cheeks. The child looking at him felt sorry for another child."[10]

His great friend, robust and vital Robert Toombs, said, "He always looked as if he had two weeks purchase on life."[11]

A newspaper description of him gave another touch: "An immense cloak, a high hat, and peering somewhere out of the middle a thin, pale, sad face. . . . If he were laid out in his coffin, he needn't look any different; only then the fires would have gone out in the burning eyes. Set as they are in the wax-like face, they seem to burn and blaze."[12]

Stephens' own letters discuss his ailments. "From the first moment of consciousness, I have never been free from pain. . . . Weak and sickly, I was sent into the world. . . . Health I have never known. . . . But this I could bear; pain I can endure. . . . Physical sufferings are not the worst ills. . . . These are slight compared with a wounded spirit. . . . The heart alone knoweth its own sorrow. . . ."[13]

This, too, was the Hamlet in him.

What did he miss? A wife and family, perhaps? It is likely. He never married. Yet women were strangely and devotedly drawn to him. And so were men. His house was usually filled with guests. The neighbors liked and loved him. So did his slave-servants.

He was born to a small, slaveless farm household. The sickly boy knew harsh toil. At the age of six his sickly body was dragging behind his father's plow, dropping corn in the new furrows. His father was an educated man, a part-time teacher, and there were a few books to interest the boy in reading. Friends helped him attend Franklin College, later the University of Georgia.[14] He led his classes. Greek was a passion with him, and he took the beauty and the precision of that language and its discipline into law, to the legislature, to the Federal Congress, and into the Confederacy, where the discord of it made his Hamlet-like mind unhappy and yet kept it constantly rationalizing the things that had to be done. He led always an inner life and an outer one. His brother Linton was the one to whom he most often turned, and to him he poured out his sad and introspective soul in letters wonderful and tragic to read.[15]

He had, like Lincoln, an almost mystic feeling about the Union and the Constitution. His great American hero was Daniel Webster, whom he put above Clay and Calhoun. In 1852 he voted, sentimentally, for Webster as president though the great man had died before that time. Webster, orator and expounder of the Constitution, was his idol.

He and Toombs were great friends. Toombs, too, was a unionist in the early days of tension. Then Toombs, Howell Cobb, and Stephens fought for the Union. That was in 1850. All opposed Calhoun's theory of nullification and secession. But, by 1860, they began to change. Stephens never did—until his own state voted to withdraw. Later Cobb was to fall out with Stephens. He did not think secession meant war. Stephens said it meant ruin.

He gave to the Confederacy the best that was in him—and if the Confederate government would not listen, then there was nothing he could do. And it did not give much heed to him. In March 1865, he headed the delegation that went to Hampton Roads to seek peace—but the restrictions imposed by Jefferson Davis made it impossible. He and Davis met later in Richmond and could not agree.

"What are you going to do?" asked the Mississippian.

"I intend to go home and remain there," he said, and abruptly left the room.[16] He survived the war for eighteen years, becoming governor of Georgia, and dying in office.

He spent most of his time writing books, and he made it plain he felt that failure might have been avoided had his own ideas been well received—and he was not a vain man. Actually, his ideas, after war began, were a mixture of soundness and unsoundness. He was not a military man.

Death came to him early on the morning of 4 March 1883. He had been governor but a short time. On 8 March, 20,000 and more persons walked past his casket in the capitol. The Legislature paid its tribute. The aging Toombs, standing by the casket, wept for five minutes before he could control himself and speak:

"He was modest, refined, learned, eloquent. . . . His life was an open book. . . . His whole life was spent in the practice of virtue, the pursuit of truth, seeking the good of mankind."[17]

He was buried at Oakland Cemetery. In the spring of 1885 the casket was removed to Liberty Hall, and he sleeps there now, on the slope of the great lawn.

It was where he would have wanted to be.

"No mortal," he wrote in his diary while a prisoner in 1865, "ever had stronger attachments for his home than I for mine. That old homestead and that quiet lot, Liberty Hall, in Crawfordville, sterile and desolate as they may seem to others, are bound to me by associations tender as heart strings and strong as hooks of steel. There I wish to live and die.[18] Let my last breath be my native air. My native land, my country, the only one that is country to me, is Georgia," wrote the prisoner in Boston Harbor, feeling that he might not again be allowed freedom. "There I wish to live and die."[19]

Notes—22

[1]Manuscript provided by Mrs. Ralph McGill from the Ralph McGill papers. A second rough sketch of Stephens was found in the McGill papers, and will be used to amplify remarks made in this essay. In that sketch, McGill wrote of Stephens: "His life was filled with greatness, kindness and with suffering. Because he suffered he tried to relieve others of suffering. His body remained small, frail. Even in summer he needed a shawl about his shoulders. His mind was great and brilliant in its activity. His courage was that of a lion. Once he fought a man three times his size who attacked with an open knife. Stephens had an umbrella. He was stabbed and all but died. Time after time he showed his courage."

[2]See "Speech on the Subject of the Mexican War," delivered in House of Representatives, 16 June 1846, in Henry Cleveland, *Alexander H. Stephens in Public and Private. With Letters and Speeches, Before, During, and Since the War* (Philadelphia: National Publishing Co., 1866), pp. 302-20. In the supplementary sketch McGill wrote: "The year 1836 found him in the legislature, leading the fight to establish the Western and Atlantic railroad to be owned by the state, and advocating a charter for Wesleyan Female College [Macon, Georgia]. In 1843 he entered the Congress of the United States to remain there for sixteen years and become one of its great figures. He favored the annexation of Texas but opposed the war with Mexico."

[3]Abraham Lincoln to William H. Herndon, 2 February 1848, in Roy P. Basler, ed., *Collected Works of Abraham Lincoln* 9 vols. (New Brunswick: Rutgers University Press, 19+3), 1:448. McGill omitted "just" before "take," and "dry" before "eyes," and substituted "tell you" for "say." The original read: "I just take up

my pen to say, that Mr. Stephens of Georgia, a little slim, pale-faced consumptive man, with a voice like Logan's, has just completed the very best speech of, an hour's length, I ever heard. My old, withered, dry eyes are full of tears yet."

⁴Abraham Lincoln to Alexander H. Stephens, 22 December 1860, in Richard Malcolm Johnston and William Hand Browne, *Life of Alexander H. Stephens* (1878; reprinted, Freeport, N.Y.: Books for Libraries Press, 1971), p. 371. McGill substituted "the" for "a" before "Republican," "a" for "A" in "Administration," and "." for "?" after "slaves." He omitted "s" at the end of "fear," and emphases of the words "directly," "indirectly," "right," and "wrong."

⁵See "Speech Against Secession," delivered before the Legislature of Georgia, 14 November 1860, in Cleveland, *Alexander H. Stephens*, pp. 694-713. From his second sketch, McGill added: "He became one of the greatest students of constitutional law in the nation. He opposed intolerance. He fought to preserve the union. He tried to hold back his own state from secession in the meeting at Milledgeville, predicting almost exactly what would happen in the event of sec[e]ssion. Yet he believed his allegiance with the state. Had the Confederacy followed his plan early to buy cotton and ship it to England for credit, the war might have been won. Until it was too late they ignored [him]."

⁶In the second statement, McGill wrote: "He dared criticise the policy of the Confederate government. He was the spokesman for the South at a conference with President Abraham Lincoln. Had not the North won the battle of Gettysburg, he might have arranged to halt the war. He was imprisoned by the North after the war in a fort at Boston. He returned to his beloved Liberty Hall. He once was elected to Congress and twice to the United States Senate, but disfranchisement of voters and the refusal of Congress to seat him kept him out."

⁷Alexander Hamilton Stephens, *A Constitutional View of the Late War Between the States; its Causes, Character, Conduct and Results*. Presented in a series of colloquies at Liberty Hall (Chicago: National Publishing Co., [c. 1868-70]). McGill amplified in the second paper: "He could have been president of the Confederate states. All he had to do was to say he would strike the first blow. He would not. They made him vice-president. 'No,' said Stephens, 'I will not strike the first blow.' Always that was his way. He was not afraid to stand by his beliefs. Often they cost him friends. Often he was misunderstood. Yet he dared tell the people they were wrong when he believed them to be."

⁸E. Ramsay Richardon, *Little Aleck: A Life of Alexander H. Stephens, The Fighting Vice-President of the Confederacy* (Indianapolis: Bobbs-Merrill Co., 1932), p. 135.

⁹Journal entry, 17 May 1834, in Johnson and Browne, *Life of Alexander H. Stephens*, p. 77. McGill omitted "net" before "weight." In his second piece, McGill

stated: "He wondered about himself. He was sick much of the time. He heard some of the neighbors, when they thought he was not listening, talking about him. They said he would not live long. His father taught school. Because the father thought the small, sickly boy would not live long, he let him go to school only when he was not needed at home. Alec helped dress the babies and watched over them. Alec helped his stepmother with work about the house. He was happiest by himself. He couldn't play games because he was not strong enough. He shrank when his father or stepmother scolded. He suffered himself so he did not like to see others suffer. He was kind to injured birds, to hungry dogs and cats. He limped through fourteen years of life. When he was fourteen his father and stepmother died. The small, thin, sickly boy was left in the care of an uncle."

[10]See Myrta Lockett Avary, ed., *Recollections of Alexander H. Stephens: His Diary Kept When a Prisoner at Fort Warren, Boston Harbour, 1865* (New York: Da Capo Press, 1971), p. 46. In Johnson and Browne, *Life of Alexander H. Stephens*, p. 73, the passage reads: "His thin chestnut hair was brushed away from a white brow and bloodless cheeks. He was leaning upon an umbrella. The child who looked at him felt sorry for another child. . . . "

[11]Rather than "he always," the quotation begins: "He never. . . ." Avary, *Recollections of Alexander H. Stephens*, p. 46.

[12]Avary, *Recollections of Alexander H. Stephens*, pp. 550-551, reads "wax-white face" rather than "wax-like face." Johnson and Browne, *Life of Alexander H. Stephens*, p. 534, have "little" before "face," "those" in place of "the" before "burning eyes," and "wax-white face" rather than "wax-like face."

[13]In his second sketch, McGill wrote: "It was while he was participating in the great debates, and packing the galleries, a newspaper man wrote a description of him: 'Mr. Stephens is slightly above medium height and painfully thin in appearance. His hair is lustre-lacking, his cheeks thin, wrinkled, and of parchment texture. His walk, his features, his figure bespeak great physical emaciation. You look in vain for some outward manifestation of that towering, commanding intellect which has held the congregated talent of the country spellbound for hours. . . . But still you feel convinced that the feeble, tottering being before you is all brain . . . that the whole man is charged with electricity of intellect.' "

[14]McGill added in his second article: "He never practiced deceit. When he was orphaned, relatives helped him. Members of his church, the Presbyterian, gave him money to study for the ministry, at Franklin College, now the state university. When he decided he would study law, he managed to stint and save and pay back the money. At the university his roommate was Crawford W. Long."

[15]Johnson and Browne, *Life of Alexander H. Stephens*, pp. 141-47. McGill amplified: "When Alexander Hamilton Stephens was born 11 February 1812, no

one paid him much attention. His mother was desperately ill. She lived but a short time. Somehow he lived. His small body was thin. His head was large. He lived on a farm in Taliaferro County although in those days it was part of Wilkes County. It was a lonely farm. Occasionally an Indian or a group of Indians passed by. The small boy wondered about them."

[16]A brief account of this is in Rudolph Von Abele, *Alexander H. Stephens: A Biography* (1946; reprinted, Negro Universities Press, 1971), pp. 244-45.

[17]Abele, *Alexander H. Stephens*, p. 316. I. W. Avery, *In Memory: Alexander H. Stephens* (V. P. Sission, Publishers, 1883), p. 32, quotes Toombs: "His life has been an open book. . . . He was modest, gentle, refined, learned and eloquent. . . . His whole life was spent in the practice of virtue, the pursuit of truth, seeking the good of mankind." In his second piece, McGill quoted from the inscriptions on the statue of Stephens at Crawfordville, Georgia: "On the north side of the statue one reads: 'He coveted and took from the Republic nothing save glory.' On the east side is written: 'I am afraid of nothing on earth, or above the earth, except to do wrong—the path of duty I shall ever endeavor to travel, fearing no evil and dreading no consequences.' There is an inscription on each of the statue's four sides, but looking up at the marble figure of the man above it, one remembers best those of the north and east. The first was said of him; the second by him."

[18]Avary, *Recollections of Alexander H. Stephens*, p. 139.

[19]Avary, *Recollections of Alexander H. Stephens*, p. 253. McGill omitted "of" before "my," "own" before "native," and "there to" before "die." He also substituted "." for "!" after "air." In his second sketch, McGill stated: "An accident, a heavy gate fell on him, crippled him so that he was confined to a wheel chair most of the time and walked only with the aid of crutches. In 1870 he and his beloved half-brother, Linton, whom he had raised and educated, wrote the platform which restored the democracy of the state to power. In 1873 he was returned to Congress, remaining there for almost ten years and winning new honors. He came home in 1882, retiring to rest. He was seventy years old. Georgia insisted he be governor and elected him by an overwhelming majority. He died in office in 1883. As he lay dying he said, 'Get ready, we are nearly home.' The sickly baby of 1812 whom no one thought would live, had outlived parents, brothers, sisters, and most of the companions of his youth. He left a name which will live forever— Alexander H. Stephens, 'The Great Commoner'."

Essay 23

Tom Watson: The People's Man[1]

America has all but forgotten Tom Watson, the irascible Georgia rebel who half a century ago led the one great Southern liberal revolt that almost succeeded. His cause—the Populist crusade—lies buried in period histories. But if you go to his hometown of Thomson in McDuffie County,[2] you will find men who mention his name with a certain reverence and others who never fail to tie a bitter or profane adjective to the man who was born near there in 1856.

Several of us were looking at Hickory Hill, Watson's beautiful old house in Thomson, watching its whiteness in the dying light of "first dark," its shuttered windows making it seem lonely and sad. "I remember him as a boy," said one in the group. "We used to run back into the woods. Sometimes he would follow us, cursing and shaking his fist."

"You know," said another, "once he was in his yard down by the gate and he saw us in the road and called to us. He put his hand on my head and he said, 'Boys, study hard and grow up loving your state.' We were shaking and scared, because he was a mean-looking old man and we were afraid of him."

"Tom wasn't mean," said an older man in the group. "Tom loved children, but Tom was fey. . . . He could go off in his mind and leave his body walking around, and it was bad to cross him when his mind was off somewhere."

One hot July day in 1936, Georgia's Senator Richard B. Russell, Jr., just out of the governor's chair, was speaking in a hickory grove across from the Watson home. He was running against Eugene Talmadge for the Democratic nomination to the U. S. Senate.[3]

On the new-pine platform erected for the speakers sat the last of Tom Watson's sisters, tall and thin and that day a little grim.[4] Talmadge was trying to claim the support of the surviving Watson followers (the "old Pops," they were called) in the district, and he was against Roosevelt. The "Old Pops" wanted none of Talmadge.

When Dick Russell spoke, he said in his climax: "I have to laugh at Gene Talmadge trying to claim the mantle of Watson. Why, the mantle of Watson would fit him like a Mother Hubbard on a jay bird. . . ." And the crowd roared.[5]

Over in Madison, Georgia, some years ago, Colonel A. G. Foster took me to see an "Old Pop" who had followed Watson.

"What *was* he like?" I asked.

"Well, son," he said, looking at me with appraising eyes, "when you heard Tom speak, you knew you were a man and that God had made you for a man's work."

"What was he like?" I asked Colonel Foster as we went back to town to his law office to talk.

"Well," he said, "you know his background. His daddy was in the Confederate war and was twice wounded. Tom was born in 1856 and so he was a boy old enough for things to burn in his mind and leave scars there when that war was done. It ruined his daddy, and his daddy had been well off. The boy Tom knew the occupying army well, because there was a troop of federal soldiers stationed at Thomson.[6]

"His mother struggled and borrowed to get him some schooling. He was good at books. His daddy drank up his last acre and opened a saloon in Augusta. Looking back at it, that was the greatest cup of bitterness he had to swallow as a boy of college age. He was to see his tenant-farmer brother lashed by an overseer in the fields. He got a pistol, Tom did, and when the planter, Shep Wright, came to town, Tom called him off his horse and gave him a thrashing.[7]

"He always said he had to fight black despair in his mind. He got to be the best trial lawyer in the state. He fought for the poor croppers, the one-gallus farmers, the Negroes, and every underdog there was here in the state and in its politics. And he took no bribes.

"He went to Congress and they stole him out of office. He raised the Populist Party up to the top, but they stole that from him and broke his heart. But, there was enough of the lion in him to go to the United States Senate in 1920 and up-end that dignified body.

"The word 'demagogue' is just a noun. It doesn't explain the man.[8] He didn't produce the forces some folks say he set in motion. They produced him.

And they destroyed him. They made him bitter and mean when he had been great and good. When he failed, a class failed and the South failed. A lot of damn fools see his story as just a man's story. The same forces are loose today and will be until somebody can conquer race, economics, and traditions cast in the furnace of history.

"I can't tell you what he was like. He was one man till 1896. He was another man after that. Both lives were tragedies, and so there have been tragic things here ever since. . . ."

In the decade before 1896—the year of [William Jennings] Bryan's first defeat and the blasting of his own hopes—Watson's course threatened to pull down the feudal house which had been reelected in the South. Those who had built it up, beginning in 1872 after the restoration of Southern home rule, were the men we know as "Bourbons" and who at that time called themselves "New Departure Democrats."[9]

They were those of the old party who deserted the agrarian leaders of the past (best typified in Georgia by Alexander Stephens and Robert Toombs) and joined hands with the industrial barons of the North in bringing "progress" to the South. In Georgia the three leaders were Princeton-educated Alfred H. Colquitt, the war hero General John B. Gordon, and Joe Brown—all veterans of the old order who had turned to welcome, work for, and do the bidding of railroads, financiers, and various promotional syndicates from the North and East.[10]

They ruled far into the eighties, and their discipline was the discipline of fear—of federal interference, of return of federal troops, of the Negro vote, of the return of the scalawag, with federal protection. They promised security. They demanded and got allegiance. And always they talked of prosperity.

Then young Watson began to speak. He alone, of all the men in Southern politics in that era, raised his voice to point out that for the most part the promoters of the new industry were simply get-rich-quick exploiters. He damned the "New South " slogan as "sycophancy to success." It was a time when men talked only of factories, and some of the articulate voices of the day were suggesting that everyone in the south move to town and work for wages, leaving other regions to grow the food. The South was going to be rich, rich, rich, the orators and editors were saying. All but Watson.

He saw the farmers getting poorer and poorer, the interest rates rising and prices falling; he heard the increasing tempo of the auctioneer's hammer.

In the late eighties, before the days of soil conservation, he was writing and speaking of gullies and the land washing away. His speeches mention "barren wastes," "ruined lowlands," "barn and gin houses leaning on crutches. . . ."[11] He was writing of the tariff and bankruptcy laws that were ruining the farmer. The farmer was in the grip of the lien system, and Watson saw the farmers, the former masters, now peons to the city banker and merchant.[12]

He saw the new mill-town shacks and the miserable people in them, while others wrote of the poetry of the new industrial smoke in the soft Southern sky. He cried out that the "New South" was forging the machinery of exploitation, but the newspapers never published his speeches in any detail, and distorted what little they did print.

A paragraph from one such speech will serve—this in 1888:

> To you who grounded your muskets twenty-five years ago, I make my appeal. The fight is upon you . . . not bloody as then . . . but as bitter, not with men who come to free your slaves, but who come to make slaves of you. And to your sons also I call, and I would that the common spirit might thrill every breast throughout the sunny land, 'til from every cotton field, every hamlet, every village, every city, might come the shout of defiance to these Rob Roys of commerce and to the robber tariff, from whose foul womb they sprang.

But, after a while, the farmers, deeply mired in the economic system which was destroying them, began to listen. Their Farmers' Alliance was forming.

It has been suggested that the paradox of Watsonism is that it tried to be radical and retrospective at once, that it was a belated agrarianism directed against the Northern industrial masters which, when it failed, made Watson cynically attack the always vulnerable minority targets, Negroes, Catholics, and Jews. In reality, Watson saw the truth from the beginning, but until the late eighties was hesitant.

Reared in the Democratic Party, he had made his early successes in it. His heroes were Robert Toombs, the great [John] Gordon of Lee's last stand, and Alexander Stephens, that acidulous little husk of a man. But Gordon had gone whooping off with the "New Departure" Democrats, who joined the carpetbagger industrialists and the railroad barons. Even Toombs was not quite sure, and neither was Stephens. The young man hesitated. But by the late eighties he was sure. So, for the record, was Toombs.

Elected in 1882 to the Georgia assembly, Watson had begun to fight the old state Democratic machine. In the late eighties he set out to destroy it. This meant he had to attack the South's old social-political structure, and its new one, too.

In December, 1889, two hundred delegates from the Southern Farmers' Alliance and seventy-four from the Northern Alliance met in St. Louis. Talk of a country-wide insurgent movement was in the air. At St. Louis also were the Knights of Labor, the Colored Alliance and the Farmers' Mutual Benefit Association. They could not consolidate because, as always, there were those to whisper "Nigger," "Rebel," and "Yankee." But the Northern Alliance men from the states of Kansas and North and South Dakota did secede from their organization and join the Southern Alliance, then to unite on a platform with the Knights of Labor.

Watson had long been urging on the Alliance. Now the Southern Democratic Party began to tremble when he embraced the Alliance platform. In 1891 he went to Congress on that platform, and out of it grew the Southern wing of the Populist Party. Next year he founded his *People's Party Paper*, which became the chief voice of the movement. Two other papers, the *Revolution* (inspired by Watson's comment on the Alliance, "Not a revolt; it's a revolution") and the *Wool Hat*, were also effective. So great was the enthusiasm for the movement that in 1892, twenty-two Populist papers were being published in Georgia alone. Watson had to leave the Democratic Party in order to go with them.

He was to be called anarchist, Communist and madman.[13] But he was not to weary of this fight for many years. He almost singlehandedly forged a third party, and he would have captured the state had there not been a steal at Augusta. Even so, he was to be the balance of power for years—the maker of governors.

He became the sworn foe of monopoly—"not in the narrow sense of the word," as he phrased it, but "monopoly of power, of place, of privilege, of wealth, of progress."[14] He had to attack not merely the old social and political structures, but the problem of race. The Populist struggle in the South was made more complex and bitter by this problem. Later Watson, in rancor, was to damn the Negro for many things, including his own political failure. But in those days he attacked the problem fearlessly, with an honesty never before seen in the political life of the cotton South—and not heard since from any man of his political stature.

The Populist program called for unity between the white and Negro farmers. Watson put his appeal in his usual simple but image-creating words:

> Now, the People's Party says to these two men, "You are kept apart that you may be separately fleeced of your earnings. You are made to hate each other because upon that hatred is rested the keystone of the arch of financial despotism which enslaves you both. You are deceived and blinded that you may not see how this race antagonism perpetuates a monetary system which beggars both."

Watson did not merely speak and write. In public appearances before farmers deeply rooted in the old pattern of race hatred and prejudice, he cried out:

"It should be the object of the Populist Party to make lynch law odious to the people. . . ."

"I nominate this man (Negro) to the executive committee of the Populist Party as a man worthy to be on the executive committee of this or any other party. . . ."

"Tell me the use of educating these people as citizens if they are never to exercise the right of citizens. . . ."

He spoke from platforms where white and colored men sat together. He spoke to mixed audiences. He never advocated social equality, saying that this was something which every person decided for himself.[15] But he did insist, emphatically, upon political equality. He held that the incident of color made no difference in the interests of farmers, croppers, and laborers.

It is fair to say Watson was the first native Southerner to give intelligent and sympathetic ear to the legitimate aspirations of the Negro to full citizenship. He urged that the Negro, with a third party open, become an independent voter and cease being a pawn in the hands of the city machines. Trembling editors wrote of "anarchy."

The entrenched Democrats set out to defeat him for reelection in 1892. Another Watson victory, said Democrats, and he would rule the state. Bloodshed and fighting grew as the primary day drew near. Watson was defeated by the results in Augusta, where the Democratic vote against him was almost double the number of legal voters.[16]

Colonel Sandy Beaver, now a distinguished educator in Georgia and a member of the state Board of Regents, as a boy watched that great steal. Negroes, hauled into town in wagons from farms and plantations, were voted repeatedly by the Democratic machine. Many more Negroes were brought across the Savannah River from South Carolina and voted.

"I remember," Colonel Beaver told me, "seeing the wagonloads of Negroes brought into the wagon yards, the equivalent of our parking lots. There were barrels of whiskey there for them, and all night they drank and sang and fought. But the next morning they were herded to the polls and paid in cash, a dollar bill for each man as he handed in his ballot."

So Watson was defeated. He ended his House career with the 52nd Congress and returned to Georgia to take up the Populist fight once more.

Politically the year 1894 marked the lowest ebb of the Republic to that time. Watson opposed President Cleveland, the Democratic "reformer" of 1884, as an agent of Eastern corporate monopoly. He advocated nationalizing the railroads and any other corporation which was of a public nature. So, with bitterness and violence flaring anew, Watson fought once more for a seat in Congress, but, again in Richmond County, he was defeated when out of a total of 11,240 registered voters, his opponent received a majority of 13,780 votes. It was so brazen a steal that even the winner agreed to a second election. This was delayed, however, until a new registration law was passed that disfranchised thousands.

Many men who knew him say it was this which turned him from a people's man into the mad destroyer whose name was later to become a byword for hate, fear, and falsehood. Once Negroes had sought merely to touch his garments and had looked up to him with a reverence given to deities. In later years he was to become one who flogged them with words and phrases which sent white men to hunting them as animals, killing them with a savage joy. He was to loose his vitriol on Jew and Catholic, too.[17]

Yet it was not Richmond County which curdled his soul. Though it did drive him to the brink of frustration, he still fought back. Lightning still was in his hands and thunder in his voice. The people still followed him, and he believed in them.

It was 1896 that broke him.

For some never-to-be-known reason, he did not attend the St. Louis convention of the Populist Party in that historic year. The Democrats, meeting earlier, had nominated William Jennings Bryan for President and thereby stolen much of the Populist thunder. Many Populists, however, feared their cause would become submerged if they fused with the Democrats. Watson was one of these. Edward Bellamy, though saying that the real issue was between "men and money," swung to Bryan. So did Eugene V. Debs. Democratic big money, meanwhile, was crying "fusion."

In order to win fusion support, the Democratic Party had pledged itself in advance to take Watson as Bryan's running mate. But, violating its pledge, it had nominated Arthur Sewall instead. In many states the Democrats obtained fusion support from the Populists in return for aid in state-office elections. So the Populist convention fell into line and chose, or rather endorsed, Bryan. For vice-president, though, Tom Watson was the nominee.

Telegraphic communication was slow, and when Watson got the news, he hesitated. Since there was little time and the convention was waiting, he accepted the nomination against his better judgment. His acceptance was grist to the fusionists' mill. Though he supported Bryan, he believed that, through the Sewall deal, Bryan had betrayed him.

From then on only a few were left to fight. The Democratic Party sacrificed itself to destroy the Populist Party. Fusion, which had been achieved in many states, meant ruin to Populists, fusionists, and Democrats alike.

After the victory of the Republicans, Watson retired to Hickory Hill. He was in debt. He felt that his mind was going. He was defeated, and for the first time in his life he accepted defeat, and crept, brooding, into his tent. He began to write, in a brilliant, erratic style, books that sold well.

Slowly but surely the bright flames of the man's passion for truth and people burned out. For a few years he flared up now and then with his old fire. But it had less and less heat. By 1904 he was seeking to disfranchise the Negro, and so violent were his tirades—which were imitated by others—that the Georgia election of 1906 was followed by the Atlanta race riot, which lasted four days, bringing looting and murder in its train.

National progressivism and Southern agrarianism no longer were going along together. Watson had taken the latter down a new path, to the dismay of men and women all over America who had followed him as the first great crusader for human rights to come in their generation. For after the debacle of 1896, the

Southern agrarian road led downhill. The South today still cries out for a balance in her economy and still seeks to break the chains of the colonial economy forged there by tariffs and credits—just as Watson had seen it.

His own paradoxes became pathological. The Populist Party disappeared. Watson retained a following, and in Georgia most of the originals, the "Old Pops," were faithful if confused by the man they no longer knew.

In one issue of *Tom Watson's Magazine* he defended the Russian Revolution, attacked monopolists, the railroads, and Wall Street, and printed a bitter attack on Booker T. Washington and the Negro race. The Catholic Church and finally the Jew came to be, with the Negro, his targets. God alone knows how many Negroes were lynched and murdered by his words. The Catholic Church fought back. Men who sought to hold the seawall against the tide of hate and who helped defend Leo Frank in the infamous trial and lynching that followed were maligned and abused.

And so ran out the sands of decency, of honor, and of greatness. The Tom Watson who walked through the doors of Hickory Hill in 1896 never again emerged. What became of him no one knew—and none will ever know.

The Watson who came out of the door moved on, through the use of hatred, violence, and his vocabulary of prejudice, to a seat in the U. S. Senate in 1920. By now he was a drunken old man, racked with asthma, subject to colds, but still a dangerous man, an opponent who knew no rules. He spoke out, now and then, for the underdog. Now and then his family saw flashes of the old sweetness they had known when he was the spokesman for the people. But mostly it was whiskey and bitterness and brooding melancholy which darkened and dominated his mind.

On the night of 25 September 1922, he died. The largest floral offering at the grave was from the Ku Klux Klan.

So far had sunk the People's Man.

The New York *Times* said of him when he died that he was "a strange and vivid public character, that already seems legendary or fabulous."[18] There were routine editorials which hit at his career, and some expressed a quiet relief that life would now be more serene.

There was one man who had no doubts whatever about Tom Watson. He summed him up with no "ifs," "ands" or "buts." This was a man who was just out of the penitentiary, and so no one paid much attention to what he said.

But in September, 1922, Mrs. Tom Watson got a letter from Eugene Debs, who wrote:

"He was a great man, a heroic soul who fought the power of evil his whole life long in the interests of the common people, and they loved and honored him."[19]

He was all Debs said—and he was also something less than Debs said. His name was to become hated and his words were to leave wounds. Yet, there was this about him—he was never afraid to get out in front and lead. At his best he was very much like Franklin Roosevelt: He flung his faith at the people and said, "Take it!"

Notes—23

[1]Reprinted by permission of *New Republic*, ©1948, Harrison-Blaine of New Jersey, Inc.

[2]At that time the county was Columbia: C. Vann Woodward, *Tom Watson: Agrarian Rebel* (New York: Oxford University Press, 1963), p. 2.

[3]Russell was not "just out of the governor's chair"; he served as governor of Georgia, 1931-1933, and was seeking an "endorsement" term to the United States Senate in 1936.

[4]Watson's sister on the speakers' stand was Mrs. Julia Mary Watson Cliatt; *Atlanta Constitution*, 15 August 1936.

[5]Interestingly, although still sports editor, McGill covered this speech for the *Atlanta Constitution* as a "staff correspondent." He may have heard this "Mother Hubbard" comment, but the one he attributed to Russell in the press was: "I want to say that if he [Tom Watson] were to come back here today and hear Gene Talmadge trying to protest the Raskobs and the du Pont wealth of New York at the expense of the Georgia farmer, he would write a piece about Gene which would send him running clear to the Pacific ocean." Also the Thomson speech was not in July but August; *Atlanta Constitution*, 15 August 1936. Earlier in the campaign, Russell said: "If Tom Watson was living today the article he would write against Gene would burn him so badly it would take half of the Atlantic ocean to put him out"; *Atlanta Constitution*, 31 July 1936. Later he repeated this latter account but adapted to the new setting by substituting "rivers of these mountains" for "half of the Atlantic ocean"; *Atlanta Constitution*, 11 August 1936.

[6]Woodward, *Tom Watson: Agrarian Rebel*, pp. 1-2.

[7]Woodward, *Tom Watson: Agrarian Rebel*, pp. 42-43.

[8]For a recent study of Southern demagogues, see Cal M. Logue and Howard Dorgan, eds., *Oratory of Southern Demagogues* (Baton Rouge: Louisiana State University Press, 1981).

[9]Bourbon is "a ruler or politician who clings obstinately to ideas adapted to an order of things gone by"; quoted in Woodward, *Tom Watson: Agrarian Rebel*, p. 56.

[10]For an analysis of how John Gordon, Alfred H. Colquitt, and even Ben Hill eventually adopted Joseph Brown's plea for accommodation with the North and Southern prosperity, see Cal M. Logue, "Restoration Strategies in Georgia, 1865-1880," in Waldo W. Braden, ed., *Oratory in the New South* (Baton Rouge: Louisiana State University Press, 1979), pp. 38-73.

[11]For related discussions, see "Speech at Degive's Opera House," Atlanta, 19 May 1894, pp. 177-79, and "Speech at Thomson, Georgia," 27 July 1898, pp. 220-22, in Thomas E. Watson, *Life and Speeches of Thos. E. Watson* (Nashville, Tennessee, 1908).

[12]See "Speech in Congress," April 1889, pp. 90-106, and "Labor-Day Address at Augusta, Georgia," May 1891, pp. 74-89, in Watson, *Life and Speeches of Thos. E. Watson.*

[13]Woodward, *Tom Watson: Agrarian Rebel,* p. 240.

[14]See "Debate at Sandersville," 9 September 1892, pp. 107-25, and "Cooper Union Acceptance Speech, New York," 18 August 1904, p. 257, in Watson, *Life and Speeches of Thos. E. Watson.*

[15]See "The Creed of Jefferson, the Founder of Democracy," Douglasville, Georgia, speech, 4 July 1893, in Watson, *Life and Speeches of Thos. E. Watson,* pp. 163-65. McGill knew first-hand the difficulty and dangers involved in speaking to racially "mixed audiences." He did so in the 1940s when it was still generally unacceptable to whites. For example, after speaking at an "interracial forum" at Spellman College he felt "like a sacrificial lamb. . . . The critics on one side damn you as supporting the Claghorn type of congressman. The Ku Klux type mind hollers that you talk to audiences with Negroes in them"; *Atlanta Constitution*, 9, 13, and 17 April 1946; 11 May 1946; 12, 23, and 27 June 1946; 5, 8, and 15 July 1946; 3 and 4 August 1946; 9 October 1946; 13 November 1946; 3 and 5 December 1946; 23 July 1947; 27 September 1947; 22 January 1948; 9, 19, 27, and 29 February 1948; 1, 4, and 5 March 1948; 14 April 1948; 30 May 1948; 19 June 1948; 2 and 20 September 1948; 7 July 1949; 20 February 1950; and 14 July 1951.

[16]Woodward, *Tom Watson: Agrarian Rebel,* pp. 241-42.

[17]In his essay, "Tom Watson: Disciple of 'Jeffersonian Democracy'," G. Jack Gravlee concluded that, while "his bitter indictment of entire population blocs is not condoned, it can be understood. The second Watson probably felt betrayed, used, abandoned. He did not desert previous supporters—they deserted him"; in Cal M. Logue and Howard Dorgan, *Oratory of Southern Demagogues,* p. 107.

[18]Quoted in Woodward, *Tom Watson: Agrarian Rebel,* p. 486. McGill omitted "almost" before "legendary."

[19]Letter of 26 September 1922, quoted in Woodward, *Tom Watson: Agrarian Rebel,* p. 486. McGill added "s" to "interest."

Essay 24

Woodrow Wilson: The President[1]

On that fourth of March, 1913, when Thomas Woodrow Wilson took the simple oath required of one assuming the office of President of the United States, the sun shone brightly. All Washington basked in the warmth of a cloudless day.

There are always those at great inaugurations and coronations who seek for prophetic symbolisms and who bend their ears to hear any whispers by whatever oracles. It was so on that March fourth. Many who wrote of the occasion noted the brightness of the day and the sunlight which seemed to be a great spotlight focused on a new figure in American political life and government.

Certain it is that his inauguration was more than ordinarily meaningful in the history of the Presidency. He was the first Democrat to take the oath since Grover Cleveland in 1893. He was the first native Virginian to repeat the solemn obligation since Zachary Taylor; the first Southerner since Andrew Johnson. He was the first scholar, student of government, and intellectual since Thomas Jefferson.

And, as it was with Jefferson, the average citizen looked to him with hope and affection. Between Jackson's second term and Wilson's start in 1913, only Lincoln appears as a President who came to office with a positive policy which he was ready vigorously and intelligently to put forward.

Since that beautiful March fourth of forty-three years ago, there have been those who looked back at that day and sought for portents and prophecies in the events of it. On that day there was no sound of the riderless horses of the Apocalypse trampling the cloudless skies. But four years later the closing sentences of his inaugural took on new significance. He spoke of men's lives hanging then in the balance. And he said, too, "Here muster the forces of humanity." When years later, the "Great Betrayal" was accomplished, there were those who, poring over that inaugural, noted that Woodrow Wilson had declared that day, "Men's hopes call upon us to say what we will do."[2]

Whether there was inspired prophecy in it or not remains for the final unlocking of all the secrets of life. Taken as a speech, it was a good one which lifted up the hearts of those who heard it. They did not know him well, but they did know he was something new in their time. He was the product of no political machine. Indeed, as governor of New Jersey, he had exposed the corruption of his party's own organization in that state. He was not at all bound by old prejudices, forms, or customs. And as he stood there that March fourth, not merely the hearts of men were stirred but their minds, too. In a very real sense, he has never stopped doing that to the hearts and minds of his countrymen.

A tree, says an old axiom, is measured best when it is down. Though this be true, the measuring of political giants is never easy and seemingly never done. Through the years that are behind us many have been busy with yardstick and tape, not merely on Jefferson, Jackson, Lincoln, Woodrow Wilson, Franklin D. Roosevelt, but on those lesser than they. Friends, enemies, and coldly calculating researchers have been active across an increasing span of years, and the measuring is by no means completed.

The difficulty would seem to be that when the real giants come down, they fall always deep in the jungle of great social and economic changes above which they towered and out of which they grew. By the time the bearers of measuring rods have hacked their way to them, the processes of change have had time to accelerate or slow down. Hindsight comes to confuse and blur the image of the times in which they lived and wrought. This sometimes causes those busy with the task of measuring the fallen great to work hurriedly, even carelessly, and perhaps, now and then, to estimate rather than apply the stick. Inevitably, the sums thus attained vary, sometimes widely.

It is so with Woodrow Wilson. Some have presented him as an enigma, which assuredly he was not. In the long, weary months of his illness while still in office, he became by the very nature of things a mysterious figure. He was secluded. Only a few persons saw him. And so he became a "mystery" as the unseen, unknown always is. But save that man is without question a complex being, he was no enigma. He was, on the contrary, an almost obvious man.

When he stood to take the oath, he was so new to politics as to be relatively an unknown. Not too many Americans had followed his career at

Princeton. His scholarly writings on government had enjoyed no popular circula-
tion. His fight against "the bosses" in New Jersey and his campaign speeches had
stirred the imagination of those who were weary of the old pattern and tired of the
static character of the Republican Party and its principles. Theodore Roosevelt
had proved that many Republicans themselves suffered from a like weariness.
But, save for New Jersey and his public writings and addresses, Woodrow Wilson
had then, on 4 March 1913 no record by which the public and the politicians could
judge him.[3]

He was one of the old "Blue Stocking" Covenanter family strains. They
bred their children to discipline of mind and character, as did those families with
the Scottish traditions, and rectitude was woven into the tartan of their being.
Porridge and predestination produce men who live by the rules. If they can laugh
and joke, it is only in the presence of the family or a small, intimate group of close
friends. His cabinet was to know the man whose severe, Calvinist, schoolmaster's
face could relax into warmth and whose tongue could tell a story reminiscent of
the Lincoln tradition.

Once a cabinet member suggested to him that a task at hand be
abandoned for a diversion toward which he knew Wilson had planned.

"My Boss won't allow it," he said.

"Your Boss?"

"My conscience," said Wilson. "It drives me to do what seems my duty.
It frowns on temptations."

Again, he said of himself, "So far as I could make out, I am expected, as
President, to be a bloodless, thinking machine—whereas I am perfectly aware I
have in me all the insurgent elements of the human race. I am sometimes, by
reason of my Scottish ancestry, able to keep these rebels in restraint. The stern
Covenanter tradition that is behind me sends many an echo down the years."

But as he stood there on 4 March 1913, taking the oath as the twenty-
eighth President of the United States, his face was stern, his lips thin, his eyes
solemn. So great was his concentration and so severely were his emotions
controlled, that he did not feel the arthritic pains in his back and shoulder. For that
matter, none of the familiar old aches troubled him on that day. But they were
there. He was never a strong man physically. The spirit which flamed continually
in his frail body was to keep him going for almost eight turbulent, testing years. It
was the inaugural face which was to become most familiar to his fellow
countrymen.

(Even as he took the oath and began the huge task of national reform,
there were men across the seas who were moving toward a bridge and a pistol
shot at Sarajevo.)

In his inaugural address Woodrow Wilson listed six specific fields
requiring reform:

1. "A tariff which cuts us off from our proper part in the commerce of the world, violates the principle of just taxation, and makes the government a facile instrument in the hands of private interests."[4]

2. "A banking and currency system based upon the necessity of the government to sell bonds fifty years ago and perfectly adapted to concentrating cash and restricting credits."[5]

3. "An industrial system which, take it on all its sides, financial as well as administrative, holds capital in leading strings, restricts the liberties and limits the opportunities of labor, and exploits without renewing or conserving the natural resources of the country."

4. "A body of agricultural activities never yet given the efficiency of great business undertakings or served as it should be through the instrumentality of science taken directly to the farm or afforded the facilities of credit best suited to its practical needs."

5. "Water courses undeveloped, waste places unreclaimed, forests untended, fast disappearing without plan or prospect of renewal, unregarded waste heaps at every mine."

6. We have not "perfected the means by which our government may be put at the service of humanity, in safeguarding the health of the nation, the health of its women and its children, as well as their rights in the struggle for existence," and he pointed out in his pledge of "alteration" the need for sanitary laws, pure food laws, and laws determining conditions of labor which "individuals are powerless to determine for themselves," and this fundamental truth that guided all he proposed: "The first duty of the law is to keep sound the society it serves."[6]

The new President could have enumerated a seventh change. He planned to lift the Presidency itself from the low estate into which it had fallen. In his book *Congressional Government*, published six years before, he had expressed the conviction that the committees of the Congress had too long been allowed to exercise increasing power. He regarded government by Congressional committees as dangerous, even vicious. "This is the defect to which, it will be observed, I am constantly recurring; to which I recur again and again because every examination of the system, at whatever point begun, leads inevitably to it as a central secret." He did not believe anything to be wrong with the basic law. His concept of the Constitution was that the President must use all the power that is his; must, in fact, stand as sponsor for the policy of the government. Too many Presidents, he felt, allowed committees "to originate, compromise, and alter it." The man, he felt, makes the Presidency, and the Presidency the man.

He sought to gird himself, in determination to be a strong executive, with a cabinet of progressives. An opposition newspaper ran a picture of them under the heading "Wilson's Cabinet! Who are they?"[7]

Wilson named William Jennings Bryan as secretary of state. He was, perhaps, a bit reluctant so to do. Certainly some powerful protests were made.

Wilson, whatever his reservations, did not hesitate. Having in mind revenue and fiscal reform, the President chose William G. McAdoo. Wilson long had been concerned about "the money power" and its influence in government. A. Mitchell Palmer, floor leader of the Wilson forces in the long convention struggle at Baltimore, refused appointment as secretary of war because he was a sincere Quaker. It went to Lindley M. Garrison, vice-chancellor of New Jersey. J. C. McReynolds of Tennessee, later associate justice of the United States Supreme Court, was made attorney general. McReynolds had caught Wilson's eye by his effective work as a federal attorney in the antitrust action against the tobacco companies. Franklin K. Lane became secretary of the interior. He had become known to Wilson by his accomplishments on the United States Commerce Commission. Albert S. Burleson of Texas was postmaster general. David F. Houston, old friend and college president with agricultural experience, took the post of secretary of agriculture. William C. Redfield, of Brooklyn, an authority on the tariff and a businessman of stature, was given the portfolio of secretary of commerce. William B. Wilson, former Congressman and an officer of the American Federation of Labor, was a popular choice for secretary of labor.

Perhaps the most unusual choice was that of a then relatively obscure newspaper publisher of Raleigh, North Carolina, as secretary of the Navy. This was Josephus Daniels. He was to become the great rock in Wilson's often weary world. His faith in people, like Wilson's, had an almost mystic quality. It never wavered. He was Puritan but never the bigot. He was simple as truth is simple. He was loyal always, and without question, to friends and principles. It is well to note he made a good secretary of the Navy; that that branch of our armed services performed well in the great war which was to come to the Wilson Administration, and that one of his reforms, that of no liquor or wine on United States Navy vessels, has come to be accepted by even the most bibulous as a necessary restriction. And, too, this would seem to be the place to say that it was Daniels who brought an ebullient, very cocksure young man in to work as an assistant— Franklin Delano Roosevelt. Young Roosevelt thought the secretary of the Navy to be a curious, hayseed sort of man and for a while, behind the secretary's back, he was condescending and critical. But he, too, learned something of wisdom, loyalty, and the Democratic principle from him, and all his days he was to love Josephus Daniels and call him "chief."

This was the cabinet.

The opposition asked, "Who are they?"

But the *New York World* said of it: "Whether strong or weak in its various elements, this is no cabinet of political trade and barter. It is fashioned to placate neither sordid political interests nor sordid financial interests. Each member stands on its own merits."

The first step, Wilson and his cabinet agreed, would be tariff reform. The sugar, steel, and other commodity lobbies geared for the fight.

The battle was begun with a precedent-breaking reading of his tariff message to the Congress. It was the first time a President had so appeared since 1796. He declared for free competitive enterprise, saying, "A duty was laid upon the party now in power, at the recent election, which it ought to perform promptly in order that the burden carried by the people under existing laws may be lightened as soon as possible, and in order that the business interests of the country may not be kept too long in suspense as to what the fiscal changes are to be, to which they may be required to adjust themselves . . . the sooner the tariff is altered, the sooner our men of business will be free to thrive by the nature of free business, instead of by the law of legislation and artificial arrangement."

The old tariff foe of that time was high protection. It was true then, as it still is true, that the nation had moved far from the "modest notion of protecting" the industries of the country and moved boldly forward, as Wilson said, "to the idea that they (the favored industries) were entitled to the direct patronage of the government."

Wilson routed the lobby. His personal appearance before the Congress gave to the message a dynamic it otherwise might have lacked.

Then, too, his approach made sense in that it was not an uprooting of protection but a change from a special privilege to the status originally conceived for a protective tariff. The average rate of duties was reduced from 40 to 26 percent. (Wilson was urging then a policy which, curiously enough, the Eisenhower administration of 1952-56 found it necessary to adopt.) Wilson said, of our goods and farm products, "American energies must now be directed towards the markets of the world." Indeed, some of our present farm surplus distress may be traced to the economic theories of the Republican protectionists of the years immediately following the first great World War. When farm prices declined in 1920, they hurriedly put together the Fordney Emergency Tariff. Wilson warned that a high tariff on farm products on which the price was fixed in foreign markets could bring no relief.

On 4 March 1921, the eighth anniversary of his 1913 inaugural and his last day as President, Wilson sent a veto message (rare for him) to the Congress.

"The situation in which many of the farmers of the country find themselves," he said in this message, "cannot be remedied by a measure of this sort. There is no short way out of existing conditions, and measures of this sort can only have the effect of deceiving the farmers and raising false hopes among them. The farmer needs a better system of domestic marketing and credit, but especially larger foreign markets for his surplus products. Clearly, measures of this sort will not conduce to an expansion of the foreign market. Actual relief can come only from the adoption of constructive measures of a broader scope, from the restoration of peace elsewhere in the world, the resumption of normal industrial pursuits, the recovery particularly of Europe, and the discovery there of additional credit foundations on the basis of which her people may arrange to take from farmers and other producers of this nation, a greater part of their surplus production."

A resurgent Republican bloc sought to pass the tariff measure over the veto, but failed by twenty-one votes. So great was the determination to have such a law that President Harding, following his inauguration, called a special session of the Congress and the emergency tariff was passed with a great show of partisan piety. The substantial increases were the cornerstone of the Fordney-McCumber tariff legislation of the next year. This, and subsequent protectionist legislation, such as the Smoot-Hawley Act, was a part of the tragic mosaic of blunders which led to the economic collapse of Europe; the associated fall of the democratic governments established there following the great war; the rise of nationalisms, trade barriers, and dictatorships, and the coming of the somber depression to our own shores.

Wilson used a phrase in his veto meessage which a people seemingly conditioned to the problem of political promises might read with profit. He said, in that historic and prophetic message, that he would not be a party to giving "the promise to the ear which has been broken to the hope."

These results of a reversal of Wilson's policies were a part of the bitter future.

The tariff reform was but one part of Wilson's over-all plan of fiscal reform. He moved next to an old idea, that of an income tax. Provision for such a levy had been voted in Grover Cleveland's second administration. It had been declared unconstitutional by a somewhat suspect overnight change of mind by a judge. Since 1896 a fight had been made by Democrats to obtain an amendment to the Constitution authorizing the levying of such a tax. They argued the cost of government ought to be apportioned on ability to pay, and not entirely on the basis of consumer consumption—as did the tariff. Wilson's floor leaders pointed out that of the hundreds of millions the government received from the tariff and internal revenue taxes, a very small percentage was paid by those who profited most from the tariff.

On 25 February 1913, the Constitution was amended to give Congress the power to levy such a tax and the Underwood-Simmons act created a graduated income-tax law. When, a few years later, the nation was pulled into the great vortex of war, necessitating the raising of billions of extra dollars, the income-tax law was the basis for finding it and for causing those industries and persons whose incomes were greatly increased by the war to pay a more equitable share than otherwise would have been the case.

In 1913, the "Schoolmaster President" turned from victories in the tariff and taxation to attack the greater citadel of reaction—the banking system. Not since Andrew Jackson in 1832-33 had boldly moved against recharter of the Bank of the United States, had any President proposed so revolutionary a revision of the currency and banking system.

His specific proposals resulted in the creation of the Federal Reserve System. He did not, of course, suggest or write the Federal Reserve Act. Senator Carter Glass of Virginia, chairman of the House committee on banking and currency, was the leader of the shock troops in the great battle that ensued. It properly is said of him that he was the "father" of the act itself. But he said, after victory, the "one man more responsible for the Federal Reserve System than any living man is Woodrow Wilson. It was his infinite patience, it was his clear prescience, it was his unsurpassed courage, it was the passion of Woodrow Wilson to serve mankind, that overcame every obstacle, that surmounted every difficulty, and put the Federal Reserve banking system on the federal statute books of this country."

It was not an easy victory.

There were those who counseled delay.

"Why should we wait to crown ourselves with consummate honor?" asked Wilson.

On 23 June 1913 Woodrow Wilson again read a message to the Congress. It was a day nagged by heat and humidity. The President noted this, but added that they, and he, were in the presence of a public duty.

His message had been long in the making. As a professor teaching political economy and "government," Woodrow Wilson had taught and written of the need of change. After the panic of 1907, a study had been made and a central bank recommended. But Old Hickory had put the mark of the monster on the central bank of his time. Wilson and his associates did not want such an institution. The existing system was, he said, "perfectly adapted to concentrating cash and restricting credit."

His currency-reform message was as lucid as one of his classroom lectures. The heart of it was this:

"We must have a currency, not rigid as now, but readily, elastically responsive to sound credit, the expanding and contracting credits of every day transactions, the normal ebb and flow of personal and corporate dealings. Our banking laws must mobilize reserves; must not permit the concentration anywhere in a few hands of the monetary resources of the country or their use for speculative purposes in such volume as to hinder or impede or stand in the way of other more legitimate, more fruitful uses. And the control of the system of banking and of issue which our new laws are to set up must be public, not private, must be vested in the government itself, so that the banks may be the instruments, not the masters, of business and of individual enterprise and initiative."[8]

So the battle was joined.

Having seen the rout of the tariff lobbyists, the opposition bankers were more coy. They wrote, telegraphed, and sent discreet emissaries to see senators and congressmen. But Washington seemed surprisingly clean of lobbyists.

But at last they could endure it no longer. When the Senate was long locked in debate and stalemate, a small carefully selected group of the nation's most powerful bankers arrived unannounced and at night in Washington. They avoided the usual suites in their favorite hotels but went instead to the Army and

Navy Club. Soon senators and others with "influence" but no Navy or Army background, began to answer summonses to the club. A young Navy officer was interested and puzzled by the presence there of the non-military strangers who were having so many visitors. He told a friend who held a minor post with the Wilson administration. This friend recognized the news for what it was and soon the names of all the visitors and the length of their stay were in Woodrow Wilson's hands. The Congress learned them, too.

The flushed bankers requested a White House conference.

Old Andrew Jackson would have applauded the President's answer. He, too, had curtly refused a somewhat similar request. The President was cold and formal. He informed them he knew them for what they were, and anyhow, did not need to discuss terms with them since he intended to fight on for complete victory.

On the floor the fight was bitter. Those earnestly seeking to give the nation a flexible currency system offered strengthening amendments.

The great banking influences sought a central bank not governed by law. One of those who voiced opposition was Frank A. Vanderlip of the National City Bank of New York. In a strongly applauded address before the American Bankers Association on October thirtieth, he said, "It starts the country on an issue of fiat currency. There is no case in our history when a nation has started an issue of fiat money but the result has been a complete breakdown of the financial system of that country."

This was the majority opinion of the nation's financial interests. Senator Carter Glass, in writing of those bitterly contested days, told of how he himself originally had believed, and urged, the banks of the country should have minority representation on the central board at Washington which would supervise the entire system of twelve district banks. President Wilson differed. Glass was equally adamant. He was, after all, the leader of those actually in the fight. It was not possible, he thought, to win the political battle without such agreement, and so convinced was he that he put it in writing to the President.

Wilson's reply was typical. He said he did not propose to apply politics to the problem.

Two days later Senator Glass obtained a conference. He took along, by agreement, seven of the leading bankers. They argued with "fervor, force, persuasiveness" and with an air of finality. Wilson listened courteously and attentively. They concluded and sat back.

Senator Glass recalled that the President said very quietly, but with unmistakable resolution:

"Gentlemen, I challenge any one of you to point to a government board, in this country or anywhere in any other civilized country, upon which private interests are permitted to have representation.[9]

"In other words, the Federal Reserve Board is an altruistic body representing all the people of the United States, put there for the purpose of supervising this great banking system and seeing that no section and class is discriminated against in its administration. Its members are not permitted to have any banking affiliation or connection at all. They are not permitted to own bank stock of any description. There is no single element of acquisitiveness in the whole formation of that board or in its operation. The board is there to represent the people of the United States; and you might as well talk about giving the railroads of this country the right of minority representation on the Interstate Commerce Commission, appointed to supervise the railroads, as to talk about giving the banks minority representation on the Federal Reserve Board—and I didn't have sense enough at first to see it."

Mr. Wilson had read his message on July twenty-third. The bill reached the Senate on September eighteenth at 6:00 p.m. On December twenty-third the gaunt, weary President signed the bill into law. "It is a Christmas present for the American people," said one of those who watched.

The old policy of concentration of reserves, carefully nurtured by the speculative interests who profited most thereby, was at an end.

Wilson was not quite finished.

Farmers historically had been the ruthlessly exploited victims of unscrupulous and harsh operators in the credit system. Under the President's leadership the Congress enacted the Federal Farm Loan Act—the nation's first long-time credit loans for farmers.

Wilson moved ahead on the more minor pledges. He obtained repeal of the law giving American ships freedom from tolls in the Panama Canal because we had pledged there would be no discrimination and the nation's integrity was at issue. It was not an easy victory. Shipping interests opposed it with the enormous influence which was theirs to command.

Among those who supported him, even, there was some muttering. The President was a very human man. But there was a quality about him which was both strength and, insofar as "practical" politics was concerned, a weakness. He had the predestined faith of the Calvinist. He instinctively trusted his own great powers. He could never accept the theory that one must convince or compromise with one's adversaries. The eight-hour day came out of such a decision.

He was well into his campaign for reelection in August 1916 when the railroad brotherhoods and management came close to a strike and paralysis of the country. Weeks of negotiation dragged on. The issue was an eight-hour day and no reduction in pay.

Wilson, believing the eight-hour day practical and proper, asked for legislation to obtain it. The Democrats supported it, as did many House Republicans. In the Senate all Republicans save Bob LaFollette voted against it. They made it a campaign issue. In the big industrial states the industrial and rail leaders fought Wilson with all they had and managed to put all of them into the Republican column in the all-but-dead-heat election in November.

It went his way.

He plodded ahead, determined to be a liberal, progressive President, seeking always to do what he believed best for people in general.[10]

He put all his influence behind the Clayton Antitrust law, which established by law the fact the "labor" is not a "commodity" but a human contribution to the economy and to society.

Every measure which he had urged upon the Congress up to the time of the crippling stroke suffered at Pueblo in September 1919 became law.

All the new legislation was standing well the test of time. Even the most violent opponents of the Federal Reserve System were convinced.

Banker Vanderlip, who had prophesied a complete breakdown of the financial system, had seen how the system had enabled the nation to finance the war and had gone to Carter Glass and said so, admitting his opinion had been wrong. All the pledges had been kept.

But on that 4 March 1913 there were no war clouds anywhere save, perhaps, in the Balkans. And already the phrase "trouble in the Balkans" had become something of a jest. They were very far away, and remote, and most Americans thought of them as somehow comic-opera countries. There was talk, too, that Germany, balked in her African colonial expansion by the French and British, was building a great navy to match that of England's. And the French still bristled over the Franco-Prussian war. But no one wanted war.

In April 1914 the Mexican problem, which President Wilson had inherited, caused some worry and embarrassment. General Victoriana Huerta had brought off a blood coup in the closing days of William Taft's administration, and that good and kindly man had soundly denounced him. President Wilson had refused to recognize Huerta, saying:

"So long as the power of recognition rests with me, the government of the United States will refuse to extend the hand of welcome to anyone who obtains power in a sister state by treachery and violence." Huerta began a series of slights and affronts. Great pressure was put on Wilson to intervene. He refused, but in April did land naval units at Vera Cruz to prevent a large shipment of German arms from reaching Huerta. There was an uproar of criticism and applause, but the net result was Huerta's flight.

Spring in 1914 was a trying one. It was hot and humid. Mrs. Wilson was not well and obviously was failing. May seventh she attended the quiet wedding of her daughter Eleanor to Secretary McAdoo. In June she was much worse.

So it was that no one in Washington seemed to pay much attention to the news of June twenty-eighth. In Bosnia an Austrian archduke had been shot.

Secretary Bryan was busy making peace treaties. In July, while Austria and Serbia exchanged notes, Mr. Wilson sent twenty of the secretary's treaties to the Congress. (Bryan was to obtain more than thirty signatures, some of them after war had begun in Europe.)

Some of the polite foreign diplomats who signed Mr. Bryan's treaties must have had great difficulty keeping a straight face. In a sense it was a somewhat ridiculous, innocent, and empty gesture. But America was an innocent country in that time, and Wilson and most of his cabinet were, in that sense, innocent men.

The pistol shot at Sarajevo sounded the death knell of innocence. The world would never know that quality again—not as it existed in the spring of 1914. It had been a time of faith and of optimism. Christian hopes were high that perhaps, after all, the brotherhood of man was a possibility.

As Ellen Wilson lay dying in the sweltering end of July and the beginning of August, they kept from her the news that Europe had flamed into war. She, too, had believed in Mr. Bryan's pacifism; and his peace treaties, so ridiculous in later and more cynical years, did not seem at all silly to her—or to millions of wives and mothers like her. When she died in the late afternoon of August sixth, the great powers of Europe had declared war and the smaller nations were coming in fast.

By the bedside of his dying wife, Woodrow Wilson had looked at the beginning of war as incredible. The deliberate speed of her approaching death and the weariness of his frail body held him in a sort of hypnosis. All else outside that reality seemed unreal.

The war was a shock. There had been across the years of peace a flowering of idealism and belief in the goodness of human nature and of civilization. America, of course, must be neutral. Almost everyone agreed to that in the early days while the armies mobilized and began their drives across frontiers.[11]

But as the funeral train took the long, sad road to Rome, Georgia, with the quiet, respectful crowds standing still and silent, hoping the broken man inside would somehow know how sorry they were, he did not think much about war. Ellen Axson Wilson had been wife and prop, comforter and friend. Such persons, when they go, leave a vacuum of pain and loneliness.

Back in the dreadful heat of Washington, neutrality began to be less popular. The agony of Belgium had begun two days before Ellen Wilson had died. It was at flood tide when the President returned to take up the burden of office—a burden which daily grew heavier. The shrilling of those who wanted war, and those who didn't, was beginning to grow in volume, insistent and discordant. But he clung stubbornly to neutrality.

So the steaming heat of August slowly gave way to the first cool breath of autumn, and the cold, raw wet of winter came and went, and it was spring again.

The war news had never been really good, save for the great, pulse-quickening gallantry of the allied troops at the Marne and the bloody struggle to keep the Kaiser's gray tide from flowing over all of France.

On 7 May 1915 neutrality became more difficult. The Germans sank the *Lusitania* with a torpedo from a submarine and 124 peaceful American noncombatants, men, women, and children, were lost. For a day the nation seemed stunned. Then the wildly protesting wrath boiled up until the nation itself seemed to shake with the poundings from pulpit, rostrum, and editorial sanctums. The grief and rage of the people were the greater because they felt betrayed. All at once those who had refused to believe all the ghastly stories of atrocities in Belgium were convinced the Germans were, indeed, Huns.

Grief and anger were a gale, buffeting the White House. Then came pictures of the dead bodies of women and children, their husbands and fathers, taken from the cold waters off Ireland where the *Lusitania* had gone down, brought ashore at Queenstown, Ireland. The gale became a storm. The hot-blooded who wanted war cried "coward." Editors who itched for battle, which others would fight, denounced the President as a human icicle, a heartless, callous man. Theodore Roosevelt, who originally had stood for neutrality, called Wilson a "Byzantine legothete," and newspaper reporters, who had hurried to their dictionaries, explained to their readers that the Rooseveltian epithet meant a person who expounded much and acted never.

Wilson, outraged and himself even less able to keep his thoughts neutral, sent a sharp-edged protest through diplomatic channels. Never again, after the *Lusitania,* did America seem so "kindly separated by nature and a wide ocean from the exterminating havoc of one-quarter of the globe."

There was a reviewing of the United States fleet off New York. It was a good show and the secretary of the Navy began to grow in popularity.

Germany's reply was not satisfactory and in June, as the cabinet discussed a second and sharper note, William Jennings Bryan resigned as secretary of state. The *Lusitania* had carried war goods and ammunition, and Bryan felt the British had unfairly allowed civilians, especially neutral Americans, to travel on her. Robert Lansing succeeded him.

Bryan's resignation made the pacifists more clamorous. Those who hated England, and they were many, accused Wilson of dragging us into war. Those who admired Germany, and they were by no means few, angrily charged Wilson was being duped by Britain. But now, Wilson was writing the notes and they were more difficult for the Germans. Their penetration and logic began to cause the American people to have a better perspective of the diplomatic struggle. Wilson, like the great mass of inarticulate people who did not want to become involved in a distant European war, was learning. A great, strong nation cannot avoid being involved, once war begins, because of its strength. Those at war will not let it be.

It was that spring, too, that Francis and Jessie Woodrow Wilson Sayre brought a grandson on a visit to the White House. A friend of the President's daughter came to call, Mrs. Edith Bolling Galt, Virginia-born, widow of a successful businessman. His friends rejoiced to see the lonely, burdened man suddenly happy in her company. But, as our political history so invariably shows, the gossip against a President almost always is scurrilous and worse. Those who hate Presidents will stoop to astonishing depths of meanness if they think they can thereby do harm. They charged, among other things, the President had written indiscreet letters to another lady, an old friend, Mrs. Mary Hulbert Peck. Mrs. Galt, worried lest the gossip harm the President, suggested they see each other no more. But the President had other ideas. The formal engagement was announced. The gossips kept on. A worried Joe Tumulty, confidential secretary, went to his chief. "Don't worry, Joe," he said calmly. "There was not a single word in [those letters] that even requires an explanation." And there wasn't.

Shortly before Christmas, Saturday, December eighteenth, at 8:30 p.m., they were married at Mrs. Galt's home in Washington. The simple ceremony was performed jointly by the Reverend Herbert S. Smith, rector of the Episcopal Church of which the bride was a communicant, and the Reverend James H. Taylor, pastor of Central Presbyterian Church where the President worshiped. They had two weeks at Hot Springs, Virginia, and then returned to Washington's cold, damp winter, and the shadow of the ever-darkening war clouds. Possessed of tact, wit, wisdom, and graciousness, Mrs. Wilson measured up always to the high standards the American people have established for the mistress of the White House. In sickness and in health, she was by her husband's side to comfort, advise, and sustain until he passed on into the great mystery and its silence.

The lonely man, the reserved man, who loved people and had for them one of the few deeply genuine compassions to be found in the history of our politics, could give personal, intimate affection only to his family and his chosen friends. He had need of such a wife and companion.

The days of neutrality were fast running out. They had begun on 4 August 1914. They ended officially on 6 April 1917—a span of 197 tortured, turbulent days.

Slowly, always slowly, Wilson and the nation moved with reluctant feet toward war. Both were isolationist, he and the country. In all the history of the United States there has been no stronger, more sincere isolationist than Woodrow Wilson.

There was a pragmatic, political argument in behalf of neutrality. More than once he said to cabinet members that war would destroy all he was trying to do—perhaps all he had been able to accomplish—for the country. War, he said, would set the country back twenty years or more. The money changers would get back into the temple. When the people's attention was distracted by war, the corruptionists would infiltrate into war contracts, and have a field day generally. The democratic processes would be strained. And, loving people as he did, the thought of casualties, with those of Europe terribly before him, had given him strength to announce neutrality, and to stand for it in those early months of the war.

He was by no means alone. In the September issue of the *Outlook* Theodore Roosevelt wrote, "It is certainly eminently desirable that we should remain entirely neutral and nothing but urgent need would warrant breaking our neutrality and taking sides one way or the other."

Wilson hoped, as 1916 began, that the warring nations, weary of the slaughter, would turn to a neutral United States for mediating their differences. It was in this spirit of hope he kept writing the notes and carrying on his negotiations.

But spring moved on towards summer and it was an election year. And the Democratic prognosis was not too favorable. Teddy Roosevelt, seeing no hope, refused the nomination of the Progressive Party and that organization, robust and confident in 1912, died. The Republicans went to the United States Supreme Court for their candidate and nominated Charles Evans Hughes, an associate justice and former governor of New York.

The Democrats, meeting in St. Louis, had only the formality of nominating Wilson. As vice-president they chose Thomas R. Marshall of Indiana, who described himself as "Wilson's only vice."

German elements, which had defended the sinking of the *Lusitania*, were strong in some areas of America, and the campaign began with emphasis on loyalty and an end to "hyphenated" citizenship.

The Democrats laid stress on their domestic achievements and the "Big Brother" policy toward Mexico—a policy severely strained that same year by Pancho Villa. In revolt against his old ally, Venustiano Carranza, and angry with the United States for recognition of him, Villa raided across the border at Columbus, New Mexico, killing and burning. General John J. Pershing led a punitive force into Mexico after Villa, but Carranza protested and Pershing was withdrawn. Wilson, having inherited the Mexican problem from the Taft Administration, was determined to reverse the policy of "dollar diplomacy."

In the East and along the Atlantic Seaboard generally, the sentiment was for war, was critical of Wilson. Candidate Hughes made no promise to go in, but denounced the methods employed in maintaining neutrality.

In the West there was strong sentiment against war. There the slogan, "He kept us out of war," used in the nominating convention by Governor Martin H. Glynn, had meaning. Wilson made it always clear that the issue of peace or war was not in his keeping. Never once did he say he had "kept us out of war."

Save for a few short trips, President Wilson remained at Shadow Lawn, New Jersey. Every Saturday afternoon he spoke from his front porch. In our time of heavy pressure campaigning, and the saturation quality of radio and television, the campaign of 1916 seems almost primitively innocent.

Candidate Hughes spoke in all parts of the country, and was carpingly critical. Wilson, reading the criticisms, said, "If you will give that gentleman rope enough, he will hang himself."

A rail strike threatened in the midst of the campaign. Wilson met it with the Adamson Law—bringing to labor the eight-hour day—which aroused all the industrial management power against him.

In the main, the candidates observed the amenities, but hardly anyone else did. It was a campaign of slander, viciousness, and bitter invective. Perhaps the worst was Teddy Roosevelt. Hot for war, he called Wilson that "damned Presbyterian hypocrite," and not so openly but still not exactly privately, flayed Hughes as a "bearded iceberg."

By nine o'clock on the night of election day. Republicans were jubilant. Impromptu celebrations began. New York, Indiana, Connecticut, and even New Jersey, traditional pivotal states, had gone to Hughes. Newspapers supporting Wilson conceded at about 11:00 p.m., and Charles Evans Hughes went to bed believing himself President of the United States. Wilson, Secretary Joe Tumulty recalled, seemed casual and carefree, though disappointed he had not convinced the people.

But by dawn's early light, the scene was not quite the same. In Ohio, Governor James M. Cox, progressive Democrat running on a distinguished record, was again returned to office, and Wilson, too, was partner in the triumph. Kansas went for Wilson. Minnesota swung back to Hughes and, finally, there were only the California returns incomplete. They would decide.

In Los Angeles, where the count was suspiciously slow, armed and vigilant men watched every box.

At last they were all counted and Wilson had a majority of 3,777. His electoral vote was 277 to 254 for Hughes and his popular majority was 568,822. He received a total of 9,116,296 votes, the largest vote ever given a President up to that time.

His inaugural was like a prayer:

"I pray God I may be given the wisdom and the prudence to do my duty in the true spirit of this great people—"[12]

In the rejoicing at that second inaugural few noted the apprehension in his voice. But it was there. The patient writer of notes, the severe man who so often had tears in his eyes, knew how exorably, and with what dread feet, war was nearing. He had initiated preparedness programs, but he knew that because of the country's inertia they would not be enough. The big wide ocean had caused us to give little attention to military aircraft production plants. Our artillery was obsolete. Our training was designed for the American terrain.

Many voices were screaming at him. The congressmen and senators with German votes in their districts and states were demanding he break the British blockade. Without doubt, it was doing some violence to American traditions of freedom of the seas, but Wilson stood firm. He admired the British for their courage and they were not sinking any passenger ships with torpedoes.

The U-boats, new and frightful weapons in effectiveness, sank some ninety ships from February to early June, 1915. Among them was the *Lusitania*.

Germany pledged to give warning to all passenger ships, but the pledge was broken. In December, 1916, Wilson asked all belligerents to state their war aims—hoping to precipitate mediation.

On January twenty-second, in an eloquent address to the Senate, he made one of his most prophetic statements, "It must be peace without victory," he said. "Only a peace between equals can last—"13

Nine days later the Germans answered. They announced unrestricted submarine warfare. They would sink all ships in the war zone—including those of the United States. It was an almost unbelievable, shocking decision.

Yet it was not hastily made. In Europe the war was deep in mud and blood, and bound by miles of barbed wire. The blockade was pinching German stomachs. And if we somehow should be able to create one, the high command believed submarines could sink most of the ships transporting it. If they struck hard enough, the war might be ended before we could produce an army worth the name. So, the Germans gambled.

In Wilson's hands, known only to his cabinet, was proof German diplomats in the Kaiser's embassy had offered Mexico the states of Texas, Arizona, and New Mexico if she would join Japan in attacking us. On 3 February 1917 the German ambassador was handed his passports.

Still, Wilson clung to the hope of peace. He would not go to war without an overt act by the Germans.

Shipping all but ceased. United States ports were crowded with ships, liners, and freighters. The docks were piled high with goods. New York City had food shortages and housewives demonstrated.

Wilson asked for authority to arm merchant ships. The House passed the bill overwhelmingly. But in the Senate eleven senators, largely from states with substantial German population, filibustered until an adjournment was forced 3 March 1917. It was an angry President who denounced the "little group of wilful men" who had rendered their country "helpless and contemptible."

Then, realizing the Constitution made him commander-in-chief of the armed forces, he armed the ships anyhow. In six days four ships were armed and steadily, then, a succession of vessels headed out toward England and France.

In March four small United States freighters, daring the seas unarmed, were sunk with loss of thirty-six men. (In that same March the Russian throne fell, and a liberal provisional government was set up. Most Americans, never caring much for Kings, Kaisers, or Tsars, were rather glad. At the time it seemed like a revolution leading towards democracy—as it might have, had other men done better thinking and planning, and had fortune been more benign.)

Wilson knew, after the filibuster by the "little group of wilful men," the temper of the people. They were no longer neutral. Nor was he.

Killing civilians was not regarded as "civilized" in 1914-16, and the submarine was the symbol of murder and of "the Hun."

And Wilson, and others, had begun to see that if we did not fight in 1917 when there were allies, we would one day have to fight the Kaiser, and his dream of conquest, alone.

If we had to fight, as we did, Wilson was the man providentially provided to lead us. We were idealists. So was he. We had been isolationist. So had he. We and he were innocents together. No dreams of empire stirred in him or us as in the minds of the French, British, and Germans.

True idealism, intellectual capacity, and honesty lead men instinctively to say the right things, to take the right course.

On April sixth, he came before a joint session of the Congress, tense, yet convinced, though nearly all there had the feeling of Gethsemane.[14]

Earnest, stern, his eyes grave, his gaunt face the more deeply lined, he was in appearance, voice, and drama the vehicle of the American spirit and dream awakened to the fact that they represented a great power which could not stand aside when a great moral issue was at stake.

It was to be, he told them, "a war without rancor and without selfish object, without revenge. . . ."[15]

He held them so still one could hear the breathing in the great chamber.

"There is one choice we are incapable of making: We will not choose the path of submission and suffer the most sacred rights of our nation to be ignored or violated. . . ."[16]

The stillness held—

"Why must we fight? Why must 'force to the utmost' be not for conquest? Why must we go to war?"[17]

"For democracy, for the right of those who submit to authority to have a voice in their governments, for the rights and liberties of small nations, for a universal dominion of right by such concert of free peoples as shall bring peace and safety to all nations and make the world itself at last free."[18]

There was no hymn of hate, no cry for blood or vengeance.

Then came his great peroration—and prayer:

"It is a fearful thing to lead this great, peaceful people into war, into the most terrible and disastrous of all wars, civilization itself seeming to be in the balance. But the right is more precious than peace, and we shall fight for the things which we have always carried nearest our hearts, for [this] democracy, [this right] . . . to such a task we can dedicate our lives and our fortunes, everything that we are and everything that we have, with the pride of those who know that the day has come when America is privileged to spend her blood and her might for the principles that gave her birth and happiness and peace which she has treasured. God helping her, she can do no other."[19]

Joe Tumulty remembered that he rode back to the White House with the President, the applause of the chamber and that of the people who lined the streets still in their ears. It was the cheers of these people which seemed to bother Mr. Wilson as he sat "silent and pale" in the cabinet room. At last he said:

"Think of what it was they were applauding. My message today was a message of death for our young men. How strange it seems they would applaud that."

Joe Tumulty wrote that this simple sentence was the key to an understanding of Wilson. "All politicians pretend to hate and dread war," he wrote in 1921, "but Woodrow Wilson really hates and dreads it in all the fibres of his human soul; hates it and dreads it because he has an imagination and a heart; an imagination which shows his sensitive perception, the anguish and the dying which war entails; a heart which yearns and aches over every dying soldier and bleeds afresh with each new made wound."[20]

This war, to which Wilson, the pacifist and isolationist, led them, had from the beginning perhaps our highest degree of unity.

And Wilson became the voice of the war and of all those opposing Germany and her allies. It was needed. The war went badly in April and May. The submarines, ordered to step up their pace, sank ships at an average of nine per day. They slowly were nullified when the Americans insisted on the convoy system, and as other antisubmarine techniques began to be developed.

The United States was prepared mentally—but otherwise there was a hopeless snarl of red tape, a confusion of effort, and a great lack of comprehension as to the size and global demands of the conflict.

"It is not an army that we must train for war," said Wilson, "but a nation."

A dismayed Congress voted the necessary authority. A war cabinet was created. Bernard M. (Barney) Baruch was called from his office to head up the War Industries Board. It established priorities, fixed prices, cut down waste, and stood off the chiselers and corruptionists with increasing success.

Slowly, surely, order emerged from chaos. Production—the vital goods to keep European allies going—began to come from the factories.

With war came high wages—silk shirts in the shipyards—and high prices. Living costs pinched the average home. There was resentment at the high war wages and the prices, and there were strikes—none serious. A National War Labor Board was established. A War Trade Board began, by license, to control exports and imports. A Fuel Administration took over the acute problem of coal. The shocked nation, never having considered the possibility of shortages, was asked to sacrifice with "heatless Mondays," "meatless Tuesdays," "wheatless Mondays and Wednesdays," "porkless Thursdays and Saturdays." "Victory gardens" sent men and women to digging in vacant lots and back yards.

They all believed in Wilson. They were inspired by his idealism, and so they did a really amazing job of following their leaders—voluntarily.

Herbert Hoover led the the Food Administration, ably and well. It is somehow revealing, in 1956, to pore over the old records and find him coming to Woodrow Wilson for help against the industrial and manufacturing groups, some of which seemed to him citadels of greed and reaction.

But over all was the keystone problem of ships. The enemy, and our allies, were across the Atlantic.

The Shipping Board, created in 1916, was joined in harness with the Emergency Fleet Corporation. Enemy ships were taken over. More than one hundred interned vessels of neutral nations were requisitioned, their owners being fully compensated.

"Ships for Victory," with haste the watchword, lost time and money with experiments in concrete ships. Yet, slowly but surely, the building program gained in momentum. Five hundred and thirty-three craft were completed in 1918.

Wilson never deviated once his mind was made up. The railroads were not doing a good job in meeting the demands on them. There were then more than thirty rail companies, and there was little cooperation between them. Indeed, so great was the competition between them, they often were at cross purposes. Management in general did not like the President because of the labor legislation he had supported over their objections. They did not like suggestions from the government and they again came into conflict with their employees. The war machine began to slow down. Continued slowness meant a German victory.

The President took over the railroads. William G. McAdoo was made director general. The opposition made hysterical protest and dubbed McAdoo, who had married Wilson's daughter Eleanor, "the Crown Prince." There was constant and unending carping. But the railroads ran. The rates were kept low. The moaning managements were guaranteed a high financial return. Economy was not a factor. Not too many persons knew that, if America could not work a miracle of production, the war would be lost. The ships had to be built. The railroads had to deliver steel. There had to be all possible speed. Winning the war, not running a cheap railroad, was the objective. The wartime deficit amounted to $862,000,000. But McAdoo got them out of their cross-purpose snarl. It cost money, but the job that otherwise would not have been done, was.

Victory loans and thrift stamps helped finance the war. George Creel came on to head up the committee on public information, and American propaganda entered the war.

Wilson was indeed training the nation for war. There were the usual cases of disloyalty—really very few, considering the great numbers of German-Americans who believed Germany's cause just—or at least as much so as that of Britain. Many Americans had believed with them—until the submarines changed their thinking. The German-Americans proved they were, first of all, Americans.

Worst of all was the hysteria and the bigotry. Gossip, rumor, and lies by hate groups caused a revulsion against things German. Some states and cities forbade the playing of German music and the teaching of the language. Stupidity and the worst in man came to the top along with the best.

Josephus Daniels and the Navy command came through with the greatest job of the war. The secretary brought off a great building program, and fended off the armor-plate cartels with skill. Some 2,079,880 soldiers were convoyed to France without the loss of a single man crossing on American transports.

Only one troopship was lost in the crossing—an almost unbelievable record. This was an English vessel, sunk near the Orkney Islands. The United States Navy patrolled the coast of France, did work in the Baltic and the Mediterranean. Late in the war it carried out a suggestion by the assistant secretary of Navy, Franklin D. Roosevelt, and laid a mine barrage across the North Sea. The plan accounted for 8 1/2 percent of the total number of enemy subs sunk or so badly damaged as to be put out of service.

Joe Tumulty, in his memoirs, wrote of the "magnificent and aggressive" leadership, so well thought-out and planned. He said that many months before war at last came, the President reached certain firm decisions. First of all, there was to be no "politics" in the conduct of the war. Secondly, no political generals were to be selected. Thirdly, all possible energy and force the nation could muster would be placed behind the Army and Navy. Fourth, every effort would be made to embargo speculators, contractors, and profiteers.

All were astonishingly well kept.

Item two of those prewar plans meant that Theodore Roosevelt would not be given a command. He was still dreaming of Rough Riders, and while he and his regiment would have been picturesque, they would never have fitted into the sort of Army needed in France. Save for the most violent partisans, none questioned the wisdom of the decision.

General John J. Pershing, named commander of the American Expeditionary Force, did not ask for General Leonard Wood, a capable officer, but in poor health. Indeed, General Pershing privately said he did not want him. It was a grievous decision, and strong was the protest. But the President, refusing to reveal Pershing's request, declared he would back up his commander so long as he was doing the necessary job.

At first there had been the usual, human hope we would not need to send an army. But from England and France came the word, "We are bled white."

On 4 July 1917 for morale purposes only, General Pershing and a small force were paraded through Paris. But there was no army. Back at home, on newly scraped parade grounds, hard by the new pine barracks, an army was being manufactured. Conscription was invoked. France and Britain sent men to help with the training. The draft, which the fearful said would result in riots, worked well because it was basically fair. The drafting, recruiting, and training went on at frantic speed. Russia's collapse, releasing hundreds of thousands of battle-toughened German troops to fight in France, gave the Kaiser numerical superiority.

It was 23 October 1917 before the first detachment of U. S. troops saw action. It was a small, token force. But thousands were taking two months of training in France. And America began to hear new songs—especially one about a fabulous "Mademoiselle from Armentières."[21]

Much of our shipping, artillery, aircraft, and other material was borrowed from the allies. "Send men," they said, when the United States programs in production of artillery, fighter planes, and automatic weapons were delayed.

Late in May, 1918, the Germans were within forty miles of Paris. United States Marines and men of the First Division, about 30,000, were thrown into the fighting at Château-Thierry. In June, the Marines won a bloody, spectacular engagement at Belleau Wood. By July, when the second Battle of the Marne began, some 140,000 United States troops were in the lines. By September, the total was almost 200,000.

General Pershing held out for a separate United States Army, and Wilson, as usual, backed him. A large segment of the front became his responsibility—a line stretching northwestward from the Swiss border to join the French eighty-five miles away.

On 26 September 1918, the allies jumped off in a great assault in what was designated as the Meuse-Argonne offensive. There were 1,200,000 Americans among the millions thrown at the Germans. There were forty-seven days of bitter, deadly fighting and the Germans, reeling under the attack, the shortages at home, the collapse of allies, and Wilson's sledge-hammer blows of the fourteen points, agreed to an armistice. The guns ceased on November eleventh.

Some 4,000,000 Americans had been put into uniform. There were 333,734 casualties, of which 130,274 were deaths. Of these, 49,000 were killed in battle. France, in comparison, had 1,700,000 dead in battle and the British empire 900,000.

Wilson had become the allied voice when he read his eloquent war message. His fourteen points as a basis for peace proved to be as powerful as guns, perhaps more so. William Allen White, critic and admirer of the President, said that the Germans surrendered to Wilson's fourteen points, and to famine, produced by the British Navy.

The famed fourteen points were set forth in a message to Congress 8 January 1918. George Creel had them translated into all the languages of Europe and sent them by cable and wireless to every receiving office and station. Planes dropped millions of copies over Germany.

There were to be "open covenants of peace, openly arrived at," freedom of seas, removal of all possible economic barriers, and equality of trade conditions. Armaments would be reduced and colonial claims impartially adjusted. Russia would receive the cooperation of the other nations for independent determination of her own political development. Belgium would be restored. All French territory would be freed and Alsace-Lorraine returned. Italy's frontiers were to be readjusted along lines of nationality. Rumania, Serbia, and Montenegro were to be reestablished. The Turkish portions of the Ottoman empire would be granted sovereignty. An independent Polish state would be erected.

The fourteenth point called for a "general association of nations" formed under specific covenants for the purpose of affording mutual guarantees of political independence and territorial integrity to great and small states alike.

Millions of weary, hungry, saddened, sorrowing, grieving people read them, or heard them read, and took them to their hearts.

From that time, until the bickering and visionless deeds of the peace treaty sessions began, the entire world was at a peak of idealistic hope and faith it had never known before—and has not since experienced. Neither before nor since has any other man occupied so firm a position as the moral leader of the world.

In his first inaugural in 1913 Woodrow Wilson had said, "Men's hearts wait upon us; men's lives hang in the balance; men's hopes call upon us to say what we will do. . . ."

Wilson's declarations for the self-determination of peoples and the League of Nations were ideas he had begun to formulate early in the war. When the pacifist, the isolationist idealist learned no great power could in fact be neutral, or hope to escape from war, he determined to find a way, if not to end war, at least to make it difficult to develop.

As usual, he acted forthrightly.

But with the silencing of the guns, the great cementing need and desire for victory crumbled. Politics, which has as its end objective the obtaining of power, reasserted itself in its most blindly partisan form. Wilson, with his mind fixed almost solely on a peace which would end war, made an appeal for a Democratic Congress to hold up his hands. Other Presidents, notably Abraham Lincoln and Theodore Roosevelt, had done so before him. But the Republicans seized on it, and called it a plea for power to establish a dictatorship—and worse.

Republican Party leaders looked ahead toward the 1920 race. Wilson, if he managed well, might enable the Democrats to win another national election. So by every known device, including the worst and most recklessly demagogic, the Repulicans set out to tear him down. "Egotist" . . . "Trying to play God" . . . "hogging the whole show" . . . "mushy sentimentalist" . . . "faker" . . . "hypocrite" . . . were some of the milder phrases. They cried, when he said he would go to Paris, that he was needed at home—they, who a day before denounced him as incompetent and unfit. They said he would be "bamboozled" in Paris. At home, in the White House, they seemed to say, he could participate much more effectively.

It made no sense, but it was politically effective. Americans, quite humanly, wanted their boys hurried home. Republican speakers argued Wilson would keep them there forever. They said, too, that Europe could make her own peace. We should give attention to our own problems.

By a narrow margin the Republicans won control of the Congress. For Wilson it was a loss of face as well.

Further cries of anguish came from the resurgent GOP leaders when Wilson announced his five-man peace commission. He had been advised to place a high-ranking Republican, even two, on the list. He refused. Some argued it was one of his fatal flaws that he refused always to see he must "convince his adversaries." Whether it was flaw or not, he would never "play politics" with a principle.

He named himself to the committee; the faithful Colonel Edward House, a practical politician who could never persuade Mr. Wilson to be very practical; Secretary of State Lansing; a military adviser, General T. H. Bliss; and a Republican, Henry White completed it. This latter choice infuriated the bitter-enders all the more. They declared they did not even know that White, a retired career diplomat, was a Republican, so quiet and inactive in party affairs had he been.

In addition there were many technical advisers, economists, and scholars, familiar with the history and peoples of Europe. This made the partisan critics wild. "Professors," they snorted. It has long been one of our national paradoxes that though we earnestly proclaim our devotion to education, and tax ourselves heavily for it, we have never really trusted our educators, or our well-educated people.

Nor did Wilson name a senator to the commission. And this, said the critics of the time, as well as the historians since, was sheerest folly because the Senate would have to ratify any treaty made.

It was not folly. There was but one senator he could have taken, Henry Cabot Lodge. He long before had come to hate Wilson. And hate is a destructive corrosive.

The harsh truth is the Republican chiefs, led by Lodge and Theodore Roosevelt, had met and agreed to "get" Wilson. In the first two years of his administration he had stepped on a lot of toes with his reforms of banking, currency, and his establishment of labor legislation. They had agreed that the man was politically dangerous. If he were allowed a triumph in Paris he might enable his party also to triumph—and, perish the thought—might himself run for a third term.

So, really, it did not greatly matter who made up the commission, though men still fret and theorize over "if" and "on the other hand."

Wilson sailed for Paris with just one long-run objective—the League of Nations. He landed at Brest, 13 December 1918.

Emotional demonstrations of almost incredible intensity and affection greeted him everywhere he went—in France, Great Britain, and Italy. But there was no action. It was not possible immediately to begin a peace treaty. France's Georges Clemenceau, hard-bitten relic of the past, nursing a bitter dream of Old Testament revenge for the Franco-Prussian war, and Britain's canny Welshman, David Lloyd George, previously had exchanged private diplomatic views. They did not dare begin a treaty with the masses of their population so fervently, almost worshipfully, hanging on Wilson's every word.

Had there been radio in that last month of 1918, Wilson almost certainly, even with the use of interpreters, would have been able to bring the conference immediately to its task. But there was no radio. And in Britain, Lloyd George had "gone to the people" and needed time for "adjustments." France, too, had a few somewhat vague, but plausible reasons for delay.

So Wilson, at their suggestion, visited Britain and Italy—with everywhere the people looking up to him as one who might be able to bring to earth that peace and good will of which the angelic choir sang on the occasion of the birth of the Messiah at Bethlehem.

In the centennial year of Woodrow Wilson's birth, events have brought him and his vision, his intentions, his words, and his views into a historical perspective rarely given one of the world's great figures. Most of what has been written of Woodrow Wilson—the biographies, the evaluations—was put down in the twenties and thirties. Those were the years of the locust. Wilson was a failure, easily discredited by the cynical and the pragmatic who so confidently "mumble the bones of the slain." He, the visionary idealist, the dreamer, who had been so helpless in contest with the strong practical men, became, in the swift rush of the twenties and thirties, a jest on the lips of those who worship the golden calf of realism. He was the "absent-minded professor." He was not realistic enough, they said. He was not a practical man. So he had failed and been left a somewhat ridiculous dreamer.

But now, it is 1956 and the centennial of his birth, and the year of vindication. One and all may see that he was the only practical man there. Of them all he was the realist, the only one dealing in cold, relentless reality.

Three days after his arrival he said, for example, replying to the French Socialist Party delegation:

"This has indeed been a people's war. It has been waged against absolutism and militarism, and these enemies of liberty must from this time forth be shut out from the possibility of working their cruel will upon mankind. In my judgment it is not sufficient to establish this principle. It is necessary that it be supported by a cooperation of the nations which shall be based upon fixed and definite covenants, and which shall be made certain of effective action through the instrumentality of a League of Nations."

This was 16 December 1918.

To the people it seemed realistic. But not to Clemenceau and George—and not to the Republican mentality then in control of Congress—all of them, in Washington, London, Paris and in Rome, were being "practical," "sound" men, looking at the future through what might be called the rear-view mirror of their experience and their political morality.

While Britain and France delayed, they sought to win Wilson to a more severe peace. They did not tell him, of course, of the imperialistic plans, of the secret treaties, already made, dividing up the rich oil land, the best of the territorial "loot." They had agreed to Wilson's fourteen points to end a war. But being "practical" men, they would not use them to make a peace. Though to be sure, they never quite said so, in so many words—the people were always demanding to see him—but then, the people, of course, were not practical either.

Speed was urgent. Wilson knew it to be so because Europe was disintegrating. Yet the Big Three worked delay so that they might obtain "title" and establish military and custom controls—to the German and Turkish colonies. The Bolsheviks had published the contents of all treaties secretly entered into by Russia. This only mildly embarrassed the European leadership of the peace conference, but did tend to make the people, suspicious of the delay, cynical, more suspicious and discontented. The Red virus was flowing westward. Already it was in the Balkans.

The peace conference was no longer truly worthy of the name. It was in the hands of "The Big Four." In truth, it usually was "The Big Three."

They shut Wilson out when they could. They did not let him know about the secret meetings, the private deals. Nonetheless, all Wilson's Scottish stubbornness came to the fore. He would not agree to their bald and bold plan for realistic imperialism—an out-right division of the spoils.

This was a violation of point five—one of the more vital ones. They were three to one—but they could not break him. At last he forced a compromise. The great powers would not receive outright title to the divisions of conquered territory, but would serve as trustees of the League of Nations. They were the "mandatories" of the League.

Had the United States come into the League, these mandates would not have become, as they did, little more than subterfuges for old-fashioned imperialism.

Wilson argued, too, for a careful determination of Germany's capacity to pay reparations. He did not believe, and said so, that France could be fully compensated without imposing a burden which would destroy any possibility of Europe's economic recovery. But the "realistic" overruled the "dreamer." And, of course, Europe's economy was never sound, and the cost in human life, suffering, and property loss was already large when Wilson closed his eyes in death. Four years later, when the cancer of the reparation plan adopted over Wilson's protest was making all of Europe ill, the troubled Republican administration came forward with a proposal—that Germany's capacity to pay be determined.

But Wilson had his League. Named chairman of the committee which drafted the covenant, he worked quite literally night and day. In ten long, emotional sessions, he obtained its adoption in a satisfactorily completed form, needing only a bit of editing.

The conference did not want it. There was an attempt, piously fraudulent, to make it the last item on the agenda. They wanted all the spoils divided up before any "League" cast a shadow on their plans to add to imperial possessions.

But Wilson would not agree.

One day he spoke so eloquently that the already cynical reporters, aware of the Big Three clique and its power, forgot to take notes. Even Clemenceau, "the tiger," ceased licking his chops. And Lloyd George, with his Welsh liking for music and words, appeared exalted, as if St. David had come back with a leek in his hat and a moving psalm on his lips.

In mid-February, 1919, Wilson won a really great victory. The League Covenant was not merely adopted but made an integral and major part of the final treaty impossible of surgery.

Years later, the practical men and others with guilt on their conscience, began to make their failure Wilson's. When the collapse came; when Europe's economy was being eaten away by the victories of the realists at Versailles, they began to blame it on him. They said he had not recognized the need for playing politics at home; that he had been bamboozled; that he had not gone to Paris well prepared; that his advisers were inadequate.

John Maynard Keynes, in his *Essays in Biography*, published in 1933, saw Clemenceau "plain." He wrote: "So far as possible, therefore, it was the policy of France to set the clock back and to undo what, since 1870, the progress of Germany had accomplished. . . . He sees the issues in terms of France and Germany, not of humanity and of European civilization struggling toward a new order. . . ."[22]

Keynes, out of his memory of 1918-19, recalled Woodrow Wilson as playing "blind man's buff" in the party (conference). Keynes, remembering across a decade, said of Wilson that "he had no plan, no scheme, no constructive ideas whatever for clothing with the flesh of life the commandments which had thundered from the White House." He was, wrote Keynes, "ill-informed on European conditions."

Keynes, with his admiration remaining with the practical men, those "informed" about European conditions, noted the President could have used the financial power of the United States, and the dependence of France, Italy, England—all of Europe for that matter—to force acceptance of what he wanted.

"But the President was not capable of so clear an understanding. . . . He was too conscientious . . . he remained a man of principle . . . but insensitive to his surroundings. . . ."[23]

And so he had. The President was indeed capable of a clear understanding of his power. But he was not a blackmailer, nor was he "clever" as was Lloyd George, or as pragmatic as Clemenceau. He did hold to principle.

Keynes published in 1933. At that time the world was in the depths of a great economic collapse. It was the year Hitler's star began to glow on the horizon of a hungry, desperate Germany. All about Keynes was eloquently accusing evidence that neither Clemenceau's ideas, nor those of Premier George, so obvious to Mr. Keynes's eyes at the conference, had been anything but ineffective.

It was plain then to many, as it is to almost everyone in 1956, that instead of being without an idea, Wilson was the only person there with a workable one. Instead of being insensitive to his surroundings and to European conditions, he was the only man at the conference who was sensitive and aware.

But the sorry, sordid show went on. They began to tear him down. Rumor and lies were "leaked" to the French press. That press, then already largely corrupted, as so much of it was revealed to be in the opening days of the second great war, began to charge Wilson was "pro-Hun"—that he had betrayed France and was trying to rebuild Germany into a great power.

There was an interlude. The President had to go home to sign bills passed by the adjourning Congress and to attend to other business. In Washington the passions of jealousy and power were rising like the temperature of a patient suffering from some deep-seated infection. Senator Lodge was the center of it. Hatred had corroded him. The man who, as editor of the *North American Review*, had greatly admired contributor Woodrow Wilson and urged him to persevere, now led the chorus of hate. The League was denounced as "League of Nations claptrap," as a dangerous "super-state" which might destroy the sovereignty of the United States and as "the League of denationalized nations." Isolationist Senators William E. Borah and Hiram W. Johnson led their following to Lodge. They were the United States duplicates of Clemenceau.

In early March these "irreconcilables" published a Round Robin. On it were the names of thirty-nine senators, or senators-elect, pledged not to approve the League of Nations. They were enough to defeat it.

The Big Three were pleased. Now Wilson would have to come to them. They drove a hard bargain.

"God gave us His Ten Commandments," said Clemenceau, "and we broke them. Wilson gave us his fourteen points—we shall see."

Even here Wilson, ill and weary, held out. For an amateur diplomat he did astonishingly well. The Saar Basin would not go to the Tiger—but would be under the trusteeship of the League for fifteen years and then hold a plebiscite. France also yielded her demands for a slice of Germany to serve as a buffer state. He was the man of principle with Italy, too, and she, like France, turned against him, when he opposed her plans for territorial looting.

The Germans signed the treaty on June twenty-eighth. They, too, charged betrayal—the fourteen points on which they had agreed to surrender, has been considerably altered. It was this "stab in the back" which Hitler used as his rallying cry. Wilson had accepted compromise to save the League. He, too, was hurt and unhappy with the treaty. But the League—it would smooth out the injustices and inequities when, and if, they began to pinch.

When Wilson reached Washington, the knives were sharpened and waiting.

Teddy Roosevelt, still nursing his dream of glory, denounced all "peace-twaddle." German-Americans, Italian-Americans, the Irish-Americans, the anti-British, the liberals, the German-haters, the isolationists—they all damned the treaty.

Senator Lodge, in July, 1919, had no hope of defeating the treaty. So he set out, as chairman of the Senate Foreign Relations Committee to "love it to death" with amendments and words. Most of the press was hostile. The people had much distortion of the pact, and not much sound interpretation. The weeks dragged on.

Wilson decided to "go to the country." His wife, physician, and cabinet protested. It was a hot summer. He was ill. The long months of harassment and work despite constant pain had depleted him physically. He went.

In the Midwest the German-American influence was then strong. The Republicans sent rabble-rousing speakers in behind him. There was not much progress.

But the West was different. That region, which had supported him in 1916, turned out great and increasing crowds, all enthusiastic. He was winning—until 25 September 1919. He spoke that day at Pueblo, Colorado, a huge crowd cheering him to the echo. That night he collapsed on the train. It was routed direct to Washington. The tide had turned.

Senator Lodge cynically produced his fourteen amendments. The Democrats voted to defeat this ruthless mockery. There was another ballot, and once more Lodge's amendments failed.

"The bitter-enders" had won.

The people, tired of idealism, assured they could always live in peace behind their great ocean, were apathetic, weary of the bitter arguments, not well informed. They did not see the fruits of victory were being thrown away. Nor, for that matter, did Lodge and his "Battalion of Death." To them, it was just politics—and a way to restore the Republican Party to power.

Wilson, sick and slowly dying, was out of touch with public opinion and the appeal of the slogan "Normalcy." He urged that the fight for moral principle and the League of Nations which could keep the peace, go on.

And the party found the candidates who would stand on that principle. They were James Middleton Cox of Dayton, Ohio, two-term governor and publisher; and Franklin Delano Roosevelt, who had been assistant secretary of the Navy.

As a preliminary to the campaign of 1920, Governor Cox and Mr. Roosevelt called on Woodrow Wilson at the White House. In the early 1940s, while engaged in the preparation of his memoirs, *Journey Through My Years,* published in 1946, Governor Cox had a talk with the Honorable Claude Bowers, then ambassador to Chile. The ambassador later went on to Washington where he saw Franklin D. Roosevelt and heard from him a story. He wrote to Governor Cox so that it might be included in his book. Better than anything else, this letter provides the clue to the Democratic campaign of 1920 and the high level of principle on which it was begun, waged, and lost. It was as follows:[24]

> Dear Governor:
>
> The other day when in Washington and with President Roosevelt, I told him I had heard from you and that you had been persuaded to write some reminiscences. "Good!" he said. "I wish you would tell him for me that there is a story never yet told, that he must tell. It is this: After the convention at San Francisco I stopped off for a conference with the governor in Columbus to discuss the character of the campaign. The governor advised that he was going to see President Wilson the next week.
>
> "I accompanied the governor on the visit to Wilson. A large crowd greeted us at the station and we went directly to the White House. There we were asked to wait fifteen minutes, as they were taking the President to the portico facing the grounds. As we came in sight of the portico we saw the President in a wheel chair, his left shoulder covered with a shawl which concealed his left arm, which was paralyzed, and the governor said to me, 'He is a very sick man.'
>
> "The governor went up to the President and warmly greeted him. Wilson looked up and in a very low, weak voice said, 'Thank you for coming, I am very glad you came.' His utter weakness was startling and I noticed tears in the eyes of Cox. A little later Cox said, 'Mr. President, we are going to be a million per cent with you, and your administration, and that means the League of Nations.' The President looked up again, and again in a voice scarcely audible, he said, 'I am very grateful,' and then repeated, 'I am very grateful.'
>
> "As we passed out we came then to the executive offices and in this very room, Cox sat down at this table"—and here Roosevelt struck the table—"and asked Tumulty for paper and a pencil, and there he wrote the statement that committed us to making the League the paramount issue of the campaign. It was one of the most impressive scenes I have ever witnessed. Tell Cox he must tell that story."
>
> Sincerely,
> Claude G. Bowers

Governor Cox and Franklin Roosevelt have been vindicated by history and events equally with Wilson. It cannot be overlooked that President Roosevelt gambled all on the United Nations, even as Wilson had on the League. He made compromises necessary to bring Russia into the United Nations, feeling, as

Wilson had in 1919, that any inequities thereby created, could be ironed out by the United Nations.

Since Governor Cox, as the standard-bearer for the League in 1920, had a more direct interest in an analysis of the League and its defeat, his conclusions are necessary to round out the story. In *Journey Through My Years*, he devoted a chapter to it. It is titled "The Great Conspiracy."[25]

Among the many letters and telegrams which came to Governor Cox when the votes were counted, and the nation had turned its back on the future, was this one:[26]

> The White House
> Washington
>
> 5 November 1920
>
> My dear Governor Cox:
> I hope that you know that no Democrat attributes the defeat of Tuesday to anything that you did or omitted to do. We have all admired the fight that you made with the greatest sincerity, and believe that the whole country honors you for the frank and courageous way in which you conducted the campaign.
> With the most cordial good wishes and, of course, with unabated confidence,
> Cordially and sincerely yours,
> (Signed) Woodrow Wilson
> Hon. James M. Cox
> Executive Office
> Columbus, Ohio

The election of 1920 found the people in one of those compulsive moods which mark our political history, both at the local and national level, in which reason is unable to assert itself as a factor. They were determined to escape back into the good old days when America was without international problems and responsibilities. So they stampeded through the door marked "Normalcy," following a bumbling second-rate President, himself soon to be betrayed by those who created him.

Now when events have reestablished Woodrow Wilson, we know that our spurning of the League was a tragedy of blindness and a hate-corroded Republican Senate leadership.

No one can prove that a League, strongly supported by the United States, would have averted the second, and greater, world war. But there is a formidable array of evidence that it would have done so. A stable Europe, with a German Republic paying reparations within its capacity so to do, and, therefore, economically strong enough to maintain itself politically, would likely have avoided the collapse of the thirties. Woodrow Wilson, in his last veto message, just before leaving office, had predicted that failure. The inability of the small, new democracies created by the principle of self-determination of peoples, might well have endured instead of being forced, as they were, to erect trade barriers in a futile effort to survive economically. The rise of angry nationalisms, and of the dictators, was the fruit of our shortsightedness.

The peace treaty was constructed with American participation as an integral part of its machinery. Its collapse was grist in the Hitler mill.

Those who had believed so greatly in the morality of American demands for peace could say in truth we wanted it only if we could have it without cost or responsibility for maintaining it.

Had we assumed the war-created responsibilities and followed through on Wilson's fourteen points and the League, we could have shaped the future of Europe toward peace and trade—and away from the path which was inevitably set toward the great depression of the thirties and the second great war.

Wilson, who had said, when the League was defeated, that "the job would have to be done over in twenty years and at ten times the cost," knew that. So did many others who shared his vision.

The sick man whom the candidates Cox and Roosevelt saw on the portico in the autumn of 1920 carried grimly on until his term was ended on 4 March 1921. Once a coarse and arrogant Senate committee, headed by Albert B. Fall, forced their way into the sickroom to investigate the President's mental condition. The political scavengers had never let up on him. The committee had to report, with obvious disappointment, that Woodrow Wilson was entirely sane and rational in every respect.

This same Fall was to be secretary of the interior in Harding's "Normalcy" cabinet and was to go to prison as a convicted felon in the great oil steal. Nor was he the only one of that administration, which conspired to defeat the peace and loot the treasury, to have that experience.

On March fourth, Wilson rode to the Capitol with Warren Gamaliel Harding. Chief Justice Edward Douglass White, who twice had administered the oath to Wilson, swore in the new President.

The public career of Woodrow Wilson was done.

When he died, many in the crowd waiting devotedly outside the house on S Street, to which he and Mrs. Wilson had retired on March fourth, knelt in the snow and prayed—for the soul of the man who was dead—and for the future of their country which had rejected him and his principles.

The principles lived. And events have vindicated them, the man who proclaimed them, and those who believed in and struggled for them.

Notes—24

[1]Reprinted by permission of Holt, Rinehart and Winston, Inc., from "The President," *The Greatness of Woodrow Wilson: 1856-1956*, Em Bowles Alsop, ed. (New York: Rinehart and Co., Inc., 1956), pp. 79-128. Copyright © by Em Bowles Alsop.

[2]McGill here is quoting from Wilson's "First Inaugural Address," delivered on 4 March 1913. He selects words from this passage: "Here muster, not the forces of party, but the forces of humanity. Men's hearts wait upon us; men's lives hang in the balance; men's hopes all upon us to say what we will do." See *Selected Literary and Political Papers and Addresses of Woodrow Wilson*, 3 vols. (New York: Grosset & Dunlap, 1926), 2:7.

[3]See John M. Mulder, *Woodrow Wilson: The Years of Preparation* (Princeton: Princeton University Press, 1978); George C. Osborn, *Woodrow Wilson: The Early Years* (Baton Rouge: Louisiana State University Press, 1968); Arthur Walworth, *Woodrow Wilson*, 2 vols. (New York: Longman's, Green and Co., 1958), 1, *American Prophet*, pp. 1-28, 70-97, 140-61, 181-99; Arthur S. Link, *Wilson: The Road to the White House*, 5 vols. (Princeton: Princeton University Press, 1947), 1.

[4]"Principle of just taxation" reads in *Selected Literary and Political Papers and Addresses of Woodrow Wilson*, "just principles of taxation"; p. 4.

[5]"Its" should go before "bonds fifty years ago"; *Selected Literary and Political Papers and Addresses of Woodrow Wilson*, p. 4.

[6]McGill inserted "our" before "government may be put at the service of humanity"; "its men and" should go before "its women and its children"; "sanitary laws, pure food laws, and laws determining conditions of labor which" should also be within quotation marks; in the sentence, "The first duty of the law is to keep sound the society it serves," "the" before "law" should be deleted; also this statement comes from an earlier passage in the address; *Selected Literary and Political Papers and Addresses of Woodrow Wilson*, pp. 84-85.

[7]Link, *Wilson: The New Freedom*, 5 vols. (Princeton: Princeton University Press, 1956), 2; Walworth, *American Prophet*.

[8]See Albert Shaw, *President Wilson's State Papers and Addresses* (New York: Review of Reviews Co., 1918), p. 13.

[9]One account of the President's words given by Glass was: "Will one of you gentlemen tell me in what civilized country of the earth there are important government boards of control on which private interests are represented?";

218 @ SOUTHERN ENCOUNTERS

Carter Glass, *An Adventure in Constructive Finance* (Garden City, NY: Doubleday, Page & Co., 1927), p. 116.

[10]See Link, *Wilson: Campaigns For Progressivism and Peace: 1916-1917*, 5 vols. (Princeton: Princeton University Press, 1965), 5.

[11]Link, *Wilson: Struggle For Neutrality: 1914-1915*, 5 vols. (Princeton: Princeton University Press, 1960), 3.

[12]Shaw, *President Wilson's State Papers and Addresses*, p. 371.

[13]McGill omitted "a" before "peace without victory"; *President Wilson's Great Speech and Other History Making Documents* (Chicago: Stanton & Van Vliet, Co., 1917-1918), pp. 147-48.

[14]This speech was not given on 6 April 1917, but 2 April; see "Address of the President of the United States," Joint Session of the Two Houses of Congress, *House Documents*, 65th Congress, 2 April 1917, vol. 35:1-8.

[15]McGill inserted the words "without revenge," taking them from an earlier place in the speech when Wilson said, "Our motive will not be revenge. . . ." See "Address of the President of the United States," 2 April 1917, pp. 4, 7. The passage, "a war without rancor and without selfish object," comes from Wilson's: "Just because we fight without rancor and without selfish object, seeking nothing for ourselves but what we shall wish to share with all free peoples, we shall, I feel confident, conduct our operations as belligerents without passion. . . ."; p. 7.

[16]McGill ommitted the words "we cannot make" before "we are incapable of making" and the words "and our people" before "to be ignored or violated"; "Address of the President of the United States," 2 April 1917, p. 4.

[17]The editor did not find these three questions in the speech.

[18]McGill ommited "a" before "concert"; "Address of the United States," 2 April 1917, p. 8.

[19]After, "for [this] democracy," Wilson said: "for the right of those who submit to authority to have a voice in their own governments. . . ."; "Address of the President of the United States," 2 April 1917, p. 8.

[20]After "silent and pale" the words used by McGill, "in the cabinet room. At last he said," were also Tumulty's and should have been within quotation marks; McGill added "of" before "what it was they were applauding", and substituted "they would" for "to" before "applaud that." Originally, then, it read: "Think what it was they were applauding. My message today was a message of death for our young men. How strange it seems to applaud that"; McGill omitted "to" before "dread war"; Joseph P. Tumulty, *Woodrow Wilson As I Know Him* (Garden City, NY: Garden City Publishing Co., 1925), p. 256.

[21]Link, *Wilson: Confusions and Crises: 1915-1916*, 5 vols. (Princeton: Princeton University Press, 1964) 4; Link, *Wilson: Campaigns For Progressivism and Peace: 1916-1917*; Walworth, *Woodrow Wilson*, 2 vols. (New York: Longman's, Green and Co., 1958), 2, *World Prophet*; N. Gordon Levin, Jr., *Woodrow Wilson and World Politics: America's Response to War and Revolution* (New York: Oxford University Press, 1968).

[22]McGill added "s" to "issue" before "in terms of France and Germany," substituted "toward" for "forwards to" before "a new order"; John Maynard Keynes, *Essays In Biography* (New York: Horizon Press Inc., 1951), p. 16.

[23]McGill substituted "on" for "as to" before "European conditions." Also, "but insensitive to his surroundings" read "He was not only insensitive to his surroundings in the external sense, he was not sensitive to his environment at all"; Keynes, *Essays In Biography*, pp. 20-22.

[24]Reprinted from James M. Cox, *Journey Through My Years* (New York: Simon and Schuster, 1946), pp. 241-42.

[25]Here McGill reprinted eighteen pages from Cox, *Journey Through My Years*, pp. 246-64. Because this chapter is available in Cox's work, the editor deleted it here.

[26]Reprinted from Cox, *Journey Through My Years*, pp. 126-27. For Cox's discussion of his purchase of the *Atlanta Journal*, see *Journey Through My Years*, pp. 387-403.

Essay 25

What Is Jimmy Byrnes Up to Now?[1]

By the time the hot, primary-peppered, deep-South summer of 1950 had dragged itself out, the Dixiecrat rebellion of 1948 had been discredited and smashed, and the party machinery was back in the hands of the regulars. But not even the more naive assumed the Southern revolt was ended.

Indeed, the more knowing privately will admit that if the national election were scheduled for November 1950, and the Republicans were running a fellow named Dwight D. Eisenhower, he would do a great deal more damage to the already slightly bedraggled political tradition of a Solid South than did Herbert Hoover in 1928. In that year, it will be remembered, the region split up into warring feuds and factions, and Mr. Hoover emerged with majorities in Virginia, Florida, Kentucky, North Carolina, Tennessee, and Texas.

This is not just city talk. It can be heard in the little towns of the South and at filling-station-store combinations along roads where the red dust is on the opened cotton bolls and the early-fall goldenrod nods by the gullies.

Indeed, there was talk through the humid days and nights of this past summer when July flies seemed to mock from the trees, that someone with some sense ought to go see that fellow Eisenhower and ask him right straight out would he rear and pitch if the Democrats themselves offered him the nomination.

"He ain't never said he's a Republican" folks would say, sitting on the gin-house porch, "and you can't tell unless you ask."

In more urbane circles, over the second martini, they eventually would get around to asking one another, "Do you really suppose there is any chance he'd take it?"

And in certain high places there were those who were beginning to plan. The story runs that the general, whose oath was taken in uniform, and who consequently has no background of party tradition or loyalties, looks toward the country as a whole and does not think in terms of parties. The word is that he feels much of the accumulated deadwood of a long administration needs to be cleaned out. This would suit a lot of Southern Democrats, who are willing to pledge themselves to help clear it away.

The revolt as it now stands is not just an anti-Truman campaign, as it was in 1948. There exists a certain admiration, grudgingly given on the part of some, for the man from Missouri. They respect his courage and his stubborn loyalty to his associates, although the latter quality seems, to some, often stretched beyond reason. But, while they don't quite understand it, they feel that Mr. Truman has become a sort of captive of a philosophy and a group which have forgotten what Franklin D. Roosevelt never did—namely, that this is a nation of regions and that each developed as such—laboriously and often heroically—with regional economics and a culture formed by economics and historical developments.

The Southern liberals share at least some of this feeling. They recall that Roosevelt once said that any national tax bill, by the time it reached his desk for signature, was more like a trade agreement between six nations than a national measure, because of the compromises forced by the chief regions of the nation. They recall, too, that he had too much common sense about government to try to govern by fiats and rigid legalistic formulas. Roosevelt knew that a fiat or formula which several millions of people have no compunction about violating isn't good either for liberalism or for government.

Liberalism, they believe, progresses only as the people will it, and not by fiats, statutes, or legal formulas. That is why Southern liberals are frustrated and fretted, dragging their feet in the eyes of those who fit liberalism into an exact, inflexible formula. The Southerners, who nevertheless like Mr. Truman, see progress in liberalism only as the people are better informed and themselves will to break down the old mores. The South's liberals, by and large, don't like the idea of a military man in the White House, although they admire General Eisenhower. But there is no mistaking the grassroots sentiment.[2]

This attitude toward the general was strongly in existence before the Korean problem developed, and events have accelerated it. It does not mean there is an inflexible conviction the former General of the Army is the only man the South is willing to follow. But it is true he is the only one to date for whom there is any regional enthusiasm, although the issue is two years away and another personality could emerge.

It does mean that a spirit of revolt still burns, but this time the leaders presently mean to make the fight within the party. If they fail to work out a compromise unification within the party and the GOP blunders up with Eisenhower or some other name which commands the respect which is his, they will quietly bring about an even more emphatic shattering of the one-time Solid South, in a manner which will make the 1928 quake seem a mere temblor. They will not do this for a Taft or a Wherry, but there is reason to believe the general would carry, if the election were this year, at least six Southern states—Kentucky, Tennessee, Virginia, North Carolina, Florida and Texas—and would have a surprisingly good chance even in South Carolina, Arkansas, Alabama, Georgia, and Mississippi. This sounds, on its face, like something straight out of Thomas De Quincey, but it still is there when you wake up.

At any rate, the Democrats were still strongly committed to revolt when they went into the 1950 summer primaries and shoved the Dixiecrats out of the line of vision. And when the dust of battle had settled, all eyes were turned either in happy anticipation or solemn calculation toward South Carolina. There stood the new symbol of the Southern revolt—imperially slim, internationally distinguished, merry-eyed James Francis Byrnes, former United States Senator, Justice of the Supreme Court of the United States, Secretary of State, "Assistant President," member of the diplomatic mission to Yalta, and now Democratic nominee for the governorship of the Palmetto State, with no opposition in a one-party state. His inauguration is set for January, the third Wednesday. Months before, when informed at a press conference that Mr. Byrnes proposed to make the campaign, and asked for comment, Mr. Truman had replied that Mr. Byrnes could do as he "damned pleased." Apparently he did.[3]

In the primary which gave Jimmy Byrnes a majority of almost 100,000 over three opponents, Senator Olin Johnston, running for re-election as United States senator, somewhat surprisingly defeated Governor Strom Thurmond, the 1948 Dixiecrat presidential nominee, whose splinter party that year had carried four states by means which had cost it much prestige. The simplest of these 1948 methods was to leave the names of Democratic nominees off the ballot. The Dixiecrats were never able to put on the garments of political respectability, save in Charleston County and those adjoining counties, but even so the spectacle of Governor Thurmond being soundly defeated in his own state in 1950 by a man he had tagged as a regular-party man and, therefore, by the governor's calculation, "a Trumanite," was astonishing. The canny Byrnes had given the Dixiecrats no aid or comfort in 1948, and in 1950 he ignored them.

In addition to his progressive state program, Candidate Byrnes told the voters he planned something else. In speeches in each of the forty-six counties, he told the people he would seek the aid of other states and governors in an effort to check what he conceived to be the trend of the national administration toward further socialization and increasing and wasteful spending.

"You can get drunk on alcohol and recover—though you may have a headache," he said. "But if you get drunk on power, you never get over it. The power to spend forty-seven billion dollars is a terrible power. I doubt if God ever made any man with enough wisdom or virtue to sit in Washington and be given the power to spend forty-seven billion dollars."

Of taxes, he said, "There is no government money except that taken out of the pockets of the people or borrowed from banks."

He wants, in this connection, to have the federal government give back to the states some of their former taxing power so that the federal government will not centralize most of the spending. This would help break up some of the concentrated power of government.

While he carefully established his interest in, and purpose to participate in, national affairs, he made it very plain that he would never be a candidate for the presidency on any ticket and would not accept a nomination if it were voted.[4]

Nominee Byrnes will not, of course, discuss his plans in a detailed way. He is too wise a strategist for that. But he does not hesitate to say he believes the Democratic Party needs certain reforms from within—reforms yet to be blue-printed, apparently. He speaks of the necessity for all parties, including his own, to return to principles. "We must make up our minds whether it is labels we want, or principles," he says, and this may be assumed to be the basis of the reforms which he hopes to force upon the party.

He has discussed strategy with friends, including some in the United States Senate, and with others in politics and business. He definitely has received encouragement from outside the state, and from sources unrelated to those which were behind the Dixiecrats. His idea is to work through friends, allies, and existing organizations, such as the National Governors' Conference and the Southern Governors' Conference. He will have opportunity to speak at conventions and dinners which will afford a forum for widespread broadcast and publication of his ideas about politics and government. Invitations come steadily and the Byrnes job is one of selection. By the summer of 1952 he will certainly be able to command considerable additional following inside the party.

From a source close to the South Carolinian, his thinking may be put down briefly as follows: He feels the national Democratic Party has come to be conducted along the same lines as a big-city machine. This, he believes, has damaged the fabric of government, because such a system puts into appointive offices and into campaigns for nomination, men who are chosen with little regard to ability and principles, but with much regard for their ability as raisers of money for campaigns and for their skill in controlling minority-group votes. Thus, he is reported as fearing, such a party conceivably can keep going indefinitely if it is able to maintain huge spending to placate the various organized pressure groups, and, at the same time, hold the minority-group votes with promises and emotional issues, cynically contrived.

The same source reports that, had the Republican Party presented any evidence of program leadership and vigorous political reform, the Byrnes state of concern would not have been so great. But the prospect did not please, and he determined to run for the governorship of his state to try to do a job for it and, if possible, to organize enough strength to be able to bring about some reforms within the party.

He will take with him into his interparty program the esteem of many men in high offices, national as well as state, and the confidence and affection of men occupying important places in industry and business.

"Jimmy," said a South Carolina politician, "fights so easily and persuasively, you don't know you are dying until your top branches begin to wilt. Then you discover your roots are cut."

Southern political decks are unusually well cleared for Mr. Byrnes, although, as a matter of course, some of the governors will want to see developments before they formally commit themselves to his leadership in the two years ahead. How many he wins will be up to him.

The South is freer of ranters and demagogues than it has been for a generation or more. The primaries put the party to a bare-knucks test. Senators Lister Hill and John Sparkman came into their home state of Alabama and led the fight which destroyed the Dixiecrat majority in the state executive committee. Senator Hill also briskly spanked his opponent. Both senators stood for seeking reform within the party.

In Arkansas, Governor Sid McMath, former marine combat veteran and a political progressive, who four years ago, as prosecuting attorney, smashed the gambling dynasty at Hot Springs, won a bitterly fought campaign for reelection against former Governor Ben Laney, and commented, in the hour of victory, "These results will kill the Dixiecrats in the South." In Louisiana, Senator Russell Long, son of the late Huey Long, having long before broken with one of the most powerful leaders of the splinter-party movement in the South, Leander Perez, went over the state saying, "The day of the demagogue is over." He honored his father, but disowned his political methods.

Even Georgia's Governor Herman Talmadge, who had remained in the party in 1948, continued to disappoint the followers of "Old Gene" by his lack of demagogic fire as he campaigned for and won renomination.

But of all the primary campaigns, no other was as strange to the South as that of James Francis Byrnes. To a South used to the shabby old political props of hillbilly grammar, jug bands, fiddler, red suspenders, jalopy cars for campaign travel, Bilbo-tirades, "feesh-egg" denunciations by "Our Bob" Reynolds, Huey Long's hammy theatricals, and various other zany and vulgar caperings, the Byrnes campaign was almost austere, despite the easy, amiable informality of the man.

Candidate Byrnes traveled the state in a shiny new high-priced car replete with white-walled tires and a chauffeur. Dressed, as always, in a neat blue, double-breasted suit, white starched shirt, handsome tie and black-and-white shoes, Mr. Byrnes toured the Carolina Commonwealth, beaming cheerily upon one and all.

Off on the far horizon one could hear the loud trumpetings of Thurmond and Johnston, whose antics were in the old mudstained pattern of recrimination. But the Byrnes tour went on its antiseptic way, calm and serene, until one fancied, even, the voice of the turtle could be heard in the pleasant, pastoral land.

South Carolina primary law requires all candidates for state offices to speak at least once in each county. The senatorial hopefuls go in one group. In another are aspirants for governor, lieutenant governor, commissioner of agriculture, and so on.

Jimmy Byrnes technically was one of some seventeen candidates on tour, four of whom coveted the office of governor. His opponents had entered before the Byrnes fedora was delicately dropped into the ring, a fact which caused the softer-hearted in the state to commiserate with them as the tour went on and they began to feel the weight of the Byrnes prestige and technique.

Candidate Byrnes, briefed by local friends, would arrive at the designated speaking site a few minutes before his turn. Without fail, much of the crowd would be waiting outside "to see Jimmy." He likes people to call him that, especially children. "That means their fathers know me," he says, enormously pleased at any chorus of "Hello Jimmy" from Carolina moppets. After the waiting voters and their progeny had spoken and shaken hands with Jimmy, and after the old gaffers, who quarreled with one another over which one had known Jimmy the longest, had recollected for him some past campaign incident, he would proceed to the platform, the crowd following him.

Usually the speaking was in the courthouse, and waiting there would be his three rivals, perspiring and often unhappy of mien. Jimmy Byrnes noted them not at all. He delivered his speech and departed. Unfortunately for his rivals, most of the crowd also would depart in the wake of the dapper political Pied Piper.

While this undoubtedly caused his opponents considerable mental anguish and private gnashing of teeth, only one of them was moved to leap up and down and cry aloud. This was Marcus Aurelius Stone, a perennial candidate for office in South Carolina. Mr. Stone, whose voice is as deep and powerful as an exhorting evangelist's, told what audience was left him that Jimmy Byrnes had been nothing but Molotov's poodle dog at Yalta; that the game was won until Secretary of State Byrnes fumbled the ball and lost the peace. This caused many dark looks to be directed at Mr. Stone. Indeed, in the final appearance of all candidates from one stage in Columbia's municipal auditorium, when Mr. Stone got around to these charges, he was booed into dropping them. They at no time ruffled the Byrnes feathers. Mr. Stone ran, finally, a very bad last.

Though the distinguished candidate entirely ignored his rivals, his friends had an answer for one question asked. The query was why he had not publicly opposed at least the beginnings of the trends he fears, while in office. Those close to him reply that he did. He had worked strenuously to end WPA and the special powers granted during the emergency. But he had, they point out, gone to the Supreme Court and then into preparation for war. Much of what he opposes he feels has snowballed since the end of the second world war.

Aiken, South Carolina, first elevated Jimmy Byrnes to office. This was in 1908, when he ran for solicitor "on nothing but nerve," he recalls, and won by fifty-seven votes. He was elected to Congress in 1911 and to six successive terms. He was promoted to the Senate in 1930 and returned in 1936. Franklin D. Roosevelt appointed him to the Supreme Court in 1941. He resigned in 1942 at the president's request to become director of Economic Stabilization. In 1942 he was director of War Mobilization, and F.D.R. referred to him as "Assistant President."

The day after Mr. Roosevelt's death, President Truman asked Mr. Byrnes to represent him at the San Francisco conference, but Byrnes insisted the delegation already named be kept intact. The next day President Truman asked him to become secretary of state, and Byrnes accepted with the understanding no announcement be made until after the conference had ended. Public announcement was not made until 30 June 1945.[5]

In the Senate, Byrnes had been regarded as having great talent for compromise and through his persuasive vehicle bringing about agreement on difficult problems. The Berlin meeting followed soon on the heels of his taking office, and Byrnes began to learn that the Russians viewed attempts at compromise as an expression of weakness. After Berlin came the London meeting of the foreign ministers, and a quip began to be heard around Washington, "The State Department fiddles while Byrnes roams."

During this period, Secretary Byrnes rode out, without too much trouble, the furious resignation of Patrick J. Hurley as the president's representative to China.

The second incident was more serious. It had the ultimate effect of summarily removing Henry Wallace from a cabinet post and liquidating any lingering influence he had with the administration. At Stuttgart, Germany, on 6 September 1946, Secretary Byrnes, having learned at last the Russian concept of compromise, made a brilliant analysis of American foreign policy, criticizing the Soviets for refusal to carry out the Potsdam agreements and declaring categorically the United States would support these pledges to the end.

On September twelfth the secretary was busy in Paris working on treaties to end the war. That evening Henry Wallace, secretary of commerce, spoke at a left-wing rally in New York and was strongly critical of the Byrnes Stuttgart speech on the basis that it was a "get-tough-with-Russia" policy. The effect was near disastrous in Paris, since in press reports President Truman was quoted as having approved the Wallace speech prior to its delivery. This the president had indeed done. Privately the president said he had merely thumbed through it after Wallace had told him he was "taking a tough line with the Soviets." From Paris, Byrnes cabled a request that Mr. Wallace be restrained from speaking on foreign affairs, or Byrnes himself relieved. Wallace countered by making public a letter, dated July twenty-third, which even more strongly criticized American-Soviet policy. Then came Senator Vandenberg's famed remark that he, as opposition leader, no matter how great his desire, could cooperate with only one secretary of state at a time. On September twentieth, the president asked for and received Wallace's resignation.

Byrnes was kept so busy with foreign conferences that he had little time to give to domestic tasks. He was able, however, because of this strength in the Senate, to break a legislative jam and push through the Foreign Service Act of 1946, a bill growing out of two years' study by the department, looking toward improving the overseas agency for the conduct of foreign affairs. This a grateful department regarded as a minor miracle.

Neither President Truman nor Jimmy Byrnes has ever told the story of what led to the latter's resignation in January, 1947. There may be no real story. In his letter of 16 December 1946 suggesting the date of his retirement, Secretary Byrnes repeated a former statement of having always received the full support of the president. But there was friction.

The best guess is the president grew a little restive because the secretary made some "report-to-the-public" radio speeches and apparently deemed it his duty to let the people hear his analyses directly, instead of indirectly through the president. Byrnes's friends say there were those about the president who kept protesting that Byrnes was too independent and was seeking to place the executive department in a secondary role in foreign policy.

In retirement, Byrnes began again the practice of law and wrote his well-received book, *Speaking Frankly*. It brought him in $125,000, and he uses the money as a special fund to assist orphan boys and girls to attend college. About fifty now are at school on the Byrnes funds. He personally assists in the selection of these students, seeking out those with "ambition, ability, a willingness to work, and a keen desire for education." He keeps up with them by letter and each year has them at his home at Spartanburg for dinner and a get-acquainted meeting.[6]

The Byrnes interest in orphans stems from the fact he has no children of his own and was himself an orphan. His father died a few months before the birth of the son who was to become "the most distinguished South Carolinian since John C. Calhoun." The young Byrnes had to quit school at fourteen to assist his mother, and he had always a burning desire for education. He got as much as he could by studying nights, and later by becoming a law clerk and absorbing enough law to pass the bar examination handily.

In Aiken, where he first ran for office, he met and married Miss Maude Perkins Busch, and she and Byrnes have had a fine, happy career together.

During his campaign, when flowers were presented at the conclusion of his speech, he would say to the crowd, "I will present these to my campaign manager. She has always loved flowers." This was always well received, a fact which surprised Byrnes until he learned that most of the candidates, on receiving flowers—an old South Carolina custom—would strike a solemn, bleeding-heart pose, and say, in a tremulous voice, "I am going to send these to those poor boys who fought for us in the world war and who now lie on beds of pain at the hospital." The crowds had begun to titter at this by the last weeks of the campaign.

Notes—25

[1]Published by permission of the author, Mrs. McGill, and *The Saturday Evening Post* (October 1950): 32-33, 183-84, 186-87.

[2]Here McGill reflects his own view that political decisions had to be realistic and result from slow, deliberate discussion. McGill stated: "A free people must be free to discuss and debate—because they have been informed." "Our system not merely permits debate," he declared, "ours prolongs it, for years, if necessary. Our process is educational." "The Jeffersonian idea is mine," McGill continued, "that the democratic way is slow, cumbersome, awkward, and inefficient—but . . . after long travail, the voice of the people makes itself heard and felt." Applying this belief to civil rights legislation McGill advocated "a fair and equitable law which will have public acceptance. It will come only because of the delay and discussion" and after "bitter, angry weeks and years of discussion and debate. When it does come it will mean something." See *Atlanta Constitution*, 10 June 1946; 20 September 1947; 22 August 1948; 1 March 1950; 16 February 1955; 2 January 1959; Cal M. Logue, "The Political Rhetoric of Ralph McGill," *Speech Monographs*, 35 (June 1968): 122-28.

[3]Byrnes was born 2 May 1879, Charleston, South Carolina, and died 9 April 1972, Columbia, South Carolina.

[4]Because he supported Franklin D. Roosevelt and the New Deal, Byrnes felt that Roosevelt "owed it to him to make him his 1944 running mate"; Robert Sherrill, *Gothic Politics in the Deep South: Stars of the New Confederacy* (New York: Grossman Publishers, 1968), p. 246.

[5]See George Curry, "James F. Byrnes," in Robert H. Ferrell, ed., *The American Secretaries of State and Their Diplomacy* (New York: Cooper Square Publishers, Inc., 1965), pp. 87-415.

⁶For Byrnes's accounts of his own public service, see James F. Byrnes, *Speaking Frankly* (New York: Harper and Brothers Publishers, 1947); James F. Byrnes, *All in One Lifetime* (New York: Harper & Brothers, 1958).

Essay 26

George Armistead Smathers: Can He Purge Senator Pepper?[1]

George Armistead Smathers, thirty-six, of Miami, whose robust challenge of Florida's controversial senior senator, Claude Denson Pepper, has the southeasternmost point of the United States vibrating like one of its palms in a storm, has come far fast. He returned home in 1945, after seventeen months' Marine Corps duty in the Pacific. The next year he made his first political offensive strike, upsetting a popular incumbent congressman.[2] Now Smathers is given a good chance to become a United States senator from Florida in the Democratic primary, May second.[3]

The challenger is a handsome, nimble-witted, smoothly-muscled young man six feet three inches tall, who wears a 7 1/8 hat and a 15 1/2 shirt, a combination of sizes which causes his father, Judge Frank Smathers, to beam happily. The judge, bedridden since 1937 as a prisoner of arthritis, allowed neither the annually increasing pain nor his substantial law practice to interfere between himself and his boys, Frank and George. His basic theory about bringing up boys was, and is, that a careful balance must be maintained between the head and neck sizes.

"You've got to be careful," he would say to young George and Frank, insisting sternly on their learning to debate and recite as well as box, "not to end up with a big strong neck and a weak little head." The boys and their playmates became used to having him limp out on the porch as they scrimmaged at football on the lawn, and call out, "Looks like your necks are getting bigger than your heads, boys! Come on in and read awhile!"

Today, political experts generally agree that young George Smathers, congressman from Florida's fourth District (Dade, Collier, and Monroe counties), has a solid opportunity to weather the expert campaigning of the left-wing, long-in-office Pepper largely because the Smathers muscles are strong and the Smathers mind sharp, due to the judge's insistence on a sensible balance between brain and brawn. The boxing matches of twenty-five years also did their part in producing a candidate who doesn't mind trading punches and who long ago learned that a very fine way to open up a fight is to jab the other fellow right slap on the nose.

In his opening campaign speech at Orlando, for instance, Smathers mentioned no names, but everyone in Florida knew whom he meant when he spoke of "those in the government who are apologists for Stalin, associates of fellow travelers, and sponsors of Communist-front organizations."[4]

This barb pierced the Pepper skin because two days later, at the St. Petersburg airport, Pepper told reporters he was not an apologist for Stalin and that he would never speak to Smathers again.

Smathers retaliated briskly, saying he assumed this also meant he would not be spoken to by either Henry Wallace or Paul Robeson, two of the senator's one-time program associates. And a few days later—after combing Pepper's public utterances, he struck again. While a partisan Miami crowd applauded, Smathers read from a postwar speech made by Pepper in Russia over Radio Moscow, a tribute to Stalin in which the senator declared his trust in the Generalissimo; from a *Daily Worker* sketch of Senator Pepper which quoted a warm tribute to the Soviet leader; and from a later Associated Press dispatch reporting Pepper as saying, "Generalissimo Stalin is a man who keeps his promises."

A search of the *Congressional Record* has also revealed a Pepper tirade against President Truman for his firmness toward Russia, to which the late Senator Charles O. Andrews, colleague of Pepper, took exception, saying, "The sentiments expressed by my colleague do not represent the feelings of the great mass of the people of Florida. I'm hoping he will apologize to Secretary Byrnes and President Truman. . . ."

These fast left jabs and subsequent readings from the pen and utterances of the senator have drawn blood, but Pepper supporters profess to be unworried. "Claude always starts," they say, "as if he did not know a ballot from a bustle, but he ends up by hypnotizing the voters and they follow him off like in that story of the Pied Piper."

Florida, generally, is delighted at the present prospects. For the first time it has something which resembles a two-party system, with the line drawn between Smathers' conception of a liberal democrat and that of the complete New Dealer platform of Senator Pepper.

The Smathers organization, which is young and vocal, wildly enthusiastic and working madly, insists that their man is in shape to make every round a fast, hard-hitting one. Many of these are childhood playmates of their candidate who still recall the unusual child-raising customs of old Judge Smathers and have for him a great respect and affection.

The judge himself is no starry-eyed amateur in the field of politics. Both his candidate son and campaign workers give close attention to what the judge has to say and see to it that he puts his eye and pencil on drafts of all the campaign speeches.

A native of Waynesville, North Carolina, where the Smathers family is "old stock," Judge Smathers, after graduating from the state university in 1903, practiced law in Atlantic City, New Jersey, and later became first a precinct worker and then one of the county committeemen. When, in September 1910, the New Jersey Democratic Convention nominated Woodrow Wilson for governor, the vote from the Atlantic County delegation was cast by Frank Smathers, chairman. Within the following year a circuit judgeship appointment came from Governor Wilson, who urged it upon the young attorney when two factions supporting rival candidates for the position could not be brought to compromise. The judgeship allowed three days' practice each week, and his modest practice burgeoned.

But so did the processes of arthritis, which had been troubling him for three years. By late 1919, Frank Smathers, Sr., was forced to give up his judgeship, abandon his law practice in New Jersey, and move his wife and two young boys to Florida, where physicians hoped the climate might halt the slow solidification of his vertebra and the tortured twisting of his hands and feet. For about two years it did, but in the third year the attacks returned.

By this time, the judge had built up a new law practice which he and two assistants could hardly handle, but annually he found himself able to spend fewer hours at the office. He gave more and more time at home to looking after his boys.

Frank and George, who were nine and six, respectively, at the time of the migration to Florida, recall now how they were wont to peer wistfully from the windows of their wide front porch after their father's arrival from the office in the afternoon, hoping that none of the larger boys in the neighborhood would show up to play. So new was Miami in those days that there was just one other house in the whole neighborhood around Northeast 39th Street, where the parental home was, and is. If any boys were observed headed in the direction of the Smathers menage, the judge would greet them fondly and then call upon George to fetch the boxing gloves. The smaller boys never showed up for the boxing hour; those who did come took great joy in cuffing the Smathers ears as a relief from the tedium of young life.

For his two rather frail, skinny boys, those first Miami years were seen through a succession of black eyes and often over split, puffed lips and tender noses. The judge would look upon their honorable wounds with satisfaction and comment, "I want you to learn to take your knocks."

So the boys learned the hard way. Both became excellent amateur boxers. George won a Y.M.C.A. lightweight title. The University of Florida, where he went to college, provided other attractions, but Frank attended the University of North Carolina, where for two years he was number one man on the varsity team at 165 pounds. He is now manager of the Miami Beach trust department of the First National Bank.

Boxing in the front yard was by no means the only home-grown idea the judge employed on his boys. Early every morning he listed the chores of the day. If there were no lawns to be cut, no old shrubs to be moved or new ones planted, the boys dug holes well back of the house. These had to be dug to the depth of the armpits, but since the soil was sandy, they could be dug in about thirty minutes by a young boy eager to get away and play. These holes were quite utilitarian too. There was no garbage collection in those days in what were then Miami's distant suburbs, so the judge had the family kitchen refuse dumped into the holes and well sanded over.

Before bedtime each night, he had his four children stand before him—two boys and two girls—and recite something they had learned from books which he regularly assigned them. One daughter, Virginia, is now Mrs. Phillip Myers, of Los Angeles, where Mr. Myers is in the real-estate business. The other, Lura, named for her mother, was killed at twelve in an automobile accident, a fact which still saddens an otherwise happy and closely knit family.

"I wanted my boys to know early that life isn't all pleasure," the judge recollects. "Also, I did want them to have good muscles and good heads. I suppose that grew out of my own frustrations, but I still think it was a good idea."

Although his father was well able to buy them, George Smathers never had a suit of clothes of his own until he went to college. He wore, instead, his brother Frank's suits as fast as they were outgrown. George is one of those tall, well-set-up men on whom clothes seem to like to hang. In his first campaign for Congress, one of his managers decided that, even though George refused to clown in the rural regions, he ought to wear clothes which looked less well-tailored. He insisted on buying same. With a reluctant George in tow, he selected for him a fuzzy item off a rack of suits which retailed at twenty-seven dollars. That was late in 1945 when suits were high.

"The hell of it was," the old manager recalls, "that suit looked swell on George, and he got more compliments on his clothes than ever. So we gave up on it. George wears good, average suits. The trouble is, anything the guy wears fits him as if all the tailors in London had joined to produce a masterpiece."

George was talking about becoming a lawyer by the time he was twelve. His father told him then that if he still wanted to when the time came to enter college, he would see him through, but it had to be in Florida.

"I would have done better had I practiced where I went to school," the judge told him. "Every year you are in school, you make friends. They may become clients. They will always be your friends. Also, the judges and the bar have a better chance to know your real worth if you have come up with them."

Young George never thought about going anywhere else. Today some of his classmates have become his clients, and in every county over the state others are heading up his campaign organizations.

Hero worship helped him attract some attention in athletics at Robert E. Lee Junior High School and at Miami Senior High. A neighboring boy named Dudley Morton, three years ahead of George in high school and a football player, had given to the then-skinny Smathers kid, who followed him about, an old varsity sweater. Freshman Smathers wore it until it was out at the elbows and ragged around the edges. Indeed, this appearance was so bedraggled and poverty-stricken that a compassionate young coed, Miss Mary Dean, would seek him out daily, insisting that he share her lunch, so sure was she that he was unfed and hungry. Dudley Morton was a good man to have as a hero. He died a hero to the nation, as the skipper of that legendary submarine Wahoo which, before her seventh and last patrol in 1943, accounted for twenty-seven Japanese ships, totaling 119,000 tons. ("We Gave the Japs a Licking Underseas," *Saturday Evening Post*, 23 July 1949.)

With Morton as his example, Smathers played football and baseball, captained the high-school basketball team, which won the state championship in 1931, and was president of his class. At the University of Florida, in 1932, he cut down on athletics and went in strongly for debating and public speaking, on orders from his father, whose last ringing words to his young hopeful trudging off to college in his first new suit had been, "You can't make a living with muscles."

He roomed there with three young men who also have done good jobs of keeping their neck and head sizes balanced. One was Phil Graham, now publisher and president of the *Washington Post*. Dr. Jack Beckwith, prominent exodontist, and John Stembler, executive of a movie chain in Georgia and Florida were the others.

The list of Smathers' honors at the university, where he spent four years in the academic school for an A.B. and two in law for an LL.B., is lengthy. He captained the basketball team, was president of the student body, won the Southern intercollegiate oratorical contest, and was one of the top debaters of his time. He was chosen the best all-around man in school, and to that he added a B-plus scholastic average.

In 1938 Senator Claude Pepper, who had been assisted to office without opposition by Governor Dave Sholtz, was up for his first real campaign. By then the oratorical ability of the young university law student had reached even the senator's ears, who paid a visit to the university and subsequently asked Smathers to manage the Pepper campaign on campus. He did. As a matter of fact, Smathers made the senator sound so good that a delighted county organization drafted him to make speeches over the county and one for good measure in Miami. That was his first introduction to politics and to the man whom he now fights for the Senate seat. Any thoughts he had, however, about politics were dissipated by his graduation and marriage, although the latter had to wait until the matter of making a living was begun.

His father, by this time, had become too crippled to practice law at all. A few months after graduation, George Smathers, Jack Thompson, and Richard Maxwell, all young lawyers, formed a firm, carefully keeping Judge Smathers' name on the door. That firm is going strong today as Smathers, Thompson, Maxwell and Dyer. David W. Dyer was added shortly before the war.

All through Smathers' last year in law school his friends had enjoyed his painful fear lest a Miss Rosemary Townley, of Miami and Atlanta, say "No." In his high-school days, Smathers had been miserably shy. Later, at college debates, the young ladies shrilled for him somewhat in the manner now reserved for crooners. Handsome and friendly, Smathers was extremely popular with Florida's fairest. Envious fellow students called him "Smooch," so successful was he as a campus Romeo. But a painstaking research of the yearbooks, of former teachers and classmates reveals him to have been too busy for much courting. Miss Townley, whose father was a real Miami pioneer, having opened that city's first drugstore, said "Yes" in 1939

The law business was slow, but in 1940 the Junior Chamber of Commerce chose Smathers as its state president, another evidence of his popularity with the young men of Florida. In the summer of 1940, Senator Claude Pepper, who has always courted the large Dade County vote, called on the state's best-known young man with the offer of a job—assistant district attorney. Smathers took it. Fate and the FBI came along with a white-slave case, a particularly depraved one known in Miami as the La Paloma Club case. When it was done, the young district attorney had sent Fred Pine, former county solicitor and a county political power, to the federal prison along with three others involved. Everyone who read the Florida papers learned the name of George Smathers and recognized him as an able trial lawyer.

He was still on the job when Pearl Harbor came along. He had one son. But the Marine Corps recruiting office was in the same building as his law office, and one day he went in and enlisted. Two days later the recruiting officer came along and informed Smathers that his qualifications made him eligible for the reserve officers training at Quantico, and did he want to go? He did, and graduated as a first lieutenant. His legal training caused the marines to keep him in Washington for some months. Mrs. Smathers won her wound stripe there. Her husband's commanding officer was Colonel R. D. Salmon, and he was called—in private of course—"Colonel Fish." All one afternoon, before a small reception she was giving for her husband's friends and commanding officer, Mrs. Smathers schooled herself against saying "Colonel Fish." But she did, in the very first introduction. From Washington, Smathers went to gunnery school at Quantico, to Sterling Island near Bougainville, with the First Marine Bomber Squadron. He was camp commander, but flew as a volunteer on more than twenty missions, serving on some as a gunner.

Some of his critics today charge that Smathers has calmly calculated all the steps of his life and that he makes no decision without due deliberation. Smathers wishes some of those who have him so figured had been with him one day at the island airbase when Lieutenant Colonel Andy B. Galatian told him to hop on in, no parachute would be needed; they were merely going over to strafe Choiseul. Jap gunners knocked out several planes, and the colonel's PBJ had one engine go sour. Ordering all craft home and radioing the rescue craft in for the crew of one bomber that was down, Colonel Galatian then rang the bell for his own crew to prepare to bail out. The ship was losing altitude badly and the engine was flickering with fire. This caused Smathers to recall that he had no parachute. He remembers hurrying up front and speaking in a very loud and plaintive voice about how naked a fellow felt without a parachute when ordered to bail out. The colonel left it up to the crew. They decided to try to make it back and did—despite forty-two flak holes in the plane.

There were other islands on the Smathers service record before he was sent home in 1945, arriving at San Francisco the day Germany capitulated.

Back in Cherry Point, he was reassigned to the Judge Advocate's office. One day Smathers read in a Washington paper that Tom Clark, attorney general of the United States, was looking for lawyers who could "wrestle with a jury." Smathers applied. Attorney General Clark recalled the La Paloma case, and when Smathers was discharged in October, the job of special assistant to the attorney general was his. Because of his ability to wrestle with Florida juries, he was assigned cases in that state.

In December some of his friends came to him and said he ought to run for Congress. This had a pleasant sound to him. His older friends voted no. They advised waiting for a while. The incumbent had been in office eight years and was popular. The veterans and other young people, however, kept urging. Smathers entered the race.

Subsequently, thirty young men formed a committee to help get out the vote. Smathers' harassed opponent one day referred to them as a "goon" squad, which was unfortunate for him, because they adopted the name, which proved good for publicity stories and pictures, and their families and friends became indignant. Indignant persons vote. The thirty who were out tearing their shirts for Smathers included tire salesmen, meat cutters, grocery clerks, two trailer-park operators, an appliance salesman, a farm-supply distributor, a filling-station operator, lawyers, a druggist, a justice of the peace, a dairyman, an optical repairman, and so on.

The Goons of 1946—one of whom is now his honor the mayor of Miami, William Wolfarth—organized the young men and women of the Fourth Congressional District into a militant group, and Smathers popped the eyes of even his closest friends, but more especially the old-line politicians, by winning almost exactly two to one.

In Congress, he was placed on the Foreign Affairs Committee, a real plum for a freshman, and vigorously supported the Marshall Plan. He opposed some of the public-housing measures, but voted for the housing bill. Florida liked one of Smathers' own pieces of legislation, which continued Title Six of the National Housing Act, authorizing the FHA to insure loans up to an additional $750,000. This boomed Florida home building, which requires no basements and, in South Florida, no heating. Smathers also introduced bills to provide long-term loans to medical and dental students. He has been a consistent opponent of the compulsory-health-insurance plan, attacked as regimenting the medical profession.

His congressional record on civil rights reveals that he was consistently against the compulsory FEPC, arguing it was coercive and unworkable, and that any effort to make a short cut to justice with police sanctions was dangerous and harmful.

Smathers says that by the summer of 1945 he was convinced someone should run against Senator Pepper, but had not at any time considered himself as the man. He couldn't get out of his craw, he says, the fact that he himself felt, and many young people and veterans felt, that Senator Pepper has so involved himself with the Henry Wallace group and with others whom he and his friends regarded as apologists for a dangerous trend in America that someone ought to run against him.

By late fall of 1949, Smathers' friends were strongly urging that he make the race. Again the political experts said no. It would be better, they said, to get more seasoning in Congress. He could stay there indefinitely without serious opposition. Pepper, they pointed out, had been in office a long time and had the enormous power cumulative patronage provides, and probably would have administration help.

They reminded Smathers that in 1944, when opposition was growing against Pepper in his race of that year, the Gandy Causeway between St. Petersburg and Tampa had suddenly been removed from toll status and that

Pepper had been allowed to make the announcement. This toll had for years been a sore spot with the cities chiefly involved, and the Pepper announcement swung newspapers and votes to him. Smathers insisted the administration would keep hands off, however. His record as a democrat, he said, was sounder than Senator Pepper's. Smathers had campaigned for the Truman ticket in 1948 and he didn't believe the administration would interfere in a Florida primary. Unless there is a last-minute change, his confidence will not be upset.

Smathers decided to run because he believes Pepper can be beat. The basis of this conclusion is the voting record of the past Pepper campaigns. In 1936 Senator Pepper had no opposition. In 1938 he won an easy 69,377 first primary majority. He polled 242,350 votes against five nonformidable opponents. In 1944 running on a "let's-win-the-war" platform, the senator's majority over three opponents was 9,604, a drop of almost 60,000 from his majority of 1938. The total vote was off, probably because the opposition to Senator Pepper was not well known and also because of the men and women still away in the war. But there was no getting around the fact that the senator's percentage was down.

The big 1944 Pepper vote came not from North Florida, the senator's home, but from the large counties, chiefly Dade (Miami), Hillsborough (Tampa) and Pinellas (St. Petersburg and Clearwater). In those three counties alone his majority was 22,672, as against a state-wide total majority of only 9,604. Without a substantial majority in those counties, he would have been forced into a run-over.

In Dade, in 1944, the newspapers supported Senator Pepper. The chief Pepper opponent of that year, Judge Ollie Edmunds, had a weak state-wide organization and did not even speak in seventeen of the sixty-seven counties. In Hillsborough and Pinellas counties, the newspapers swung to Pepper because of the Gandy Causeway. This year the Dade County and Hillsborough papers are supporting Smathers, and in Pinellas County the dailies are split.

The Smathers board of strategy also checked the North and West Florida counties, often regarded as Pepper's chief source of strength. In 1944 he carried fifteen by clear majorities and lost eleven, including Duval (Jacksonville). He had a plurality in eight, including Escambia (Pensacola), but was topped in all by the combined votes of his opponents.

These and other 1944 figures helped Smathers, his father and friends make up their minds that there was a real chance. Smathers' formal announcement came in January, 1950, and by the close of the day, the young man's committee, largely augmented for the state campaign, was active and the issues publicly drawn.

Close on the heels of his announcement came one from Labor. Pepper, it said, must have the support of all labor in Florida. The labor press attacked Smathers as "Pretty Boy" and "Gorgeous George." The fact that he outshines many of Hollywood's handsomest male stars annoys some persons. His vote for the Taft-Hartley Law meant, said the labor editorialists, he was part of a conspiracy seeking to destroy labor. The fact that a typographical-union strike at the Miami newspapers had been going on for more than a year has added to the flame of attack against Smathers. Labor has rarely voted as a bloc in Florida, but this time its leaders will make their greatest effort to deliver it against Smathers. Labor claims 90,000 members in Florida, with an estimated family voting strength of about 125,000. Smathers remains confident he will get a good share of it. "They know I don't want to destroy labor," he said. "I voted against the original Hartley bill, and I will vote to amend this one where needed. But we need a labor law."

Meanwhile, President William Green, of the A. F. of L., and the head of the A. F. of L. Amalgamated Meat Cutters and Butchers have urged the Florida electorate to defeat Smathers. This pleases him immensely.

"Kingmakers from outside Florida will not dictate to the voters," he declares confidently.

Smathers' support of the Taft-Hartley Law was bolstered by the coal strike and allowed him to say in his speeches that, when either labor or business becomes too big and too·powerful, we obviously need legislation to curb either, pointing to the antitrust laws, to the Wagner Act and to the Taft-Hartley legislation as illustrations.

Some of Senator Pepper's ultra-left-wing friends were shocked when the senator, in replying to Smathers' discussion of the FEPC [Fair Employment Practices Commission] during the war, said he twice since had voted against it in committee. This Smathers called one of the best-kept secrets of the post-war years.

Another issue between them is Social Security expansion. Senator Pepper advocates continued expansion of Social Security and welfare programs, despite federal deficits. Pepper also supports the Townsend Plan and calls for a national sales tax to support it. Smathers calls this appeal to the old people—our "senior citizens" is his phrase for them—a "cruel deception." He insists that we must keep the money sound and not expand Social Security until we can pay for it, lest all pensions and security blow out the window of inflation.

These, plus their difference on the compulsory-health-insurance bill, are the chief issues between them, although their basic philosophy differs. Smathers opposes forthrightly any welfare state whose expansion is accomplished by deficit financing. He also declares the drift leftward must be halted when those in the drift become too chummy with those who are openly friendly to, or members of, the Communist Party. He insists that no liberal can take that route and remain a true liberal. It is these differences which provide almost a two-party senatorial primary in a state which is in many respects a political curiosity.

Students of Southern politics say Florida ranks high in "political atomization." It provides but another illustration of the fact that in the Southern states where the one-party system dominates, each state presents its own complex factional system. Florida is known as the "every-candidate-for-himself" state, a state "unbossed and unled." In 1944 it elected Senator Pepper, with a strong pro-labor record, and in the same balloting enthusiastically chose as its attorney general Tom Watson, a labor baiter who had announced he would smash the closed shop.

Geographically, Florida is in the South. But Florida is unlike any other Southern state, and save for some of its northern counties, close to the cotton states, it is not truly Southern. Its peculiar shape as Uncle Sam's lengthy chin whisker has made state-wide organization difficult. It is as far from Miami to Pensacola as from Atlanta to Washington, D. C., or from San Francisco to Portland. Its population has increased far faster than its neighbors'.

It has no agriculture as other states know it. Its citrus and muck-land vegetables factories are not "farming." Florida has the smallest farm population of any Southern state. Its urban population is largely confined to five widely separated counties. The counties with the five largest cities—Miami, Tampa, St. Petersburg, Pensacola and Jacksonville—contain about 45 percent of the state's population. The exact figure was 43 percent in the 1940 census and the cities have all grown. There are estimated to be 240,000 more voters this year than in 1944 because of the returned veterans and new citizens.

This wide separation and the highly diversified economic interests of each make for varying local political interests. This has largely prevented the demagogic pattern seen in other Southern states. It also has helped keep the state remarkably free, compared with her neighbors and regional associates, of Negro-baiting. Only in a few of the northern counties does this appeal make votes.

Early in his campaign, Smathers, after consulting with his Negro friends, refused to go on with a scheduled speech at a Negro church at St. Petersburg where a small crowd had gathered with photographers in waiting. Smathers had been informed that pictures were to be taken of the meeting and distributed in the few northern counties where anti-Negro propaganda has been used in other campaigns.

"I wanted none of that in my campaign," he said, "so my friends and I agreed to prevent it by not holding the meeting."⁵

Senator Peppers' organization, while admittedly working harder than ever before, and running a scared race, is confident their man's genius for campaigning will pull him through. They take a wry sort of pleasure out of the fact that many businessmen who detest Harry S. Truman and the politics of Senator Pepper will go along with him because of what they say the senator has done for many Florida businessmen. Pepper lieutenants also count heavily on help from the state administration, which is expected to make no public demonstration, but to pass the word on to the county organizations. They rely on the lack of professional experience in the Smathers committees to make them ineffective.

On the other hand, Judge Smathers and the young Goons remain equally assured. "George is doing all right," the judge says calmly. "Hat and shirt size are still in balance."⁶

Notes—26

[1]Published by permission of the author, Mrs. McGill, and *The Saturday Evening Post* (22 April 1950): 32-33, 141-43.

[2]Senator Claude Pepper helped Smathers get a job as assistant United States district attorney and thus be discharged early from the United States Marine Corps. Pepper also supported Smathers for Congress in his defeat of Pat Cannon in Florida's Fourth District.

[3]Smathers defeated Pepper by 60,000 votes.

[4]Although known as a liberal politician, a labor candidate, a progressive, and a Claude Pepper supporter in the mid-1940s, in 1950 Smathers reversed his stance and campaigned against the liberal ways of Senator Pepper. Using extremist tactics, he warned Florida voters of "socialists" and "fellow travelers," and attempted to win votes by referring to Pepper as a "shameless extrovert" who would "practice nepotism with his sister-in-law," and whose "sister . . . once" was a "thespian." See Robert Sherrill, *Gothic Politics in the Deep South: Stars of the New Confederacy* (New York: Grossman Publishers, 1968), pp. 147-48, 150.

[5]In the United States Senate Smathers, like most Southern politicians of the time, "vigorously opposed civil rights measures." But in 1964 when 300,000 blacks were added to the voting roll, he changed stances again, even voting for the Voter Registration Act of 1965. See Eleanora W. Schoenebaum, ed., *Political Profiles: The Truman Years*, vol. 1 (New York: Facts on File Inc., 1978), pp. 500-501; Sherrill, *Gothic Politics in the Deep South*, pp. 154, 172.

[6]In 1956 McGill wrote what was to be the foreword to an autobiography by Judge Frank Smathers. McGill wrote: "I am delighted that Judge Frank Smathers and his brother John and sister Lydia have done us all the favor of giving us the story of his grandfather, John C. Smathers"; manuscript provided from McGill papers by Mrs. McGill.

Essay 27

Walter George Picks the Most Important Decisions of His Time[1]

    Sitting there in the quiet of his Washington apartment, talking of the past, present, and future, one thought inevitably of how much Walter F. George had had to do with the first two of these, and of what his influence would be on things to come.

    When he went to the Senate of the United States in the fall of 1922, the state still echoed to the last Wagnerian frenzies of Tom Watson, whose range always was between heaven's gate and hell's abyss.[2] When Walter George left the Senate in January of 1957, having determined for reasons of health not to seek another term, he already was serving as the President's ambassador to the North Atlantic Treaty Organization (NATO). He continued in that field.[3]

    The senator, now ambassador, had been asked to think back on his almost thirty-five years in the top house of our Congress, and to select from them decisions and events which he considered the more important. It was a panorama of years in which much of the nation's greatest history was made. It involved the crushing forces of a world-wide depression in which the United States, losing none of its liberties, found its inspired Constitution resilient enough to make the changes necessary to the people's wishes. It included the second great world war and its aftermath.

The senator sat there thinking, quiet, dignified, as is his custom.

The reporter knew there would be no claims made for recognition of accomplishment. He knew, too, the senator ambassador would understate and be most modest in any recollections of accomplishment. Here was a man who, in the present Senate, had for a generation been perhaps its most influential man. Here was one who had, for Presidents Roosevelt and Eisenhower, been a great bulwark of strength, and often the shadow of a great rock in a weary land.

The Georgia boy who had gone from a small tobacco farm to school at Mercer Law School, to the practice of law at Vienna, to the Supreme Court of Georgia, and to the Senate of the United States, had never lost his humility; had never sounded his own trumpets.[4]

"It was from the first," he said, "a gripping experience. All the years seemed to come at a great period in our history. When I came here the first world war had but recently ended. There were some of the same old problems which have plagued us after the second great world war. At the request of the leadership of the party at that time, I went into finance. The tax laws and tariffs were most important in those postwar years. I plunged into that. Out of that came, I recall, the first comprehensive legislation for the protection of veterans of the war."

"Not too long after that," he said, his thoughtful quiet voice revealing none of the drama of his beginning, "they asked me to go into foreign relations and I gave up my place on the military affairs committee to do that."

What the senator had not said was that he had within a few months revealed so great a capacity for the technical affairs of legislation having to do with finance and with intricate ramifications of all sorts, that he was in demand. And what specifically was at hand was the gigantic and complicated task of funding the debt of the allied countries.

Harding, being an inept man and in the hands of his betrayers, had bungled things. Cal Coolidge, the careful man, had declared a moratorium.

Walter George helped the Republican Party steer its way through its many contradictions of that period. Even then he was being recognized as one of the more able men in the Senate. Not many Georgians recall, for example, that it was he who joined with Senator Bennett Champ Clark of Missouri to take the burden of writing the veterans' legislation, and with others to handle the financial legislation made necessary by the new pressures of the time.

Having wrecked the League of Nations, the Coolidge and Hoover administrations nonetheless found themselves compelled to deal with the problem of international relations and of peace. Senator George now believes that had we gone into the League with a "will and purpose" we might slowly have built up precedents which would have been of value. He feels the same about the World Court. But we modified our own membership to such an extent that membership was but an exercise in futility.

The Senate leadership, of both parties, continued to find use for "George of Georgia." Of fourteen major revenue bills adopted by the Congress in his period, Walter George did major work on all of them.

As a boy he remembered his own thirst for an education. He recalled, too, the many boys who could not go to college. Busy as he was with finance and foreign relations, he found time to make his weight felt in this field.

It is typically ironic of politics, and a sad commentary on the memory of man, that when Senator George retired from the Senate he was regarded by most of his fellow Georgians as a man whose primary interest had been in foreign affairs.

The record reveals the contrary facts. Not only did he do much of the burdensome work on veterans' legislation; he was one of the authors of four basic bills which set up a system of vocational education in trade and agriculture. The bills bear his name. When the second great world war came, the value of such education was recognized and the government itself set up, with industry, vocational training schools. Senator George was a pioneer and when the need came the basic law long had been on the statute books—bearing George's name.

Meanwhile, because of the League failure, the second great world war, which a sorrowing Woodrow Wilson said in 1920 would have to be fought over again within twenty years, was rushing toward us.

Senator George regards the "Lend-Lease" legislation as "one of the most important acts of my time." It was. It is not an exaggeration to say that Lend-Lease, by providing England with the sinews of war, enabled her to remain strong enough to fight.

But what the average American perhaps never realized was that Lend-Lease brought our own military machine into being. Without Lend-Lease we would not have had the industrial capacity at the time it was so desperately needed. As it was, the Japanese sneak attack on Pearl Harbor badly crippled us. Had it not been for the fact that Lend-Lease orders had put our industrial production into high gear, the disaster at Hawaii would have been much greater than it was. The Lend-Lease legislation was complex and technical. It was to Walter George the White House and the Congress turned when the pressure for its construction and passage came. Preparation of the legislation was arduous and long. So was the debate.

There occurred then a vivid illustration of his value which, because of the clamor of war, largely was overlooked. He is the only man who was chairman of both finance and foreign relations, serving from 1940 until 1941.

Senator George produced, as we talked of the great battle for Lend-Lease, a footnote to history. "The administration was, of course, urging it," he said, "with Cordell Hull speaking strongly for it. But I do not believe it has ever been told that the man who suggested the idea and plan for Lend-Lease was Henry L. Stimson, who served as secretary of state and of war under Republican administrations and in various other diplomatic posts. He was the first to seek to try and halt Japanese aggression in Manchuria. He saw that we could not, as a nation, make adequate preparation unless we could begin to expand our industrial production for war. He never doubted the Japanese would bring us in. And, so he privately provided the inspiration for Lend-Lease."

This is but another reason for the nation to feel grateful to Henry Stimson. Had we heeded his advice about using force to stop the Japanese aggression in Manchuria in 1932, we might have prevented the expansion into China—and the Nipponese drive to World War II.

We turned to talk of senators—and their abilities.

"What about Senator Robert Taft?"

"Senator Taft was a real student of government. He was stubborn but did not have a closed mind. He was open to conviction. He became a real friend of the President, despite their differences before the convention which nominated Mr. Eisenhower."

"What do you think Taft would be doing now had he lived?"

"It is my firm conviction Senator Taft would now be supporting the President and his policies. He could meet change and change his mind."

"Who was, in your opinion, the best orator?"

"I think Senator (William) Borah was the best advocate, or pleader. Senator Joe Robinson was a man of great ability in this field. He was also a man of very considerable parts."

"Who are some others you remember for their special abilities?"

"George Norris I remember as perhaps the most tireless worker I have ever seen there. George W. Pepper, of Pennsylvania, was not too successful as a senator, but was a man of really great abilities. (Senator Pepper served from 1922 through 1927.)

The senator remembered an amusing incident about Henry Wallace.

"During the long debate on Lend-Lease," said the senator, "we had to be patient. There was much at stake. It was neither possible nor desirable to hurry. Yet we could not waste time. Senator Taft was opposing the measure. He did not believe there would be war. Vice-President Wallace, who, of course, presided, would listen to the debates and become disturbed. He would relay his fears to the President. Mr. Roosevelt would telephone me and I would reassure him.

"At last we had it about ready for passage, but it was necessary to accept one really innocuous amendment. We agreed and the amendment was attached. This upset Mr. Wallace.

"That night the President called. 'Senator,' he said, 'you know Henry is the world's worst politician. And he is nervous. Is there any reason for me to be?'

"I assured him there was not. And there wasn't."

The senator paused and reflected.

"I am sure," he said, "from what military leaders of our own country and those of Europe have told me, that Lend-Lease shortened the war by at least a year, maybe more. It saved many thousands of lives, perhaps hundreds of thousands, and millions of dollars in property. I suspect that because of this fact, the lives and property saved, the war shortened, it is the greatest single piece of legislation of those years. I am rather proud to have been one of its architects."

We sat and talked a while longer.

Here was the man who had talked of orators and advocates, of students of government, and tireless workers whom he had met as fellow senators.

What he did not say was that his reputation in all these fields was at the top. Senator Walter George, for example, is described in William White's *Citadel*, recently published best-seller book on the United States Senate, as the most commanding figure in it.

It was White who pointed out, too, that it was Senator George who gave the Eisenhower administration the opportunity to open discussions with Russia when the White House and the State Department were impotent and, apparently, fearful of action.

One thought, saying goodbye to the senator when the talk was ended, that few are the men of whom it may be said they shortened the second great war by a year, and that later they provided the *modus operandi* for enabling the powers to meet with the Russians, breaking a deadlock which seemed then leading to the third war.

There are those senators who, throughout their careers, have by sensationalism in the field of race prejudice and by demagoguery of the worst and most flagrant kind, occupied the headlines year after year, in season. They have made of themselves "personalities" who ranked with the Hollywood divorces and scandals as "news."

But Walter F. George, after almost thirty-five years in the United States Senate, has been one of the real architects of his country. His contributions are in its major legislation in almost every aspect of our life, domestic, national, and international.

In a time which called for ability, deeds, and character, he had all three to give. And he gave them without stint, and without any sound of brass or tinkling cymbal.

That always has been his way.

Notes—27

[1]Reprinted from *Atlanta Journal and Constitution Magazine* (17 March 1957), by permission of the author, Mrs. McGill, and Atlanta Newspapers, Inc.

[2]See article on Tom Watson by McGill in this book.

[3]Walter Franklin George was born 29 January 1878 and died 4 August 1957.

[4]George was graduated from Mercer University, 1900, and Mercer Law School, 1901. He began his law practice in Vienna, Georgia, 1901; was solicitor general of the Cordele Judiciary Circuit, 1907-1912; and judge of the supreme court of that circuit, 1912-1917. In the United States Senate, 1922-1957, he was chairman of the finance committee, 1941-1947, and 1949-1953.

Essay 28

Sam Rayburn[1]

Sam Rayburn is dead in Bonham, Texas, in the autumn season of harvest and fulfillment:[2] "Don't ever count the crop until it is in the barn," he used to tell young, impatient congressmen. The crop of his life is now in eternity's barn, and it can be counted and measured.

Sam Rayburn was not an average man. He was not, as some thought, taciturn and short of temper. He was not a man for small talk. He did not tolerate fools easily. Now and then he annoyed the more idealistic newcomers to the House by telling them that the "way to get along is to go along" (He did not mean it as cynically as it sounds.)

As we begin to look at the harvest of Rayburn's long, rich life, we discover that in the years of the New Deal, the Fair Deal, and the first of the New Frontier, it was he, the small town, rural conservative, who labored most success-fully in the vineyard of social reform. He could be, and was, both conservative and liberal. But, what he really was, was a man of great sensitivity and feeling for the needs and rights of people. He had no patience with those who proposed legislation which he thought had for its purpose merely the coddling or rewarding of people. But, when the real needs of people were at issue, Mr. Sam was on their side.

Had it not been for him, President Kennedy, for example, would have been brought to disaster in the first months of his administration. The rules committee was in defiant, hostile hands. It would not permit bills which established a new minimum wage, expanded Social Security payments, a housing act and other legislation pledged by the Democratic administration to be voted out to the floor. To get them there Sam Rayburn had to do battle with an old friend, Representative Howard Smith, of Virginia. He defeated that austere, vain, and dogmatic man when the experts said it couldn't be done. It was a close vote—217 to 212. But the margin was wide enough—especially in a battle which might not have been won at all.[3]

This was in early January, 1961. It was in late summer that what seemed like an old man's lumbago pains began to bother Mr. Sam. He went home. Worried doctors found it was not lumbago at all, but cancer, already spread through the lymph system, and impossible to cure.

In the sorrow which welled up at the news, men began to remember that he had served well three presidents—Franklin D. Roosevelt, Harry S. Truman and John Kennedy.[4] They each learned to lean on him. They encountered his sometimes irascible stubbornness. They knew moments of irritation and anger. But, none doubted his loyalty. They knew that when the chips were down they could count on his complete loyalty to the Democratic Party and its basic principles. He might, and often did, refuse to accept presidential urgings and proposed legislation. Not even his enemies ever suggested he was a rubber stamp. But he was unfailingly a Democrat.

There are many examples of this presidential awareness. On 18 February 1942 Franklin D. Roosevelt sent a personal note to Speaker Rayburn:

> Dear Sam:
> I understand you have been invited to be the principal speaker next Monday at the George Washington Dinner to be held in Fort Worth, Texas. Because of the importance of legislation before the House at this time—legislation urgently needed because of the war—I feel that it would be better if you stayed in Washington . . . . I feel it is my duty to ask you to stay here with me at least until the House has disposed of much needed legislation. In other words, the nation needs you a lot more than Texas does right now.[5]

One weekend when a VIP caller telephoned Washington he found the president and the vice-president were away. He reached the president in a distant city and asked, "Who's tending the store in Washington?"

"Rayburn," said the President. "The country's safe with him there."

In his autobiography, *That Reminds Me*, the late Alben Barkley, the Kentuckian who for so long was majority leader of the Senate for the Democrats, and war horse in national conventions and in debate, wrote of Rayburn: "When I consider Sam Rayburn's tenure in the House and think how valuable his long, unbroken experience is to the country, it makes me realize how, in one respect,

British parliamentary customs have been superior to ours. I have always felt the British had the best of it in keeping their good men in Parliament for long periods—Gladstone, Lloyd George, and Churchill—to mention a few examples—instead of replacing them every few years as we do in many cases."[6]

Even Harold Ickes, "the old Curmudgeon" and gadfly of the Roosevelt years, though he quarreled often with Sam Rayburn (and with everyone else), wrote that Roosevelt's most vital legislation could not have been had without Sam Rayburn.

The president did not obtain all he wanted. But in the field of public utility reform, for example, strong legislation was enacted over the bitter fight of the powerful electric and gas industry lobbies. Rayburn was storm-tossed and under terrific pressure from interests in his home state. Yet, he held on.

Rural electrification came via the Norris-Rayburn bill. Here again, the electric companies fought hard to prevent passage of it. Rayburn put it through the House, and the Senate followed this leadership.[7]

This was the period when President Roosevelt said, "I am fighting Communism, Huey Longism, Coughlinism, Townsendism. . . . I want to save our system, the capitalistic system; to save it is to give some heed to world thought of today. . . ."

In all these things Sam Rayburn was a stalwart.

Perhaps he remembered his own harsh boyhood. He was the eighth child of eleven, born on a rocky farm in East Tennessee. When he was a child the father, a Confederate veteran, made the long move to Texas for a new start. There, on an isolated forty acres, young Rayburn grew up. He recalled the far stretching, level emptiness of the plains, and the hours when he swung on the gate on Sundays, hoping to see some rider coming on a visit. (Once he said of those days, "I have known loneliness that breaks the heart.") He toiled hard in the fields. He read history books at night.

He wanted school. His father wanted it for him and all his children. When it came time for Sam to go to East Texas Normal, the young man had perhaps $5.00 saved from the meager amounts which came his way. His father waited until the train was in. He then silently handed his boy $25.00.[8]

"God knows how he saved it," said Rayburn, in talking about that day. "He never had any extra money. We earned just enough to live. It broke me up, him handing me that $25.00. I have often wondered what he did without, what sacrifice he and my mother made beyond those which every day demanded of them."

At the Normal School he swept floors and did odd jobs for his room and board. He studied hard—especially history. He managed to get to law school. Politics were always in his mind. He once said that at ten years of age he was determined to go to Congress. In the Southern states law is regarded as a necessary stepping stone to politics.[9]

He went to Congress in 1912, the year Woodrow Wilson became president. Wilson was ever one of his heroes. He never thought of the Senate, and never aspired to it. To him the House, the legislative body, was the most important and meaningful. One way to earn a rebuke was to speak to the House as "the lower body." To him it was the highest. The senate always waited on the House to originate and clear the air with debate.

He was often at odds with Democratic presidents. But he never even considered bolting the Democratic Party. He thought it not unusual that the country turns to Democrats when there is trouble. "I am perfectly serious about it," he said once, in talking of this. "Democrats somehow seem to have more instinct for government and for keeping the country running right than the Republicans. I think this is because they are, for the most part, closer to the people and think in broader political terms. The Republicans have a tradition of representing business—not people."

This perhaps helps explain his support of legislation, attacked by the GOP Old Guard as socialistic, which enabled "people" to have a better life. REA [Rural Electrification Administration] is a perfect example. He pushed it hard. "It will take some of the harsh labor off the backs of farm men and women," he said, perhaps remembering the worn, tired father who, at the train, had given his son an unexpected $25.00, saved "God knows how." "Can you imagine what it will mean to a farm wife to have a pump in the well and lights in the house?"

He was elected Speaker in 1940. He held that position until his death, save for the first Eisenhower administration. He respected President Eisenhower, and believed him to be an honest, well-meaning man. But, he also thought him a Republican in the sense that Mr. Eisenhower's image of wisdom and "the best brains" seemed to be any man who had attained financial success. He privately predicted that, in the years ahead, Mr. Eisenhower's indecision, his refusal to come to grips with the dangerous problems which were fast building up, would cause his administration to be compared with that of Buchanan's.[10] In the years before the Civil War it, too, called for men of good will to join hands for the common good. But the Buchanan administration never grappled with the big issues.

Nor did Mr. Sam care much for vice-president Nixon, who previously had been much in the House and Senate. He never had an open quarrel with Mr. Nixon. But he said of him that he could not bring himself fully to like or trust him. "I never saw a man with such cold, mean eyes," he said, once, in discussions of the then vice-president.

There was a long, fast friendship between him and Lyndon Johnson, now vice-president. The current vice-president first came to Washington as a congressman and it was his fellow Texan Rayburn who schooled him and taught him the ropes. At the 1960 convention it was Rayburn who placed his protege's and friend's name in nomination for the presidency. It was Rayburn, too, who was one of those who gave the green light to Senator Johnson's surprise acceptance of the vice-presidential nomination.

Sam Rayburn's life was not Spartan; it was rich. Yet, he lived simply. He never took congressional junkets. Indeed, the record shows that he never left the United States but once. He went once to inspect the Panama Canal. When Congress adjourned he went home. He had two farms. On one he raised cattle. On the other he grew corn and cotton. He liked to fish and read. But he was not a man who had to be entertained. He could live with himself.

"Many a time," he once told the writer, "I sit on the front porch of my home and think about the old forty acres on which my father wore out his body and his heart. I have wished a thousand times he could have lived to be an old, old man and sit with me on the porch."

It is proper, in seeking to sum up the life of the man who served with (not under) Wilson, Roosevelt, Truman, and Kennedy, and who gave to each advice which was wise and politically pragmatic, to note that he is the last of his breed. He came quite literally from the frontier. The last president he served projected for the country a new frontier in a time of growing population, automation, computers, and industrial techniques which approach the miraculous.

Sam Rayburn came from the old frontier. Yet, none was more alert or at home in the new frontier than he. His mind was so resilient that he could serve the presidents in whose administrative years the nation made its greatest social changes. The tremendous reforms began with Wilson—the eight-hour day, and the various legislative acts which made the capitalistic system itself more flexible and strong, at a time when the first world war was about to bring the changes which would pull down ancient thrones and kingdoms and loose powerful revolutionary forces which are yet out of control. Our system has endured because the profit dollar developed, in the years spanned by Rayburn's life in the Congress, a social conscience. American capitalism came to mean, among other things, public education, Social Security, unemployment insurance, aid to crippled children, to the blind, and, through hospital construction aid, the sick. Capitalism pays the bill for disasters; it subsidizes farmers; it builds dams and irrigates deserts. It clears slums, finances housing, guarantees bank deposits. American capitalism resembles almost not at all the classic capitalism of Queen Victoria's day. It is almost unbelievable that one man's legislative experience spans these tremendous reforms—from 1912 until now. And rare is the important bill which does not bear his name or the stamp of Rayburn's advice or influence.

It is easy to see that he was, and that the sum of his life is, greater than that of any one of the presidents with whom he served. "Don't ever say a Speaker of the House serves 'under' a president, son," he once told a young reporter.

In writing about men who have served for a long number of years, it is too easy to slip into the trite conclusion that an era has ended and that it is perhaps as well that death has come to save a man from heartbreak and disappointment.

This is not true of "Mr. Sam." Until the lumbago pains would no longer respond to aspirin or mustard plasters, he could sniff the battle from afar and go forward confidently to meet it. He was a magnificent field commander. He grew old, but his mind, his political tactics and strategies did not. He was not losing his grip. The fact is there is none to take his place in the House. And, in certainty, he will stay on in the hearts of the thousands who knew and loved him.

Notes—28

[1]Manuscript provided by Mrs. Ralph McGill from the McGill papers.

[2]Samuel Taliaferro Rayburn was born in Tennessee on 6 January 1882 to Martha Clementine Waller Rayburn and William Marion Rayburn. He died 16 November 1961.

[3]See C. Dwight Dorough, *Mr. Sam* (New York: Random House, 1962), pp. 3-15.

[4]For Rayburn's interactions with Roosevelt, Truman, and Kennedy, see Dorough, *Mr. Sam*, pp. 219-82, 348-403; and Alfred Steinberg, *Sam Rayburn: A Biography* (New York: Hawthorn Books, Inc., 1975), pp. 115-29, 227-34, 257-69, 311-48.

[5]Roosevelt to Rayburn, in Elliott Roosevelt, ed., *F. D. R. His Personal Letters, 1928-1945*, vol. 2 (New York: Duell, Sloan and Pearce, 1950), pp. 1286-87. McGill omitted "night" after "Monday."

[6]Quoted from Alben W. Barkley, *That Reminds Me* (Garden City, NY: Doubleday & Co., 1954), pp. 99-100.

[7]See Dorough, *Mr. Sam*, pp. 244-47.

[8]Rayburn moved to a farm in Flag Springs, Texas, 2 November 1887; studied at Mayo Normal School, Commerce, Texas, 1900; passed the bar examination after enrolling in courses at the University of Texas, 1908. See Dorough, *Mr. Sam*, pp. 43-67; Steinberg, *Sam Rayburn*, pp. 3-12.

[9]Rayburn was elected to the state legislature of Texas, 1906-1912.

[10]For Rayburn's interaction with Eisenhower, see Steinberg, *Sam Rayburn*, pp. 270-95.

Essay 29

Why Atlanta Keeps Electing Mayor William Berry Hartsfield[1]

In January 1962, unless dispatched in answering a fire or police call or by a stroke brought on by a furious argument over the merits of the city, William Berry Hartsfield will have been mayor of Atlanta for 24 1/2 years, a record for American cities of more than 300,000 population. Dan Hoan served the city of Milwaukee for twenty-four years and presently holds the title of municipal political longevity.

Before his first election as mayor in 1936, to take office in January 1937, Mayor Hartsfield was six years an alderman and four years a state legislator. This means he has been before the electorate for thirty years. His latest victory, on last December 4, was by the largest margin in all his career.

Any man that long in politics, especially a successful one, picks up opposition. Defeated candidates and their friends rarely feel warmly toward the winner. Citizens of any and all cities who are angry because the fire department was tardy in getting the family cat out of a tree, who are morose because they didn't get, or lose, a beer license, or a street repair contract, and those who are unable to fulfill certain underworld functions common to many other cities, always feel the city should have a new mayor. Mayor Hartsfield has his share of these.

The mayor also picks up others because he is of an intense and impulsive nature. This causes him to create unnecessary foes and frequently to exasperate even those who regard him most fondly. He is a stubborn, often impatient man, who usually knows what he is talking about—a fact which makes him difficult in debate. He certainly is one of the best students of municipal government in America. He is so regarded by his fellow mayors who, in 1953, elected him president of the American Municipal Association, and who still retain him on the National Airport Committee. The U. S. Conference of Mayors keeps him on its advisory board.[2]

In late 1957 the thesis that Mayor Hartsfield knows more about efficient management of a city was confirmed by the completely nonpartisan computing machines which now are called upon to provide us with so many analyses of statistics. Certain ideas which rather effectively constitute what might be called an X-ray machine for peering at the organic operations of a city were fed into a computer by researchers at *Fortune Magazine*. They revealed Mayor Hartsfield to be one of "the nine best mayors in the United States," a fact which surprised no fair-minded resident of the city, since Atlanta's well-managed affairs are obvious to the naked eye.

Robert Snodgrass, an Atlanta businessman, put the mayor and his methods in good perspective a few years ago when serving as president of the city's Chamber of Commerce.

"At times," he said, "Bill acts as if he actually owned the town. And that's exactly why he is one of the most effective mayors in the whole country. He looks after the city's interests exactly the same way a homeowner looks after his property. Naturally, this does not always please some of those who encounter him in those moments. But it appeals to most taxpayers and businessmen."[3]

It still does. In his most recent campaign, Robert Maddox, Atlanta's only living full-term ex-mayor, who served from 1909 to 1912, led a great body of business and professional endorsements of Mayor Hartsfield.[4] In fact, in almost all his campaigns, the mayor's opposition has consisted largely, but not entirely, of extremist groups represented by the Ku Klux Klan and the more rabid White Citizens Councils.[5]

His business, labor, and white collar support was earned by solid accomplishment. He took office in January 1937. Atlanta was then $3,000,000 in debt and near outright bankruptcy. It was operating under the even then outmoded "anticipation of revenues" system which invites new deficits and increases old ones. The fire and police departments had almost no equipment and that which was in use was in a bad state of repair.

Hartsfield had already won a considerable amount of public confidence as an alderman and state legislator. As mayor he had the immediate support of bankers who provided the money to an all-but-bankrupt city to refund the more pressing obligations. The county's legislative delegation introduced suggested legislation setting up a model budget system for the city. Under its provisions the city may not budget more than ninety-nine percent of the receipts of the previous year. Council usually holds to about ninety-five percent, thus providing a carry-over.[6]

Under this cash system the city annually saves around $35,000 by taking two percent discounts on bills. One of the things which fascinates many other mayors is that Atlanta makes a clean, if modest, profit on its garbage. A good many years ago the mayor persuaded the council to buy and install in Atlanta incinerator equipment he had heard about in Copenhagen, Denmark. It was the first of such plants in this country. The city sells enough steam and reclaimed scrap to make a profit. The mayor discusses the garbage plant in the ecstatic terms employed by orchid growers in describing some new and beautiful plant.

The airport is closest to his heart—and with reason. As chairman of a new aldermanic committee in 1924, he had selected the site of the airport and had, with vision and enthusiasm, led the way to enable Atlanta to be ready when the aviation industry began to find its feet. He obtained the first city appropriation to do work on the airport—the sum of $5,000. It was widely attacked as extravagance by those in the city administration, and some businessmen, who did not believe airplanes would ever be more than personal playthings or attractions at state fairs. By resisting all the "hurry-up" pressures, the mayor has saved the people of Atlanta about $5 million on the present airport expansion. He and the Municipal Association were trying to get the government to assist. Once it did, the plans long-made and awaiting the most propitious time were activated.

Atlanta's record of financial soundness has been maintained through years of war, inflation, recession, and shortages of material and manpower. It was, however, Atlanta's successful "Plan of Improvement" which attracted new and admiring attention to the city. This was a team effort, with all groups, save the usual "do nothing" factions, lending a hand. Atlanta, like almost every city in America, had been living in a sort of suburban strait jacket. Atlanta was more severely restricted than others. With the exception of small bits of acreage, the city limits had not been extended in almost forty years. Thousands of persons had moved outside the boundaries and the competing city and county services were each year becoming more and more burdensome. The "Plan of Improvement" began the consolidation of some duplicated services, regrouped others, and enlarged the city limits from thirty-seven square miles to 118, increasing the population by about 100,000. Lower fire insurance rates, better police and fire protection, were among the many benefits.

The plan is regarded by the American Municipal Association as one of the most workable and practical ever devised. In 1952, the first year of the plan's operation, the National Municipal League singled out Atlanta for special commendation. A fine system of express, or freeways, is moving toward completion. A project of the county, city, and state, all have worked well together and made excellent progress, despite inflation in materials, wages, and land condemnation costs.

The mayor refers to Atlanta as the "showcase" city of the Southeast. It just about is, and in no other field has it offered a better look than in that of race relations. Good race relations just don't happen. They are the net result of a lot of work by decent, well-meaning people of both races. Atlanta is not a city of hates, but there are those who keep trying to make it so. The mayor, with the help of an excellent police chief, the city's daily newspapers, and a great majority of its citizens, has enabled Atlanta to retain a standard of civilization which is rather high in the Deep South. Atlanta is a cosmopolitan city of schools, churches, businesses, and the arts. The Negro citizenship is perhaps the highest in the United States. The result of all of these factors is that common sense, decency, and honesty have a chance to express themselves. But all of this requires direction and this the mayor has given with, of course, the assistance before noted.[7]

The mayor is, fittingly enough, a native of Atlanta. He was born 1 March 1890 about five blocks from Five Points.[8] His father, Charles Green Hartsfield, son of a Confederate veteran, was one of the many young men who came to the city which was being rebuilt out of the ashes of war, to seek opportunity and work. Here he met and married Victoria Dagnall, whose parents had moved to Atlanta from South Georgia. As a small girl she had seen Sherman's troops march through her part of the state on the tremendous march to Savannah and the sea.[9]

Hartsfield's father became a skilled tinsmith with the old Conklin tin plant. He wanted his son to go on to college, but the urge was strong in the boy to make his own way. In his senior year at Boys High he entered the Dixie Business College and became a secretary. Moving slowly up with each job he felt, on the fifth, he was financially able to marry a young lady he had long been courting, Miss Pearl Williams. She has been ever since his quiet adviser and has shunned the spotlight to supervise the home and the two children as they grew up.

The sixth job was as a secretary and law clerk in the then outstanding firm in the city—Rosser, Slaton, Phillips & Hopkins. Luther Rosser's name still is a legend in Georgia bar circles and John Slaton became a famous governor of the state.

It was there, Hartsfield recalls, that he realized his father had been right about getting more book learning. He took a typical approach. He wrote the deans of a dozen colleges, honestly telling them he was a fool to quit school too early. He asked for suggested reading in English literature, history, and corollary reading. When the answers came he gave all the books a thorough study. He acquired thereby the reading habit, and newspapers, magazines, fiction, and biographies are a part of his habits. This helped make him a fluent speaker. He is really excellent as a master of ceremonies and is very quick with repartee and debate.

In 1918 the young law clerk passed the bar examinations and in 1921 opened his own office. Active in that same year in support of a friend campaigning for the aldermanic board, he ran himself the next year and was elected to the first of two three-year terms.

The next year he became fascinated with aviation, and as chairman of the first aviation committee, he helped persuade Asa Candler to allow use of the oval inside the race track on the outskirts of town as an airport. From that time on the mayor has felt a great personal interest in it. In those early days he helped repair planes, spieled for customers for the barnstormers selling rides, and finally learned to fly. Had he possessed the necessary money, he would have gone into aviation as a career, but a young married man with a new law office couldn't afford it.[10]

In 1928 he dropped out of politics rather than play ball with a newly effected organization of city and county politicians, in and out of office. A year later the exposure began, led by the *Atlanta Constitution*, a job which earned that newspaper the Pulitzer Prize for public service. His elevation to the mayor's office came in the primary of 1936. His only defeat in seven primaries and one election came in 1940. An unusually severe traffic judge had aroused a great deal of enmity and, as is always the case, the mayor became the target. He lost by 111 votes, and despite well-sustained charges of fraud in some precincts and evidence of certain irregularities, he was refused a recant. The winner, Roy LeCraw, a state guard officer, had run on a pledge to go with his regiment if it were called to service. When it was called in 1942 the city administration was at a low ebb and Hartsfield won the special election in June 1942, polling more votes than the eight opposing candidates had together.[11]

The mayor has a vast reservoir of energy and he always is on the go. He shows up at hospitals, fires, wrecks, and at the police station. He knows the town and what goes on in it. He thrives on meetings and personal appearances. He has toured Europe on a number of occasions. In England he took a soapbox and spoke at London's Hyde Park on the free enterprise system. In Germany he made friends with mayors and with Chancellor Adenauer. Everywhere he personally checked directors of police and finance, and methods of operation.[12]

Atlanta, which is a city remarkably free of any organized underworld activities, enjoys that status because of the mayor's interest. No scandal has touched the financial administration or the chief of police office. In 1957 seven of the city's more than 500 police were indicted in a federal lottery, or numbers, probe. All were found not guilty by the trial jury. But these few cases served only to emphasize how remarkably free the department is, and for how long it has been, of any scandal in its administration.

One of the Hartsfield axioms is, "Be sure your police chief has the citizen's type of viewpoint." He and his department must protect property and people. Chief Herbert Jenkins always has met that requirement.

When Mayor Hartsfield was elected to the term ending with 1957, John O. Chiles, then president of the Downtown Improvement Association, said:

"After all, when a city elects a man to serve 20 1/2 years as its mayor, it becomes apparent that the story of the town and the man has become one and the same."

When the same city extends it to 24 1/2 years, and by the largest majority yet, there would seem to be no doubt about it at all.[13]

Notes—29

[1]Reprinted from *Atlanta Journal and Constitution Magazine* (19 January 1958) by permission of the author, Mrs. McGill, and Atlanta Newspapers, Inc. In this article, McGill revised a former piece, "You'd Think He Owns Atlanta," *Saturday Evening Post* (31 October 1953): 28-29, 94, 96-98, 103. Material from that earlier article is quoted with permission.

[2]In "You'd Think He Owns Atlanta," *Saturday Evening Post* (31 October 1953), McGill added: "For example, shortly before the nonpartisan primary which renominated Mayor Hartsfield last June, he and an executive of Atlanta Newspapers, which publishes the *Constitution* and the *Journal*, almost came to blows. The mayor was denouncing the papers for what seemed to him an unreasonable bit of surgery on his opening campaign statement, and was threatening dire reprisals. Only the fortuitous arrival of a second executive prevented a fight. Managing editors and city editors of Atlanta papers are used to seeing the mayor, who buys and reads every edition of each paper—a custom adhered to in whatever city he may be—appear at their desks, his face reflecting accusation and great hurt, criticizing what seems to him an example of poor news handling or emphasis. The mayor has made such a study of news stories that he is a good critic, if prejudiced, and tough to handle in a news argument. Naturally, not all these little visits endear him to the editorial staffs."

[3]McGill wrote: "His friends, on and off the newspapers, know that before any of the mayor's campaigns are well started it will frequently be necessary for them to remove the candidate to some quiet spot and lecture him on staying away from newspaper offices and all meetings where his appearance is not necessary. They keep a wary watch on him, for the mayor is drawn to controversy as the bee to clover. Despite frequent clashes and editorial opposition to some of his measures,

the newspapers and a majority of voters generally have supported him on the basis of his ability as an administrator, and the resultant excellent financial condition of the city and its general civic health. But, as George C. Biggers, president of Atlanta Newspapers, Inc., said before the most recent primary, 'Sometimes Bill makes it hard to keep remembering the record' "; *Saturday Evening Post* (31 October 1953).

⁴See McGill's article in this book on Robert F. Maddox. McGill provided an example of Hartsfield's independence: "He attracted attention at the Sistine Chapel in Vatican City. Peering upward for a while, he suddenly turned and walked to an ancient bench by the wall, pulled it out and stretched himself upon it for a solemn, searching view of the masterpiece. Since the bench likely had not been moved since Michelangelo climbed down from his scaffolds, the attendants were torn between admiration for this passion for art and the rules of order. They stood in nail-biting indecision while tourist groups stared questioningly at the recumbent American. At làst he arose, put the bench back where he got it, and gave the custodians a friendly tip. A few cots such as are·used by sun-bathers on roofs of health clubs, he told them, would, if strategically placed, allow those interested in the magnificent panorama to view it properly." *Saturday Evening Post* (31 October 1953).

⁵"Conscious of," McGill wrote, "the city's Ku Klux Klan background of the early '20's and of the fact that for some uninformed Americans the title of Erskine Caldwell's play *Tobacco Road* has been rubber-stamped on the state, the mayor tries to interest all hands in keeping the showcases of their city clean, particularly in the sensitive area of race relations. In this field, with its explosive political and social possibilities, the mayor has acted with boldness and common sense. A conservative progressive, he prefers to roll with the punches and win victories on points, avoiding a knockout when one is not required. Agitators have found the pickings lean in Atlanta." *Saturday Evening Post* (31 October 1953).

⁶"This record of financial soundness in all city affairs has been maintained through years of war, inflation, and shortages of material and manpower," McGill wrote, "and it explains why Atlanta enjoys one of the best credit ratings in the nation. During the latter years of Democratic federal administrations, the mayor would please visiting bankers and presidents of large corporations interested in locating new branches or plants, by giving them the financial story. He would cite the then relatively low tax rate of eighteen mills for all city expenses save schools, and conclude, 'We operate this city here in the heart of the Democratic South in a most un-Dealish fashion.' (The rate in 1953, including all school and bond costs, is twenty-five mills)"; *Saturday Evening Post* (31 October 1953).

⁷See Harold H. Martin, *William Berry Hartsfield: Mayor of Atlanta* (Athens: University of Georgia Press, 1978), pp. 49-52.

[8]Hartsfield died 22 February 1971.

[9]McGill stated: "Mayor Hartsfield believes some of his success stems from the fact that he is a native of Atlanta and does not mind at all the occasional remark from some disgruntled critic that sometimes he acts as if he had been born to be mayor. He was born . . . about five blocks from the present traffic horror of Five Points, where once the town well was located"; *Saturday Evening Post* (31 October 1953).

[10]"His interest in aviation began," McGill explained, in 1924. "Three or four wealthy young Atlantans who owned planes had been using the oval inside a race track on the outskirts of the city as a landing field. Asa Candler, of the Coca-Cola Candlers, owner of the track, offered it to the city for development as an airport. Council named Hartsfield as chairman of the committee to investigate. His ringing report inspired council to appropriate $5,000, which was used to level a triangular space of 1,500 square feet. From that time on, Hartsfield regarded it as his airport. He helped repair planes, rode in them, aided barnstormers by spieling for customers, and chased cows and cars off the landing area. Finally he learned to fly. Had he been able to afford a plane of his own, he likely would have become a barnstormer, but he didn't, and he stayed on with politics and law. The next year he got through a $20,000 appropriation and fought off an injunction which denounced the act as a wasteful use of taxpayers' money 'to build a playground for a few wealthy college boys to use for their expensive sport.' The suit also charged there was never a chance of the city benefiting from the airfield. Through these and succeeding years the newspaper files testify the mayor was a prophet predicting great days for commercial aviation. The result is that Atlanta from the start had an adequate airport, and became the aviation center of the Southeast"; *Saturday Evening Post* (31 October 1953).

[11]"As chief executive of a city remarkably free of any organized underworld activities," McGill wrote, "Mayor Hartsfield offers a basic formula: 'Stay hard on organized gambling and you'll keep a clean town.' 'Gambling,' he says 'cannot exist without protection. Once gambling has corrupted law enforcement, then come vice and all the other features of a town with an underworld.' Another Hartsfield fundamental is to 'be sure your police chief has the citizen's type of viewpoint. He and his department must protect property and people.' (He is fortunate to have such a chief in Herbert Jenkins, who is highly respected by both the white and the colored populations.) 'A man in political office must open his political mail every day and learn from it' is another of his rules of political life"; *Saturday Evening Post* (31 October 1953).

[12]McGill concluded: "The mayor is effective in all his activities because of a vast reservoir of energy and a willingness to use it. He rides herd on his city, night and day, and friends are never surprised to have their telephones ring around

midnight and to hear the soft voice of the mayor saying, 'It's a wonderful night. Feel like riding around awhile and looking at the town?' . . . The mayor, who has a police radio in his car, shows up at hospitals, fires, wrecks, and at the police station. . . . He has no private, unlisted number. He enjoys the office of mayor so much that he rarely refuses invitations involving public appearances. Being aware of the value of the right sort of publicity, he greets legitimate publicity agents warmly and will go to great lengths to assist them. Convinced that television is creating new political listeners and viewers, and is, therefore, the political medium of the future, he has, as president of the American Municipal Association, led that organization in petitioning the FCC and the National Association of Broadcasters to work out policies permitting candidates in local elections the use of prime time at reasonable rates. 'Television will avail the nation little if it merely teaches the people what commodity or car to buy, and at the same time fails to enable the people to be informed about the issues of local government,' he said. The fact that he is himself a really effective television performer may have influenced the mayor's enthusiasm for it"; *Saturday Evening Post* (31 October 1953).

[13]Prior to 1963 McGill wrote a piece that was to be submitted to *Airlanes*, the international in-flight magazine. In this article, McGill discussed William Hartsfield, aviation in Atlanta, and his own experience flying. Manuscript from McGill papers provided by Mrs. Ralph McGill.

Essay 30

LeRoy Collins: Florida's Nominee for Governor Started Out in a Grocery Store[1]

On the night of May 15, about 10:30 o'clock, in Tallahassee, Florida, LeRoy Collins turned to his wife and to Mr. and Mrs. Rainey Cawthon, who were with them, and said, "Let's go down to the church."

So through the streets of Florida's capital city they walked to historic old St. John's Episcopal Church, entered its dark interior, lit only by street lights coming through the windows, and knelt in one of the pews in prayer.

A few minutes before, LeRoy Collins's political opponent had conceded. Barring a political upheaval highly improbable, November will find the young man of forty-five, who went to pray with his wife and friends when his nomination was assured, as the next governor of Florida.[2]

Collins's personal story has a Horatio Alger turn to it. And certainly it fits the American legend and is a part of the American dream—that a poor boy may find opportunity in this country if he seeks it and is willing to work for it. His grandfather was a circuit-riding Methodist preacher in the pioneer days. His father, Marvin Collins, moved to Tallahassee from Tampa and opened a small grocery store. With the income from it he reared his six children. There were few luxuries in that home, but there were love and integrity and a way of teaching a boy to get along.[3]

"If you want to go to college you will have to earn at least half the cost," the father said. "I'll match dollar for dollar."

Mrs. Leslie Bogan of Atlanta was in the same class with Collins at Leon High School in Tallahassee. She remembers him as a popular class leader, the one always chosen to make the presentation speech with the class gift to the teacher.

All through high school LeRoy Collins was a part-time clerk at Bernard Byrd's grocery store. When he had graduated with honors he went to work there full time until he had saved up $500.

There is a story from that era which pretty well demonstrates that father Collins's theory of sharpening the wits of his young with competitive endeavors was paying dividends. Early in life it paid son LeRoy fifteen cents, but to make this modest profit was an almost sensational triumph. He turned disaster into victory.

There had come, in an order to the store, some new and strange jars of *pate de fois gras*, and the price was one large dollar. And in those non-inflated days a dollar was a right respectable sum. The customers of the Byrd grocery store almost lost their minds wondering about goose liver in jars with a Paris label and name, and costing what, not so many years before, had been a day's pay.

One day they found out. But not for free.

Clerk Roy, in sweeping out the store, let the handle of his fast-flying broom bang into a shelf. Down came one of the jars of goose liver.

Roy stood for a moment looking at the cracked jar, and carefully picked it up.

Then he took a dollar from his pocket and paid the awed Mr. Byrd. He next took out a nickel and bought a box of crackers. These he opened with slow deliberation.

"Gentlemen," he said to the curious ones in the store, "for months you have been wondering about this goose liver that costs a dollar a jar. All of us have been dying to know what it tastes like. I now am going to offer an opportunity—at five cents a cracker."

There was a rush of buyers. By carefully spreading the goose liver thin, young Collins not only had one for himself but came out with a profit of fifteen cents.

There is another story from his boyhood which he regards as having contributed to his maturing processes. He was still in high school and a member of the town band, playing the trumpet. The band picked up small change now and then by playing for special occasions. One of these was to furnish music at a real estate auction in a new Tallahassee subdivision. One parcel was offered for sale in a section where lots had been selling at around $30.00 and $35.00 apiece. For some reason the top on this particular lot stopped at $20.00.

In the band the trumpet player was all excited. Somewhat to his own surprise he found himself calling out $25.00. To his consternation the auctioneer slammed down his hammer and said, "Sold."

Collins was too young for a contract, and he had to work extra time to add to his savings and buy the lot. He learned then about contracts, and also that there is a time to play the trumpet and a time to attend to business. He held on to the lot. Years later he sold it at a substantial profit.

There was a family emergency and college was not possible when the honor graduate left high school. He didn't whimper. He took his $500 and went to business school.[4] When that was done he worked as a shipping clerk in a wholesale grocery and later as a bank teller. And he kept on saving. His father was able to match this money and the young man went to Cumberland University for a law course, graduating well up and being voted by the students as the outstanding member of the class.[5]

In 1931 he took the Florida bar examination, as well as those of Arkansas and Tennessee. He made the second highest mark then made on the Florida tests.

He began practice in early 1932. The great depression was on and in Florida, where it followed hard on the heels of the tremendous real estate boom collapse, times were harder than elsewhere in the nation. Young Collins supplemented his really very meager law income by working in the attorney general's office as a filing clerk.

He was deeply in love with one of Florida's finest and most attractive young ladies, Mary Call Darby, whose great-grandfather, Richard Keith Call, was one of Florida's early territorial governors. He was out of Tennessee and was one of Andrew Jackson's friends and Army leaders. In the early 1820s Richard Keith Call built a handsome brick house on a wooded knoll hard by the little Indian trading village of Tallahassee which, in the Creek language, means "Old Town."

It is a house with an ancient beauty and sweetness which have survived hard times. The house long ago passed out of the hands of the Call family. It became, even, a boardinghouse, and a tourist attraction.

In 1932 when young Collins and Mary Call Darby married they had, among other dreams, that of buying back "The Grove." In 1941 they managed to do just that. They both worked at clearing the grounds and putting the house back in condition. One day as LeRoy Collins was cutting down the high weeds in the spacious front lawn a tourist and his wife came in. The wife went on to look at the house. The man stayed behind.

"I guess some smart son of a gun will put this in shape and make a lot of money out of it," said the tourist to the handyman who was cutting the weeds.

"I sure hope so," said the handyman, with a fervency which startled the tourist, and went on cutting the weeds. But they, of course, made it home and not a tourist lure.

As Collins says, "The house has just about kept us broke." But they have never regretted it. "It's a matter of where you put your values," he explained. "The old place means things to Mary Call and me. We wanted our children to grow up in it. We think it will mean something to them later."

There are four children, LeRoy Jr., a midshipman at Annapolis; Jane, fifteen; Mary Call, eleven; and Darby, three. Collins, remembering his own boyhood when malaria was rife, and public schooling inadequate, especially in the rural regions, has devoted much of his legislative effort to a better deal for Florida's children. Health insurance measures, too, including malaria control, have been among his other legislative concerns.[6]

The Collinses, LeRoy and Mary Call, long ago memorized a quotation from Socrates as one of their guideposts:

"Could I climb to the highest place in Athens," the old philosopher said, "I would lift up my voice and proclaim: 'Fellow citizens, why do you turn to scrape every stone to gather wealth and take so little care of your children, to whom, one day, you must relinquish it all?' "

When Nominee Collins becomes governor in January, 1955, he simply will walk across the street from "The Grove" to the governor's mansion.

He will carry with him his enormous store of idealism, which is complemented and strengthened by the pragmatism of his upbringing. There is no trace of the demagogue in him, nor will there be. A successful lawyer, he has in him the strength of an unusual integrity which has made it impossible for any mud thrown at him to stick.[7]

The church, an orderly career, devotion to duty, to state, country, and family are a natural part of his life. He has been a vestryman at St. John's for a good many years. His family has always been one close to the homespun virtue in which love of family and country are the essential ingredient. He has served the state as legislator and senator for eighteen years. His record is one which has won him almost annual awards. Typical were those won last year. He was voted "the most valuable senator," "most valuable all-around member," and "outstanding in debate."

He had led the fight to elect his good and able friend, the late Dan McCarty, governor of Florida. He steered the governor's legislative program through the senate. And when an unexpected heart attack struck down his friend, LeRoy Collins walked every day to his bedside in the hospital and later to the governor's mansion, to counsel and to ask what the governor wanted. And they put it through. This was one of the real reasons why Florida gave him such a tremendous majority in the recent primary.

This victory was enormously significant. It was said that no man from the capital could be elected—that the courthouse cliques were too powerful.

Then Florida defeated the old country courthouse machines and named Collins to Dan McCarty's unexpired term.

Collins's nomination was a great lift to all those in Florida who dream of a steadily improving state. This, the political wise men say, will assure a Collins's election in November.

Notes—30

[1] Reprinted from *Atlanta Journal and Constitution Magazine* (18 July 1954) by permission of the author, Mrs. McGill, and Atlanta Newspapers, Inc.

[2] Collins did serve as governor, 1955-1960.

[3] Collins's mother was Mattie Brandon Collins.

[4] He attended Eastman School of Business, Poughkeepsie, New York.

[5] He attended Cumberland University, Lebanon, Tennessee, 1931.

[6] Collins was elected to the Florida House of Representatives, 1934, and the State Senate, 1940-1954. He served two years in the United States Navy during World War II, was president of the National Association of Broadcasters, 1961-1964, and was Under-Secretary of Commerce, 1966-1968. He practiced law in Tampa, 1966-1968, before moving to a law practice in Tallahassee in 1970.

[7] Later McGill quoted from Collins's inaugural address: " 'I have no feeling of hate for any man. But I do hate the things some men do. To fight for right is the easy half of the battle for progress. The hard half is to fight against wrong. But this we must do if we are to be worth our salt.' . . . I believe every American of any sensitivity of heart or mind knows that what Governor Collins said is the truth. Without that quality in our political system, it may fall"; McGill, "The Gizzard of Society," *Georgia Review* 10 (Spring 1956): 6-7.

Essay 31

Robert F. Maddox Has Helped to Make Atlanta Great[1]

On his eighty-sixth birthday, 4 April 1956, Robert Foster Maddox, Sr., could, and did, look back with considerable satisfaction on a life which had paralleled that of his native city—Atlanta.

His eyes have seen the city grow from a straggling town of about 30,000 persons, living under military rule as a conquered province, to its present status as a burgeoning city of some 600,000 persons—the transportation and distribution center of a great Southeast—in the travail of growth and change wrought by the continuing industrial revolution.

In a very real sense, Robert F. Maddox, still slim, debonair and erect, is more a part of his city than even he, perhaps, realizes, though he loves it well and has given it and its institutions more years of loving attention than customarily are given to so inanimate and impersonal a thing as an incorporated municipality.

It is said of an institution which progresses and endures that it is but the lengthening shadow of those who have served it. This is even more true of a city. There are cities which are spiritless and dominated by inertia. They reflect a certain shabbiness and bankruptcy of municipal pride in the physical appearance of their city, in their government, and in those qualities which lift a municipality out of the ordinary—a spirit of doing, a determination to have parks, libraries, concerts, an awareness of, a respect for, and a place for the arts.

This is because those who have served it, especially at the critical moments which come to all cities, have themselves lacked vision and entertained no affection or ambition for the people they served. At the critical moment when Atlanta sought to free herself from such shackles, Robert F. Maddox was available. He already loved his city. In fact, it seems to him he loved it from the time he, as a boy, began to look about him.

Atlanta's Peachtree Street was then, in its downtown blocks, an avenue lined with spacious lawns, wrought-iron fences, hitching posts, and homes in the architectural designs of the time. Robert Maddox likes to recall the almost pastoral beauty of that street.

At the busy corner where Davison-Paxon Company's department store stands today was the "second John H. James mansion." It was so-called because at the northern end of the block was the first big home built by Mr. James. He had completed it in 1868 and sold it to the state as the governor's mansion in 1870—the year Robert Maddox was born.

In between the two homes built by the enterprising James were the red brick and terra cotta Robert H. Richards home, complete with gargoyles, and the Leyden home. General George Thomas had used it as his headquarters during the period General William T. Sherman occupied the city. (The house was torn down almost forty years ago, and its columns later were used in the construction of Woodbury Hall, 149 Peachtree Circle. This later became an apartment house.) There were but four houses in that block of Peachtree Street.

Robert Maddox's father had been a colonel in the forty-second Georgia Regiment, which had a distinguished record in the great war of his time. He returned to the city when it was in ashes. He served in the state legislature and in the city council. He taught his son never to look backward, or to long for the "good old days" but to create better ones for the future. He founded, too, the Maddox-Rucker Banking Company. The bank was located on Alabama Street just across from the then "new" *Atlanta Constitution* Building.

His son came along in the public schools, the University of Georgia, and Harvard. In 1889 he entered his father's bank, beginning as a collector. He filled every position in the bank up to the vice-presidency, which position he held when it was converted into the American National Bank. Robert Maddox yet recalls the pleasure that was his in meeting and knowing Henry Grady, Joel Chandler Harris, Frank Stanton, and others of the *Constitution* staff who were his banking neighbors.

In 1890 Mayor James G. Woodward, a "diamond in the rough," according to his friends, was nominated for another term in the city primary of that year.

The mayor-nominate not yet elected, elected to celebrate. His celebrations became too frequent, too public, and too flagrant to go unnoticed.

A great crusade was organized, culminating in a tremendous rally at the Kimball House, and the young banker, Robert Maddox, was drafted to run as an independent. In the general election he was returned the victor by a huge majority.

At a critical moment Atlanta had a man of intelligence, courage, and one who loved the city and had a vision for her.

Atlanta was a shabby, neglected, spiritless city. Her municipal services were archaic and inadequate. Her school system was a disgrace.

Robert Maddox took office in January 1909, and served two years—refusing nomination for a second term, even though enthusiastic public opinion already had caused a legislative change in an old law which limited mayors to one two-year term. This had been one of the evils, causing each two-year term to be a long political "grab" session.

One of Robert Maddox's great achievements was to get the people behind the city's first big bond issue—one of $3,000,000. For 1910 that was a huge one. It was honestly used. The city's inadequate sewer system was increased and improved with the construction of disposal plants. The educational system was vitalized by the building of twelve new schools. Grady Hospital was renovated, improved, and an addition completed. The waterworks plant was greatly improved and new mains laid. There was vast improvement in the physical "plant" of the city. Those achievements alone would have established him as a successful mayor.

But they were by no means all.

Piedmont Park was then a run-down fairgrounds, with dilapidated, neglected buildings.

Mayor Maddox was able to persuade the people and the city government to tear down the old buildings and make Piedmont Park the beautiful place it is today. He established sixteen playgrounds for children in various areas of the city.

He was early interested in public health. He knew that many diseases began in neglected youth. It was he who originated the system of requiring that all school children have a physical examination—a rule never abandoned and today recognized as one of the more valuable regulations of the school system.

The City Hall was a shambles—dirty, deteriorating, and inadequate.

He began a movement to obtain from the federal government the old post office building at the corner of Marietta and Forsyth Streets. The government was preparing to move to its new and palatial plant further up Forsyth. The lot had been given to the government many years before with the proviso that if it ceased to be used for a post office building it would revert back to the city.

The government was willing to return the lot. But there was a large, well-kept building on it. The property, lot and building, were valued at $500,000.

The government finally put a price of $70,000 on the building. This was good and generous of the government, but the city had been spending to make itself over, and while the budget was in balance, there was no surplus.

Robert Maddox gave the government his personal check for $70,000 and turned the building over to the city for its municipal building. He was repaid across the next several years in installment fashion.

During his administration the municipal auditorium-armory was completed and formally opened with a big civic "possum dinner," at which President-elect William Taft was a visitor. The hall in which the dinner was served was named in his honor—Taft Hall.

With the auditorium completed, Mayor Maddox joined with other leaders to bring Grand Opera to the city. The fabulous "Met" did not leave New York in those days. But the Atlanta committee persuaded it to come south, and gave this city another distinction. At a critical moment in her history Atlanta had been given a spirit and a soul.

These were the highlights of a great and inspiring two years. Robert Maddox refused a sure second term, saying he had offered at the behest of the people confronted with a crisis, and that he wished to return to his business career. "When my term expires, I will give my constant and sympathetic support to the Atlantan who succeeds me."

He did just that—filling many positions of trust and honor with ability, dignity, and success.

A magnificent silver service was purchased with money raised by public subscription and presented him when his term came to an end.

Today, Robert Maddox is pleased at the growth of the city. The acceleration of it surprises him somewhat, but not the fact of it.

He recalls that in 1914, still a young banker, he got the inevitable yearning of the city man to "move out to the country" and have a garden and chickens.

He found a tract of land on an old ferry road—Paces Ferry—and bought seventy-five acres at a modest price. It was totally undeveloped. He built a small house and the family lived there in the summer. But it was so far in the country that they moved back to town in the winter so the children could go to school.

There was just one store—of the general variety—at Buckhead. The nearest drugstore was at Fourteenth Street and Peachtree.

Later on, of course, as the city expanded, Paces Ferry Road became noted for its beautiful homes, including the present Maddox residence. Theodore Roosevelt was entertained in that home.

While banking was his career, Mr. Maddox did not neglect his city. He continued to serve.

In 1916 his bank was combined with the Atlanta National, and he became president of the new institution. Later, through other mergers in the developing financial life of the city, the bank emerged as the First National and he was chairman of its executive committee. He was president of the Georgia Bankers' Association in 1912 and of the American Bankers' Association in 1918.

But he gave generously of his time to public affairs. He was a member of the State Board of Health for thirty-three years, and its chairman twenty-one of them. He was a director of many important corporations, hospitals, and on the boards of educational institutions, including Berry School, Vanderbilt University, and the High Museum of Art. In 1946 the Atlanta Chamber of Commerce gave him its Distinguished Service Award. He was one of the committee which located the Federal Reserve Bank in Atlanta. He served as chairman of major civic drives for community funds. The list of positions he filled with honor and ability is a long and distinguished one.

He was, and is, a friendly man, and ever the impeccable gentleman. He is a life member of the Piedmont Driving Club and the Capital City Club. He is one of the oldest members of the First Methodist Church, a steward and member of the board of trustees.

On 12 June 1895 he was married to Miss Lollie Baxter, of Nashville, Tennessee. A son, N. Baxter Maddox, is vice-president and a director of the First National Bank. A daughter, Mrs. Edward Devereaux Smith, is also a resident of Atlanta. A second son, Robert F. Maddox, Jr., succumbed to a heart attack in 1949. Mrs. Maddox passed on in 1955 after a long illness.

Now, in 1956, with his eighty-sixth birthday behind him, Robert F. Maddox still has a zest for life, and a satisfaction in it. He has been an integral part in the growth of his city, and this, too, pleases him, though with genuine modesty he deprecates his contribution.

But those who join him in love, affection, and hope for Atlanta know that more, even, than the great tangible contribution he made to it, was the intangible gift. At a time when the city was floundering, down at the heels and lacking in purpose or pride, he came along and lifted it to firm ground.

He gave it direction, purpose, pride, and knowledge that a city must be much more than bricks, stones, and pavements. No matter how great the city may become, the hallmark of Robert Foster Maddox, Sr., will be on it.

Notes—31

[1]Reprinted from the *Atlanta Journal and Constitution Magazine* (6 May 1956), by permission of the author, Mrs. McGill, and Atlanta Newspapers, Inc. Known as "Mr. Atlanta," Robert F. Maddox died 10 April 1965 at the age of ninety-five. Formerly president and chairman of the board of the First National

Bank of Atlanta, Maddox had been director of the bank for seventy-two years when he retired. He was a life member of the Capital City Club, elected to membership in 1892. He served as president of the Capital City Club from 1912 to 1914.

Essay 32

George Wallace: Tradition of Demagoguery[1]

George Corley Wallace, the "Mister" of the tandem-tableau at the governor's suite in Montgomery, Alabama—where an ailing Governor Lurleen Wallace is less and less able to sit in her office and increasingly leaves things to George—has started his Western "presidential" campaign.

Californians and their fellow Westerners may have been entertained or dismayed, amused or angered by his two visits there this fall. But they should know that George Wallace was prepared from birth for the role he played there. The ritual performances of Dixie politics are a folkway art akin to the elaborate ceremony of the Chinese or Japanese theater, where the same actor assumes different masks to play a variety of roles—comedy, drama, the buffoon, the redeemer, the protector of the downtrodden little man, the executioner, and the prophet.

Californians and their neighbors probably saw most of the masks in the Wallace baggage and heard the different voices behind them. George Wallace, his friends and enemies agree, was not "behind the door when the brains was passed out." He is shrewd with a shrewdness born of the bitter soil of poverty and isolation that is found in the backward rural areas of the old cotton South, where so many Dixie demagogues "are born." Their names make a long list. Those who come most readily to Southern minds are Tom Watson, "Pitchfork Ben" Tillman, James Vardaman, Theodore Bilbo, Cotton Ed Smith, Cole Blease, "Old Gene" Talmadge, Huey Long, Ross Barnett, and Orval Faubus. The elders among them participated in the several devices that disenfranchised the Negro. They also were motivators of the so-called "Black Codes" and the doctrines of white supremacy and inferiority of the Negro.[2]

Some of them lectured around the country on these subjects. Vardaman and Tillman were in demand outside the South, speaking on the theme that the Negro was somewhere between a human being and the missing link. All of this was a facade of attitudes and beliefs that became a part of the sect religions that flourished in the South from 1865 on. As God himself had ordained black men to be slaves, so, later, was God found to be the first segregationist. Since 1945 the successors to the elder demagogues have fought to retain segregation with the same non sequiturs, false premises, and religious absurdities that were employed to defend slavery.

It is helpful to understand some of the forces that shape George Wallace before one considers what he is and why. He fits into the old line of Southern politicians who historically used raw racism, or some degree of it, to further their political advancement.

George Wallace was born at Clio, Barbour County, Alabama, in the southeastern corner of the state. It was then a poor farming area, given largely to cotton, timber, and turpentining. Today, it is somewhat more prosperous, with cattle, soybeans, and some small industry. Clayton, the county seat, is near Clio, and it was there the family moved after his father, a small-time farmer, died and the mortgage had been foreclosed. The boll weevil, which hit the area in the twenties, and the depression that followed hard on its heels, had a profound effect on the cotton South. Eufaula, a river town on the Chattahoochee River, is the largest city in the county, part of what was a slave-holding aristocracy with large plantations and steamboats that loaded thousands of bales of cotton.[3]

There were legends about local heroes for the young George Wallace to hear and grow up with. There was a streak of Populism in some and, in all, a flavoring of race and a fierce commitment to the South and "our way of Life." The town of Clayton itself, for example, is named for Augustin G. Clayton of Georgia, one of the hot-headed secessionists of the period when John Calhoun was advocating secession and nullification of federal law in protest against the tariff and federal "interference" with state rights.

Wallace no doubt also heard the story of Clayton's town bell. It stood for more than a century in the square, summoning the volunteer patrol and their bloodhounds to hunt down run-away slaves. The patrol also checked to see if slaves had proper passes when they were away from their plantations. The slaves called these patrollers the "patter-o'ls," and generations of Clayton youngsters grew up knowing verses of a song:[4]

> Run nigger, run, the patter-o'ls 'll catch you,
> Run nigger, run, it's almost day,
> Run nigger, run, patter-o'l 'll catch you,
> Run nigger, run, you can't get away.

The story of old man Jefferson Buford of Eufaula and Clayton was a favorite and admired bit of local history. When political control of Kansas became a national issue, Massachusetts Free Soilers sent men there to vote against extension of slavery. Jefferson Buford recruited and financed 500 stout slavery men to go settle there and vote for slavery. They made their way to Montgomery, New Orleans, and finally Kansas. They accomplished nothing, save to spend most of the Buford fortune. But he had done his best for the South and states rights.

Other, similar legends out of the past reflected attitudes of the old South, the South of the small cotton towns, the South of isolation, of pride without substance, of a defensive hip-on-the-shoulder style, a South that felt an inexpressible resentment against life, a sense of guilt and anger. [William] Faulkner was the first to put it into words. He wrote of the Sartorius and Snopes families, the miasma of the past and of how, by a sort of osmosis, this past became part of the mind, the psychology and religion of the people. It gave them a curious mixture of attitudes, of tolerances and intolerances.

George Wallace, at five feet six inches, is something of a delight to the Freudians and others who probe into what a man reveals or hides about himself. Wallace is asking Americans—including Californians—to "stand up—stand up tall for America." He will pay great tribute to the "little man." Indeed, it is seemingly his code that the "little man" is the repository of all that is good, "moral," and "right," and that such belief makes one stand up tall.

Wallace speaks a great deal about "individual rights," "bedrock principles," "Constitutional rights," "law and order," and against the "meddling of the federal government in local affairs."[5] Alabama is a state that would be bankrupt without the many forms of federal aid for the education, agriculture, welfare and the numerous other state activities. "It's ours," he says glibly, ignoring that much of it comes from the more prosperous Yankee states.

He also insists that today the little people are unheard and alone, that the government has ceased to be their servant and has become their callous and uncaring master. He will speak passionately of the "little man" and his property rights and of how freedom lovers are not protected in this "God-given" right to defend their home.

He is rather sure to adjure "those who don't understand me" to "ask the little man," the taxi driver and policeman. "They know what I'm talking about!" he shouts.

And they do. In all his crowds are a few who don't know—usually a housewife. She will whisper to her husband and ask. And he will grin, and bend down and whisper into her pink little ear, "He means niggers. . . . He means niggers moving next door or trying to buy in your neighborhood."

Wallace also, without fail, bitterly condemns the President and the government and the courts for not protecting policemen and firemen from hoodlums, thugs, and rioters. The Little Giant does not want federal troops or "interference." But somehow, he always blames "Washington," not governors or local government. It is not surprising the Little Giant is much admired by many firemen and policemen.

Hippie-weary Californians no doubt had to brace themselves for broadsides about the "bearded beatnik bums," the "intellectual moron," the immoral "beatnik professors," liberals, and the liberal newspapers, none of whom are for the little man, according to Wallace.

"They think you don't understand," he tells his crowds. "They think you and I are dumb." He sometimes answers himself by saying, "You and me, we understand them. . . ."

Mr. Wallace's skill with the verbal counterthrust some years ago discouraged his opponents from bringing up the fact that after he was honorably discharged from the Air Force in 1945, he soon started drawing $10.00-a-month compensation for ten percent "damage to his nerves," reportedly growing out of combat fatigue. (So far as the writer knows no one has seen the exact government language determining this compensation.)

Senator Wayne Morse was the first to mention Mr. Wallace's compensation for ten percent "damage to his nerves." When asked about this by reporters at the time of his primaries in 1964, Mr. Wallace was quoted as saying, "Why the hell shouldn't I take the money? At least I have got papers certifying my mind is ninety percent sound. Can Wayne Morse say that?"[6]

In 1964 he also was quoted as saying he still was accepting the $10.00-a-month compensation. If he has since discontinued it, he has made no mention of it.

Beards seem to fascinate him. He speaks so often of beatnik beards. He arouses laughter by saying that if he were President, he would grab some of those beatnik intellectual morons by the beards and yank them in front of a grand jury.

There is always lots of laughter at a George Wallace speech, but it almost never is real, loose, happy, belly laughter. It tends mostly to be somewhat strained, as he conjures up images of unfit judges, the President, or what he and freedom lovers who stand on bedrock principles would do to those beatnik, intellectual morons—especially the moron professors.

Washington's mass war protest last October disturbed all thoughtful persons because the vast majority of the students were so ruthlessly exploited by a hard core of disciplined groups like the old Trotskyite Progressive Labor Party (now Maoist), the W. E. B. DuBois clubs, the new SNCC leadership, and some of the minority who were so vocal at the recent New Politics convention in Chicago. Every development in this vein provides Wallace with new material. Dissent plays into his hands. There must have been enough beards in Washington to make Wallace dance with pleased anticipation.

Direct racist excitements now are out of his campaign vocabulary. One has to know the new dialogue of our time to understand what is meant when candidate Wallace says, after a ringing paragraph about individual rights, property rights, freedom, and federal interference, "If you don't know what I'm talking about, ask the taxi drivers or the policemen. They'll tell you." They know.

But the dialogue is lofty with clichés, homilies. It was not always so.

In 1958 Wallace lost the nomination for governor to State Attorney General John Patterson. Their platforms were similar, but Patterson had seized the racial issue first and had obtained endorsement of the Ku Klux Klan. With that ground lost, Wallace appeared to be—but wasn't—the more moderate of the two. He lost.

He now denies a statement attributed to him at that time: "They out-niggered me that time, but they'll never do it again." Undeniably, however, others of his supporters said it for him, including former Governor "Kissin' Jim" Folsom. George Wallace once had been one of Folsom's campaign managers in the Folsom gubernatorial victory.[7]

From 1958 on, through the winning campaign for governor in 1962, no one did "out-nigger" George Wallace. His inaugural address in 1963 is an illustrative sample:

> Today I have stood where Jefferson Davis stood and took an oath to *my* people. It is very appropriate then that from this cradle of the Confederacy, this very heart of the great Anglo-Saxon Southland, that today we sound the drum for freedom as have our generation of forebears before us time and again through history. Let us rise to the call of freedom-loving blood that is in us and send our answer to the tyranny that clanks in chains upon the South. In the name of the greatest people that have ever trod the earth, I draw the line in the dust and toss the gauntlet before the feet of tyranny, and I say: "Segregation now—segregation tomorrow—segregation forever."

A mighty, screaming yell went up. It rebounded from the hills into the flats where the city stands. The mind that produced that speech bore the memory of boyhood days in the back-eddy county seat of Clayton, the stories of Confederate heroes, the myths and preachments about Anglo-Saxon supremacy, the romance of the old Ku Klux Klan, and stereotype images of the slave and the plantations.

Six months later the University of Alabama was desegregated. The story of it is revealing. President Kennedy had been privately in frequent touch with Southern governors. He was using all his persuasiveness in an effort to win them over to preventing violence. He did not want to send troops or to nationalize their National Guards. The governors, he said in personal talks and messages sent them, surely must already know that neither they nor their people gained by violence and resistance to courts.

There already had been foreboding violence in Birmingham. In April and May, demonstrations in behalf of jobs and an end to the more flagrant discriminations against individuals in that city had been brought to crisis by the bombing of a motel where Dr. Martin Luther King was a guest and by the threat of more dynamiting.

It was against this dark curtain that two qualified Negroes were ordered admitted to the University of Alabama at Tuscaloosa. Governor Wallace was enjoined against interference. He announced he would "stand in the door" seeking to prevent entry.[8]

June 11 was a hot, humid day in Tuscaloosa. Damp heat lay heavily on the land and the people. College registration was at Foster Hall. Two Negro students, Vivian Malone and James Hood, approached. Attorney General Nicholas deB. Katzenbach and other federal officials also were present.

Governor Wallace had drawn, or someone had drawn for him, a circle in which he was to stand in the doorway. The symbolism of the governor standing in the confining circle was not lost on the more observant. Governor Wallace read what was, in reality, a long campaign document, addressed not to those present, but to the voters of Alabama.

The words were largely routine condemnation of the federal government, of the courts and all who differed with Governor George Wallace. He announced that under the Tenth Amendment Alabama had complete authority to maintain segregation.

The picture, there at the door, was not to be forgotten by those who saw it in person or even on television. The tall, heavy, shaggy figure of Katzenbach and that of the dapper little governor made an enduring image and philosophical contrast. Katzenbach was calm, scholarly, legal—Wallace oratorical, political.

When Wallace refused, Katzenbach departed. A few hours later he was back. The National Guard was federalized. Wallace deserted the door. The young Negroes entered. Segregation had lasted only a few months despite the "forever" pledge by the governor.

In autumn of that same year, the governor again moved to halt locally determined desegregation of elementary and seconday schools in Birmingham, Tuskegee, Mobile, and Huntsville. Because of the Wallace sound and fury, President Kennedy again nationalized the state guard. It was not needed. Wallace stood physically in no more doors.

But five days later, on a warm, sunny Sunday morning, at the hour of Sunday School, a dynamite blast ravaged an all-Negro church in Birmingham. Four little girls, dressed in their neat Sunday best, were killed as they heard a lesson of Christ, love for mankind. A half dozen others were wounded.

In a public statement the next day, President Kennedy said: "It is regrettable that public disparagement of law and order has encouraged violence which has fallen on the innocent."

Everyone knew what the President was talking about.

The 1964 [Barry] Goldwater campaign and that of Governor George Wallace had no visible umbilical cord, but it was there. Indeed, this contest saw the beginning of a solemn, cynically pious, freedom-loving new arrangement of the old states rights, anti-Negro litany in Dixie. The generations-old tune and words of *Nigger! Nigger!* and the competitiveness of candidates in trying to "out-nigger" one another changed first in Alabama.

Newsmen who cover Alabama and reporters from "the outside" who "do not understand us" generally agree on what happened. One-time Democrats James Martin and John Grenier—but by 1964, Goldwater Republicans and also Wallace "friends"—too, were a part of the new strategy. John Grenier, indeed, was selected by the Goldwater national committee to conceive and direct the "Southern strategy."

Grenier and Martin are generally credited with the strategy of eliminating the raw and vulgar "nigger" theme from the campaign. It was never believed that Senator Goldwater would do well in states with large cities. Hope of victory lay, therefore, in sweeping the South. To do this, it was necessary to win independents and as many Democrats as possible to the view that Senator Goldwater was a statesman and not a racist-minded, reactionary states right fellow. But the strategists did not want to go too far. Out of their strategy conferences came the new litany. The old, ugly, and naked prejudices were clothed in the new right-wing semantic styles. Like some of the modern feminine apparel fashions, these new words and phrases revealed more than they covered. To the rednecks and peckerwoods of the rural areas or to the disenchanted in the cities, the many phrases about individual rights, and the tyranny of the courts mean "Nigger."

Sometimes Senator Goldwater, in making such speeches to Southern audiences, seemed completely surprised by the burst of understanding cheering they evoked. Since he had not written them, it is possible the strategists had never explained the subleties of the new dialogue.

George Wallace, however, wants to be sure. "I'm not a racist," he has said. "A racist . . . despises the handiwork of God. A segregationist is a man who likes people but knows God made some black and some white and separated them from the beginning."

The Little Giant entered three primaries in 1964—Wisconsin on April 7, Indiana on May 5, and Maryland on May 19. He campaigned on a racial theme—

the right of each state to say what it would do about segregation—federal law and the Constitution to the contrary notwithstanding. This was freedom for freedom-loving people. He said property rights would disappear from freedom-loving people if they did not stand up for individual rights. Wallace ran strongly in each state. If the nigger bloc vote hadn't gone against him, he said, he might have won. He was determined then to go on into November.

There were many, many stories of what happened before the announcement of 19 July 1964. The real one isn't yet known. But four days after Senator Goldwater won the nomination, Governor Wallace withdrew as a presidential candidate. It was perhaps just a coincidence that in Georgia the then-active segregationist restaurant man, Lester Maddox, now governor of Georgia, announced that Senator Goldwater's position on "race" suited him. Mr. Maddox headed up a group that worked for the Republican nominee.

As Marshall McLuhan or one of his disciples has said, "The message is the massage."

Next year—1968—will offer another chapter. During the months of his ailing wife's gubernatorial campaign, Wallace repeatedly expressed his intent to run for the presidency next year. He left a small opening. "If both parties run the folks they're talking about now, we are going to get in the race." He has an organization and headquarters. The latter is in the Ten High Building. Seymour Trammell, an old Clayton boyhood friend of the governor, is fund raiser.

He will run, Wallace says, "because the steelworker, the paper worker, the rubber worker, the small businessman, the cab drivers are getting tired of the intellectual morons in Washington and in the liberal newspaper offices and the federal judiciary telling them when to get up in the morning. . . ."

But, of course, the winds of change may blow. Governor Lurleen Wallace's illness is a source of concern to her family and of regret, even, to those who do not know her. Many women in Alabama somewhat resent her having been pulled into the demands of a state political campaign and the governship when she was not well. If her health should worsen and the twice-operated-on cancer condition should not be cured, it is possible that George Wallace, not really believing in his heart that he can win the presidency, would elect to compete with veteran Senator Lister Hill. The senator has, as of this writing, done no campaign mending of fences and has not said what he will do. There is a strong feeling that if he should find Wallace his opponent, he might not offer for renomination.

So, as winter comes with the promise of spring in it, it will be necessary to wait and see what the winds of change do to politics in general and George Wallace in particular.[9]

Meanwhile, all bearded beatniks, all intellectual morons such as liberal professors and newspapermen, all who are not freedom-loving segregationists, and all who do not wish to get back to bedrock principles, good Christian teachings, and other associated virtues had best brace themselves. The Little

Giant campaigns vigorously. And if you don't know what it is he is saying, ask your taxi driver. He and all "little people" know. Or, at least, George Wallace so believes with a fervor that brooks no doubt.[10]

Notes—32

[1]Published by permission of the author, Mrs. McGill, and the *Los Angeles Times*, 17 December 1967.

[2]See Cal M. Logue and Howard Dorgan, eds., *Oratory of Southern Demagogues* (Baton Rouge: Louisiana State University Press, 1981).

[3]*See* Marshall Frady, *Wallace* (New York: World Book Publishing Co., 1968), pp. 49-63; George C. Wallace, *Stand Up for America* (Garden City, NY: Doubleday & Co., 1976), pp. 10-17.

[4]See Cal M. Logue, "Transcending Coercion: The Communicative Strategies of Black Slaves on Antebellum Plantations," *Quarterly Journal of Speech*, 67 (February 1981): 31-46; Logue, "Rhetorical Ridicule of Reconstruction Blacks," *Quarterly Journal of Speech*, 62 (December 1976): 400-409; Logue, "Rhetorical Appeals of Whites to Blacks During Reconstruction," *Communication Monographs* 44 (August 1977): 241-51.

[5]See Waldo W. Braden, ed., *Oratory in the New South* (Baton Rouge: Louisiana State University Press, 1979), pp. 8-37.

[6]Wallace, *Stand Up for America*, pp. 47-49.

[7]Robert Sherrill, *Gothic Politics in the Deep South: Stars of the New Confederacy* (New York: Grossman Publishers, 1968), pp. 267-78; Wallace, *Stand Up for America*, pp. 62-70; Frady, *Wallace*, pp. 122-29.

[8]Sherrill, *Gothic Politics in the Deep South*, pp. 270, 281-83; Wallace, *Stand Up for America*, pp. 71-82.

[9]In 1968 Wallace campaigned for President within the American Independent Party. His running mate was General Curtis LeMay. See Wallace, *Stand Up for America*, pp. 121-37; Jack Bass and Walter DeVries, *Transformation of Southern Politics: Social Change and Political Consequence Since 1945* (New York: New American Library, 1976), pp. 57-86.

[10]For more by McGill on Wallace, see Logue, *Ralph McGill: Editor and Publisher*, 1:241; 2:426, 432, 493, 510.

Essay 33

Lester Maddox: "Ole Lester and Atlanta's Fat Cats"[1]

It is not quite true, as some of the more realistic said when the 1968 session of the Georgia Legislature ended amid the traditional swirl of papers tossed high, the loud cheers, and the usual number of alcoholic belches, that politically, at least, Governor Lester Maddox resembled a bedraggled duck.

He is a short-legged little man with a large head that is growing less and less hair. His hands somehow look to be oversized. His torso is short and plump. But he does not quite waddle when he walks. In point of fact, he gets about very well, indeed. He probably holds the speed record for going a full block in a country town, shaking all the hands, urging one and all to go to church on Sunday, telling ladies they look mighty fine, and assuring them that all he wants to do is make everything pickrick in Georgia.

"You mean everything will be peaches down in Georgia?"

"No, sir, everything will be pickrick, man, not peaches. Pickrick!" (Pickrick meant, restaurateur Maddox said, "to pick what you want and we'll rick it up." This meant, he said, a generous helping.)

There is nothing in Atlanta today that even remotely resembles the Pickrick, home of skillet-fried chicken. It now is a legend. Even the governor seems to be trying to reshape his image and make people forget. He gives visitors gold-plated cuff links with crossed chicken drumsticks on them and the word "Pickrick" written below them, as if it had all been good clean fun. But it wasn't. And people remember. It was in front of his Pickrick skillet-fried chicken restaurant that he was photographed waving a pistol and chasing after a Negro customer who had sought to enter and eat. It was at the Pickrick that he once armed a group of feverish "segs" with ax handles to repel expected Negro customers. It was at the Pickrick, too, that one could pick up Klan literature, White Citizens Council pamphlets, right-wing publications attacking the U. S. Supreme Court and the government as being run by liberals, socialists, Communists, and traitors. One also could find there "Impeach Earl Warren" car stickers.[2]

The appearance of this Mr. Maddox as governor was perhaps "pure theater," as some said. But it also was a mixture of comedy, tragedy, farce, and shock—especially for Atlanta.

It is an oversimplification to say that Atlanta was not quite prepared for the switch from Pickrick to governor. There had been eight years of competent, progressive state government. When the Legislature had at last elected him, the people having failed to provide a majority in the state-wide balloting, Atlanta viewed him as a potential disaster.

The city's "Forward Atlanta" campaign had, across a long span of years, been gratifyingly successful. All the slogans had come true. It was a city too busy to hate. There were problems, to be sure, but the inflammatory gases of hate were not much in evidence. Sleek, contemporary office buildings had for years been springing up like April flowers. A sensational hotel, John Portman's dynamic Regency, just opened on Peachtree Street, was being talked about all over the nation. Financial institutions were moving in or enlarging their branches. Atlanta was rated as the hottest growth city in the Southeast. It also was the "money" town of that region. Its "money" does not touch a competitor until it reaches "Big D" down in Texas. A $9 million cultural center, including a concert hall, a theater for the performing arts, a museum, and an accredited art school, was nearing completion. So was a modern auditorium with adequate halls for general exhibitions.

"Imagine it," said one of the editors of the Chamber of Commerce's nationally known, award-winning *Atlanta Magazine*. "Just imagine it. It is into that sort of stage setting that there walks the stumpy little man with the balding head, the big hands, and the ax-handle, pistol-waving reputation. A proper director would have had him come on with a Bible in one hand and an ax handle in the other, his mouth wide open at high pitch in an old fundamentalist hymn."

If Governor Maddox did not look like a windblown duck, he was bereft, as the 1968 Legislature departed, of any substantial control over that assembly.

His assistant floor leader in the Senate, Robert A. Rowan, had quit, making his mea culpa speech on the floor and saying he could no longer go along with the governor. For this and other related reasons, Governor Maddox failed to get what he wanted in the 1968 session, but, as legislators reflected, he really hadn't wanted much. His Santa Claus budget had been cut. The Legislature and its officers had done more leading than had the governor. Members had assisted in a Maddox parole board reform, but had quietly gone to him and told him he could not keep a major appointee who had a conflict of interest problem. The governor was furious. So was the appointee. But he resigned, denouncing the Atlanta newspapers as a propaganda machine. He did not, however, designate them as liars, thus abandoning a favorite phrase of wounded or exposed politicians in past years who usually have taken refuge in the phrase, "Them Lying Atlanta newspapers."

In Atlanta there was a feeling that things might have gone worse on Capitol Hill with the city and state. There was consequent appreciation for the Legislature's independence.

No governor of Georgia has been able really to hurt Atlanta—and some have tried. Georgia's iniquitous county unit system, which allowed governors and other candidates to be elected even though they had fewer votes, was outlawed in the U. S. Supreme Court in 1962. That freed the state from political bondage and gave the cities more voting power. Reapportionment decisions gave cities additional representation. Georgia's 1968 Legislature obeyed a court order to carry out further reapportionment to more nearly produce the one-man, one-vote ideal.

America's cities, for so long dominated by petty rural provincialism and greed, are freer than they have ever been of "capitol punishment."

This year's Legislature saw some of the young men from rural counties making alliances with city representatives. They know that to get what they want in the future and thereby build political careers, they must be with the city—not against it. Some of the older legislators still have an anti-Atlanta grudge, as did their fathers before them. But they can't do much.

Governor Maddox could hurt the state with poor appointments in key purchasing positions, on the courts and the Board of Regents of the University System, and in failure to improve the quality of secondary and elementary education.

As for what he had done or might do to harm Atlanta specifically, there was concern for the state's name and reputation. But it was not felt that Governor Maddox could halt the city's economic momentum.

Atlanta, even in the days of blackmail, and county-unit politics, played things cool. Atlanta was the first major urban renewal project, having been rebuilt on the acres burned by General William Tecumseh Sherman's "Burn, Baby, Burn" troops in 1865. Being burned was the best piece of luck the city could have had. It had to start over. To do so it had to call on all the spirit its people possessed. There was a further necessity—to obtain and use managerial skills and capital, both in very short supply in 1865. Atlanta did not, therefore, chase off or jail its carpetbaggers who had come in during the Reconstruction years to make money out of rebuilding and in putting down new rail lines. The city winced, but kept the know-how carpetbaggers on and thereby grew and prospered. Atlanta was the only Southern city in that period to obtain capital and managers of money. The "Redeemer" Democrats eagerly joined in to help. The city has had the good fortune, therefore, never to have been a traditional "Southern city," nursing its wounds, myths, and romance, and running spring pilgrimages to see the old antebellum mansions. It has in it the best of the South and little of the worst.

Atlanta will, of course, join with others in the state who can't shake off a sense of apprehension in a day-to-day analysis of the governor. He does not appear always aware of what some of his old pals are doing. But in candor, one must say he has shown no inclination to punish Atlanta. He would, of course, be a fool to do it. Atlanta provides by far the largest percentage of state taxes paid in by metropolitan areas. There is no reason for him to be hostile to the city. He may hurt the state with poor judgment, but there is no expectation of war or even sniping against the Capital City.

This being so, the Forward Atlanta organization has taken a deep breath and marched forward with its old-time confidence, elan, and allure. The city still is great, gleaming, and growing.

The governor not unexpectedly has created a new and crowded avocation in Georgia—Maddox watchers. They keep careful records of the governor's verbal and policy flights and migrations.

At his inauguration in January a year ago, Governor Maddox made a speech over which a number of ghosts had sweated. They wanted, and he wanted, to move away from the old ax-handle and pistol-waving image of Pickrick. They did. But right away the House refused to make sharp reductions in the university budget left by former Governor Carl Sanders. The governor learned very soon that he wasn't the take-charge type.[3]

There was a flurry of prison reform action. Escaped convicts presented themselves at the governor's mansion, surrendering to the guards, and asking to see the governor. He saw them. He heard their stories of cruelties, poor food, poor living conditions, grievous working conditions, and undue punishments. He promised action. A couple of the worst work camps closed. But in Georgia, county work camps are a county asset and a vested political interest. When the noise stopped, not too much had happened in the way of reform.

Word got around after a while that God alone knew to whom the governor was listening. Maybe he was listening to God. He held prayer each morning. He preached and talked to Sunday Schools. Christian ladies in small towns began to write letters to the editors about how nice it was Governor Maddox had brought God back to Atlanta. A few irritated ministers said they didn't know God had been away. The governor went along, apparently confident he had a hotline to God. His first twelve months, when all was said and done, were an unexpected but gratifying "nothing" kind of a year.

There had been time, however, for a good look at Lester Maddox. He was on various TV programs and was interviewed by members of the press, including those unfair liberal reporters and some of those prejudiced Yankees from up North.

In one respect the governor never wavered. He was a segregationist. He believed God had ordained it. He could quote chapter and verse, opening up the large Bible on his desk. He could point a finger and one of those godless reporters could see right there in Deuteronomy: "Thou shalt not plow with an ox and ass together." And anybody but the godless, unconstitutional liberals knows what God said about the purity of the races. Genesis 24, verses three and four, spells it out. The Lord told Isaac, "Thou shalt not take a wife unto my son a daughter of the Canaanites." If he had the old Pickrick days to live over again, a reporter asked, would he do the same thing? He would.

There was a sort of pathos in the man and his predicament. He was himself a white Southern stereotype—as clearly delineated as is the stereotype of the Southern Negro which segregation and discriminations produced. Segregation has been a two-edged blade, cutting down the quality of Southern education, the economy and life in general. Segregation has condemned its white people to live in an environment below that of residents in other regions. The 1954 United States Supreme Court decision freed the white Southerner even more than the Negro. But the majority would not have it so. The governor is of that majority.

Lester Garfield Maddox was born 30 September 1915, to Dean C. and Flonnie Maddox, in Atlanta, Georgia. Dean Maddox was employed in a small steel mill, then given over largely to manufacturing steel bands for baling cotton, nails, and other small items. He was himself a typical Southern story. He had been born near the small town of Rockmart, in Polk County, Georgia. A nearby slate quarry gave the town its name and provided a few unskilled labor jobs. All about it were small farms. Dean Maddox, as so many Southerners before and after him have done, "went to town" in search of a job and opportunity. He found a job. He met a young girl named Flonnie Castleberry at a Baptist church meeting. She was fifteen. Three years later they were married. (Neither knew nor comprehended it, but both were caught in the South's dilemma of educational and opportunity lacks.) Seven children were born to them.[4]

"I just raised my children the best way I could and had a tough time," the governor's mother remembers. "Lester had a tough time, too. . . . Everybody had tough times then. . . ."

They did.

Mrs. Maddox, Sr., is a quiet, dignified lady. A well-worn Bible is her closest companion. Her faith is unquestioning, based on an unwavering fundamentalist belief in the efficacy of prayer. Her faith has a part in much of her conversation, but it is in no sense pushed on others or "advertised." She is a fine old woman, given sincerity and endurance by living through "tough times."

Mrs. Virginia Maddox, the governor's wife, also is deeply fundamentalist in religious belief, finding in it a rationale for all Southern attitudes. But neither she nor her mother-in-law is exhibitionist with their beliefs in the manner of the governor, who offers prayers, homilies, and sermons on morality, "Christian life," and so on, to audiences in his offices or to church congregations, usually Baptist.

In 1925 young Lester Maddox was ten years old. At that time the burning crosses, silent, hooded paraders, and preachments of the Ku Klux Klan were familiar Southern spectacles, especially in Atlanta. In small towns its influence was huge. Lester could hardly have missed hearing talk of the Klan, of lynchings and of "killing."

For all young Southerners, ten years old in 1925 and fifteen years old in 1930, the Klan and its prejudices were a part of the fabric of life. Many who believed in all the Klan preached never joined it. Their reasons for not doing so were varied. For many it was the initiation fee of $10.00 and a further cost of robe and other accessories. As far as is known, Lester Maddox never joined the Klan, but the Klans openly and ardently support him and known Klansmen are in and out of his office.

Money always was scarce in the Maddox family. Young Lester opened up a "store." His business house was an old pigeon house set up in front of his home. There he sold candy and grape soda. Later he took a job in the steel mill where his wage was $18.00 a week—when there was work. He was twenty when he married Virginia Cox, aged seventeen. They moved the old pigeon coop to a vacant lot corner and expanded it to add hotdogs, hamburgers, and ice cream. There were four stools. The bride and groom were the entire work force.

In 1947 the two young merchants bought a weed-grown lot in a deteriorating section. The faded for-sale sign testified to how long the owner had gone without a buyer. They got it cheap. There they built a drive-in. The Pickrick was born.[5]

The Pickrick flourished. Lester expanded with it. The place was his life. He was a moving part of the decor, going about, beaming and happy, asking "Is everything Pickrick?" He was the main attraction. He began to advertise, always in the Saturday papers. The ads were the thoughts of Lester Maddox and were as sacred to the fanatic racists as are the thoughts of Mao Tse-tung to the faithful in Peking.

A sample will do: "I think that the most horrible thing ever to be said by a president of the United States was when our president (Johnson) told Southern Baptists to come back to the South and, from the pulpit, try to lead patriotic Americans to accept the unconstitutional, ungodly civil rights legislation that the politicians, Communists, and Communist-inspired agitators are trying to pass in Congress that will enslave all Americans."[6]

Pickrick attracted the admiring faithful, the curious, and those who like the price of the drumstick special. The faithful urged him to run for mayor. He did, in 1957 and in 1961. He got the red-neck and extreme right-wing votes. In 1962 he ran for lieutenant governor, and failed. In 1966 he ran second for governor, and the Legislature, not the people, elected him.

In the summer of 1966 Lester Maddox had abandoned his restaurant and his ax handle business rather than obey the congressionally enacted public accommodations act. He blamed socialists, Communists and left-wingers for "forcing me out of business."

Later, as owner of a new furniture store, he announced as a candidate in the Democratic primary for nomination as governor. He announced because a political vacuum had been suddenly created.

There followed an unbelievable set of circumstances.

There was no majority in the election itself because of almost 100,000 write-in votes for former Governor of Georgia Ellis Arnall.

In the gubernatorial campaign Atlanta's financial and business community had begun with almost total support for Howard (Bo) Callaway, the GOP nominee, who, himself, had been a former segregationist Democrat. But even the committment of the business-financial leadership was diminished by the confusion of events and the personalities of the candidates. In the end the business-financial leadership sought chiefly to influence appointments. One such success, that of a competent man of integrity, Peyton Hawes, as revenue commissioner, has contributed much to the Maddox consensus—"He ain't as bad as I thought he'd be." Aside from a few temper flare-ups, the barring of the press, and a small number of other antics, the consensus has an uneasy validity.

In retrospect, perhaps the unkindest cut of all was from Barry Goldwater, whom Mr. Maddox had supported in 1964. On a CBS Walter Cronkite show in December before the courts gave the Georgia state Legislature authority to elect, Mr. Goldwater said: "Georgia was a most progressive state until all of a sudden they have that fellow that belongs back in the Stone Age, and I really think that if the Legislature of Georgia were really true to their state's reputation, they'd see to it that Maddox went back to serving hotdogs, because he certainly is not going to be a credit to the United States."

"It was fried chicken," said Cronkite.

"Fried chicken. Is that right? And baseball bats. . . ."

Mr. Cronkite did not have time to correct the last item. It was ax handles, not baseball bats.

So, here we are in the spring of 1968, the state of Georgia, the progressive city of Atlanta, and Governor Lester Maddox. And there are almost three more Maddox years to go.

Any city that survived William Tecumseh Sherman isn't likely to be disturbed by that.[7]

Notes—33

[1]Copyright © by the *Institutional Investor*, and reprinted by permission of the author, Mrs. McGill, and the *Institutional Investor* (May 1968): 49-51, 53, 55, 88, 91.

[2]Lester Garfield Maddox, *Speaking Out: The Autobiography of Lester Garfield Maddox* (New York: Doubleday & Co., 1975), pp. 49-69; Bruce Galphin, *The Riddle of Lester Maddox* (Atlanta: Camelot, 1968), pp. 55-85.

[3]Maddox, *Speaking Out*, pp. 95-132; Galphin, *Riddle of Lester Maddox*, pp. 168-91.

[4]Maddox, *Speaking Out*, pp. 1-12; Galphin, *Riddle of Lester Maddox*, pp. 5-14.

[5]Maddox, *Speaking Out*, pp. 13-36.

[6]Maddox, *Speaking Out*, pp. 27-28; Galphin, *Riddle of Lester Maddox*, pp. 15-25.

[7]For more by McGill on Maddox, see Logue, *Ralph McGill: Editor and Publisher*, 2:426, 432, 494, 509.

Interview

"Reb" Gershon Talks About Ralph McGill[1]

Logue: Reb, it's certainly a pleasure for me to be in your home. I appreciate your giving me this opportunity to chat with you about your relationship with Ralph McGill. To begin with I would like to ask you when you first really got to know McGill and just what was the nature of your longtime relationship.

Gershon: Well, Ralph and I met in February of 1913 on his fifteenth birthday and I was just past fourteen a couple of months. We met at an inter-preparatory school discussion group. You have mentioned in your account[2] these inter-preparatory school discussion groups and I made a note to tell you just how they functioned if you were interested enough.[3]

L.: Good. Yes, I would like to know exactly.

G.: On this particular occasion Ralph was representing McCallie School and I was representing Girls' Preparatory School, each of us having won in our own school in the intra-school discussion thing and the topic for discussion, I think, was Panama Canal tolls.

It was just when the Panama Canal had opened, just prior to its opening and there was discussion, Congressional I believe, as to whether to make it a toll affair or not. Now that's all I remember about the topic itself and after the thing was over there was always a social hour and Ralph asked to meet the girl who had sufficient presence of mind to change her talk midstream because of something that a prior speaker had said. I don't even remember that, and we became acquainted. Ralph was, without any exception, the most superlatively shy person I've ever known in my life. I just never saw a teenager who was as shy as he was. So the first six or eight times he came for a date with me, he came with somebody else. Well, then, eventually he got so he could come alone because he felt very much at home with my family and in my home, which he describes in the *South and the Southerner*. Well, the nature of the relationship was just a perfectly on-a-par-friendship deal. I don't think there ever was—there was nothing like what we used to call a crush. You mentioned the night we were at Mrs. McGill's that when he went to join the Marines he left his fraternity pin with a Jewish girl and I told you I was that girl. But leaving the fraternity pin was a matter of sort of safeguarding it. I mean it wasn't "pinning me."

L.: Well, don't you think really that the average reader reading that column McGill wrote would probably have different connotations?

G.: Probably. But I think what he meant was that he was sufficiently friendly to deposit his pin with her. I kept it until, oh I don't know, I don't even remember—but I had it for a number of years. But it didn't really imply anything like a pre-engagement. That, I'm sure, was in neither of our minds. This was a devoted friendship that remained devoted over the years. We had many things in common—reading, interests, outside-of-school interests as we got older. I suppose when we were first friends it was reading, in-school interests, football, glee club, dramatics, and some of the things that these two schools did together.

L.: What was the name of your school?

G.: Girls' Preparatory School.

L.: Do you remember the plays in which he participated, like *What Happened to Jones?*

G.: I remember some of them and I remember a couple of them which these two schools did together and which we took to a couple of surrounding small towns. I think we went on the train. These days you can go in no time flat in a car. But I remember very little about them except the coach that he mentions in, I think he mentions it in his book. And you have it again in your—[4]

L.: Mr. Wilcox?

G.: No, Mr. Wilcox was in a different relation, a man by the name of Bobby Strauss.

L.: Oh, yes, that's right—

G.: Who had been on the stage himself in minor parts.

L.: Can you amplify what you said about McGill being shy? Not just the fact that he was shy, but can you give us any more insight into the kind of young man he was at that age? Do you remember other traits?[5]

G.: He always read voluminously. He remembered extraordinarily well. He could quote poetry by the page, not poets whom we think of as particularly highbrow poets these days, but Kipling, Robert W. Service, maybe some Tennyson. Ralph could quote page after page after page. He was also interested in football. Other sports I don't recall. He was terribly shy of girls. Not only shy in general of everybody but shy of girls and I remember not too long ago he had a column about taking a girl to a movie and not being sure he had enough money to get her home if it rained and he had to take a taxi.

I wrote him a note after that column and signed it *Name Withheld by Request* and said to him, "I must have come before your movie stage. I don't remember you ever taking *me* to a movie;" I remember glee club concerts and school plays and basketball games at the old Armory between the schools with dances afterwards in which he never participated because he never danced.

L.: How many years are we talking about here in this first stage?

G.: Ralph for years would say to people, referring to me, "We've known each other since we were thirteen." Well, this was an error. We met in 1913 when I was just past fourteen and he was just fifteen; as a matter of fact, we met on his birthday, February 5. But I never corrected him and said it was 1913, not age thirteen. What difference did it make? I mean by the time you've gotten to know each other over forty or fifty years, what difference does that make? And I just let it ride. But I've never been able quite to coordinate the dates.

L.: Other than being shy, was he a pretty friendly fellow? Did he get along well?

G.: Yes, he got along well; once he felt at home he was friendly; he was forthright; he wasn't afraid to express his opinions once he felt at home. But it was hard for him to learn to feel at home, I think.

L.: What shortcomings, if any? I know it's difficult to judge a man, but do you recall any that he had at that time?

G.: Well, he was always what somebody in a writeup called "baggy." Always.

L.: In his dress you mean?

G.: Yes. He could put on a suit that was freshly pressed and it looked rumpled.

L.: Like a storekeeper, as someone said.

G.: That doesn't mean anything to me but rumpled. And I don't think this is a fault; it's a mannerism. He always pulled at his hair when he talked and the more interested he got the more he did this. I remember on a long library table in the living room of my house we had one of these scissors-paper knife things, and he would take the paper knife and . . . I can see him.

L.: Curl his hair?

G.: Sort of. I don't know. I remember him as being completely agreeable and in addition to just the two of us there were two other couples. The two boys went to McCallie, the girls were friends of mine at school, and the six of us did things together a great deal. One of these boys, Ken Whitaker, had a car or at least had the use of a family car.

L.: Who was the other boy. Do you remember?

G.: Yes, Sam Eaves, whom we called Keith. Ken Whitaker is no longer living. He died a number of years ago and the last time I heard Ralph say anything about Keith Eaves he was a wheelchair patient in some nursing home in Texas. Ken Whitaker's widow is living and has been down here not too long ago. She is a semi-invalid now, but Ralph kept up with her. As a matter of fact, she was the first person who called the morning after Ralph's death.

L.: Can you describe for us McGill as he might participate in this discussion league? What kind of participant was he. Was he quite aggressive?

G.: I do know that his voice was always the husky voice that he had in later years. He always had that. Now I can't say that it didn't wax and wane more or less, but he always had that voice.

L.: Let's move on and get any remarks you'd like to make about McGill's stay at Vanderbilt University in Nashville.

G.: Of course, this would be information that he told me, because I wasn't there. I think Ralph must have been one year—one scholastic year—behind me because I went to Smith College before he went to Vanderbilt. I know that he always supplemented his funds by working at various things. And when he first went to Vanderbilt, his idea was to take a pre-med course. He wanted to be a doctor. And he did start with a pre-med course. How long he took it I no longer recall. But I do remember his throes of decision as to whether to go on with it or switch to something else. He simply thought that medicine still had allure for him and all his life he was interested in talking to doctors.[6] He was very much interested in experiments, medical experiments, new discoveries, and I don't think this came out of any family illness. I think this was from his boyhood on. But as he looked at it from his pre-med course, having to supplement his finances, he said, I can remember distinctly his saying it was just too long a pull going through med school, then internship, residency, 'til you got on your feet. It was just longer than he could face.

And I remember you have something about his taking law next. I have no recollection of that. If I knew it, I have forgotten it completely.[7] I know that one of the things he did by way of amplifying his income was working on the *Nashville Banner*, and I think he started out as a copy boy and then he had some of these assignments at outrageous hours like late at night or early in the morning. Those were the days when the trains from the East came in at way past midnight or early morning. And he took those assignments because they were very hard to get anybody else to take and he got an enormous bang out of them because he met actors and actresses and singers and speakers and people he'd read about. Apparently he got through his work all right.

But my recollection is that his initial interest in the paper was—he started out as a copy boy, then he did this strange assignment, and then he did some sports. Then he did a Vanderbilt journal of some sort, newspaper sheet, in which I think he initiated a column, and then he got a better job on the *Banner*, and he just stayed on until he was eventually sports editor on the *Banner* with a strange interlarding of politics. When there would be a political campaign, he'd go. Those years he was living in Nashville because when he finished school he went on to the *Banner*, but he'd come home for vacations and I would see him. I remember his enthusiasm about some of these political campaigns and some of the tales he told. He was always, as I recall it, an excellent raconteur. Now for years he wasn't a good speaker and I don't know that he was ever really a good speaker. He was never an orator. He didn't have the things that make a speaker, a building up, climaxes, and dramatic things, but he was a good talker and he was an excellent raconteur. He could sit in a group of people and tell tale after tale after tale. And some of them we heard many times, some of them we heard once, some of them we never heard at all. But I can remember his telling about some of these political compaigns that he covered in Tennessee.

I know he went with a much larger crowd in Nashville than he ever went with in Chattanooga. I would think that he greatly overcame this shyness and learned how to mix with people better. He also played football at Vanderbilt. He was very lightweight in those days; he was very thin, almost gangly thin. No one who knew him in his later years could picture him as thin as he was.

L.: Reading some of the accounts that even McGill wrote, it seems that he was getting to be quite independent, almost a rebel—his protesting at the halftime of football games the high prices of clothes in Nashville, things like this. Do you remember this coming out in McGill? Was there a transition when this began to develop?[8]

G.: No, I think he probably was always a rebel. He just learned to express it. Now, I can't give you any proof of that, but I have a feeling that he was never a conformist because the things he did when he was an early teenager weren't the things that were routinely done by teenagers. A teenager didn't sit and read poetry by the ream either to himself or out loud to somebody who would listen. This wasn't the typical teenager. But he combined football and this, so nobody could say, "you're a sissy."

L.: I'm sure you've read my accounts of McGill as to why he was asked to leave Vanderbilt before graduation? Can you shed any more light on this?

G.: No, the only thing I know is this story about the fraternity thing. I've always had a sneaking suspicion that it might have had something to do with some of his rebellious utterances, but I don't know that and I never heard him say that.

L.: He wrote once that he indicted the administration for misuse of funds that were to go to what they called a student lounge or a student union building. That may have had something to do with it.

G.: I always had the feeling it was something a little bit more serious than the fraternity dance thing. For years he didn't mention this. The fact that he actually hadn't gotten a diploma from Vanderbilt—I think it hurt him psychologically and he just didn't talk about it. Afterwards I remember his referring to it. Although I can't say that he said it in words of one syllable, I always had the impression that it was some balking at the administration, or tripping up the administration or having something on the administration or something of that sort, rather than only the fraternity thing, although I don't know.

L.: One of the striking things one learns in reading about this period is the kind of people he worked with and associated with.

G.: You mean like the Agrarians?

L.: —The fugitives. Sims he said, wrote "Popeye"; later, critic Allen Tate, Robert Penn Warren, do you remember him mentioning this at all?

G.: I'm sure he must have mentioned them, but they weren't well known names then. I do remember the first time I ever read anything of Robert Penn Warren. Ralph was already living here, and I said to him, "Don't I connect Robert Penn Warren with you in some way or other?" But he would mention them just the way you'd mention John Jones or Bill Smith, and they never stuck in my mind.[9]

L.: There's some confusion, at least in my research, as to how long he stayed at Nashville after leaving Vanderbilt. Some brief biographical sketches will say after leaving Vanderbilt about 1921 or 1922 he went to the *Nashville Banner* full time and then in 1929 he moved to the *Constitution* in Atlanta. Is it true that he stayed in Nashville all that time?

G.: I think so. I left Chattanooga in the fall of 1921 but I think Ralph was in Nashville all that time—working on the *Banner*, working up to sports editor. Exactly when he became sports editor I don't know. Then he did come to Atlanta in 1929. The first time that I remember seeing him in Atlanta he came down as sports editor from the *Banner* to report a Vanderbilt-Georgia Tech game. I remember my husband and I met him at the train and took him to lunch before the game. Some of us who knew Ralph over the years always felt that it was very strange and we felt a little bitterly about the fact that Vanderbilt never gave him any sort of an award.

L.: Did they not give him an honorary degree?

G.: I don't think so. Not that I know.[10]

L.: So McGill came to Atlanta in 1929.

G.: The fall I believe. Anyway, he came to Atlanta in 1929 and he was married then. . . .[11]

L.: Here you had an associate sports editor, soon to be sports editor and all of a sudden by 1938 he returned from Europe and he's writing his own column commenting on cooking, politics, Eugene Talmadge. What's happening to this man at this time?[12]

G.: When McGill was a sports writer both on the *Nashville Banner* and here in Atlanta, he was an atypical sports writer. His interests and knowledge were far wider than sports. And every now and then he would do a story about something else. He did some stories on some farm situations. I don't know whether it was Georgia only or whether it was the South in general. In 1937 or even earlier, one of the representatives of the Rosenwald Fund was traveling through the South and he came across these articles of McGill's about agriculture. He was interested, and he made it his business to meet Ralph and talk to him about them. He persuaded Ralph to make an application for a Rosenwald Fellowship, and Ralph did make an application and did a special article as an exhibit for the application. I can remember his telling me about this man coming to see him; I don't remember what his name was. I remember when he sent the thing off to the Rosenwald Fund office, and I remember when he was notified that he'd received the fellowship. He was still sports editor but the *Constitution* gave him a leave of absence.

He left sometime after the late spring of '37. I know he was in Europe in '38. I know that his wife went with him and I know that he and Mary Elizabeth returned in the later spring of '38. The first thing he did was go to Denmark and write about the farm situation in Denmark and the connection between the practice of agriculture and the Danish folk schools. This was much in the news at that time, and then he went to Sweden following the same thread. Then he went down into Austria and Germany and the last part of their trip was in the British Isles.

Shortly before their return, Francis Clark, who was managing editor of the *Constitution*, had pneumonia and died. When Ralph came back, he stepped into that position. I don't remember the date when he was made editor. I have a letter here that Ralph wrote from Essen, Germany, in March 8 of 1938.

L.: Would you read a little of that for us?

G.: Yes. It isn't of any tremendous significance.

L.: It's of historical significance.

G.: He says "My dear Reb, it was awfully nice of you to remember my birthday." I always did—the fifth of February.

L.: Now, could you date this letter once more for us?

G.: March 6, 1938, written from Essen, Germany on hotel stationery, the Hotel Reichshof, Germany. "The letter caught up with me in Germany, and I am sorry to be a bit late answering it." This is a characteristic line. I don't think I ever got a letter from Ralph that wasn't a bit late in answering it and apologetic. "I came to Germany with a prejudice which remains. I cannot understand the German people at all. But the fact remains that Hitler is stronger than ever before and there is no sign of weakness, that is, no apparent sign. If there is one, it is in the economic fabric. I keep thinking they will laugh but they don't. I keep waiting for a break in the armor of some individual, but there isn't any. On entering a shop, a hotel, a barbershop, a bookstore, an elevator, the clerks, attendants, etc. raise the right hand and say 'Heil, Hitler,' and the one entering responds in the same fashion. No one laughs. He has given them an arrogant morale. Germany is busy building roads, building streets. We saw all the big day of February 20 when he paraded to the opera for his speech, talked with some of his body guards. They're just boys such as died in the last world war. I seem to feel a weight pressing down and I can remember that I grow old and small things such as repeated pictures of Hitler, Göring and others in every shop store lobby annoy me. Well, later we will talk about it. The Scandinavian countries, especially Sweden and Denmark, are the most civilized of all the countries that I have seen but they are not utopias. Mr. Childs was not fair. He ground a few axes." And I think that's Marquis Childs who had recently published *Sweden: The Middle Way*. This too I think is typical. "My

articles won't come fast enough. I hope one or two are all right."
With this leave of absence that the *Atlanta Constitution* gave him,
there was this commitment to send back articles from these
countries. Then he simply says, "God help a poor penman when
he gets a poor pen. I hope you can read this. Mary Elizabeth joins
me."

L.: Very interesting letter. Just a side note here. He wrote of how to
supplement his funds to go on this trip; he wrote several articles
about Greece and published them and he sold them for several
hundred dollars. And I have never been able to find where they
were published. Do you happen to know?[13]

G.: I don't know of any articles about Greece.

L.: This was back in '37 and '38. He didn't go to Greece on this trip, did
he? No, this was before. He got the money before that to help pay
expenses. When do you think that McGill first began to become a
well known individual throughout the South, throughout Georgia,
and finally throughout the world?

G.: I do know that it was in the middle 1950s before he got real
reception—I mean real appreciative response. Between the early
and the middle 1950s, a local group sparked by a man and a
woman asked people whom they thought were favorably disposed
toward McGill to write appreciative letters. And they wanted to
leave a big bundle of them at his door on Thanksgiving of that year.
This was approximately, I would say, between 1952 and 1956,
somewhere along in there. There had been so many hate things
that this was an effort of some people who liked him to give him a
feeling, *There are some people who appreciate you.* They did do
it, and he got the letters on Thanksgiving. How many there were I
don't know.

Then in the period after the Supreme Court decision in
the spring of '54—it was in the late 50s or 1960 when the schools
were desegregated here. But he had done many a fighting column
in that interval and he had many, many violent detractors because
of it. He spoke at the Tower Theatre for a meeting of HOPE, the
group that worked for peaceful desegregation of the schools in
Georgia. The letters stood for Help Our Public Education. He
spoke at a big rally meeting for HOPE, and he got a tremendous
ovation. This seems to be one of the first times that he got this
tremendous acclaim locally. Shortly after that he was asked to

speak at West Georgia College at Carrollton. And a local radio station had spot announcements every fifteen minutes, something against his coming. I don't remember who drove him from here, but some miles out of Carrollton the president of the college and two or three other people met him and they rode in between these pennants from the school that said, "Welcome, McGill." He got an acclaim at that performance.

Now this seems to me to be almost the beginning of his going around speaking at schools. He'd spoken locally for different things, but he hadn't done as much going about as he did later.

L.: You mention several times about the hate letters, spot announcements. What kind of fellow was McGill that he could put up with this? I mean to read about it is one thing, but to live it from day-to-day—what kind of man was he?[14]

G.: He was often times depressed by them. I don't think he was ever stopped by them. But equally I am sure that they never ceased to hurt him. Up to his last days, a letter that attacked him, a letter that didn't understand what he was trying to do, a letter that spewed venom—these hurt him. But it didn't stop him in his tracks.

And then I've had Mary Elizabeth tell me—and I mean Mary *Elizabeth*, the first Mrs. McGill—tell me about phone calls, garbage dumped on the lawn, and excrement put in the garage and that sort of thing. Occasionally something like this would happen and Ralph would laugh. But I've seen him many a time sit and shake his head and say, "I don't know why they said something like this. What did I ever do to them? Why can't they understand?"

I remember a novel that a young advertising man wrote back in the 1950s sometime when the main character was undeniably based on McGill. Then it went off on a tangent that seemed to have no connection with McGill at all. It was very unkind, and I remember Ralph's reaction to that. He said, "I don't know why he ever wrote that way. I never did anything to him. I tried to help him. I tried to help him get a job. Tried to help place him. What do you suppose made him react like that?"

L.: If some of these letters did stay with him and did hurt him, what motivated McGill to continue to do what he knew would bring similar responses?

G.: Because it was far more important to him to do what he thought was right, to follow what was the principle of not only his living but his newspaper work. I have had the theory for years that his sensitivity, almost the sensitiveness of a child or a very young person who has his feelings hurt, was part and parcel of the sensitivity that made him so attuned to somebody else's hurt.

L.: If he's willing to go ahead and write and take his stand even though he will be hurt, then what's he driving at? Are you saying he was a crusader?

G.: Yes.

L.: You say he was a crusader?

G.: I say he was a crusader. He said he was not a crusader because he could always see both sides. And I guess he could and I don't suppose he was a crusader for a person, ever. He was a crusader for a principle, what he thought was a basic right. I wish I knew another word that would mean the same thing.

L.: Usually a crusader often had a connotation—not just a purpose but his method. For example, I say in this book that he was not a crusader in the sense of a William Lloyd Garrison, a Wendell Phillips where he would burn the Constitution—McGill was more really kind of a teacher in his crusading. But you like that word pretty well, don't you?[15]

G.: No, I don't. I would rather use another word for crusader. Because crusader to me has some sort of an aura of fanatic and he was not fanatic. At least as I saw him, he wasn't fanatic.

L.: What is there in that word that you do like? Just forget the word "crusader." What are you trying to say he was? He was willing to go ahead and fight for something even though he would be hurt and even though he was sensitive. What was it that drove him to this?

G.: I think his own definition of a good newspaperman may help here. A good newpaperman is part teacher, part preacher, always interested in what's going on, and curious about what makes it. He took that a little deeper than many newspapermen. He took it into psychology, into history, into sociology. What makes these people in this region respond the way they do? What are the backgrounds? What are the forces that have helped make them so? He almost never did it right off the top of his head, or theirs. He tried to dig into the historical and sociological. He had a pricking conscience; there was no doubt about that. I guess all these things go together—the conscience, the sensitivity. I think the sensitivity was in a measure responsible for his wanting to see all around the person, even the person whose actions he condemned, his desire to see why they did behave that way. Think about some of the people in this regional scene whose actions he condemned in no uncertain terms. He frequently tried to see the things that were responsible for their behavior, for their reactions.

L.: Earlier you mentioned that even as a child he was different when he was reading poetry. Don't you think McGill was really a poet at heart?

G.: Yes. He and Gene Patterson and Harold Martin every now and then would get together and read poetry.

L.: In recent years?

G.: Yes. Sometime within the last very few years, he and I were talking about poetry. I said, "I don't read poetry the way I used to because mostly I can't get anything out of this contemporary poetry." He said "Well, there are a lot of them I don't get anything out of either. But now I've come across somebody that I think you'd enjoy," and he gave me the name and a few days later he sent me a paperback of Eberhart, Richard I believe. With several of his poems marked.

L.: You ask why an evangelist like Billy Graham is driven to go all over the world. Well, it's kind of simple. Some person would say it's to make money; one guy would say it's his love of God. You ask why a businessman is motivated. Maybe it's profit, maybe it's service to humanity. It's just interesting to speculate why McGill could do all he did within one lifetime. What was the driving force?

G.: The driving force was such an essential part of him that if you thought about him, if you knew him, you accepted the driving force.

L.: I'm not sure these questions are answerable, but they're fun to deal with.

G.: Yes, they are.

L.: Many people who would oppose McGill at a very basic level— would say that as soon as he saw that the race question would be a popular question in the late 1950s and 1960s that he took it, latched on, and became much more liberal. He could see that this was the way to become well known, win many awards, and become well respected among liberals and intellectuals. Their explanation

would be very simple: it was purely selfish. This was what motivated McGill. What is your comment on that?

G.: Nobody who knew him could have said that. Nobody who knew
the antagonism he aroused in those years could have believed
that. And his awards didn't begin to come until around 1960 or
1961. When they started they came in a flood but they were
long-starting. I don't think he ever expected awards. He was just as
surprised in an almost naive way when these awards began to
come. If he ever expected to get an award, like an honorary
degree, I was certainly blind to that. He was surprised and he
seemed to contine to be surprised when people thought that
something he did was specially good. I found McGill exactly the
same man in the last couple of years that he'd been years before.

L.: Back in the 1940s he supported, strongly, separate-but-equal
schools for the races. Then in 1954 and 1955 after the Supreme
Court decision, he began gradually to support the law which
meant racially integrated schools. Do you think there was ever a
real change in his thinking, say, on race relations?[16]

G.: I don't think there was. And I'll tell you why I think that. This is very
hard to prove, because as the times changed there were different
ways of manifesting your interest and your advocacy. Back in the
1940s Ralph was interested in the old Commission on Interracial
Cooperation and in the development of that into the new Southern
Regional Council. It has become the thing in these free days to be
very slurry about the old Commission on Interracial Cooperation.
But that old Commission, judged in its own context from 1919
when it was formed to 1943 when it gave over to the new organization, Southern Regional Council, was something else again. I think
the people who were interested in it in the 1930s and the early
1940s were evidencing their stand on race relations which was just
as far in its day as a different sort of manifestation, as it was in the
late 1950s, if that makes things clear.[17]

L.: Yes, it does.
     What do you think McGill meant by his frequent state-
ment, "I don't think anyone could have a policy of integration."
Quite often after speeches there would be a question and answer
period and the people would press him on this. "Why are you
taking this stand? Why are you supporting this daily in your
column?" And he never made excuses. He was quite proud of his
stand, but he would always say, "I have never had a policy of

integration," or "I don't think anyone could have a policy." He always stressed that word *policy*. Can you shed any light on that?[18]

G.: He made a distinction between the terms, "desegregation" and "integration," which I think is a valid distinction. You can legislate desegregation. Integration has more to do with people coming together because they want to, because of some interest in common, some activity in common, some mutual liking or understanding. And my guess would be that he meant you can't legislate this latter sort of thing. You can't even have a policy for it.

L.: Your explanation is very consistent with some of his other stands. Many people indict McGill for opposing many of our federal laws back in the 1940s, 1950s, and 1960s, all kinds—of anti-lynching. And they never take the time to understand. He wanted the South to solve these problems, and that goes along with what you said. He knew we would have better relations if we solved our own problems.[19]

G.: I don't know how much he ever thought about the fact that you do not lead your constituency if you get too far ahead of them. Now I don't know that I ever heard him say that, but it must have been in his head.[20]

L.: He told me that in a taped interview.

G.: Heaven knows, plenty of them thought he was too far ahead as it was.[21]

L.: In my interview with McGill I asked questions for about forty-five minutes. The only time he became a little impatient was when I asked him what he considered his own role in society to be. I got the idea he wanted to leave that to history. He just didn't want to comment. What do you think his role was?

G.: I just don't know. I would guess that he thought he lived his role. He didn't have to verbalize it because he lived it. I don't know if he ever saw himself in a role in his mind's eye. I don't believe he ever would have expressed that. He was a combination of the unusually joined qualities of genuinely deep humility and great strength. If he was sufficiently committed in his own mind on something you didn't budge him. But as far as his accomplishments were concerned, he had this very deep humility.

L.: What do you mean by great strength? Was he tough? Can you amplify that?

G.: I think the very fact that he wasn't sidetracked by the various things and people who tried to sidetrack him shows strength. I'm thinking of the kind of strength that comes out of conscientious commitment, of dedication to the few basics that you think are right, come hell or high water.

L.: Many people probably shared his convictions, but the reason that McGill stands out was his ability to stand by some of these publicly.

G.: Now that, I think, indicates strength. This is the kind of strength you can't measure or weigh on a scale or even color by injecting into the veins. You can't X-ray it. But it seems to me that this is evidence that that kind of strength was there.

L.: Most people thought of his role as being tied chiefly to civil rights, particularly the Negro in the South and in this country—did he see himself primarily in that role? Did this occupy a great deal of his time and thought as far as you knew?

G.: I don't know. I couldn't measure how great these interests were. But he had great interest in international affairs, the United Nations, its potential, and its failure to reach its potential. He was interested in a number of things.

L.: Politics?

G.: Politics, nationally. As you know, he went to the conventions. He went along with several of the campaign trains or planes. He was also interested in foreign affairs. He was interested in India. He had one fairly long stay there and then a couple of other returns. He was interested in the Middle East. He was very much interested in the state of Israel after his visit there in 1946 and 1950 or 1951. His little book, *Israel Revisited*, is a small book but I think a significant one. I was amazed all over again when I read it again a few weeks ago at the depth of his perception and understanding. He was interested in Middle Europe before, during, and after World War II.

L.: Most of his awards seem to come through minority groups— bombing of synagogues, burning of churches, etc. Apparently this was a theme of the time.

G.: I think that's true. But the people whom he knew in foreign countries were often not public figures. He would have met the public figures, but he also knew *little* people—the ordinary reporter or a woman who had worked in some area of interest to him, if not newspapers, medicine, children. He's introduced me to people hither, thither, and yon. Almost always they were people who were interested in books, newspapers, some sort of work for children, education, medicine—but medicine in the experimental field, in the area where it's reaching out to know more—not just a plain practicing doctor, although I'm sure he respected the plain practical doctor. I suppose that what you say is true, that most people think of him in the field of civil rights. I think of his interests as being so much broader.

L.: Oh?

G.: Yes, I think of his interests as stemming out of a warmth for people who in any way suffered deprivation, unjust treatment or unusual difficulties. I think some of his interest in India fell into that category. This was a nation with phenomenal potential and so much going against it.

L.: McGill sounds more like a missionary, a humanitarian, a man with a cause, not just a reporter.

G.: He could have been any one of those things, but there would have been some of these same elements—the same thing that made him more than just a reporter. He was a reporter who wanted to go beneath the surface, to see what made these things come out the way they were. His interest in international affairs came through the human channels, not just moving places around on a map. But he knew an awful lot because these various national committees he served on put him in touch with a great deal of information that frequently didn't come out in the public press. For years every time he went to Washington, he'd have lunch with Admiral Rickover. He has described to me Admiral Rickover's lunch. They sat at Admiral Rickover's desk and Admiral Rickover had a hard boiled egg and a piece of lettuce and a slice of tomato. I can't be sure whether it was a glass of milk or not. And Ralph would say, "And me, if I had cottage cheese I was starving by 3:00. But I didn't have the nerve to eat much more than that when this little bit was on this little thin man's desk."

He knew Adlai Stevenson personally. He was a long time friend of Ted Weeks, as you know. These were people whose information, whose attitudes towards things, whose sparkling minds sent out signals to his own. He had an excellent mind, not only this gift for organization. His secretary [Grace Lundy] said that he almost never wrote a column and did it over and underlined and changed it. If he did a column on the typewriter, it was almost always clean. Or if he dictated it to her in person or over long distance as he did frequently when he was away, it was all done in his mind beforehand and it would come out just perfectly. He would expect her to catch any grammatical errors. But the meat of it and the expressions he had already worked out in his mind.

He had a fantastic memory. If he didn't remember exactly what it was he wanted to refer to or quote, he knew where to find it, and he could go right to the bookshelf and find it. Or he could go to a stack of notes he had taken and find it.

L.: What do you think McGill was most proud of in his life?

G.: Probably his son, I don't know.

L.: What was Mrs. Mary Elizabeth McGill like? Can you tell us about her?

G.: I liked her and I thought she was a warm, generous person, terribly misunderstood and very unkindly treated. I don't mean by Ralph; I mean by others. She had a lot of tragedy. She had I don't know how many miscarriages and a couple of stillbirths, lost an infant child, and then lost this little girl who was adopted. This little girl, Virginia, was buried out at Westview, died at four or something, and they adored her. Mrs. McGill took these things terribly, terribly hard and in some of her periods of depression she had difficulty with alcohol which she completely overcame. But I don't think people ever forgot that she'd had it or ever credited her with having overcome it. And they were very unkind, the way they talked about her. I think many people just didn't think she was Ralph's equal. But equal is such a stupid word. She was different. She was not an intellectual—made no pretense of being—but she had marvelous horse sense, common sense, good salt-of-the-earth sense, and a fantastic sense of humor and nobody could ever have gotten a blown-up impression of themselves living with her. I don't think Ralph ever would have. I don't think it was in him to do it, but if he had, she would have punctured it. And I thought she was really a great person and I thought she was a much, much better companion for him than somebody more like him. But people were never fair, were not kind to Mary Elizabeth.

L.: Did you ever hear McGill discuss his mother or father? We find something in his writings, but not too much really.

G.: I heard him discuss his mother more than his father. I've heard him say again and again and again, "I never had any feeling that I wasn't wanted or that I was being mistreated, or anything. That was just left out of me entirely. I never had any of that when I was growing up at all."

I don't know too much about his father. I think his mother was the strength in the family. And she must have been a remarkable woman even to her very latter years. I have the feeling that there was more of a channel of communication between Ralph and his mother than between him and his father.

I'm going back to the "What was he the proudest of?" question. I was one of the four people whom he invited to go with him to Washington when he got the Freedom Award Medal. This was before he knew Mary Lynn and after Mary Elizabeth's death, and each recipient was permitted four people. I think there were some twenty-odd recipients and the event was in the East Room of the White House. He took Mr. and Mrs. (Jack) Tarver, and Grace Lundy, his secretary, and me.[22] And I was so proud I just couldn't quite hold it. And he was just as calm about it. And he wouldn't put the little button hole thing on, and wear it. They put the medal around his neck when they gave it to him. He took it off and we went to lunch and then he wouldn't wear the other thing at all; we couldn't make him.

The President [Lyndon Johnson] gave them in the East Room of the White House, and that night the assistant secretary of state, George Ball, and Mrs. Ball, had a reception for the award winners and their guests at which Mr. Ball made a brief statement about the Freedom Award Medals. Ralph had been asked to respond to it which I thought was pretty much of an honor when you looked around at all the other people. I think he was pleased, but he didn't do any showing off about it, bragging. I don't know what he was proudest of.

L.: When we were talking about the young Ralph McGill back when he was a teenager, you said about the only shortcoming you could recall was he was rather rumpled. There are very few perfect men, as I think we would all agree. Can you recall what would be his shortcomings as a man later in years? If he had limitations, what were they?

G.: He always took on too much. He wore himself out. He took himself away from people he would have enjoyed; maybe he even took himself away from his family more than he should have. He had such a large correspondence he never kept up with it. He frequently offended people because he didn't say "thank you" for something they had done for him. I mean he'd say "thank you" if it was a friend, but if it meant sitting down and writing . . . he sometimes even forgot to turn up where he was supposed to to address a group. I guess that happened less in later years and I think after he got Miss [Grace] Lundy as secretary she saw to it that fewer of these things happened. Sometimes he would be invited to dinner and the hostess would get a telegram or a long distance phone call just before time to sit down to dinner that he was in Washington or Des Moines or San Francisco or Oshkosh and had been detained. He probably had forgotten all about the engagement until the last minute. This was all a problem of taking on more than any one person could do.

L.: You probably read in recent months, *Time* magazine, recognizing McGill's obvious capabilities, said that one of his strengths was not being a [decisive] publisher or an editor when he was in charge of other people. Did you ever hear him mention this?[23]

G.: The only time I can really think of was when the announcement was made that he was going to become publisher. I asked him, "What does this mean?" And he said, "It means that I'm going to have the time to do what I like best and can do best and not have to bother about the things I hate and don't do well." I took this to mean the administrative part of a paper he didn't enjoy and he didn't think he did well. The writing and the editorial policy of the paper, the discussion of policy and so forth he did like and he did think he did well.

L.: One thing that concerns me is that as years come and go there will obviously grow up a McGill myth. Most people will . . . forget [that he had] many . . . interests. The interview with you has helped keep us honest in that respect, has shown more of the man, of the total picture. Any final comments that you think history should know about McGill?

G.: I have here a note of Gene Patterson's. It says the same thing about Ralph's sports stories that I said Grace Lundy said about his columns. Gene is quoting an old Atlanta Morse Code operator. "We used to fight to get Ralph McGill's football copy," the operator recalls. "I must have worked with him twenty-five or thirty games. Most writers would edit, X out and draw lines all over their copy. McGill would roll in the story, type it clean, tremendous flow of words. Because it was easy to read, we could glance two or three words ahead and then watch the play on the field while we sent the word. It was nice to work McGill's copy and see the game besides."

You know what Carl Sandburg said about McGill:
"Sometime I may try to figure out who are the ten richest men in
the country, and you would be one of them."

Notes—Interview

[1]This interview by the editor of Ms. Gershon was tape recorded in her home in
Atlanta in 1969.

[2]Calvin McLeod Logue, *Ralph McGill: Editor and Publisher*, vol. 1, (Durham,
NC: Moore Publishing Co., 1969).

[3]Later Ms. Gershon amplified the nature of the discussions: "The participants
were from those four schools and a topic was assigned for a month and each
school had its participants. They chose one to represent them in this interscholas-
tic deal and the thing may have been at one of the schools or at the courthouse if it
had an auditorium where we oftentimes had plays. . . . You presented your aspect
of the topic. I don't remember whether there were questions from the floor or not.
. . . You planned, you prepared your talk and you gave it and afterwards you have
a social hour. Sounds awful dull doesn't it? There was no decision; it wasn't like a
debate. . . . I also remember that one of the topics once when I participated was
Judge Ben Lindsey's advocacy of companionate marriage. Judge Ben Lindsey
was a judge in Colorado, I think in a Denver court, juvenile court—I'm not sure,
but he was very prominent, and he made an enormous splash. This was sensational because what he was advocating was young people experimenting on living
together before they married to see if it would work. Well, this was horrendous
back that long ago."

[4]Logue, *Ralph McGill: Editor and Publisher*, 1:25-44.

[5]McGill wrote: "I do remember my own childhood, and the hours I used to
spend all by myself, just thinking about things; wondering about clouds and the
mystery of the night and a lot of things I didn't understand and was too shy to ask
about"; *Atlanta Constitution*, 12 February 1948.

[6]See McGill's article on Robert Woodruff in this book.

[7]McGill wrote that he enrolled in law where he "sat at the feet of Judge Ed.
Seay, an erudite, somewhat eccentric man whose subjects were wills and real
property." But "as an unreconverted ex-Marine in 1919," he wrote, "the law bored
me. At the time I considered myself to be one of the lost generation, discovering
Mencken, Sandburg, and all the new poets and novelists of the time.

. . . Anyhow, I did not gain ten yards on torts, and failed on a first down on contracts"; *Atlanta Constitution*, 23 December 1946; 19 December 1961.

[8]In the spring of 1920 "there was a demonstration at a Vanderbilt track meet in which Tom Sims, Ralph McGill, and other students appeared in overalls as a protest against clothing prices"; *Atlanta Constitution*, 23 August 1948. Critic Allen Tate, classmate of McGill's at Vanderbilt, remembered that McGill "had a very pleasant personality." "I believe I thought then—and his career confirms it—that he would become a powerful journalist rather than a 'creative writer' "; letter to Logue, 12 July 1966.

[9]Logue, *Ralph McGill: Editor and Publisher*, 1:39-41.

[10]McGill received approximately twenty honorary degrees, but not a degree from Vanderbilt University. For more by McGill on his Vanderbilt experience, see article on teachers in this book.

[11]"It was 2 April 1929," recalled McGill, "At 10:00 AM, I walked into the [*Atlanta*] *Constitution* feeling excitement and anticipation"; *Newsweek* 53 (13 April 1959): 102.

[12]See Logue's taped interview with Ralph McGill, 29 December 1965, in Logue, ed., *Ralph McGill: Editor and Publisher*, 2:18-21.

[13]For a speech by McGill on "The Greeks," see Logue, *Ralph McGill: Editor and Publisher*, 2:52-61.

[14]McGill wrote: "Most of the days I love it in there with my head through the canvas and everyone privileged to pay his five cents and throw three baseballs at said head." "They will try to smear you and everything you say. They will try to terrorize your family and annoy you with anonymous calls. That isn't important if you know how to shrug it off and regard it as part of the game." *Atlanta Constitution*, 17 July 1946; 28 January 1949.

[15]For McGill's view on "crusading," see Logue, *Ralph McGill: Editor and Publisher*, 1:66-69; 2:taped interview, 21-22.

[16]Logue was incorrect in his emphasis here; McGill began preparing Southerners for racial desegregation as early as 1949; see Logue's essay on McGill's stand on civil rights in an anthology of McGill's writings on the South and civil rights, in press.

[17]See Morton Sosna, *Southern Liberals and the Race Issue: In Search of the Silent South* (New York: Columbia University Press, 1977).

[18]*Atlanta Constitution*, 22 January 1948, Logue, *Ralph McGill: Editor and Publisher*, 1:159, 195-196, 2:120; *Augusta Chronicle*, 4 February 1959.

[19]Logue, *Ralph McGill: Editor and Publisher*, 1:73-81.

[20]Logue, *Ralph McGill: Editor and Publisher*, 2:15-23.

[21]Some critics didn't; see Robert Sherrill, *Gothic Politics in the Deep South: Stars of the New Confederacy* (New York: Grossman Publishers, 1968), pp. 49-52, 150-51.

[22]See article on Jack Tarver in this book.

[23]See *Time* (14 February 1969), p. 68; "A Conversation with Ralph McGill," *Atlanta Magazine*, February 1969, pp. 44-46. Celestine Sibley, writing in *Saturday Evening Post* (27 December 1958): 51, concluded that McGill welcomed opposing views "as sort of friendly whetstones on which to sharpen the edge of his own arguments and persuasions."

Index

MUP SOUTHERN ENCOUNTERS

Designed by Margaret Brown

Composition by Omni Composition Services, Macon, Georgia
    formatted by Janet Middlebrooks and Joan McCord
    the text was "read" by a Hendrix Typereader II OCR Scanner
        and formatted on an Addressograph Multigraph Comp/Set 5404,
        then paginated on an A/M Comp/Set 4510.
    set in Souvenir (text) and Kompact (display)

Production specifications:
    text paper—60 pound Warren's Olde Style
    end papers—80 pound Warren's Olde Style
    cover (on .088 boards)—Joanna Kennett 49601
    dust jacket—100 pound enamel, printed PMS 282 blue and varnished

Printing (offset lithography) by Omnipress of Macon, Inc., Macon, Georgia
Binding by John H. Dekker and Sons, Inc., Grand Rapids, Michigan